Race and the Forms of Knowledge

Race and the Forms of Knowledge

*Technique, Identity, and Place
in Artistic Research*

✦

Ben Spatz

NORTHWESTERN UNIVERSITY PRESS
EVANSTON, ILLINOIS

Northwestern University Press
www.nupress.northwestern.edu

Printed in the United States of America

10 9 8 7 6 5 4 3 2 1

Library of Congress Cataloging-in-Publication Data

Names: Spatz, Ben, author.
Title: Race and the forms of knowledge : technique, identity, and place in artistic research / Ben Spatz.
Description: Evanston : Northwestern University Press, 2024. | Includes bibliographical references and index.
Identifiers: LCCN 2023041861 | ISBN 9780810146587 (paperback) | ISBN 9780810146594 (cloth) | ISBN 9780810146600 (ebook)
Subjects: LCSH: Performing arts—Research. | Performing arts—Technique. | Art and race.
Classification: LCC PN1576 .S63 2024 | DDC 790.2072—dc23/eng/20230907
LC record available at https://lccn.loc.gov/2023041861

for Becca

CONTENTS

AUTHOR'S NOTE

I have been lowercasing the words jewish and judaism since 2017. I do this to mark a molecular approach to jewish identity, avoiding the assumptions of coherency and wholeness that attend the capitalization or uppercasing of nouns; in this case, particularly those of religious orthodoxy and state nationalism.[1] For a similar reason, I lowercase lineages named after individuals (e.g., deleuzian and grotowskian).

In this book I extend the practice of lowercasing to a wider range of identities, including the religious, the geographical, and the racial. Those who argue for the capitalization of Black (and sometimes also "White") include structuralist theorists of afropessimism, as well as scholars and journalists who aim to emphasize the political and ontological force of distinct racializations.[2] I respect this, but here follow the practice of those who lowercase blackness to resist its assumed fixity.[3]

With blackness lowercased, so too must be the rest of the (de)colonial or racial grammar of colors, certainly including whiteness.[4] More ambivalently, in this volume I also lowercase indigenous and indigeneity, as well as the names of indigenous tribes and nations. While recognizing the political value of uppercase Indigenous politics, I aim here to think indigeneity alongside blackness, whiteness, and jewishness, emphasizing the porous, contested, and profoundly asymmetrical boundary practices of each. I also lowercase place names in this book, to avoid a troubling reinforcement of state-enforced geographies.[5]

I have applied this orthographic approach to transcribed quotations, while retaining, of course, the capitalization of identity terms within textual quotations.

Introduction

✦

Materialities in Artistic Research

You know when people say: "I'm gonna slap the black off of you."
(Well, maybe *you* don't.) What they mean is that they're gonna slap
you so hard that they will decouple you from your genetic code. They
will slap you down through all the mothers of your mother, so that
your color will go flying off you, like cheap clip-on earrings. That's
how hard they're gonna slap you. Now, if you could, like, really, like,
slap the black off . . . Where does it go? Like, on the floor? Or does
it spread through the air like little particles of black that get sucked
back into your lungs? Or does it splatter all over you like hot oil, like
a dank rain puddle, like spit?[1]

It is not only that Okwui Okpokwasili describes here something like a
molecular blackness, literalizing identity as chemical substance to posit a
deracialized body, uncoupled from its color and code; but also that this text
appears within a work of contemporary performance, which arrives to me
only belatedly, through its appearance in a documentary film. I can transcribe
the spoken words, but I cannot bring Okpokwasili into this book, neither her
artistry nor her blackness nor the angular force of her movement, nor their
inextricability, nor the slap and its violent threat. But isn't the videographic
trace itself a kind of splattering of blackness, the performer's audiovisual
body a particulate substance that flows across space and time to where it
hits me, splatters on me, blackening me in some way? And what then exactly
happens when this blackness comes into contact with my jewishness, itself
perhaps "a concentrated dye," a "minute quantity" of which "suffices to
give a specific character—or, at least, some traces of it—to an incomparably
greater mass"?[2] What is the nature of this chemical reaction, this molecular
encounter?

Writing this introduction, I extract Okpokwasili's words from the film
Bronx Gothic, which is both more and less than a tracing of the live performance, and reel again from the density and complexity of mediated
communication and the politics of audiovisuality in the present historical
moment. The film contains words in various forms—spoken aloud, printed

on-screen, dubbed as voiceover, captured and recorded, enframing the work—but as a videographic work it is much more than those texts. Through it, I encounter excerpts from the dance-theater work *Bronx Gothic*, alongside other material of the kind that makes the film a documentary and not just documentation: the artist driving from one venue to another, involved in a postshow conversation, spending time with her family. This material adds to my understanding of the performance, but its presence also makes me aware of how much is missing. There is so much to understand about the processes that lie beneath and behind this performance, so much that cannot be found in the film, not because the artist or the filmmaker refuses to show it, but because the tools do not yet exist to unfold all that I might wish to know about the work of performance.

Within the documentary frame, we cannot settle down into the rhythms of daily rehearsal; we cannot excavate the histories that lie beneath the movements; we cannot descend into the memories that enable the performance; we cannot grasp the rhythms underneath the rhythms. As much as the performance itself is an excavation of memory and embodiment, it is also necessarily a fixed object, a "work" of performance. The same goes for the film. Both performance and documentary only scratch the surface of the knowledge processes that subtend this work—or that, in a continuous rather than discrete sense, *are this work*. Is there another form or medium that could more adequately render that epistemic depth? Is there a mode of explication, a genre of book or video, that can short-circuit the moment of performance to the interweavings of knowledge, cutting through the personal and family histories that the documentary genre foregrounds to offer a richer, more layered, more grounded or "earthed" articulation of the work? And wouldn't this require a radically different approach to performance and to video, a different framing of the project, or even an entirely different methodology of practice?

In a special issue of *International Journal of Screendance* addressing issues of race and nation, Melissa Blanco Borelli and Raquel Monroe set Okpokwasili's *Bronx Gothic* alongside Janelle Monae's *Dirty Computer* and Childish Gambino's "This is America" as instances in which racialized artists take control of the means of audiovisual production, which for so long have implemented a subject-object split along white supremacist lines. "Artists of color have a paradoxical relationship to the screen," they write. "From the dancing blackface minstrels of the nineteenth century to the contemporary insidious depiction of Muslim terrorists, white supremacist ideologies have deployed the screen as a weapon to maintain the oppressive order of enslavement and colonization endured by people of color." In contrast, "when a black or brown subject controls their power of representation different images and imaginaries emerge."[3] Exactly such changes in the structure of embodied and audiovisual practice are my focus in this book. But what does it mean to control the power of representation? To appear onscreen, as these editors acknowledge, does not mean that one possesses full control over one's audiovisual embodiment. Nor is it clear that absolute control over one's audiovisual body is possible, or desirable.

In the film *Bronx Gothic* Okpokwasili's performance is doubly composed by others: both the director of the film and the director of the show. There is no question that the work is hers, with her embodied knowledge at the heart of it. But what about the matter of genre and form? What formal constraints are imposed by the theatrical frame, and then by the filmic documentary frame, within which the embodied artist composes her appearance? Screendance and music videos, as Borelli and Monroe suggest, are forms that push the boundaries of contemporary audiovisuality, working outside and beyond the conventions of narrative film. What other forms might remain to be discovered, as part of the reconfiguration of knowledge that the contemporary explosion of audiovisuality makes possible? And what are the implications of such a reconfiguration for the university as a privileged site of thought, knowledge, and research?

To say that artists not only draw on but also generate knowledge through processes of artmaking is by now commonplace in cultural and performance studies, as well as in anthropology. Foundational work by scholars like Diana Taylor and Tim Ingold allows theorists of performing arts to assert without hesitation that artistic practices constitute ways of knowing.[4] Yet a wide gulf remains between this critical assertion and the activation of its implications, which in their implementation imply nothing less than an epistemic revolution. I am interested here in a particular manifestation of the gulf between theory and practice, which from my perspective has both disciplinary and geographical dimensions: namely, the distance between activist-oriented critical theories of embodiment and identity, which have developed largely in north america, and the emergence of what is called "artistic research," especially but not only in europe and canada. This book comes at the shifting relations between performance, identity, and audiovisuality with a specific interest in the politics of the claim to knowledge. I want to know why, despite the richness of dialogue between artistic and scholarly production in the united states, this particular claim has so rarely been activated or instrumentalized as an intervention into the structure and form of the university. Even more urgently, I want to know what can be done with artistic research and its cognates: practice (as) research, performance (as) research, performance-based/led research, research-creation . . . What are the limits and potentials of these proposals and what can they be made to do, especially in relation to the hegemonically white and implicitly racist and colonial structures of academic knowledge production?

This book is written in apprenticeship to black studies, understood as an urgent and fundamental "critique of Western Civilization."[5] I call this relation an apprenticeship to emphasize that I make no claim to mastery (which could only be perverse in relation to black studies) or even to substantive intervention in that field. Rather, I am attempting to learn from critical black studies—on its own and in dialogue with critical indigenous studies, critical whiteness studies, and critical jewish studies—how to think about the relationship between identity and knowledge. This is not a book about black performance. Although I focus on some examples of black performance in this introduction and in chapter 1, the overarching aim of this book is to put the predominantly white field of university-based artistic research into a wider decolonial framework. While in some places I may apply insights from the emerging field of artistic research to a discussion of black performance, more often I take black and indigenous theories of knowledge and identity as philosophical guides in my efforts to rethink whiteness and jewishness. In other words, I attempt in this volume to take up what Katherine McKittrick calls "the gift of black studies": "a conceptual frame that draws attention to and critiques racism and other practices of discrimination but does not remain beholden to the system of knowledge that profits from oppression." In doing so, I mean exactly to ask: "How has this world already been radically reimagined by and through black thought?"[6] Following McKittrick and others, I recognize black studies as profoundly "method making": generative of a potent transdisciplinary methodology that overturns established structures and forms of knowledge.[7] I do my best here to respond to the prophetic invitations, made by scholars in black studies and other explicitly political fields, to let myself be transformed by the radical epistemic proposals that they offer, as I endeavor to reimagine the meaning and politics of artistic research.[8]

I begin from a commitment to learn from black thought about what artistic research could be. Such a commitment requires a clear statement, at the start, that artistic research, in the rich and fundamental sense of *knowledge making through artistic practice*, exists and has always existed primarily outside the university. It also exists and has always existed primarily outside whiteness, in the precise sense that the term "global majority" intends to reclaim. Yet the phrase "artistic research," with its specific and strategic claim to knowledge production, has come to prominence only in the past two decades, as a debate unfolding largely within predominantly white academic institutions in europe and canada, as well as in australia and south africa. My aim here is to grasp and apply torque to this phrase, foregrounding the institutional and epistemological paradox by which it refers both to a relatively recent trend within academia and to an immensely larger context, the overarching and long-standing lineages of artistic and embodied ways of knowing that far exceed those developed by the modern university. In this sense, artistic research resonates not only with the idea of the global majority but also with what Fred Moten and Stefano Harney call "study" and what José Esteban Muñoz refers to as the temporality of a *brownness* that is not in the future but very much already here.[9] What might be the relationship between these very different meanings? Does academic artistic research—which is also overwhelmingly white artistic research—activate, absorb, appropriate, acknowledge, reconstitute, disavow, learn from, make reparations to, or let itself be remade by artistic research in a broader sense? What happens when we recognize that contemporary black studies, for example, already performs a kind of artistic research in its grappling with the limits of scholarly form?

To center blackness as a mode of knowledge production is a radical "displacement of normative methodologies."[10] Thus, Omise'eke Natasha Tinsley begins a monograph with the instruction: "Read this book like a song."[11] Elsewhere, A. D. Carson submits a rap album as his PhD dissertation, later revising it to become the first such album to be peer reviewed and published by a scholarly press.[12] Of course, the radical methodological interventions of black studies are not without compromise. As Manning Marable writes: "In theory, Black Studies was initially advanced as an interdisciplinary mode of critical investigation, employing tools and resources from various disciplines. In practice, the curricula of most African-American Studies programs are taught in the same parochial manner as the traditional, discipline-based departments we have criticized."[13] Keeanga-Yamahtta Taylor concurs: "In most African American Studies departments, you connect yourself to a 'traditional discipline' for the study of research methodologies."[14] What might happen if the institutional interventions of black studies and other nominally identity-based fields were put into closer conversation with the methodological innovations of artistic research? Could the latter become a point of contestation, or even leverage, by which the vastness of alternative knowledges might arrive (again) at the university gates, this time carrying not only a critique of power and a grounding in the politics of identity but also a further challenge to the epistemic structures by which the social world is mediated and institutionalized? What kind of tool, what kind of weapon, is artistic research, as an intervention that not only raises questions about who possesses knowledge but also aims to develop concrete alternatives to its very forms?

These are the kinds of questions that compel me to reconsider artistic research and its cognates. I will not be overly concerned here with the divergence of those terminologies, which often derive from national institutional models and the whims of funding bodies rather than the ontological and epistemological questions that concern me here. There are significant and interesting differences between artistic research, research-creation, practice (as) research, performance as research, and the like, but in the present context these are minor in comparison to the core issues of knowledge, power, and medium that I want to address.[15] Moreover, the majority of books that mobilize such terms are edited collections. This likely results from the decentering of writing that is the primary move of artistic research, with the book chapter being more accessible than the monograph to many scholar-practitioners and artist-researchers. It may also suggest a valuable commitment to diversity of method. Whatever the reason, there are countless descriptions of artistic research and as many different ways of practicing it, but relatively few clearly established positions in the field and even fewer extended arguments about what might constitute its best or boldest practices. My own previous work has foregrounded the concept of embodied research, through which I have intended to reject the prevailing definition of artmaking as the production of separable artistic "works" in favor of a broader notion of embodied practice that could be contextualized in a wider and less white world of embodied arts: performing arts, martial arts, healing arts, ritual arts, sexual arts, and more.[16] Part of what this book chronicles is a shift in my understanding from an exclusive emphasis on embodied practice toward a realization that the contemporary concept of embodiment is itself unthinkable without the rise of audiovisuality, which has profound implications for how we understand the materiality of race and identity. The need to highlight form, especially audio-visuality, is why I have taken up the term "artistic research" in this volume, sometimes writing "embodied artistic research" when I want to foreground the centrality of embodiment in artistic practices. This choice is strategic and should not be taken as a rejection of other cognate terms.

What I mean here by artistic research is the questioning, challenging, and transforming of the structures and forms of academic knowledge production by practitioner-researchers who straddle or synthesize multiple worlds, being associated both with the university and with artmaking and the artistic. Just who those practitioner-researchers might be is a central concern of this book, since "art," like knowledge, on the one hand can refer to the widest possible fields of human activity and, on the other, can consolidate dominant structures of power through hierarchical distinctions like those that separate it from craft, tradition, or culture.[17] In the former, broader sense, artistic research and artistic production are not two different types of processes at all, but only different frameworks for examining embodied creative processes, or perhaps different moments in the cycling of such practices. But the term "artistic research" enacts a kind of leverage, opening a channel between art and knowledge and inviting a thorough reconsideration of each in terms of the other. This is because the word "research" both invokes and reappropriates the respect and power that is afforded uniquely to written knowledge in a logocentric society and world.[18] It invokes academic disciplinarity, but only to reattribute epistemic depth and richness to knowledges that have never been recognized within that framework. It stakes a direct claim to knowledge production, but in a way that fundamentally troubles the culturally specific (white) assumption that research can or should be strictly separated from the rest of life. The pivot point of this move is the crucial claim to knowledge on behalf of that which is not recognized as such, a claim activated in various ways by critical theory, cultural studies, social epistemology, and other fields that work to reappropriate and redistribute the attribution of knowledge to what has conventionally been excluded from the epistemic category. Crucial to artistic research, however, is that this claim is made not on behalf of others (as in most ethnography), but for oneself and one's own communities of practice. Furthermore, this is done using new tools and media of articulation, new *forms of knowledge*, which appear in different ways—perhaps not taking the expected form of an argument—and in which the status of writing itself may be radically decentered.

Artistic research can thus be understood broadly to encompass massively diverse worlds of knowledge making that far exceed the boundaries of whiteness, modernity, and the modern university, even while what calls itself "artistic research" today is much narrower. The "research" in artistic research, practice research, research-creation, and related terms implies a specific type of claim about the possible forms in which knowledge can be archived and transmitted. In one of the best-known books on practice research in the united kingdom, Robin Nelson observes that "the 'problem of knowledge' has been a topic for debate in the Western philosophical tradition since Plato." He continues:

> Some practice-as-research (PaR) projects that advance the idea of "embodied knowledge" pose a challenge, as we shall see, to the privileging of mind over body in the Western intellectual tradition in respect to the locus of knowledge. Furthermore, the project of bodily dissemination of knowledge from one community to another—for example, the passing on of a movement vocabulary in the workshop from one dance or physical theatre community to another—challenges the dominance, if not virtual exclusivity, of writing (or other codified symbolic language) which has long since established itself as the appropriate means of storage and distribution of knowledge.[19]

The connections drawn here—between the "problem of knowledge," the dichotomization of mind and body, and the challenge to writing as the sole legitimate medium of thought and knowledge—suggest the extent to which the project of artistic research is inherently related to the decentering of whiteness. One way to extend this idea could be to compare the development of artistic research with the development of identity-based interdisciplines in the united states, as charted by Roderick Ferguson. Both Nelson and Ferguson cite abstraction and textuality as key tools of academic disciplining. Both speak on behalf of "that small and insignificant thing called the body," the material substrate of embodiment, practice, and performance.[20] If Ferguson's interdisciplines are politically radical but also methodologically constrained by the cultures of academic institutionality, then artistic research has more recently been developing a set of radical methodological proposals without grounding them in any substantive politics. We could then perhaps see contemporary theater, dance, and performance studies, as well as cultural studies more broadly, as fields with the potential to bring the radical politics and methodological limitations of identity-based fields together with the radical methods and political limitations of artistic research.

As an epistemological intervention, academic artistic research can also be aligned with the development of new materialist philosophies and with social studies of science. Both of these, without transforming the role of the researcher as does artistic research, attempt to come to grips with the agency and complexity of matter, or materiality, which to a large degree had been left out of prior theoretical turns that emphasized the symbolic, discursive, or representational aspects of things. As Barbara Bolt writes in the introduction to *Carnal Knowledge: Towards a "New Materialism" through the Arts*, "each artistic form has a unique relation to the matter of things":

> Dance, theatre and fashion, as embodied practices, engage the matter of bodies. In music, the material bodies of composers, musicians and singers co-collaborate with instruments and other technologies in spaces that allow music to emerge. Film-making is an intense relationship between a myriad of human and non human actants—lights, cameras, editing machines, actors, editors, film-makers and directors, to identify just a few in this complex assemblage. Finally the visual arts engage all manner of material processes in making and assembling art. The material facts of artistic practice appear so self-evident and integral to our understanding of art that it may seem unremarkable to frame them in terms of the material turn. What then are the stakes for art in invoking the material turn?[21]

Among the stakes of such an invocation is certainly the claim to knowledge. If "the arts" enact substantial investigations of material processes, then they offer distinct knowledges that cannot be replaced by those scholarly or scientific disciplines that are more often recognized as epistemic. The relevance of new materialisms here is precisely to underscore the epistemic character of artmaking practices as accomplishing much more than giving expression to ideas or composing diverse elements in compelling ways. Artmaking here is a continuous process of encounter, investigation, and searching, sometimes leading to discovery. This idea can be further developed through an explicit parallel with science, as proposed by the editors of *Dialogues between Artistic Research and Science and Technology Studies*, who write: "The past two decades have witnessed a new convergence between artistic and scientific ways of knowing and making. Artists not only increasingly draw upon developments in science and technology, but artistic practices are also seen now as the locus of research, presented to and evaluated in art worlds and academia."[22] These two volumes, like many others, collect chapters that combine theoretical argument with detailed case studies, foregrounding in various ways the knowledge claims at the heart of academic artistic research. But, to reverse Bolt's question: What are the stakes for knowledge in invoking the artistic turn? What does it matter whether art generates or merely applies and incorporates knowledge?

According to the latter set of editors: "The debate on art as research addresses fundamental philosophical questions of epistemology and methodology and issues of artistic agency and autonomy, as well as institutional and educational strategies."[23] I agree with this framing, but I question the reach and scope of academic artistic research as it has developed thus far within academic institutions that are not only predominantly white but also neoliberal, capitalist, and otherwise bound up with structures of control and extraction. I am wondering to what degree these "questions of epistemology and methodology," which are not only fundamental but also tremendously urgent, and which are not merely questions but also battlegrounds, can be posed within existing frameworks?[24] What are the limitations of present conversations around artistic research, new materialism, and science studies, and how might the questions they raise be answered even more thoroughly through means that have yet to be invented? To put this more pointedly: What are the geographies and geopolitics of artistic research? And what does the artistic turn in research amount to, if both the world of "research" and the world of "art" are still constituted by and immersed in whiteness? What are the stakes of bringing artmaking practices into academic epistemologies, if the territory of "art" remains circumscribed by colonial assumptions? The frames of reference for the discourse linking artistic research to science studies are predominantly european and are especially strong in belgium, the netherlands, germany, and finland—countries where the long history and powerful legacies of colonialism may be even more thoroughly disavowed than in north america.[25] Bolt writes, of the *Carnal Knowledge* book project, that it "began as a quiet conversation between a group of Australian and Finnish scholars" before expanding to embrace a more international group.[26] Given these geographies, it is perhaps not surprising that race and colonialism have been largely absent from discussions of artistic research, despite their omnipresence in and as the material ground of modern academic institutionality.

Neither new materialism nor science studies offers sufficient tools for dealing with the materiality of race and identity as understood in black studies and critical race theory.[27] The former approaches develop powerful and sometimes poetic grip on the vibrancy of matter: "For materiality is always something more than 'mere' matter: an excess, force, vitality, relationality, or difference that renders matter active, self-creative, productive, unpredictable."[28] Yet this same focus on materiality can—ironically or fittingly, depending on one's assessment of the fields—go hand in hand with a dematerialization of race, a capacity to pass over racialization, colonialism, and whiteness, if not a tendency to actively dismiss the politics of identity as overly reductive.[29] This is not to reject new materialisms or science studies, which are essential to my own thinking about race and identity as well as about artistic research. It is rather to point to the absence, the immateriality, of racialized difference, and the histories such difference embodies, in these predominantly white fields. Strikingly, race and racialization would appear to be precisely immaterial in many "new" approaches to materialism, despite their crucial material role in european colonialism and its ways of knowing. As Tiffany Lethabo King pointedly remarks, much "nonrepresentational and posthumanist discourse disavows Indigenous worldviews that don't (and for centuries did not) rely on the western boundaries between human and things in order to discover these white 'new materialisms' as if they had not existed before."[30] Thus, when a leading theorist of european artistic research defines artistic research as a relationship between academic knowledge and "the art world, the artistic universe," or calls it "an opportunity to address specifically the interrelationship between what is at stake within art and other domains of life," we have to ask what "art" indexes here and what its contact with academia heralds: an epistemic revolution, or merely the conjoinment of two historically distinct yet both predominantly white and ongoingly colonial disciplines?[31] Is there a real collision of interests here, a confrontation with the potential to enact ethical and political change? Or are we watching something like what happens when two galaxies collide, so full of empty space that they pass through each other leaving most of the stars untouched?

If, like the university, the "art world" consists of institutions that are actively and daily "working to reinforce and center whiteness," then perhaps the debates over artistic research are merely white on white, amounting in the end to just another form of what Aruna D'Souza calls "whitewalling": "a neologism that expands in many directions: the literal site of contention, i.e., the white walls of the gallery; the idea of 'blackballing' or excluding someone; the notion of 'whitewashing,' or covering over that which we prefer to ignore or suppress; the idea of putting a wall around whiteness, of fencing it off, of defending it against incursions."[32] The immediate response to pointing out the massively predominant whiteness of academic artistic research might then insufficiently grasp what is at stake, as so many white institutions have done in recent times. Examining a set of protests around the 2017 Whitney Biennial, D'Souza describes the response of one staff member as "mistaking, perhaps understandably, what was at stake for the protesters: reading their outcry as a plea for *diversity* at the museum, as opposed to an insistence that the museum face its own structural *antiblackness* and its complicity in centering whiteness."[33] Nothing seems easier, from the perspective of artistic research, than attempting to include artistic practices beyond whiteness in the formulation of artistic research. But such inclusion runs the gamut only from missing the mark to actively hampering the much more difficult and deeper processes that could realize the radical epistemological potential offered by the concept of artistic research.[34] As Janelle Reinelt observes, responding to the question whether performance studies as a discipline is imperialist, there is a massive difference between internationalizing the "*objects* of study" to which a field or discipline attends and transforming the "*production* of knowledge" to articulate a more global or planetary perspective.[35] Indeed, if artistic research centers the experience of the artist, and if this artist is the same person as the researcher, then it actually runs the risk of reducing some of the critical potential of performance studies and cultural studies, recentering and "whitewalling" both the object and the means of study. This is the risk and danger of white artistic research.

But there are other views on artistic research that position it as simultaneously epistemological and political, making strategic and potentially far-reaching interventions into the structure of academia and, by extension, of knowledge itself and of the socially shaped material world. In one of the few essays examining european artistic research that draws attention to the whiteness of the field, Paula Kramer and Stephanie Misa observe that, out of a survey of recent artistic research projects, "only a few are overtly critical or *political* (in the sense of explicitly driving towards social change, speaking out against injustices, demanding equal access to resources and so on)." Indeed, some theorists of artistic research explicitly reject the impulse to position it politically. Kramer and Misa acknowledge both sides of this point, noting that artistic research can "provide excellent tools for reflecting on, and intervening in blatant structures of dominance and exclusion that structure our social worlds on a daily basis. But it unfortunately tends to not apply its tools towards this endeavour."[36] A roundtable on research-creation in canada goes further to articulate a range of explicitly political fields and movements with which such approaches might align themselves: Erin Manning mentions neurodiversity, black life, and the political; Stephanie Springgay names gender, sexuality, race, disability, and indigeneity; and Nathalie Loveless refers to feminist and decolonial practices.[37] The position articulated by Loveless is closest to my own, approaching artistic research or research-creation "as an intervention into *academic* discourse and production" that is also "genealogically tied to earlier interdisciplinary and social justice interventions into the university landscape that worked to challenge which research methods and vocalities could be understood as scholarly."[38] This suggests a very different framing of artistic research: not as a confrontation between the different but equally matched forces of the (white) "art world" and the (white) university, but as a critical and deconstructive intervention into power/knowledge, via the university, that is allied at least potentially with those earlier critical interdisciplines that also sought to launch a "generative inquiry" into the form of academia by interrogating long-established "relationships between textuality and institutionality."[39] My aim in this book is to explore such possible alliances between artistic research and black studies, critical race studies, critical indigenous studies, and critical whiteness studies, as well as feminist and queer theory, via a shared investment in what Zakiyyah Iman Jackson calls "dissident ontological and materialist thinking" that exceeds logocentrism and centers "the philosophical thought that occurs in/as expressive culture."[40]

A handful of recent projects, written from the global south and/or in solidarity with current black-led protest and struggle, point to the decolonial or decolonizing potential of academic artistic research. Manola K. Gayatri writes about performance as research and decolonization, touching on theaters and artist hubs between india and south africa, with land issues and the "Fees Must Fall" protests in mind. She wonders if perhaps all we can do today is practice a kind of "notemaking," like Antonio Gramsci in prison, but she concludes with the fire of poetry blurring love, sex, worship, and travel.[41] About decolonization, she asks: "Is it really possible to decolonise the university or this discourse?" In the same collection, Juan Manuel Aldape Muñoz tracks his embodied participation in Black Lives Matter "die-ins" and offers similar concerns about the growth of performance as research. That mode of research, he writes, has the potential to sidestep the distancing effects of performance studies analysis and to bring the researcher out into the space of praxis, into the street and the protest. On the other hand, "the type of academic justice and liberty we seek with this research orientation can manifest as a version of colonization that masquerades as liberatory politics."[42] As Muñoz concludes, the "bifurcation" between the political protest of social movements and the epistemological protest of artistic research is not easily bridged, as

> the two modes of anticolonial resistance refuse to constitute each other. As such, when we look to performance as research as a methodology of the oppressed, we must engage this movement through a problematically personal and physically dis-embodied entry point into research practice, one focused on analyzing, understanding, and giving account to the injustices that we perpetuate as researchers both inside and outside the White, Westernized university.[43]

Both these chapters, in different ways, foreground a certain ambiguity or double-edged quality of artistic research. Both investigate a relationality to blackness, black thought, black struggle, and black practice, from a position that is neither black nor white and from margins of the university that are at once racial, political, economic, and disciplinary. Breath is also central to both of them, a notable correspondence insofar as breath may represent, in different contexts, embodiment, universality, and/or the political.

Perhaps the most important volume published thus far, when it comes to the decolonial potential of artistic research, is the conference proceedings from an event hosted by Arts Research Africa at University of the Witwatersrand in January 2020. While the initial call for contributions mentioned decolonization only as one of several invited topics, by the time of the conference that topic had become central and generated a new title for the event: "How Does Artistic Research Decolonize Knowledge and Practice in Africa?"[44] As conference director Christo Doherty writes, this title links two strategic choices made by the organizers: to use "artistic research," rather than any of the other cognate terms, and "to fasten the theme of the conference to the imperative of decolonization" in the wake of the #RhodesMustFall and #FeesMustFall student-led protest movements.[45] Prompted by the form of the question (as Doherty notes, "not just 'how can?', but 'how does?'"), these proceedings foreground the political-epistemological power of artistic research to act in concert with social movements by shifting and reconfiguring the basic principles of knowledge production. A number of them highlight the ways in which artistic research contests the primacy of writing, not only as the sole legitimate medium of academic thought, but also within the arts themselves—for example, in european approaches to music as "in essence, a form of writing."[46] In the context of south african universities, the colonial lineage of written thought, often glossed in relation to the "Cartesian" subject-object division that writing so powerfully affords, stands in marked contrast to the vastness of african epistemologies that remain largely unwritten. As ethiopian artist-academic Berhanu Ashagrie Deribew suggests, the concept of artistic research has the potential not only to adjust relationships among academic disciplines, or between academia and an equally colonial art world, but also to refigure the very institutionality of the university as a social and material site. In that case, "it is not only art education or artistic research that will be liberated as a 'practice of freedom,' but also the distorted mentality of research institutions toward local and embodied knowledge production systems and the pedagogy of the land."[47] Samuel Ravengai speaks for many contributors to this volume when he claims that "arts research challenges the dictatorship of *logos* and privileges embodied ways of knowing"; and that, as a result, "artistic research has the potential to decolonise the curriculum in Africa" and beyond.[48] Artistic research has something to offer decoloniality.

By decoloniality, I mean a revisionist historical reading of european modernity as inextricably linked to violent global colonialism—a radical overturning of the triumphalist narrative of european hegemony—along with the massive implications of such an epistemic revolution.[49] As I will suggest throughout this book, political decolonization at the level of state and nation is an essential aspect of decoloniality, but there is no neutral platform or medium of thought by which to imagine or debate fundamental changes in the structure of politics. Hence, epistemic decoloniality—a grappling with the *forms of knowledge* to which, I propose, artistic research may contribute—necessarily goes hand in hand with political decolonization. Foluke Ifejola Adebisi quotes Joel Modiri: "Decolonisation is an insatiable reparatory demand, an insurrectionary utterance, that always exceeds the temporality and scene of its enunciation. It entails nothing less than an endless fracturing of the world colonialism created." In response, Adebisi asks:

> What then is this world that colonialism created? And was this world not done away with at the end of empire? This is where people confuse the passing away of political colonial structures with the permanence of the colonial logics that drove the process and continue to drive and structure our institutions and our world.[50]

The matter of "colonial logics" and forms of knowledge is, I will argue, inseparable from the concept of artistic research. Moreover, decolonial forms and logics are distinct from, not metaphors of, political decolonization.[51] It is this move that takes artistic research beyond an unmarked (white) "conflict of the faculties" and toward a deeper engagement with the racialization of knowledge, in recognition that the battle over epistemic legitimacy unfolds both within and against the assumed whiteness of the university and its ways of knowing.[52] A decolonial turn in historiography and politics is essential to this reframing, because it transforms the grounds on which the question of artistic research is asked. This may be relatively obvious in a place like south africa, where political decolonization, after long struggle, became a reality in 1994, but where epistemic and other dimensions of decoloniality remain contested and unfinished projects. But it is no less important in europe or north america, where academic artistic research can all too easily develop without awareness of the university as a contested colonial (or neocolonial) space.

Meditating on the 2016 Brexit vote via the words of Frantz Fanon and Aimé Césaire, Priyamvada Gopal introduces a decolonizing perspective on europe with clear relevance to a consideration of how artistic research could position itself in the global north:

> Europe is a paradoxical formation. We recognize, among other things, that the same Europe that imposed the nation-state form across the globe, and effected innumerable lethal partitions of land in doing so, also contains within itself the seeds of a countermovement, as all large entities and ideas inevitably do. The paradox of Europe, as the European Union, is that it has both one of the globe's most lethal borders, between itself and the darker nations, and internally the relatively recent practice of a great idea: the free movement of peoples and their right to choose where they give their labor. Many South Asians like me, who have had to live with the hard, impermeable, and violent borders imposed by a retreating British Empire, are drawn to the idea of dissolving those borders. To take this possibility to its logical conclusion, however, Europe must decolonize. Ending free movement in Europe is not the way to extend free movement to the rest of the world. Decolonization invites us all to think about how we might undo some of the lethal legacies of empire: the concentration of wealth, income inequality, resource grabbing, sweated labor, hard borders, and selective free movement. "Another Europe" must be a decolonized Europe in a decolonized world.[53]

Elsewhere, Gopal offers an extended treatment of decolonization in relation to the university, tracing the argument that decolonization does not end with political revolution to earlier articulations in the work of Aníbal Quijano and Ngũgĩ wa Thiong'o.[54] Following Gopal, I understand epistemic decolonization—what Walter Mignolo calls decoloniality—as requiring a change in the narrative of modernity: a transformation of prevailing and hegemonic assumptions about the large historical forces that have shaped the planetary situation over the past five, six, or ten centuries. All current political demands to change curricula, take down monuments, transfer land, or otherwise dismantle colonial institutions follow from this revolution in the historical narrative—which is, of course, not a revolution at all for those to whom a decolonial perspective has always been obvious. If the Arts Research Africa volume claims for artistic research an intrinsic entanglement of artistic research with decoloniality, then its implications necessarily extend beyond the geography of africa.

As Gopal observes, quoting Fanon: "Europe is literally a creation of the third world." Fanon was referring to "the wealth that was the foundation of that continent's prosperity, wealth brought in 'from the ports of Holland, the docks of Bordeaux and Liverpool,' and extracted from the labor of millions of enslaved Africans, as well as colonial plunder." But among these extractions and this plunder must also be counted a substantial portion of that which is most radical in western art traditions and thus in artistic research—and it is here that the methodological and epistemological revolution proposed by artistic research offers a way to rethink certain contemporary questions about artistic production and cultural appropriation. D'Souza writes: "The question of when, and on what terms, a person is justified in taking up the cultural forms and historical legacies of groups (races, ethnicities, genders, etc.) to which they themselves are not a part is always fraught, but especially so in the art world where cultural 'borrowings' are the cornerstone of the European avant-garde tradition we've been taught to admire."[55] This comment resonates with Brett Pyper's suggestion that "decolonial critiques of the very knowledge project of the traditional university require that we simultaneously *address the coloniality of (much) art* even as we recognise its affordances with regard to decolonial knowledge production."[56] With that in mind, it is essential to understand that at least some of what is happening in artistic research—and part of what makes the very idea of artistic research possible—is that practitioner-researchers, often working at various margins of predominantly white academic institutions, are carrying indigenous, diasporic, and colonized knowledges in our bodies and practices, often without fully recognizing this fact or having the tools to articulate it.

Precisely because of long processes of cultural appropriation, usually in the context of explicit political and structural colonialism, these knowledges may be held in the body, where they are registered as individual capacity ("creativity" or "artistry") while being cut off from their social and political histories and contexts. What are the implications of recognizing such appropriations as the lifeblood of artistic research? When researcher and object of research appear easily separable, it may be possible to resolve such relations of appropriation by severing the link, so that researchers who do not have sufficient ties to a community are asked not to speak on its behalf. But in acknowledging the embodiment of knowledge—the extent to which researcher and object of research are inseparable—we encounter the limits of such a solution. Then it is no longer possible to sever that link, because the epistemological foundations of the research itself are entangled with colonial histories. In that case, what the field of artistic research needs to do, if it is to be honest with itself, is to patiently and committedly return to its own sources and lineages, reconnecting its methodological and epistemological radicalism with appropriated and cut-off flows and sources of embodied and artistic knowledge.

At this moment in the history of the species and the planet, artistic research offers methodological leverage that can be joined with decolonial and anti-racist politics, as well as those of queer and feminist and trans and disability-led social movements. But for such links to be forged, artistic research must learn from black studies and other identity-based fields how to connect epistemological and methodological radicalism with a wider grasp of historical and social context, beyond eurocentrism. Black studies as an academic discipline emerged alongside and out of a radical social movement and, for Robin D. G. Kelley, from "its inception was dangerous, highly contested, a potential threat to the status quo, an epistemological revolution, and barreling toward institutionalization."[57] Artistic research has no such history of radical politics, but in taking aim at some of the core principles and structures of academia, it also carries tools for an "epistemological revolution." Artistic research struggles with some of the same problems of institutionalization that have confronted black studies and other identity-based interdisciplines, including how to deal with "the academy's transformation of minority cultures and differences into objects of institutional knowledge."[58] Indeed, Ferguson's detailed history of the institutionalization of the interdisciplines reveals the extent to which methodology itself is political: "As quantification became the standard by which to incorporate racialized subjects, race would be read ironically as an abstraction divorced from historical contexts."[59] The potential radicalization of artistic research, as an intervention targeted specifically at the level of methodology, should therefore not be underestimated. While its focus on methodology allows it to develop in problematically depoliticized ways, that same focus may offer distinct kinds of leverage in relation to academic institutionality, and upon the forms of thought itself.

In a dialogue on the idea of reparations, Frank Wilderson and Saidiya Hartman consider the difference between the alternatively depoliticizing or radicalizing ways in which such a double-edged concept can be activated. According to Wilderson, when advocates for reparations frame their demands in terms of quantifiable redress for "an essentially historical phenomenon that ended," they "*waste* a political weapon, they dull the knife," trying "to simultaneously *mobilize* and *manage* black rage." On the other hand: "If reparations were thought of not as something to be achieved, but as a weapon that could precipitate a crisis in American institutionality, then it could be worked out a lot differently from the way it's presented."[60] The double-edged idea of artistic research, too, could be worked out very differently. If understood as a fundamental questioning or shaking of the founding principles of hegemonic thought, it too might be "a weapon that could spew forth in untold directions" and "precipitate a crisis in American institutionality." Such a conception of artistic research cannot be limited to the inclusion of artists within a university that continues to operate largely as before. Instead, it is a call for a radical reexamination and reformulation of "research" (knowledge, thought, rationality, the mind, discourse) and equally of "art" (creativity, discovery, skill, understanding, craft, life, practice).

Who can be recognized as knowing? What forms constitute knowledge? In what form and on whose behalf are epistemic claims mobilized? What are the relations of artistic research to whiteness, institutionality, and colonialism, not as "an essentially historical phenomenon that ended" but as the ongoing structure of knowledge and power? Can artistic research be an *undulled* knife? What could it mean to demand that a live performance, a recorded album, or a video be the final outcome of a research project, the assessed form of a doctoral dissertation, or even the founding document of a new kind of institution?

> HARTMAN: At the very least that would entail a transformation of the social order.
>
> WILDERSON: Yes, they would have to call for revolution.[61]

If artistic research were to grapple with its own materialities, then perhaps it could participate in the demand for a kind of epistemic reparations in the second sense: not a quantifiable exchange, in which globalized "art" is allowed to benefit from academic legitimacy in exchange for exclusions marked as merely historical, but a revolutionary reformulation, in which planetary practices that have never accepted the division between art and knowledge are recognized as no less urgent or real than the hardest of sciences. Whether artistic research can be undulled in this way will depend on what is grasped and invoked through the leverage points of the "artistic" in artistic research, the "practice" in practice research, and the "creation" in research-creation. Do these terms summon the vast outside of the university, opening the floodgates—"they would have to call for revolution"—or do they act instead to contain by including, to incorporate by quantifying, to mobilize and to manage? Do they call for an epistemic revolution or enable a further expansion of the colonial machine?

A full accounting of decolonial artistic research as epistemic revolution is beyond the scope of this book. To begin moving in that direction, what I hope to develop here is a preliminary account of some of the ways in which present histories of racist and colonial power dynamics are present in spaces and practices of artistic research, even when they go unacknowledged or are actively dematerialized, rendered immaterial. I begin from the premise that race is present in practice, whether or not it is named. This premise is learned from black studies, indigenous studies, critical race theory, critical whiteness studies, trans and queer of color critique, decolonial studies, and related fields, which perform crucial work that new materialist philosophy and science studies have not yet undertaken. "Race" in this context, as I discuss in chapter 1, embraces a broad, radically asymmetrical and historicized range of materialities, including institutional contexts, physical environments, and technologies, as well as techniques of the body. Embodied identity, thought from blackness and extending outward from there, is in this sense inclusive of class, religion, gender, language, body shape, and more.[62] Neither the term "race" nor "identity" can do all this work, although I continue to employ them in this volume. What is clear, however, is that artistic research cannot claim to work with materialities—cannot claim to grapple with the real of the world, or with the entanglement of knowledge and power—unless it faces the materialities of embodied and emplaced identity through a thick and critical engagement with the racial. Moreover, black studies today "urges us to redefine the human through our racial attachments, for the sake of not just our collective selves but for the planet," because "our environmental decline, climate change, is tied to the enslaved moving across the Middle Passage" as well as to ongoing colonial dispossessions across the globe.[63] What if black studies, black thought, and black poetics were understood to be central and essential, rather than marginal or secondary, to both new materialisms and the evolving concept of artistic research?

Artistic research has much to learn from black studies—and other fields in which embodied histories of violence, resistance, extraction, and celebration are tracked across and beyond the level of individual bodies and identities—about the ways in which those histories and presences materialize today. Such present materialities are not always easy to name and recognize. They are often illegible as well as painful. Poet Caroline Randall Williams writes in the *New York Times*:

> I have rape-colored skin. My light-brown-blackness is a living testament to the rules, the practices, the causes of the Old South. If there are those who want to remember the legacy of the Confederacy, if they want monuments, well, then, my body is a monument. My skin is a monument.[64]

No stronger statement could be made about the embodied presence of racial histories. And this is part of what must be meant when we talk about materialities, new or old: the literal presence, written on and through the body, inscribed in skin and blood and hair, in trauma and in hope, as well as books and walls and computers and textiles, of past practices that flow into the present moment and with which present materialities seethe. No one can say to Williams that a body is unraced, that histories are not carried in our bones, or that slavery is only in the past. Artistic research must come to grips with what it means for someone with "rape-colored skin" to inhabit and redesign spaces of knowledge practice. It must learn to deal with the diversely layered and intergenerational traumas that are carried differentially by those who enter such spaces and by those who undertake artistic research without having access to its formally designated spaces.

To come to grips with history means to know how to address it by both direct and indirect means, how to name it and how not to: a *know-how* that ought to be a core methodological concern of artistic research. Somatic practitioner and anthropologist Kesha Fikes describes a certain

> slippage, something discontinuous, between 1) the structural and historical realities of race as something that precedes me, is actually in advance of me, and 2) the interactive relational fields in which we engage, where resonant connection in the present moment can momentarily appear or feel as if this past is distant from us: these unresolved colonial, enslaved, migratory, or geo-politically shifted events are in the past. But they're actually still with us. And here, I'm not just speaking about interactions across two or more racial locations, like between someone black or brown and white, as this easily applies to what happens in encounters between two or more people who are white, or two or more people of color, for instance.[65]

Fikes illuminates the ways in which race and identity are always in the room, in the encounter, in the material moment. The developments I am calling artistic research could be a site at which to "consensually engage," as she suggests, "in communicative practices, where we transparently and reverently make reference to and engage with what's both present and not yet realized, or what's present and not yet dismantled in interaction." Fikes calls such practices "racial transparency" or "extimacy": not the final undoing of racism, because "we're not there yet," but an "embodied awareness of our ongoing unresolved historical material realities" and "a mutual and reciprocal reckoning with the unspoken." How can artistic research, as an intervention in academic institutionality, become such a site?

Race is not something carried by certain people, or reducible to histories of black and white racialization. If black studies today offers the most powerful critiques of race and, at the same time, the most rigorous tools by which to recognize how race ongoingly matters, that is because it teaches us that the ways in which blackness might materialize in a body, or in a room, or in a moment, can never be the same as the ways in which whiteness might materialize there. What are the implications of this radical asymmetry, beyond the binary of black and white, for more complex ontologies or grammars of color (black, white, brown, red, yellow . . .) and other modes of embodiment (jewishness, indigeneity, trans/queer . . .)? Black studies highlights the continual materialization of antiblack racism in the present, in the "wake" of slave histories that continue to exert power over "those whom the state positions to die ungrievable deaths and live lives meant to be unliveable." This is "antiblackness as total climate," a climate of "structural silences produced and facilitated by, and that produce and facilitate, Black social and physical death."[66] Black studies also teaches the dignity and even the "sweetness" of life under conditions of constant violence, "the *life* in the *bare life* compound," the "sorrow songs, smooth glitches, minuscule movements, shards of hope, scraps of food, and interrupted dreams of freedom that swarm" the apparatus of legal and everyday violence, the unkillable plenitude of the world and of the flesh.[67] And black studies also teaches the centrality of ritual and ceremony in the transformation of the world, the epistemic power of dance and song as modes of living research: "The hum of the chorus, the interweaving of textiles, the shared drum skin that beats out a new dance and the praising and calling forth of shared gods offer some of the most poignant moments, utterances, knots, kinetics, gestures, and modes of thinking" through which new worlds might be created.[68] Perhaps most importantly for my argument, black studies teaches the impossibility of thought without poetry and the need to radically transform the *modes* of thought, the *ways* of thinking, the *methods* of inquiry, to escape and unmake the pervasive climate of white supremacy, colonialism, and anti-blackness. If artistic research is to be a mode of fabulative counterscholarship that develops alternative ways of knowing, such teachings must be the starting point for a thorough reexamination of the materiality of whiteness, including the whiteness of the university, and the racialization of knowledge. This does not take us into a full or complete accounting of racial identity, which is impossible, but it does locate race and racialization at the center rather than the margins of investigation. The task at hand is to uncover what is present, to recognize what is material, in spaces and moments of experimentation, and to look beyond colonial models in framing that question.

The seed of this book was planted in 2012, when, in my song-based theatrical performance practice, I decided to stop working with invented, nonlexical songs and to begin working with jewish songs. The question of what counts as a jewish song, which ones to work with and how, led me on a journey to rethink my own relationship to jewishness and to reimagine my songwork practice as a mode of critical artistic research. It became apparent to me that, on a critical and political level, I could not theorize jewishness without disentangling it from whiteness; could not examine whiteness without putting myself in apprenticeship to black studies; and could not learn from blackness without placing it in relation to indigeneity.[69] At the same time, my commitment to centering songwork practice as a research method, and my unwillingness to accept writing as the sole legitimate medium of critical thought, led me to rethink the relationship between these four "identity" categories and the forms of media through which they are continually reworked in scholarly and popular discourse. The resulting book weaves back and forth between—or, if I have been successful, weaves together—critical theories of race and of media, not solely from a perspective of distanced scholarship but always also in reference to questions of research design, laboratoriality, and the structure of the university. There is no sense in which this book treats a topic, subject, or archive that is figured as external to the production and transmission of knowledge. Rather, it is intended as a critical intervention into the framework of knowledge production and the idea of research. By deploying a decolonial reading of history inspired by black and indigenous studies, I attempt to rethink relations between identity categories and media forms, in service to genuinely new ways of thinking.[70]

Dylan Robinson, whose work is central to chapter 3, defines "hungry listening" as a colonial, extractive approach to song and music: a desire for music that devours, captures, contains, museumifies, and incarcerates song.[71] In the research process leading to this book, I have tried to avoid "hungry reading": the reading of theory in a mode of engulfment or capture. In the writing process itself, I have tried to avoid what I call "white writing": the logocentric usage of alphabetic writing to inscribe a dominating sense of prior reason and truth. Instead of these, I have attempted to cleave to a different technique of reading and writing, one that illuminates life without attempting to control it, one that is fervent without becoming "hungry" in Robinson's sense. This other technique is what I now imagine, following Martin Buber, Jacques Derrida, and others discussed later in this volume, as a hasidic or jewish mystical approach to reading, in which letters are flames and readings are shards of light.[72] This is a jewishness of critical theoretical practice; a lineage I claim as knowledge or technique, rather than property. I am no proper hasid but critical theory, which I theorize in this volume as extended talmud, is my home. These days, I annotate texts heavily as I read them, whether in paperback or digital form. In fact, I no longer feel that I am fully reading unless I am simultaneously writing onto a text. I call this a practice of fervent reading: a continual back and forth of inscriptive layers, writing that accrues rather than systematizes. Methodologically, this improper lineage powers my engagement with the unavoidable paradox of writing a book that aims to critique the hegemony of writing. That same practice, carried into the realm of audiovisuality, gives rise to a form of "illuminated video" that I discuss toward the end of the book.

I want also to note that this book was also written in huddersfield, an economically depressed town in northern england whose land I would like to acknowledge as the backwaters of the former british empire. (I am currently developing a practice of land acknowledgment for northern england.) Being based in huddersfield since 2014 has given me some distance on the politics of identity as they have developed in the united states, allowing me to appreciate the brilliance of those debates and perhaps also to approach them from a slightly different angle.[73] Writing in and from huddersfield forces me to acknowledge not only my apprenticeship to black studies but also the blackness that is in me. Somehow, without claiming (or claiming to speak for) blackness, I must ethically acknowledge the blackness that makes me who I am. To ignore this would be to deny the extent to which american identity is black, just as it is jewish, often without knowing or acknowledging this truth. The ways in which I have come to experience myself as white and as jewish are inconceivable without the great epistemic rivers of blackness and indigeneity. These terms here name not divisions, not separate boxes as on a census form, but lineages, traditions of knowledge, and revolutionary techniques. Acknowledging this blackness without claiming it, recognizing my indigeneity to the earth while at the same time grounding myself in a diasporic condition that is properly indigenous to no place, and simultaneously acknowledging the saturating whiteness through which I move, is part of what allows me to speak back to whiteness and to jewishness in the ways I have tried to share here.

The rest of the book unfolds in three large chapters. The first chapter begins from recent debates over theatrical and cinematic casting and proposes a different way of understanding the relationship between technique and identity—through an expanded notion of the molecular—in a world increasingly articulated in audiovisual forms. Drawing on black studies and black performance theory, in conversation with deleuzian approaches to new materialism, I expand on a key argument made in my first book—that *identity is made of technique*—by considering how *technique is made of identity*. I argue that we cannot think artistic research without identity and we cannot think identity without race. Moreover, we cannot think art, research, identity, or race without also thinking media ontology as forms of knowledge, since the contemporary meaning of all these concepts is inextricable from the rise of audiovisuality. The second chapter deploys audiovisuality indirectly to break, through triangulation, the dominant mind-body and theory-practice binaries (along with many others) on which colonialism and whiteness are founded. Refusing to separate technique and identity, I develop a concept of "white writing" and then use this to analyze a range of historical and contemporary approaches to white experimental practice, including those of predominantly white university-based artistic research.

The third and final chapter moves toward a different way of thinking, a concretely different mode of thought, which arises from the ethical and political synthesis of decoloniality and audiovisuality. Foregrounding my own embodied artistic research over the past decade, I offer an audiovisual ontology of song as a videographic way of thinking in which diasporic or even decolonial jewishness is not merely an object of study but also a method of thinking and a form of knowledge. The book concludes with a proposal for *earthing the laboratory* that draws on critical indigenous studies in attempting to reconnect technique and identity with place. Taken together, these chapters propose to reformulate and radicalize artistic research as an intervention into the racialized forms of knowledge. In this book, artistic research operates as a potential meeting point or bridge between (racial) identity and (mediated) forms of knowledge—or, in simpler terms, between race and media. This, I suggest, is not the culmination but perhaps a new beginning for artistic research.

Chapter 1

✦

Molecular Identities

Race and the Dramaturgy of the Body

"Cultures are not anyone's property," declares white french director Ariane Mnouchkine.[1] She makes this statement in response to criticisms of the 2018 production *Kanata*, devised by white canadian writer-director Robert Lepage with the actors of Mnouchkine's company, Théâtre du Soleil. The project took its name from an indigenous word that "gave its name to Canada" and its "subject matter ranged over a two-hundred-year history of First Nations Canadian native peoples."[2] Yet despite dealing with the ongoingly urgent political matter of colonialism and cultural genocide in canada, the performance included no indigenous performers. Nora Armani explains:

> Part of the agreement of this co-creation was that the international and fully diverse cast of Théâtre du Soleil was to be used for the new work. (This is the first time they were directed by someone other than Mnouchkine.) Therefore, no special auditions were held for *Kanata* and no new cast members hired. And since there are no Native North American actors in the current company, it was natural that other actors—Afghans, Persians, Arabs, Africans, and indigenous and refugee members of the troupe—would play all the roles, including those of the Native Americans.[3]

As suggested by the problematic phrase "fully diverse," which treats diversity as an abstract quality that attends the company independently of context, the terms in which the debate around *Kanata* was framed leave little room to grapple with the complexity of the issues raised by the project and its criticisms. Both Mnouchkine and Lepage are major figures in white avant-garde theater, paradigmatic examples of white artistic research developed largely outside the university. Yet despite the explicitly ethical and political orientation of the project, Mnouchkine acknowledges no risk of cultural appropriation in response to the critique. Disavowing the very possibility of cultural appropriation, she invokes a number of tropes that frequently recur in such debates: that being accused of racism is itself "very scary"; that "we" (artists? white people?) are "not 'only' French or 'purely' white," not only "racists and colonialists," but also "human beings, carriers of universality," who should not "bow our heads to an ancestral curse"; and that closely examining the ethnic composition of a theater company "cannot help but recall what the Nazis did."[4] I disagree with Mnouchkine's position, which refuses to engage the critique of cultural appropriation mounted by indigenous artists and activists, claiming for artists a kind of privilege or immunity in the name of an unrealized but potential universal.[5] But I also recognize that the framework and language through which charges of cultural appropriation are forced to articulate themselves often fails to articulate what is at stake in such cultural moments, as the dominant model of how performance relates to identity blocks nuanced analysis.

Although *Kanata* was temporarily canceled in canada and premiered in france instead, this was not the intention of the open letter by indigenous artists and activists who mounted the critique. They had instead called for inclusion in the creative process: "It's not a question of the actors—the cast could remain the same," said abenaki filmmaker Kim O'Bomsawin. "But having an (Indigenous) co-writer or co-director could have avoided the feeling of inauthenticity. A vision from the inside would have allowed the team to go deeper, avoid stereotypes."[6] That a request for inclusion and participation was interpreted as a call for cancellation is indicative of the ways in which controversies over specific artistic works are flattened and reduced by a conceptual framework in which identity is understood as a fixed attribute of individuals rather than a central concern of artistic practice. Again and again, the cultural politics of identity are reduced by this framework to a matter of casting—the dominant paradigm for popular cultural analysis of the politics of performing arts, including film and television. In the casting model, performers as living beings are selected, matched, and inserted into a set of roles or characters that preexist them and are defined by a separate work of art, usually textual in form.[7] Among the effects of this model in shaping public debate is that focus can be redirected away from critiques of the production process and creative team and toward "diversity" as a static attribute of the cast. The cast of *Kanata* can then be referred to as "fully diverse" even when its production is directed by Lepage and Mnouchkine. Such containment of the politics of identity within the framework of casting is often implicit, although it sometimes crosses over into an explicit policing of the line between diversity in performance and structural change at the level of institutional power.[8] Additionally, the casting model serves to flatten the debate by severing the complexity of what happens inside an artistic process from its outcomes in public performance. As a result, both sides of the argument are misunderstood and polarized in ways that reflect broader cultural debates over identity, embodiment, performance, and knowledge. In other words, the way in which a nuanced critique of *Kanata* was reduced to a problem of casting reflects a broader impasse around the politics of identity.[9]

Despite the narrowness of its cultural and aesthetic lineage, the casting paradigm is tenacious. Following the etymology and root metaphor of the term, casting is "a manufacturing process in which a liquid material is usually poured into a mold, which contains a hollow cavity of the desired shape, and then allowed to solidify."[10] In performing arts, this means that role and performer must be conceptualized as entirely separate entities, each possessing its own distinct qualities that preexist and remain unaltered by the artistic process. The "liquid material" takes on the shape of the mold, but the two substances remain separate. As Angela Pao notes, there is nothing natural or inherent about this model. It is rather "a peculiar situation created by modern realistic and naturalistic acting traditions whereby two more or less fully constituted identities—that of the actor and that of the character—inhabit the same body."[11] The casting paradigm is fundamentally eurocentric in its assumptions about what constitutes a performance work, how such a work is brought into live performance, and the relationship between performers and roles.

Analyzing another recent casting controversy, Amanda Rogers and Ashley Thorpe describe "two seemingly antithetical systems, of colour-blind and authentic casting."[12] Those on the "colour-blind" side include not only the predominantly white and often culturally or economically powerful artists who control production, like Mnouchkine and Lepage, but also sometimes the artists working within those institutions, including artists of color, who may point to the ways in which the critique of casting in a specific production misses longer-term processes of artistic exploration, as well as less visible kinds of diversity, that may be at work within a performing ensemble.[13] On the other hand, those wishing to use such instances to highlight racist institutionality may find themselves forced to rely on a tenuous concept of authenticity. As Brandi Catanese suggests, the cultural politics of performing arts have in many cases hardly advanced beyond the terms laid out in the well-known debate between black playwright August Wilson and white director Robert Brustein in the 1990s, which hinged on opposing concepts of cultural appropriation and cultural authenticity that are still prevalent today.[14] Those dynamics continue to inform not only the casting model in performing arts but also the predominant model of identity itself. Mainstream debates, and many scholarly debates as well, remain trapped in an impasse between the abandonment of identity and its overdetermination, rarely moving through these apparently opposing alternatives to ask, with Catanese, about the specific "philosophy of race (in and as performance)" that grounds a given artistic practice.[15] As long as identity is understood as a fixed attribute of individual performers and roles, the meaning, force, and complexity of its materialization in artistic process remains illegible.

The paradigm of casting continues to limit controversies around artistic production because it is based on an underpinning epistemology of identity that likewise remains in place despite numerous critiques. When controversies around casting and other forms of cultural appropriation break down into superficial debates over the politics of individual productions, rather than substantive investigations of institutionalized power, this is most often because those wishing to launch a critique of power find themselves constrained by a prevailing *census* or *demographic* model of identity, in which identity is conceptualized as a stable, permanent, and perhaps even biologically rooted quality of an individual person. In a census epistemology, epitomized by the form of a checkbox survey, individuals may perhaps check multiple boxes, but a box cannot be half-checked, nor can the labels on the boxes be changed. This epistemology (or indeed ontology) of identity has been extensively critiqued, notably in a much-cited passage by Brian Massumi, who describes how identity as "positioning on a grid" ("male versus female, black versus white, gay versus straight, and so on") can lead to a kind of "gridlock":

> Of course, a body occupying one position on the grid might succeed in making a move to occupy another position. In fact, certain normative progressions, such as that from child to adult, are coded in. But this doesn't change the fact that what defines the body is not the movement itself, only its beginning and endpoints. Movement is entirely subordinated to the positions it connects.[16]

Massumi's critique is often understood as demonstrating the general insufficiency or even fundamentally misguided approach of something called "identity politics." But this interpretation can lead to an unfortunate rejection of identity itself, not only by conservative white cultural institutions, or even by universalist humanist artists like Mnouchkine, but also by political thinkers like Asad Haider, who, despite being nominally committed to a politics informed by racial histories, nevertheless concludes that "we have to reject 'identity' as a foundation for thinking about identity politics." According to Haider: "In its contemporary ideological form, rather than its initial form as a theorization of a revolutionary political practice, identity politics is an individualist method."[17] I agree that methodological individualism is the problem in both the casting paradigm and the broader politics of identity. Census or demographic epistemology is too coarse to grasp the complexity of embodied identity. But neither can identity be discarded or translated into something else. The problem lies not with identity itself, but with an onto-epistemology of identity that renders it fixed, discrete, and symmetrical, rather than mobile, continuous, and radically asymmetrical. Doing away with identity and its politics is no better than attempting to lock it down through a quantifying, census-style approach. This is perhaps most clear regarding blackness, which

has been theorized in recent black studies as a fundamental category super-
seding anything that might be said about race in general.

Black studies offers at present the richest and most pressing formulations
of the problem of embodied identity, especially where it draws on black feminist thought to analyze race in relation to gender and other modes of identity.
Marquis Bey formulates the problem as a "double bind" that pertains equally
to the black (or "Negro") and the trans:

> To say that the Negro, or the trans, is an actually occurring self-
> evident entity in the world concedes to the very logics that someone
> like Du Bois is trying to oppose. That is, to concede uncritically that
> there is something called the Negro and that it exists, that it is obvi-
> ously called and known as the Negro, is to affirm the logics behind
> the entity of the Negro, which brings with it also the violently racist
> formulations of it that would adhere to those hailed by that nomi-
> native. On the other hand, to say that the Negro, and the trans, are
> merely concepts is to bereft them of any kind of essence; to deem it a
> concept would, in a way, be a radically anti- or nonessentialist move.
> Theoretically and philosophically, such an argument might be fine,
> but *politically*—in an environ wherein something called the Negro
> and some people called transgender are deeply felt to exist and, on
> the grounds of that existence, are pulverized in so many ways—it
> is quite dangerous. In other words, the Negro cannot exist, but the
> Negro must exist. Black is . . . an' black ain't.[18]

If Mnouchkine's claim, on behalf of the privilege or immunity of (white)
artists to practice in ways that exceed and complicate existing identities, resonates with the first part of Bey's double bind, the other side of the coin—the
weight and inertia of identity—is no less important. Among the interventions
of current black studies is to remind thinkers of race that a turn toward the
movement, malleability, and fluidity of identity does not always serve the
aims of democracy, justice, or liberation, especially when anti-blackness per-
sists without being named.

Jared Sexton demonstrates the limitations of census epistemology through
a critique of the proposal, active during the 1990s, to add the category "multiracial" to the US census. While at first this might appear as a welcome
move toward acknowledging the fluidity and malleability of the taxonomic
categories that subtend racism, Sexton highlights the ways in which the multiracial came to represent, at least in that instance, not anti-racist solidarity
but the displacement of blackness.[19] Although the historical case studied by
Sexton involved the actual census, it reveals many problems around identity
and identification that extend much further, including what Sexton calls an
"inverse historical relation between white supremacy's tolerance for multiracial formations and the relative strength of black liberation struggle."[20]

Behind the allegedly liberating politics of the multiracial lies an assumption that the historical violence named by racial categories is best counteracted by denying the validity of those categories as quickly and thoroughly as possible. The same approach is evident in much contemporary discourse, where it continues to create a fatal bridge between the genuine but naive liberal desire to transcend racial difference and the cynical manipulation of "colorblindness" as a mask for white supremacy. While ostensibly aiming for equality, such approaches are easily mobilized to avoid the naming of identities or to replace politicized identities, especially blackness, with depoliticized ones.[21] Such warnings provide ample reason to hesitate before joining in "celebrations of hybridity, biraciality, multiraciality, and postraciality," which may too easily abandon the politics of racial identification in the desire to escape the "gridlock" of reductive identity politics.[22] Bey's work on paradox and "paraontology" demonstrates the force of this impasse in the present moment and the way in which articulations of identity are corralled into one of two positions. Either identity is real and immutable, or else it is illusory and subject to superficial (nominal or "cognitive") change. Either "black is" or "black ain't." But foregrounding embodied and artistic practices suggests another way to move through this dichotomizing impasse.

As Sexton shows, the premise that identities have material force and reality cannot simply be abandoned. The marking of racial identities, for example as part of civil rights compliance monitoring, can be an essential tool in struggles for justice. Race, understood as "neither a biological index of natural kind nor an illusion produced in culture," is socially and materially real, while at the same time its "political ontology exceeds the terms of sociological investigation."[23] Sexton's reference here to "sociological" inquiry is important, because it reveals the extent to which the current impasse around identity politics results from a problem that is fundamentally methodological and epistemological as much as it is political. There are situations in which a census or checkbox epistemology may be appropriate. When one is attempting to implement remedies for injustice through the existing mechanisms of the nation-state, what disciplinary frameworks could be applied other than those of sociology and law? On the other hand, these same epistemologies may fail, or even do harm, when applied to other kinds of processes. Roderick Ferguson's tracking of the academic institutionalization of identity-based interdisciplines reveals a similar problematic: The mapping of identities according to an essentially sociological and quantitative methodology has worked both to develop and stabilize new academic fields and to constrain their potential. Arguably, it is the abstraction from "race as a mode of becoming" to "quantified race"—the process by which "race is fixed in discrete units" and the application of "bureaucratic metrics and protocols in matters of diversity"—that generate both the straw figure of "identity politics" that so many scholars and pundits lambast today and the hidden paradigm that makes debates around cultural appropriation in artistic practice so unproductive.[24] Put simply, sociological and legal epistemologies of identity may be appropriate for intervening in the policy and legislation of the modern state apparatus, but they do not address and cannot account for the multivalent ways in which identity materializes in artistic work or embodied practice more generally.

As noted above, the casting model locates performer and role on two entirely separate tracks, each possessing a stable and coherent identity. (The idea of "colorblind" casting names the most extreme separation between these tracks, wherein the identity of one supposedly has no relation at all to that of the other.) This model profoundly limits the ways that the politics of identity can be tracked through artistic processes, making the complex materialization of identity in practice impossible to grasp. In the logocentric and eurocentric world of script-based theatrical production, characters have identities but no materiality, while performers have fixed, sociologically defined identities. Traffic between these two levels is then impossible. What is left out of such a model is precisely the materiality of embodied practice that enables performance to be a kind of research, including research in identity itself. To understand this materiality and that research, we must conceive the relationship between performers and roles in a different way: not as two tracks, each with its own identity that may or may not align with the other, but as mutually constituted through flows and fields of practice. The census epistemology by which human beings are categorized into fixed and stable identities, whatever purchase it might have in a sociological or juridical context, is inadequate for grasping embodied processes such as those of performing arts. This is not a rejection of identity, but rather an affirmation that the way in which identity accrues to a person is nothing like checking a box. Identities are not *yes-or-no* things, except when they are made to be so by particular epistemologies. To think beyond casting is to bypass the individualist framing of identity as that which a given person is or is not and to think instead about how racial and other identities cut through a given moment, event, or practice, at levels both above and below the individual.

Identity, in this expanded sense, is all around us, inside us, material and embodied, continually structuring and being transformed in and through practice. To grasp racial and other identities in this way is to move beyond the impasse generated by a sociological, juridical, demographic, or census-style account of identity. It is to take seriously the claim that performing arts practice, and other practices foregrounding the materiality of embodiment, constitute not merely an expressive mode for the representation of identities that are factually constituted elsewhere (in the real of sociology or of the law), but in fact a different mode of thinking, a distinct onto-epistemology. We are then faced with an entirely different set of problems around the politics of identity: problems that can be set in relation to those of sociology and law, but which have their own temporality and spatiality and must be examined in different ways. To formulate alternative models for how identity is practiced, we might turn to a pair of recent works written from the perspective of theater and dance dramaturgy. Both focus on specific processes of artistic creation and production, unpacking the detailed ways in which they negotiate the materiality of identity in creative and experimental practice. Taken together, they suggest a much-needed shift away from the outdated and eurocentric paradigm of casting and toward an emerging paradigm of dramaturgy, in which the materialization of identity happens not once but countless times, through a sustained engagement with material relations at all levels.

The authors I refer to write about performance from an intimate and proximal position, referring less to reified artistic works than to ongoing processes of exploration and creation that take place over many years. While such a position could be called ethnographic, the role of the dramaturg in these processes goes further than that, exceeding participant observation in ways that only a concept like artistic research adequately names. The dramaturg here is one who brings critical, scholarly, and indeed even sociological knowledge to bear on performance practice, not primarily in order to describe or evaluate it but to support and enrich it. Through extended partnerships and collaborations with performers, directors, and choreographers, such a dramaturg works through the daily materialization of embodied identity in a sustained and iterative way. This distinct temporality allows the dramaturg and the dramaturgical to offer a more nuanced engagement with the materialization of identity than is available through the casting model. For it is the focus on the public performance of singular works that necessarily misses the most important processes of embodied research taking place in performing arts, including the materialization and dematerialization of race and identity in moments of practice. By the time a "work" of performance appears in public, before a small audience or a large one, the pressure of the imaginary public sphere overcodes and overdetermines the myriad problems and solutions that have been found along the way. A dramaturgical perspective corrects for this overdetermination by drawing attention to the layers of process and experimentation that have not merely generated the public performance work but also remain active within it, as the very materiality of its repeatable existence.

In *Worldmaking: Race, Performance, and the Work of Creativity*, Dorinne Kondo begins from "the strong argument that, as theater artists are creating their art, they are also making and unmaking race."[25] This is common knowledge in some areas of contemporary theater and performance studies, but Kondo leverages her own role as dramaturg to move from a general framework of "ethnography's *corporeal epistemologies*" to "richly specific, granular insights into *race-making*" in the context of performing arts practice. The concept of race as socially constructed has become foundational, she observes. "*But how*, specifically, do we construct race in our everyday scholarly and artistic practice, and under what structural, historical conditions?" If theater making not only represents race but also intervenes in its constitution—"We made, unmade, remade race"—that is because the techniques explored in artistic practice are none other than the same embodied knowledges that make up larger-scale social formations of culture and identity, out of which they emerge and back into which they sediment.[26]

When Kondo asserts that *race and gender pervade aesthetic form*," we might then hear a different kind of rejoinder to Mnouchkine's declaration that cultures cannot be property: namely, that elements of culture do not lose their identities in being rendered technical or aesthetic.[27] On the contrary, what becomes mobile and manipulable in artistic processes, precisely because of the materiality of artistic craft, is identity itself. Race and gender, among other fields of identity, are not abstracted and represented in performance, but materially worked, practiced, and altered. The power of theater-making processes to make, unmake, and remake race is dependent on this unavoidable materiality of form. The dismissal of "identity politics," Kondo writes, "arises from a power-evasive notion of identity, occluding the racialized, gendered, colonialist power through which that identity comes into being." To avoid such an approach, while still recognizing the capacity of artistic practice to do more than just reproduce existing power relations, we must recognize with Kondo that "the arts are not separate from 'the world'; they are zones where power relations—[and] race in particular—are reproduced and contested."[28]

Who better than a dramaturg to articulate the innumerable ways and moments in which identity is stretched, twisted, consolidated, and reconfigured in everyday practices of performance making? The dramaturg, for Kondo, is one who brings "a scholar's critical faculties" into the rehearsal room. But unlike a distanced scholar-critic or ethnographer, the dramaturg's intellectual work is oriented primarily toward the artistic process itself, working in proximity to it and aiming to support and augment it rather than to assess it from a distance.[29] Kondo explains: "My abilities as a cultural critic are precisely the skills I could offer the creative team. Unlike the position of the critic, however, the position of dramaturg meant *full* participation, bearing responsibility for what goes onstage and having a stake in what happens." In recounting her work as dramaturg with Anna Deavere Smith and David Henry Hwang, Kondo emphasizes the conflictual or "agonistic" nature of the process and what is materially at stake in them:

> Unlike liberal versions of dramaturgy that prize harmony, our creative process suggests that incommensurability, conflict, and partial connection offer more politically progressive ways of thinking about dramaturgy and political coalition. The dramaturgical theorizing of *process* interrupts capitalist fetishizing of the final product and promotes theoretical attention to open-endedness, always fraught collaborative labor, and the possibilities of imagining otherwise.[30]

The interactions that Kondo describes are not always easy: "A complex matrix of power was in operation during our work in the rehearsal rooms." But this power matrix, for Kondo, ultimately serves reparative rather than violent ends: "Our backstage battles debated the meanings of race at that historical moment. We may have reenacted the race wars, but our conflict was ultimately generative, even reparative."[31] As Kondo's work shows, a good deal of what Kesha Fikes calls "extimacy" or racial *transparencing*—learning to name and work through the materialization of race through embodied practice—takes place in some processes of artistic creation.[32] In such contexts, an artist like Smith, in collaboration with her creative team, wrestles with the representation of "various racial groups, conventionally defined," while at the same time "keeping in mind the inadequacy and multiplicity of the categories themselves." These categories include whiteness, so that exchanges between Smith and her white institutional hosts can raise issues resonating with critical whiteness studies, including the role of white identity and affect ("white fear, white guilt, white righteousness," and even "white love") in a critical anti-racist or decolonial context.[33] Kondo's dramaturgical lens allows us to understand how artistic processes like those led by Smith continually grapple with the materiality of race, not in a single moment of casting but on a continual, iterative basis and in an experimental mode.

To extend from casting to dramaturgy, and from representation to materialism, as a model for the politics of theatrical performance, is not to downplay the importance of the former. The matching of a performer with a role at the level of an overall production is, as Kondo notes, "both an issue of the politics of representation—where most academic critique rests—and a labor issue."[34] But casting is only one instance of a process that happens repeatedly, even constantly, in the linking and delinking of identities on multiple levels throughout a theatrical process—especially those that are open-ended, exploratory, or research oriented. Dramaturgy in this sense reveals a crucial aspect of artistic research, namely the way in which the materialization of identity is ongoing, dynamic, and emergent, rather than being fixed at the particular moment in which a performer is assigned to a role. Kondo's analysis of Smith's process in the creation of a solo performance takes us deeper into what such a model could reveal.[35] This process involves no "casting" in the traditional sense, because it is established from the beginning that Smith is both director and sole performer of her works. Yet the relationship between identity and performance, the politics of representation, the power dynamics of artistic control, and the material labor of acting are all very much at stake.

If there is a "casting" process in Smith's verbatim solo performance work, it happens in reverse, when Smith selects individuals to interview. Rather than slotting actors into roles, she chooses individuals to become roles for a preselected actor. Diversity, representation, and race making are all present in this process, not least in how Smith's own gendered and raced body matters in relation to the identities of those she interviews. Yet what exactly Smith performs is not grasped by the concept of casting. These are not theatrical "roles" in the standard sense; but neither, of course, can Smith literally become another person. As Kondo shows, Smith's performances are built using a method she has developed, linking quasi-ethnographic interviews to a certain kind of acting technique. This process is enabled by the extent to which identity is rendered technical. The transmissibility of bodily technique allows Smith to perform other people, representing individuals and identities across difference. But equally important is the material interaction of those technical elements with Smith's own identity, so that "de-essentializing race and gender does not mean disavowal. Smith avers that her own gendered, raced body plays into her cross-racial performances; we never entirely forget the performer's subject position or its political histories."[36] What takes place, not only in moments of public performance but across the entire process, is much more than casting: It is a continual negotiation of the materiality of identity, as each living individual Smith interviews is translated—often by audiovisual means—into embodied technique, which is then absorbed and re-presented by her in performance.

As a playwright as well as a dramaturg, Kondo writes explicitly from the position of "scholar-artist."[37] With regard to scholarly form, her positioning of a playscript as the "culmination" of a scholarly monograph marks a valuable "exploration of how the artistic and scholarly can intertwine, meld into and strain against each other."[38] At the same time, that very structure sustains a binary division between the two modes of writing and highlights Kondo's emphasis on script-based drama and the centrality of the textual. To dive deeper into the race-making capacities of performance practice, we might shift from theater dramaturgy to dance dramaturgy, following Katherine Profeta into the long-term research-oriented artistic practices led by choreographer Ralph Lemon. Here is another "intercultural rehearsal room," in which "collaborators come to the process with a mix of identities and cultural alignments," including those of "race, gender, religion, class, ethnicity, politics, and geographical location, which may be expressed in ways both conscious and unconscious, visible and invisible, performed by subjects or imposed upon them," and together generate an emergent "ecology of the working process."[39] Like Kondo, Profeta is explicitly in dialogue with the discourse of artistic research and the argument that "artistic practice creates new cultural knowledge, possessing an analogous value to academic research." Her analysis of Lemon's work is grounded in her experience of performance as "a laboratory for everything else: ontology, epistemology, anthropology, sociology, politics."[40]

Profeta's account invites us to move even further away from the framework of casting, in which performers are matched up with roles, into a dramaturgical framework that turns, I suggest, on a complex and iterative relation between *identity* and *technique*. In this model, the individual performer is no longer taken for granted as a premise or starting point but is recognized as a nexus or site at which multiple layers of technique and identity intersect. In other words, the performer no longer simply "has" identities in a fixed or discrete way but is composed of and intersected by a variety of embodied lineages and histories, including those glossed as racial. By the same token, that which performers confront through performance practice is no longer reducible to a "character," or even a "role," but opens up to incorporate the widest fields of embodied technique. Instead of two parallel tracks, performer and role, there is now a potentially infinite array of combinations and recombinations linking identity and technique, each of which ultimately constitutes the other.

In his decade-long *Geography Trilogy* (*Geography*; *Tree*; *Come Home Charley Patton*) and in works created afterward, such as *How Can You Stay In The House All Day And Not Go Anywhere?*, Lemon has guided members of his ensemble through a series of investigations of identity and technique that can be taken as exemplary models of artistic research.[41] Some of these investigations have focused on the most violent and public spectacles of antiblackness, such as lynching and blackface, but I want to draw attention here to some more subtle aspects of the work, following the assertion by Profeta that the company's "nitty-gritty experiments with physical technique were the most interesting, and arguably most radical, aspect of *Geography*'s intercultural project." Building on some of what Patrice Pavis has written about intercultural performance, while setting aside his discredited "hourglass model," Profeta emphasizes the political and historical significance of "corporeal techniques." In her words, "because the physical body and its techniques are never abstract, but rather ineluctably located within a historical moment and a cultural/political system, any confrontation between two or more physical techniques has unavoidable historical and political resonances." Among those resonances are the materialities of racial identity, manifesting as the dramaturgy of the body in processes of artistic research. Profeta carefully describes how

> the political and historical implications of intercorporeal exchange were often felt in *Geography* and *Tree*'s rehearsal rooms. Frequently work on a tricky flight of dancing would spawn yet one more involved cast discussion about the dancers' reasons for dancing, the tensions between individual and group, the notion of "freedom," the residues of colonialism, or the connections between dance and spirituality. These topics bubbled up easily from just below the surface of the daily work, because they were so often implicit in the reasons for which one moved this way instead of that.[42]

For my larger argument, it is important to underscore that the relationship between this kind of sustained artistic research process and any kind of public performance is never one of direct presentation. Theatrical performance can be one way in which to present the results of such research, but it is not the only one. If we change the orientation of our questioning from performance to research, many other possibilities appear. Processes like those described by Profeta can only be reductively seen as instrumental strategies for generating material to be used in public performance. Instead, we would do well to take seriously their epistemic substance and to ask, with Profeta, how "the knowledge gained in the rehearsal room" might be "effectively disseminated" and shared with those who were not present.[43] Such a change in perspective further suggests that moments of creative failure—those "rehearsal room experiments" that "were never performed in the eventual stage piece," because the choreographer "never figured out how to stage them safely, or with enough cultural respect, or to turn them into something that an American theater audience could metabolize"—are as much part of the research process as whatever is eventually presented in public.[44]

Acknowledging failure as epistemically generative not only displaces the idea of creativity as flowing completed from the mind of an artistic genius but also crucially reframes artistic practice as a research process. Any artist or craftworker knows that aesthetics is not a matter of free composition but a painstaking process of experimentation to discover what works. Even in performing arts, the materiality of artistic research extends far beyond the biophysicality of the body to include what is too often externalized as merely cultural or sociological. When we ask *what a body can do*, we do not only mean physiologically, in terms of how it can literally move, but neither do we mean something separate from that, the "cultural" as a merely metaphorical question of what a body is allowed or permitted to do. Within dramaturgical processes, I argue, we are confronted by embodiment in a way that pragmatically exceeds such dichotomies, so that the question of what a particular body can do, in a particular time and place, becomes a material question precisely insofar as it is always also cultural. The question then is how the results of such experiments—which take place not within but alongside the technoscientific investigations of biology, physiology, and neuroscience—can be shared.

As much knowledge is transmitted by Profeta's written account, but not in the publicly performed stage works, as vice versa. Indeed, Profeta acknowledges a "gut feeling that the dialogues, tensions, and provisional solutions of our process, all of which I was attempting to archive in my notebook, were always going to be more interesting than any scene we might stage inside a proscenium frame."[45] Such comments reveal the onto-epistemological implications of shifting from a casting model to a dramaturgical one. Processes of embodied research that are often glossed as "training" or "rehearsal" now become central to the meaning of what takes place, not only in how they contribute to a "final" performance but in all the ways that they enact a substantive investigation of bodies and worlds that are always both material and cultural. This is the significance of Kondo's remark that a focus on "corporeal epistemologies" compelled her "to shift focus from the analysis of representation, the conventional work of drama and cultural studies criticism, to spotlight what I learned as a *participant*: backstage creative processes, the artistic labor that *makes, unmakes, and remakes race*."[46] As the work of both Kondo and Profeta demonstrates, to share and disseminate the embodied research undertaken in performing arts requires more than the staging of performances and more than the writing of books; it demands a continual reinvention of the very forms of knowledge.

The reduction of the (racial) dramaturgy of performance practice to a matter of casting and representation makes embodied research legible at the cost of badly diminishing its value. Of course, it will sometimes be strategic, or even analytically salient, to focus on the particular moment in a production process in which a defined "role" is mapped onto the living organism of a given performer. But more often than not, a reduction of the (racial) dramaturgy of performance practice to a matter of casting and representation detracts from what is most at stake in performance: the ongoing and iterative processes through which a performer's embodied identities—the ways in which they are constituted by larger flows of history and sociality—interact and intersect with particular bits of those same flows that have been rendered technical as the craft of performance. These mappings are far less easy to capture, interpret, or assess than those of casting, but through them we might begin to understand how identity is constituted beyond the textual modes of sociology and law.[47]

The performer/role dichotomy of the casting model offers a stark choice between what Kondo calls "power-evasive" analysis and, on the other hand, what we might call a "knowledge-evasive" analysis: one that is overdetermined by power relations to the extent that the epistemic content of the artistic process is ignored. A dramaturgical model, following the work of Kondo and Profeta, shifts the performer/role dichotomy into a more complex but no less material relationship between technique and identity, which in turn supports a critical analysis of relations between knowledge and power. To develop such an analysis, two reciprocal claims must be honored: first, *identity is made of technique*, there being nothing in identity that cannot be made to circulate as knowledge; and, second, *technique is made of identity*, there being no such circulation that fully escapes the power relations that enable it. To hold both assertions together is not easy, particularly in an increasingly complex media landscape defined by the circulation of technique and identity through unprecedented channels and forms. Yet this is what we must do, since significant risk of harm attends the foregrounding of either claim without the other.

Technique and Identity

To think technique and identity in relation to each other requires an analytical framework that is both intersectional and radically interdisciplinary. In other words, one must be able to undertake both a power analysis and a knowledge analysis, without letting either supersede the other. Some recent discussions of intersectionality criticize its analysis of power for assuming a static concept of identity. Drawing on the same passage from Massumi quoted above, Jasbir Puar has described intersectionality as a framework that "demands the knowing, naming, and thus stabilizing of identity across space and time, relying on a logic of equivalence and analogy between various axes of identity" and which "simply wishes the messiness of identity into a formulaic grid."[48] Yet, as Tiffany Lethabo King points out, this critique is based on a narrow reading of intersectionality that centers the work of Kimberlé Crenshaw and Patricia Hill Collins over a wider range of black feminist theory. Crenshaw is a legal scholar, Collins a professor of sociology, and these disciplinary contexts shape their thinking about race and gender. "As a legal scholar Crenshaw is engaging with the terrain of juridical discourse. Her specific task as a critical race and legal theorist is to explicitly deal with the construction of the liberal human and interrogate the very concept of the rights-bearing subject of law."[49] By the same token, "Collins, as a sociologist and someone concerned about Black women's lived realities," while clearly recognizing the limitations of individualist analyses, "at some point must abandon this nebulous contingency and make race, class, gender, sexuality, and other identity categories knowable in order to address them."[50] In light of this argument, it seems not entirely fair to critique this particular lineage of intersectionality theory for its adherence to an epistemology of identity that is fundamentally juridical and sociological, as Puar does. Within the disciplines of law and sociology today, it is not possible to mount arguments for justice based on a concept of identity that is fluid and mobile or dramaturgical. Such an argument would risk losing all political bite.[51] A more careful reading of intersectionality, King suggests, would link it to "non-identitarian" traditions that already exist within black feminism, for example in the work of Hortense Spillers, Saidiya Hartman, and the Combahee River Collective, to which the concept of identity politics itself may be traced. It is this lineage of *interdisciplinary intersectionality* that I follow here.[52]

What might an intersectional analysis of performance processes look like if it were truly interdisciplinary, carrying forward the analytics developed in black feminism beyond the epistemological constraints of sociology and law? And what might constitute an intersectional analysis of identity and power that does not take the individual as its primary unit? Much contemporary black studies already does this and what it looks like is nothing other than a recognition of artistic methodologies as ways of knowing—that is, artistic research in the broader sense of that term. In her articulation of black feminist "radical interdisciplinarity," Rosamond King refers to Hartman's "critical fabulation" alongside her own method of "critical biomythography."[53] Like Hartman, King grapples with absences in the historical archive and with the failure of conventional methods. In such cases, conventional historiography doesn't work: "Whenever I tried to write narrative, linear, scholarly prose," King recalls, "poetry would interrupt me and temporarily take over the page." She was therefore compelled to develop "hybrid critical-creative methodologies," which she describes as "not so unusual in women of color feminist writing at the edge or outside of the academy." In terms that closely align with artistic research, King defines

> radical interdisciplinarity as the use of methodologies that combine traditional scholarship with that which is not traditionally considered either scholarship or even part of an academic discipline. As I conceive of it, one aspect of radical interdisciplinarity entails accepted methods of scholarly research and writing, and the other aspect is creative work, such as poetry, performance, or film.[54]

As might also be claimed by the more radical wings of artistic research, King states that "critical biomythography is itself protest: not only against traditional methodologies, but also against colonialism and the racist heteropatriarchies that established methodologies and the disciplines."[55] This then is already a form of radically interdisciplinary intersectionality: a critical practice that does not assume that a rigorous power analysis can only be undertaken through prevailing sociological or historiographic methods. The starting point for such a practice is the recognition that power and knowledge, however much they might be strategically distinguished in particular moments and cases, are always tangled up in each other and undergoing processes of mutual transformation.[56] Such interdisciplinarity is radical not only because it is intersectional (power sensitive and power aware, rather than power evasive), but also because it proposes a profound questioning of the forms of knowledge. We are not only talking here about mixing sociology with history or law but also about song as knowledge, dance as knowledge, sexuality as knowledge, disability as knowledge, land as knowledge.[57]

The synthesis of interdisciplinarity and intersectionality, in my usage, is a call to hold onto, or continually oscillate between, both a *power analysis of knowledge* and a *knowledge analysis of power*. On the one hand, when we encounter what seems like "knowledge"—circulating understandings and ideas, frameworks, discourse, thought, and technique—we need to analyze that knowledge also in terms of the power dynamics that enable and constrain it. This is intersectional interdisciplinarity: recognizing that the ways in which we know things are always also structured by relations of power. By the same token, when we encounter what seems like "power"—structures of domination and capacity, institutions, laws, rules, violence, oppression, inequality, and the positionalities of cultural-material identities—we need to analyze that power also in terms of the circulating forms of knowledge through which it moves and of which it is made. This is interdisciplinary intersectionality, based on a realization that the power relations that structure social and material worlds are always also formulated and embodied as fields of knowledge.

To conduct both a power analysis of knowledge and a knowledge analysis of power means that neither term can be reduced to the other; or, rather, that both terms can be reduced to each other only temporarily and provisionally. As conceived here, a knowledge analysis of power could mean analyzing the identity of a performer or practitioner as if it were made up of the same kind of stuff as a role, that is, of circulating and transmissible knowledge; while a power analysis of knowledge could mean analyzing performance technique as if it were made up of the same kind of stuff as performers, that is, of intersectional identities defined by power relations. Restating this more concisely: *Identity is made of technique* and *technique is made of identity*. To acknowledge the differential speeds or inertias of these layers, we could also say: *Identity is sedimented technique*, while *technique is desedimented identity*. The rest of this section is a warning against the serious risks that I believe attend the foregrounding of one of these claims without the other. In describing these risks, I also hope to make clearer what I mean by technique and identity, as a premise for the rest of this book.

In several publications over the past decade, I have attempted to think about embodiment and identity in terms of technique, drawing out the knowledge dimensions of social and corporeal phenomena that have previously been analyzed in terms of materiality and power—for example, by restoring to concepts like *habitus* and *performativity* their crucial epistemic dimension or knowledge content. To summarize my prior arguments: Pierre Bourdieu develops his concept of habitus in contradistinction from knowledge, writing: "What is 'learned by body' is not something that one has, like knowledge that can be brandished, but something that one is." Similarly, Judith Butler influentially distinguishes between "performance as bounded 'act'" and performativity, "insofar as the latter consists in a reiteration of norms which precede, constrain, and exceed the performer and in that sense cannot be taken as the fabrication of the performer's 'will' or 'choice.'"[58] My earlier proposal for an "epistemology of practice" emphasized the need to recognize the ways in which, on the one hand, knowledge absolutely is something that one "is" and becomes, rather than merely "has"; and, on the other, the "norms" that "precede, constrain, and exceed the performer" (including the "performer" of gender or racial identity) are never wholly divorced from will, choice, agency, and indeed fabrication, but rather are the results of prior investigations, prior research, which has been sedimented until it becomes the unconscious and material basis for later choices. Bourdieu's habitus and Butler's performativity are thus forms of "sedimented agency" that in an important sense remain epistemic, still being *made out of knowledge*, even when they are no longer directly accessible to be "brandished" or wielded in a "bounded act" of agency. Technique, I have argued, is knowledge that structures practice. We can visualize it as "a network of fractally branching pathways that vein the substance of practice."[59] Whereas practice is unrepeatable, always taking place at a specific time and place, technique is defined by its transmissibility. Thus, "epistemic practice," including that which has the potential to generate new embodied identities, "involves a continuous and mutually constituting transformation, back and forth, between the two categories of conscious and unconscious knowledge, or what one *has* (knowledge) and what one *is* (identity)."[60] I stand by the claim that identity is made of technique, but my project here attempts to counterbalance my previous focus on technique and knowledge with a fuller consideration of identity and power.

My prior examination of identity focused on gender rather than race. Specifically, I theorized gender as technique and argued that the development of new gender identities requires not just "catachrestic" (Butler's term) misuse or deviation but substantive and sustained embodied research.[61] Looking back, it seems clear that my emphasis on gender, in the context of theorizing technique as knowledge, was due not only to my own embodied experience but also to the fact that, in current leftist politics of identity, gender is articulated through strategic voluntarism, while race is articulated through strategic essentialism. While the political emergence of trans and nonbinary gender identities has at its core a commitment to the authority of the individual in naming their own gender (although debates over the importance of biomedical frameworks continue), the parallel assertion of "transrace" identities has been rejected by many who operate within the same scholarly and activist communities.[62] This does not mean, however, that transgender and transrace identification operate or function in the same way. If the very terms "race" and "gender" index not individual attributes, or even merely histories of struggle and oppression, but complex material histories and historically sedimented technique, then we should look to understand their relation in ways that far exceed either equation (race and gender are the same; if gender is technique then race is technique in the same way) or opposition (race and gender are different; transgender identities are truths while transrace identities are false).

When theorizing gender as technique, I already aimed to ground cultural, discursive, or semiotic analyses of gender in the materiality of embodiment, attempting to think embodiment itself as shaped by communities of knowledge. But I did not reckon with the kinds of massive geopolitical histories of colonialism, enslavement, and genocide that inform the contemporary materialities of racial identity. My approach was one of caution when it came to applying a technicizing or knowledge analysis to racial identity.[63] Not only was I more cautious about theorizing race as technique in *What a Body Can Do*, but further, when I began to focus more explicitly on racial identity through my artistic research, I found that an emphasis solely on the technicity of identity was not tenable. The demand to think identity in terms of power relations, especially as articulated in black feminism, has required me to rethink the concept of technique once more, with a greater emphasis on power analysis. It has required me to think technique as identity and not only identity as technique.[64]

Nina Sun Eidsheim's study of black music in *The Race of Sound: Listening, Timbre, and Vocality in African American Music* offers an analysis of sound and voice that has much in common with my theorization of technique. Eidsheim argues that thinking technically can help to resolve an unproductive "split" between those aspects of the body that are understood to be essential and unchanging and those that can be trained (or experimented with) to develop in various ways. "Through daily vocal practice, voice in its material presentation as flesh, ligaments, and tissue is encultured according to its constant comparison" with what Eidsheim calls the "figure of sound," the categories of meaning that we assign to sound:

> Because the voice is formed in conjunction with the body, it too broadcasts the social attitudes and values of the trained body. Every interaction, from state educational systems to the informal lessons imparted when a person receives positive or negative feedback on his or her voice, entrains (auto-)listening and vocal behavior. I believe we may take a crucial step toward untangling the "politics of frequency," to use Steven Goodman's apt term, by considering—through a systematic examination of the micropolitics of timbre, how vocality, a learned physical behavior, is trained and perceived. Part of the micropolitics is to begin *to render all vocal activity as learned physical behavior*; through such activism, vocal timbre and any given categories of it that we know can be denaturalized.[65]

The categories and figures that Eidsheim aims to denaturalize include not only those of quality (better and worse voices) and gender (male and female voices) but also of race and, in particular, blackness. Like me, she draws an analogy between professional and everyday identities, observing that racial and ethnic vocal timbre is trained through daily interactions, just like the various "schools" of professional vocal technique. Eidsheim's technical analysis of identity resonates with my arguments for embodied and artistic research. Indeed, when Eidsheim claims that "race and ethnicity are aspects of a continuous field of style and technique," or invokes "the infinity of possible styles and techniques and the infinity of ways of naming a given pattern drawn from these styles and techniques," she undoubtedly invokes the most profound capacities of embodied and artistic research to reach beyond established norms and categories in the discovery of truly different ways and worlds.[66] This is precisely the hope demonstrated by Kondo's idea of "world making" or "race making" through performance and it powerfully articulates the argument that *identity is made of technique*.

However, I am uneasy with the way in which Eidsheim's argument develops, particularly given its focus on blackness and black music. Even more than my own prior arguments for technique as knowledge, Eidsheim's technical analysis of identity disallows a concomitant identitarian analysis of technique. *The Race of Sound* offers a knowledge analysis of power while in several places explicitly rejecting a power analysis of knowledge. In favoring technique to the exclusion of identity, a political reading of the voice becomes impossible, and we are left not with "the race of sound" but with *sound instead of race*. Ultimately, for Eidsheim, sound as vibration replaces the racialization of sound. As a result, what unfolds is a problematic displacement of race and blackness via fluidity and flow, perhaps similar to that critiqued by Jared Sexton.

To develop a theory of sound as enculturated but denaturalized vibration, Eidsheim has to claim not only that voice is "cultural" rather than "innate," but also that "sound in general, and vocal timbre in particular, have no a priori meaning."[67] The aim of her analysis is to deconstruct and avoid a "micropolitics of timbre wherein vocal events are heard with a constant comparison to preestablished categories," instead developing the capacity to hear each vocal event "in its unrepeatable and unpredictable co-unfoldings between vocalizer and listeners." Through repeated reference to "style and technique," she hopes to sidestep the assignment of identity to singers and to "open a space for completely new interactions" in an "unknown territory." Not coincidentally, this approach allows us to recognize that "artists are sources, not objects, of knowledge."[68] Eidsheim's call for radically open-ended embodied research resonates with the kinds of research-oriented artistic practices that I am committed to supporting. There is even a shared reference to the sky as an image of this wild and wide-open potentiality.[69] Yet these similarities rub up against important differences in our approach, which I would hazard to associate with our personal and professional trajectories. Both Eidsheim and I returned to academia following years of professional artistic activity, to which we maintain a strong allegiance; hence our shared commitment to bringing concepts of embodied training and technique to bear on debates over the construction of identity. But Eidsheim's journey has carried her from europe to north america, while mine has led in the opposite direction.[70] I wonder if this may partially account for the different ways in which we unpack the politics of the technical analysis of identity to which we are both committed.

In my understanding, following the work of Sexton and other thinkers in black studies, the loss of a capacity to analyze technique in terms of identity, in favor of analyzing identity in terms of technique, is not trivial. This is evident even in a passing example that Eidsheim offers early on when she addresses the alleged or perceived racial identity of Barack Obama's voice. While it is true that a binary debate over the "color" of Obama's voice is misguided, that problem is not resolved by simply discarding the association of voice with race, as this makes it impossible to acknowledge either the blackness of black vocal technique or the hegemonic whiteness of "standard" english as other than incidental. Obama's accent and timbre may indeed not detract from his blackness, but they certainly played a role in his election and presidency that is more than merely vibrational. In this example and others, the politics of the voice developed in *The Race of Sound*—as much in what is left aside as in what is examined—are those of "colorblindness": a call to escape and transcend power relations by rejecting the analysis of technique in terms of identity. As the very possibility of racially identifying voices is dissolved into an analytics of "style and technique," the anti-racist ethos that motivates Eidsheim's project likewise dissolves into that of "colorblind" liberalism, which deactivates any specifically racial politics. Strikingly, for a book that focuses centrally on african american music, the politics of blackness are on multiple occasions explicitly set aside to deconstruct racial identity in terms of technique. I will mention three such occasions, to show how an overemphasis on technique can displace the analytics of identity. My aim is not to single out Eidsheim's work—which, as noted, is closely aligned with my own—but to warn against a certain danger that arises when identity is theorized as sedimented technique without simultaneously theorizing technique as desedimented identity.

The first example is Eidsheim's discussion of the relationship between renowned black singer Billie Holiday and a young, white, norwegian girl who is able to sound just like her. At the start of Eidsheim's analysis of this girl (and others who imitate or impersonate Holiday), she explicitly sets aside "the complex politics arising from [these] impersonators' various racialized dynamics."[71] Instead of engaging with those politics, Eidsheim advances a widespread but superficially cognitive account of race and racism, according to which we have only to "enumerate the errors" of racial categorization to do away with it. In Eidsheim's formulation: "If the myth of essential vocal timbre is debunked, voices become immune to racialization." The intentions here are anti-racist and include that of freeing Holiday from the burden of representation—from being confined within her identity as a black woman and hence underrecognized as a masterful artist of the voice. As Eidsheim points out, "a careful listener can deconstruct the vocal act into stylistic choices and technical prowess. This listening practice debunks vocal timbre as autobiography, gender, race, and expression of the deepest essence, allowing listeners to understand vocal timbre as skill, artistry, and communicative intention."[72] But the desire to free Holiday from her identities in this way is double-edged. On the one hand, an artist like Holiday cannot be understood solely through her biographical identities, nor should her vocal technique be reduced to her situated life experience. But what does it mean to dissolve Holiday's race and gender so thoroughly that there is no longer any substantial difference between her voice and that developed through the "dedicated practice" of a white norwegian girl? Instead of removing blackness from the equation, might we not want to stand up for it and assert that the norwegian girl's voice, even if it is sonically indistinguishable from Holiday's, is nevertheless importantly *not black*? Or, on the other hand, that if this girl's voice does become materially black, in a certain sense, then that transformation amounts to a circulation not only of technique and knowledge but also of identity and power? The vocal, after all, is only one kind of embodied technique. In severing the audible voice from the rest of embodiment, including all those other dimensions of perceptibility and experience that might be said to constitute blackness, have we not lost any possibility for a politics of the voice?

Much later, in the book's conclusion, Eidsheim recalls a personal anecdote from her childhood, in which a white norwegian boy points to her in public and calls out: "Look, an African child!" Eidsheim identifies herself here as "an individual born in South Korea and transported by my adoptive parents to homogenous Norway." The boy, she guesses, "must have thought that all people with black hair came from Africa." She observes that she did not feel offended at the time, but that she did take offense, many years later, as an adult teaching in California, when a child asked why she and her son spoke Norwegian when they did not "look" Norwegian. In this latter case, she writes: "I felt offended that I had not been seen for who I was."[73] The phrasing of the first interpellation, "Look, an African child!" hauntingly recalls Frantz Fanon's well-known meditation on a similar address.[74] Yet the situations are very different, Fanon is not cited by Eidsheim, and the conclusions she draws are nearly the opposite of his. Rather than grappling with the ways in which race is ascribed to individuals without their consent—that is, how "the fact of blackness" (Fanon's phrase) circulates materially as part of social structures—Eidsheim draws from the difference between her two experiences a critique of her own commitments to particular identities. The difference between the two events, she finds, is that as a child she was "unaffected by external labels" and "operated outside the cult of fidelity"; whereas as an adult she "was offended and thus affected by labels," because she "had switched to operation within the cult of fidelity." The problem in the latter case, she suggests, is that she "was clinging to a stable and seemingly knowable category about myself." It is this misguided clinging that for Eidsheim leads to the feeling of "dissonance," rather than any racial or social realities, because in the moment of interpellation, which Eidsheim abstracts from all social contexts, whether each child's "assessment was actually correct or incorrect did not matter."[75] But what is lost in this not-mattering of racial, ethnic, and national identity, when these are said to be fully dissolved by the misrecognition of a child?

Eidsheim is free to account for her own identity as she sees fit, but again the dissolution of blackness in this sequence of passages is troubling: For whom does it matter or not matter whether sound and image escape their racial and other identifications, or whether they continue to be linked to those social and material relations of power? My concerns about the potential anti-blackness and generally anti-identitarian (hence anti-antiracist) effects of a solely technicizing analysis of identity come to a head in the following passage, which applies such an analysis to no less pivotal and defining a political event than the 2012 murder of Trayvon Martin at the hands of George Zimmerman. This killing, and the subsequent trial of Zimmerman, who was acquitted of all charges, was a turning point in the development of the Black Lives Matter movement.[76] Yet Eidsheim's analysis here only extends the strangely abstracted symmetry according to which she might as well be african because someone thinks she is, to embrace the allegedly symmetrical positions of the mothers of Martin and Zimmerman. Both women apparently testified "that they heard their own son calling for help" on an audio recording of that night's events. It may be true that neither woman is intentionally lying, but what does that mean about the recording, the voices it captured, and the bodies of the individuals involved? Again, in this analysis, the blackness of Martin, with its crucial relationship to anti-racist social organizing over the subsequent decade, simply disappears. Through "listening beyond identification," Eidsheim suggests, we may hear every cry as though the vocalizer were our own child." Thus, by "dissolving the reference points so that the pain of social injustice is also my pain," we can begin "hearing the cry as composed of styles and techniques," so that the question of who exactly cried, and what their racial identities may have been, no longer matters.[77] With this step, it is race and blackness specifically that no longer matter, and the important political claim that "Black Lives Matter" becomes impossible to distinguish from another utterance that formally embraces it while in practice displacing it: "All Lives Matter."

In pointing out the possible antiblack effects of a solely technical analysis, I am of course not suggesting a foundational grounding of technique in identity. I am not suggesting that identity is *not* made of technique and instead has some fundamental being, force, or power that exceeds all possible knowledge. The desedimentation of identity into technique is an important analytical move, found not only in Eidsheim's work and my own but also in many political theorists of race, including some who identify as black.[78] My aim is rather to warn against the danger of asserting that *identity is made of technique* without in the same breath acknowledging that *technique is also made of identity*. For every deconstructive and desedimenting move to analyze power relations in terms of knowledge, highlighting the mobile epistemic flows of technique that exceed and transform relations of power, there must be a parallel grounding and sedimentary move that acknowledges how these circulating and fragmentary flows of technique are historically and materially linked to structures of power. It is true that black and white voices, as well as male and female voices and young and old voices, are comprised in any given moment by "styles and techniques" of bodily activation, which can never be ruled out as permanently inaccessible to a given individual either on political or ontological grounds. *We do not know what a body can do.* But it is also true that circulating particles or technical "molecules" of the voice (the latter concept is developed in the next section) are raced and gendered, abled and disabled, documented and undocumented, national and foreign, classed and trained in particular ways. Vocal utterances, even in their tiniest fragments, like the unintelligible sound of a voice calling for help on an emergency services recording, must then remain at least potentially classifiable as black or white, male or female, young or old—not in permanent or static ways, but precisely in their material relations. Eidsheim's technical and epistemic analysis of identity is full of sharp thinking based on sustained artistic practice. It is also "colorblind" to the extent of risking anti-blackness.[79] I highlight this here because, if academic artistic research does not undertake a much more thorough power analysis of identity, such as that offered by critical race theory, intersectionality, and black studies, it will almost certainly follow along this path. On the other hand, there are ways of thinking that risk the opposite danger: They assert that technique is made of identity without in the same breath acknowledging that identity is also made of technique. I turn now to an influential example of such a theory.

Frank Wilderson's "unflinching paradigmatic analysis" of racial relations and identities, as developed in *Red, White & Black: Cinema and the Structure of U.S. Antagonisms*, offers an important counterbalance to the knowledge analysis of power and the technical analysis of identity.[80] As Linette Park observes, this book has "made a profound impact in not only Black Studies, but also a type of rupture in other areas of study."[81] Wilderson does not simply describe the ways in which artistic technique is formed and constituted by larger configurations of identity. He goes much further and fully, explicitly, formally rejects any analytics of knowledge, technique, or interdisciplinarity that would make it possible to think the malleability of race. This is why his work stands as a warning here. A radically interdisciplinary intersectionality, or a materialist theory of identity that grapples with both power and knowledge, cannot be "paradigmatic" in Wilderson's sense. What Wilderson means by paradigmatic is what I would call structuralist: In his conception, it is not possible to think (let alone to act) beyond a particular set of structural power relations that define the world in a fundamental or "ontological" way, as "inaugural division."[82]

This means, among other things, that Wilderson effectively mounts an argument against artistic research—not against the white artistic research of european universities, which he has no reason to consider, but against even the possibility of black artistic research in cinema. While drawing on black scholars of history and literature like Saidiya Hartman and Hortense Spillers, Wilderson's argument, as he acknowledges, is much more directly a response to Karl Marx and Jacques Lacan. It is also much closer to the latter in its formulation, often taking on a masculinist and ableist tenor in its narrow definition of the real. In theorizing "the Black position," Wilderson comes close to the kind of gridding of identity that Massumi and Puar critique, but in a more far-reaching way, without hedging or apology and with even less allowance for mobility. "The Black position is indeed a position, not an identity," he writes.[83] As a result, Wilderson's structuralism of race, which he develops to replace a marxist structuralism of economic classes and a lacanian structuralism of gender, is no more tenable than those in its strict collapsing of technique into identity.

For Wilderson, there are only "three structuring positions of the United States (Whites, Indians, Blacks)" and "these different relationships to violence are structurally irreconcilable."[84] Basing his argument not only on the history of chattel slavery, which is essential for all contemporary black studies, but also on the absolute equation of slavery with blackness ("Blackness cannot disentangle itself from slaveness"), Wilderson defines the organization of contemporary life and society, hemispherically if not globally, as fully continuous with that of antebellum slavery.[85] This is Wilderson's formulation of afropessimism, which

> explores the meaning of Blackness not—in the first instance—as a variously and unconsciously interpellated identity or as a conscious social actor, but as a structural position of noncommunicability in the face of all other positions; this meaning is noncommunicable because, again, as a position, Blackness is predicated on modalities of accumulation and fungibility, not exploitation and alienation.[86]

It is important to examine the problems raised by the ontological positioning of blackness as radically distinct from all (other) identities, as well as the resulting ontological fixity of whiteness and "Red"-ness (indigeneity) that Wilderson develops. This is particularly relevant for any attempt to activate artistic research as a substantive intervention into the forms of knowledge, since a side effect of Wilderson's structuralism is to reduce the transformative power of art to zero. The formulation developed by Wilderson can be mapped directly onto what I am calling the relationship between technique and identity. His claim is the opposite of "colorblindness," in which technique and identity are radically severed from each other. What Wilderson offers is instead a racial structuralism in which the "structural" and "ontological" identities of performers are so rigorously overdetermined that character, role, performance, and technique can never be more than secondary expressions of that underlying reality. While in a sense opposing colorblindness, since technique is mapped directly onto identity rather than freed from it, a similar result unfolds: It becomes impossible for close attention to be paid to the dramaturgical ways in which technique and identity mutually constitute one another in specific events and practices. For Wilderson, technique can only ever be an expression of identity. It follows that no depth or degree of technical or aesthetic research can make a dent in the materiality of (racial) identities.

This rigid mapping or structuralism of the relation between identity and technique is made explicit throughout *Red, Black & White*. It develops via a series of oppositions between the world of whiteness—which, for Wilderson, effectively includes all identity positions other than black and red (he names and lumps together jewish, latinx, and asian people, women, and all "postcolonial" subjects) and is structured by merely cultural "conflict"—and the "structural antagonism" of black and, to a lesser extent, red positionalities. A generous reading of this opposition might imagine a kind of spectrum between conflictual encounters and antagonistic ones based on whether resolution without recourse to physical violence seems possible. But Wilderson takes great pains to reject such a spectrum, positing the difference between the conflictual and the antagonistic as strictly dichotomous. Indeed, he goes to considerable lengths to ensure that the diverse modes of suffering, oppression, and violence experienced by many different historical communities are not considered in any way commensurable with the social death of blackness—a commensurability that he calls the "ruse of analogy"—and, further, that this incommensurability is not even one of degree or extent, but of fundamental ontological kind.

Building on Lacan's psychoanalytic model to a degree that may be surprising given his larger argument, Wilderson links cultural or conflictual identities to the symbolic, or language, and ontological or antagonistic positions to the real, understood as material force or violence. Native/indigenous or "red" positionality is for Wilderson fractured precisely along these lines, half-aligned with white (and postcolonial) "human" subject positions and half-aligned with the black positionality of slavery and social death. The former includes everything that we might associate with knowledge or technique—culture, heritage, subjecthood, and relations to land—whereas the latter contains only death itself as the incarnation of material force, that which is "beyond the symbolic."[87] As a result, for Wilderson, "there can be no such entity as Black culture."[88] Culture itself is a property of white people and their "junior partners." It is defined from the beginning as fully contained within whiteness and no act or discovery of culture can disrupt the structural or ontological relation of these positions. There is then no such thing as black technique or black knowledge, for these could only ever be direct expressions of black slaveness and death, which would amount to no culture or knowledge at all.

There is considerable rhetorical force in such an approach, especially given how it allows one to recognize the profoundly white and even white supremacist foundations of social institutions that continue to hide behind illusions of neutrality and universality. But the cost of claiming this degree of exceptionalism for any category or position is too high and ultimately undermines Wilderson's own argument. The problem is not only that the experiences of nonblack people of color and other marginalized populations are described reductively as having a merely conflictual relation "to the Settler/Master, that is, to the hemisphere and the United States," regardless of time, place, or context.[89] An even more fundamental problem is that, in replacing economic and psychoanalytic structuralisms with a structuralism of race, Wilderson repeats the impossible attempt, common to all structuralisms, to write from an untenable position of textual completion and mastery.

Consider how strictly Wilderson cleaves essence from experience and law from history:

> We really have to stop thinking slavery, definitionally, through the lived experience of it. And until we can stop doing that, we really can't understand—which is not to say agree with—we cannot understand the Afropessimist argument. Because the essence, the *essence*, not—I've got a whole book here about lived experience, so don't get me wrong—but the essence is not in the lived experience. And the Marxists had to learn, from the Gramscians and from the Negrians, how to think at a level of abstraction that does not need the factory floor to theorize the laws of capitalist oppression. You've got to be able to think at a level of abstraction that does not need whips and chains and fields of cotton to theorize the laws of slavery at the level of abstraction of the *relation*, the relation. And for that, you've really got to, for a moment, put aside historical so-called fact and empiricism.[90]

Such an approach takes no interest in the material relations between experience and essence, history and law, empiricism and abstraction—precisely those interactions of technique and identity that I argue a radically interdisciplinary intersectionality must track. Wilderson's afropessimism cannot be used to track such relations and in fact explicitly rejects their existence. For Wilderson, there is no traffic between these levels. Essence is radically distinct from experience, not generated by it. Law is not a matter of hegemonic power (which always, contra Wilderson, implies a threat of violence), articulated through technologies of mediation, but something deeper and more fundamental than history, which it entirely contains. Fact and empiricism are more likely to get in the way of grasping the abstract relations that define the real than to contribute to an understanding of them. More than just a resuscitation of structuralism, Wilderson's afropessimism is a case against experience and history, dismissing them as superficial. It is anti-interdisciplinary: a power analysis that forcefully rejects a concomitant knowledge analysis, never more clearly than in the analysis of cinema through which Wilderson develops his ontological claims.

Given his interest in the largest possible "structural" phenomena, it might be surprising that Wilderson's argument turns around cinema. After all, as I will argue more fully in this book, films are nothing if not multifaceted cultural-material objects that immediately reveal and intervene in the complexity of identity. But Wilderson's aim is not to unpack what films can do, it is to demonstrate that films can do nothing substantial. Because, in his model, technique and identity are locked together—because identity entirely structures and determines technique, at least to the degree that variations in technique are minor and "inessential" in relation to power—there is no possibility, in Wilderson's account, that a film could enact a transgressive intervention into the structure of the world, let alone make a dent in the ontology of power. Wilderson's goal is actually to deprive film of its "status," "coherence," and "interpellative power," by questioning the very idea that cinematic representations can have material effects.[91] To be clear, Wilderson is not critiquing a representationalist approach to film in order to offer an alternative with more bite, for example by foregrounding the materiality of film production processes. For Wilderson, there is no such alternative. Film is of the "world" and therefore cannot express black subjectivity or culture, only black death and fungibility.

Like writing itself, Wilderson argues—including that of afropessimism—film has no "interpellative" power, only "explanatory" power: "Explanatory power is all that Afropessimism has to offer. Explanatory power. It does not have to offer tactical suggestions. It does not have to offer a vision of the new world. It's simply an explanation of the structure of pain and suffering."[92] Cinema, in this framework, can either hide the real or "unflinchingly" reveal it. As a film analyst and "ontologist" of race, Wilderson looks to film not to intervene in the structure of the world, which he deems impenetrable, but merely to reveal and display those structures: "In the images, editing, and camera work of even the most sentimental socially engaged films one finds confirmation of structural violence."[93] Wilderson writes in detail about filmic technique, including the ways in which sound and lighting design, camera work, and editing exceed and sometimes even contradict the more commonly analyzed work of narrative and script. But, in his analysis, the result of such cinematic workings can only either express structural positionality or fail to do so. Films and filmmakers, for Wilderson, are "cinematic prisms" of the real, which can be altered and contested solely through the ethical violence of armed struggle.[94]

One of the concerns raised about Wilderson's work is that it does not offer any positive routes forward or suggestions for actions to be taken.[95] Indeed, the epilogue to *Red, White & Black* acknowledges that the question "What is to be done?" cannot be answered within Wilderson's conceptual framework, or perhaps can only be answered by reference to a desire for an unspecifiable "end of the world."[96] Another serious concern might well be that Wilderson's treatment of black and white racialization as structurally ontological leads him to casually dismiss the jewish holocaust, the armenian genocide, and other moments of historical brutality as mere exploitation or contingent violence, producing what almost reads as a caricature of nonblack suffering as contained within discourse.[97] But I want to focus here on the conceptual corner into which Wilderson paints himself by refusing to acknowledge the materiality of technique and knowledge. What does the strictness with which

Wilderson divides the ontologically structural from the merely cultural imply about the possibility of thought and the positionality of the thinker, including Wilderson himself? If black subjectivity and culture are impossible, then how is it possible even to advance the "explanatory power" of an afropessimist analysis?

This problem is not specific to Wilderson and has nothing to do with blackness as such. It is a result of structuralism, owing more to Lacan than to Hartman, and it is precisely complementary to the problematic dissolution of identity for which I criticized Eidsheim above. In strictly binding the cultural to the ontological, not as mutual construction but as a structuralist hierarchy in degrees of the real, Wilderson paints theory itself into a corner, untenably positioning the critical thinker as wholly outside politics, capable of analyzing the world but unable to act on it. It might well be objected that Wilderson's own work has already had material effects: It has already circulated as knowledge in ways that, however modestly, remake race and rewrite the material world. That this is evidently true underscores the limits of Wilderson's own argument and his trenchant attempts to dissolve technique into identity. The very fact that Wilderson's afropessimism evidently has more than merely explanatory power demonstrates that, his own claims notwithstanding, identity and technique continually remake one another. Wilderson's own work demonstrates that there absolutely can and must be black knowledge, black culture, black subjectivities, and black institutionality, even if the meaning of such identifications cannot be pinned down.

In a sense, both Eidsheim and Wilderson are right. Eidsheim is right that identity is mutable and that no part of identity is immune to the possibility of being rendered technical. But this does not mean that identity can be reduced to pure technique, because the technical always remains connected to the larger and slower structures out of which it desediments. And Wilderson is right that identity is inertial and heavily laden with power relations, from which there is no possibility of complete escape. But this does not mean that a schema of ontological structure rigidly determines the development of that which is cultural, experiential, or epistemic. If we are to recognize the technical aspects of identity without losing all hope of a power analysis, we must acknowledge that, in a raced world, even vibration may be raced. At the same time, if we are to learn from the force of an afropessimist critique, we have to understand blackness beyond the census category: a blackness that does not attach in a simple or direct way to any population that might be grasped demographically, but is rather something that operates beyond the level of the individual, a materiality that cuts across bodies in ways that structuralist theories cannot grasp. In the terms I am proposing: *Race is made of technique; but technique is also, in its very circulation as knowledge, made of race.* To grasp the implications of this dynamic two-way relation, it is worth noting that neither Eidsheim nor Wilderson explicitly examines the qualities of the specific media forms that make their analyses possible, in contrast to the form of writing in which they both (as I also do here) articulate their arguments. As a prelude to later and more detailed examinations of the differential racialization of media, it is worth noting that Eidsheim and Wilderson build their theories on analyses of differing media, to which they accord differing statuses and capacities.

Wilderson reads films as mediated reflections or "prisms" of the whole structural situation of society and world: cultural objects in which the identities of directors, performers, other creators, and narrative techniques all come together in heavily overdetermined ways that reveal but never change the world. Eidsheim, in contrast, reads audio recordings as effectively dissolving the world, ending identity, transcending power, and entering a plane of pure vibration, pure immanence: the plane of consistency, the sky. The "technique" into which (black) identity dissolves in Eidsheim's analysis is that of an *audio ontology*. It does not include movement technique, for example, let alone techniques of kinship and care, or even skin color, but isolates the technique of sonic vibration: that which is captured by the technology of audio recording.[98] In contrast, the "identity" into which black technique (culture) dissolves in Wilderson's analysis is defined by the *audiovisual ontology* of cinema, often in contradistinction from script and narrative. Wilderson repeatedly points to how a film's images and soundtrack "act contrapuntally to the screenplay," revealing the truth of an underlying structure that its "conscious narrative strategies" work to hide. In this way, "the sensory excess of cinema lets ordinary White film say what extraordinary White folks will not."[99] Although Wilderson's model for the world is structuralist, the mode in which the real of structural violence is revealed to him is audiovisual: Individuals are literally and materially positioned by their audiovisual appearance, often in ways that contradict their narrative role, such that no depth or degree of technical innovation can make a difference. For Eidsheim, the audio or auditory is effectively omnipotent, displacing any possibility of a real substrate beneath it; for Wilderson, in contrast, the audiovisual is effectively impotent, static, and transparent, at best revealing and confirming the real of structural violence. I return to issues of media ontology in the last section of this chapter. For now, I will simply point out that neither Eidsheim's audio ontology nor Wilderson's filmic ontology are able to recognize what Kara Keeling describes as the potential of audiovisuality to be a "house of difference": a site within which differentiation is held without being dissolved or congealed.[100]

By closely reading the opposing ways in which Eidsheim and Wilderson respectively dissolve and reify blackness, I have wanted not to reject their arguments but to collide and combine them, pointing toward an account of identity that is both interdisciplinary and intersectional—synthesizing a knowledge analysis with a power analysis—all in the name of recognizing the complex materialities of embodied and artistic practices in which identity is undeniably present yet still not adequately grasped by prevailing theoretical frames. While Eidsheim accords the artist an impossible freedom to escape the structures of power and identity, Wilderson reduces the artist to merely reiterating and reinscribing paradigmatic structures of power. Eidsheim, in a move similar to mine in *What a Body Can Do*, opens up the limited concept of performed "role" to acknowledge how much further training, technique, and style extend into the bodies and identities of artists than can be accounted for by the casting model with its census epistemology. Wilderson, in contrast, fixes the embodied identity of the performer so tightly within the dynamics of white supremacy and antiblack racism that any attempt at transformation via artistic research must be dismissed as superficial, if not entirely illusory. Both moves make the work of the *artistic researcher*, as imagined here, impossible. The first assigns to the artist a kind of immunity from social determination, which at the same time removes them from the world, so that any discoveries or innovations they make become effectively meaningless. The second deprives the artist of all agency. But if there is such a thing as artistic research, it must consist of interventions that take place through the practical materialization of power-knowledge and identity-technique: working with, rather than dissolving or reifying, both identity and technique. With these considerations, risks, warnings, and examples in mind, the next section takes a further step in critically and theoretically imagining those workings via a rethinking of the molecular.

Thinking the Molecular

Natasha Myers begins her study of molecular biology and the life sciences by asking:

> What are you made of? Look at your hands. Draw one palm across the other. Feel the density of your tissues, the bones, musculature, and sinuous ligaments. What gives your tissues substance and form? You have probably been told that your body is composed of trillions of living cells. But what are your cells made of? What is the stuff of life?[101]

There are many senses in which human embodiment is biochemically molecular. The discovery and definition of biochemical molecules as "the stuff of life" has revolutionized the scientific understanding of human embodiment and, like other technoscientific developments, led to the invention of biochemical technologies with far-reaching impact. As Myers explains: "In the twenty-first century, life and living bodies have been rendered thoroughly molecular," so that the word "life" can in some contexts be almost synonymous with an analysis of the cells, tissues, and molecules investigated in biochemistry, neuroscience, and physiology. On the other hand, the concept of the molecular begins long before the modern scientific map of the body. A "propensity to parse the world into molecular components has a long history that extends back to ancient philosophers who postulated that the worldly stuff we could see and feel had an unseen 'inner constitution'; matter, it was thought, was made up of subvisible atoms or particles."[102] In her ethnographic study of protein crystallographers, Myers continues the important work of social epistemology, revealing how laboratory scientists do not simply discover preexisting material objects, but also "render" them in ways that are at once material, social, cultural, aesthetic, embodied, and performative. Such studies have been crucial to my own attempts to wrest from technoscience the crucial claim to knowledge.[103] But recognizing the cultural construction of technoscientific knowledge is only one side of the coin; it is also necessary to recognize the materiality and relative reliability of that which is known by nontechnoscientific experts.

Several recent studies make clear that even the most rigorously quantifiable and technoscientifically specified molecules are also thoroughly sociocultural. The most astute of these highlight the ways in which positing such molecules as merely biochemical objects not only entrenches the power of scientific ontologies but also reinscribes the racial, gender, and other hierarchies that come with them. DNA, for example, remains central to contemporary scientific, political, and critical debates because of its powerful yet still not fully understood relationship to the organic development of bodies. As Kim Tall-Bear explains, while DNA is typically formulated as that which defines racial and ethnic heritage, as in the popular practice of DNA testing for individuals to determine genetic ancestry, the mapping of inherited biochemical links also depends upon the prior grouping of populations. DNA thus does not cause or define racial identity any more than it is caused and defined by social processes of racialization. In human genome diversity research, faith in "molecular origins" refers back to "ancestral populations," which are defined in terms of contemporary "reference populations." But "each of those constitutive elements operates within a loop of circular reasoning. Particular, and particularly pure, biogeographic origins must be assumed to constitute the data that supposedly reveals those same origins."[104] In my terms, DNA is *knowledge* or *technique* in multiple senses: It is analyzed biochemically in terms of information; it is increasingly subjected to alteration at the micro-level through specialist technologies; and the technoscientific disciplines that claim authority over it understand themselves as fields of knowledge. As such, DNA is not only the stuff out of which racial and ethnic identities are constructed; it is also constructed out of racial imaginaries and the study of racialized populations. The "loop of circular reasoning" that generates a "material-semiotic" object like DNA is not a glitch or bug but an inherent feature of the relation between knowledge and power, which continually constitute each other, not all at once in a deterministic block but iteratively, through iterations of practice.

A similar kind of sociopolitical context surrounds testosterone, even though its molecular structure and biochemical function are very different from those of DNA. Rather than being thought to constitute race (while in fact also being constituted by race), testosterone is typically understood to constitute gender (while in fact also being constituted by gender). Paul Preciado's theory-memoir *Testo Junkie* makes this clear in its investigation and contextualization of testosterone, or "T," within a vast social and political matrix of gender and sexuality. The makers of the Testogel brand, for example, assume that the user of testosterone "is a 'man' who isn't producing enough androgen naturally and who, obviously, is heterosexual." This man is presumed to have his preexisting but insufficient manhood augmented and consolidated by testosterone, similarly to the way in which ancestry is assumed to be preexisting but insufficient before it is confirmed by DNA tests. Biomedical renderings of transgender as a medically approved passage between two preexisting genders further sediment the link between testosterone and gender, since "in order to legally obtain a dose of synthetic testosterone, it is necessary to stop defining yourself as a woman."[105] What Preciado wants to introduce as gender "piracy" or "hacking" is a destabilization of the relationship between technique/technology (in this case, testosterone) and identity (manhood or masculinity), opening up other possibilities through an embodied research process that bears more than passing resemblance to artistic research, being based on "the invention of new techniques of the self and repertories of practices."[106] Of course, the molecule at the heart of such research cannot be simply biochemical. Testosterone is analyzed and produced through technoscientific practices of biochemistry, but its meaning is also constructed through cultural and embodied practices of gender and sexuality. Drawing on Peter Sloterdijk and Donna Haraway, Preciado locates the principle of *self-experimentation* at the heart of the development of liberation movements, so that "anyone wishing to be a political subject will begin by being the lab rat in her or his own laboratory."[107] The counterpart to this claim is to recognize the materialization of gender, racial, and other identities in all experimental practices, even the most radical. After all, the purpose of experimenting with a molecule like DNA or testosterone—not in a technoscientific laboratory but in a laboratory of everyday life—is not merely to change oneself by changing one's own techniques and technologies but also to invent new techniques and technologies that, because they are made of the "stuff" of political identity, have the potential to be shared and to develop a politics of their own.

Two further examples illustrate this point. Mel Y. Chen tracks the animate journeys of the metals lead and mercury, examining how these too, despite occupying "the lowest end of the animacy hierarchy," can nevertheless become racialized, both constituting and being constituted by racial formations.[108] Here, lead is not only the chemical element Pb but also a "material-semiotic" substance that becomes "animated in new ways," taking on "new meaning and political character" as it shifts racial identities: from a disabling pollutant raced and classed as black and poor to an invasive asian or chinese toxin endangering the presumed intelligence and innocence of white children.[109] Going even further to theorize the biomythography of racialized molecules, Tiffany Lethabo King explores the relationship between black bodies, concepts of blackness, and the materiality of indigo dye as portrayed in Julie Dash's film *Daughters of the Dust*. King describes "Blackness as coterminous with a series of chemical reactions and as porous bodies that exceed the humanist ontological boundaries that would separate plant, objects, and human flesh from one another." This

> creates an opportunity to reflect on other kinds of cosmologies—more specifically, Indigenous and Black ones—that radically reimagine the body's relationship to life forms that have been taxonomized as plants or nonhuman. . . . Moreover, theorizing Black bodies as forms of flux or space in process rather than as human producers, stewards, and occupiers of space enables at least a momentary reflection on the other kinds of (and often forgotten) relationships that Black bodies have to plants, objects, and nonhuman life-forms. A focus on the fungible flux of Blackness can temporarily arrest the tendency to assume that Black life always already orients itself around the human as the center of space and life. As an open and porous state, Blackness possesses various openings, entry points, and ways of orienting itself to social and organic constellations.[110]

In Dash's film, and specifically its biomythographic portrayal of "blue-handed people," we find not merely a portrayal of black labor but also a project of artistic research that investigates "a molecular process of a body becoming both flesh and indican." While the "indigo stain is knowable only at the molecular level"—"slaves are poisoned and die," but the chemical does not really appear as a bluish tint on the skin—it becomes "perceptible to the human eye . . . through decolonial art such as Dash's," which makes visible forms of molecular violence that colonial regimes of knowledge hide. Here, as in Chen's work, toxicity itself is racialized in ways that biochemistry cannot explain. "In the nether regions of the indigo plantation, Black bodies may merge/mate with plants and create the commodity dye." These bodies are "embedded within ecotonal processes that tropicalize the landscape of the plantation" and "present new racial and sexual coordinates of human alterity."[111] It is not only that the biochemical molecule *indican* helps to construct the meaning of blackness; equally, the indigo dye is itself blackened through a historical retelling that refuses to exclude slavery and colonialism from the realm of the material.

My claim here is that a racial analysis of molecules, or a molecular analysis of race, does more than reveal how material objects and substances are swept up into social and cultural discourse. The latter acknowledgment could be made while keeping intact an ontological distinction between culture and matter according to which sociocultural forces act upon preexisting material substrates. No scientist would deny that this is the case. What critical thought contributes, however, is a further claim: that molecules are themselves materially constituted by sociocultural practices, there being no way to know or access a pure substrate of materiality outside the sociocultural. If this is the case, then no absolutely distinct biochemical model can be separated from the racialized and gendered contexts in which it is mobilized. Instead, what we encounter are relatively distinct yet overlapping disciplines, each with its own methods and onto-epistemologies for storying the material: molecular biology, with its technoscientific quantification of matter; anthropology, with its studies of the work that molecules do in particular situations, including those of the scientific laboratory; cultural studies, analyzing the entanglement of the biochemical with other discourses on a larger scale; and others even farther afield, such as the biomythographics of artistic research. A truly interdisciplinary perspective is one that recognizes the legitimacy of all of these disciplines—as well as, crucially, those still excluded from academic recognition—in making claims about what a given molecule means or does.[112] Moreover, a radical interdisciplinarity—one that is also intersectional—also recognizes the differential power dynamics among these fields and critiques the prevailing hierarchy of knowledge by which they are accorded differing ontological force. It is, after all, social and political history that determines why some disciplines are understood as defining the most fundamental reality, others as studying the merely cultural, and others (with even less epistemic legitimacy) as merely forms of culture themselves. To approach the question of what is material therefore demands an inquiry into the differential legitimization of diverse forms of knowledge.

I have introduced the molecular through the relatively "hard" molecules of technoscience only to appropriate it for a range of molecules that are not measurable or localizable in this sense: that which I am calling *technique*. A gesture, a melody, a joke, a dance, a rhythm, a habit, a gait, an exercise . . . By what right do we exclude such chunks of embodied knowledge from the realm of the material? In whose interests is it to assume that aspects of embodiment that cannot be reliably located and measured by technoscientific means are therefore immaterial? Would it not be more accurate (and more ethical) to name those aspects of material embodiment that are localizable and quantifiable as such, lauding the extent of their reliability and the technologies they afford but not for that reason according them greater ontological reality? Taking the primary example developed in my own artistic research practice: A song, as embodied technique, cannot be extracted from the body using the type of anatomical and anatomizing methods that found modern science by extracting natural objects from their temporal and geographical contexts.[113] But this does not mean that we cannot work with songs or that they do not push back against us in material ways. Obviously, we can and do work with songs and other kinds of embodied technique, even without the technologies of notation and recording. Nor is such an extended conceptualization of the molecular to be taken as metaphorical. Embodied technique is literally material, even if it cannot be anatomically isolated. Songs are components or elements of our bodies. They are inside us and constitute us, just as biochemical molecules do, even if they cannot be extracted or manipulated in the same ways. What must be rejected is a definition of materiality that requires anatomical dissection. Hence, it is right to say that *technique is molecular identity* in the same way that biochemical molecules might be. A gesture, a movement, or a fragment of melody is a molecule of gendered and racialized material, or is formed of gender and racial molecules, as much as are testosterone or DNA, lead or indican. They constitute the matter of identity in a way that operates both below and above the imaginary of the individual with its checkbox-style identities.

There is no need or possibility to draw a strict line between those molecules that can be isolated by technoscientific methods and those that cannot. The former, as it turns out, are just that: molecules accessible to technoscientific methods. This does not make them more real or more material. A wider concept of the molecular would include many other relatively reliable patterns: flows of repeatability that subtend, enable, and compose organisms and societies, whether or not they can be chemically or anatomically isolated. Even within the "hard" (quantifying) sciences, the "stuff" of life and the world is not as symmetrical or epistemologically stable as the folklore of scientific positivism would suggest. It is already not possible to handle or manipulate an atom of hydrogen and an atom of iron in the same ways as each other, to say nothing of a photon or a quark. Such particles are "real" not in a self-evident way that can be easily grasped or tested, but precisely in the highly specialized ways that have been discovered and invented in the field of particle physics.

Something like breath itself is then equally an epistemic object: Everyone breaths, just as everyone is made up of quarks, but not everyone has access to the epistemic depth of breath or to its possible uses, developments, and transformations. Neither is there any single science of breath; rather, there are fields of breath, disciplines and techniques of breathing. The metaphor of "building blocks" that still informs the commonsense positivism of everyday scientism is based on the beautiful symmetries that sometimes appear within science, such as those of mechanical physics or of the periodic table of atomic elements.[114] But the "laws" or relative reliabilities that describe quarks, photons, atoms, and molecules cannot be neatly integrated even at the level of the basic forces of physics, let alone in terms of their measurable behavior or potential application. There is no symmetry in practical chemistry; no molecule is precisely the functional opposite of another. When calculative methods fall by the wayside and are replaced by experimental ones, this does not make the objects of study less real. Epistemological and hence ontological gaps already exist within even the "hardest" of scientific fields. It is therefore no wild flight of fancy to theorize technique and identity as molecular.

We might then observe that, while blackness, whiteness, brownness, indigeneity, and jewishness all circulate as molecular substances in practice, they are no more functionally symmetrical or equivalent to one another than are water, diamonds, and neurotoxins. As we leave behind the elegant symmetries of mechanical physics and the periodic table—not rejecting them, of course, but recognizing their situatedness within particular disciplines based on techniques of quantification—so we must also reject any "grid" model of identities. This is not a rejection of identity; on the contrary, it is done only to reclaim those same identities in a resolutely nongridded and nonbinary formulation of the molecular. Such a reclaiming would allow us to speak of how racial and other identities operate in particular moments and instances, including on the largest scales: flexible like rubber, flickering like flame, impenetrable like diamond, or any of the other properties of bone, ebony, steel, ice, sand, glass, hair, plastic, concrete. . . . Such imagery is already present in Okwui Okpokwasili's evocation of molecular blackness as a substance that may "splatter all over you like hot oil, like a dank rain puddle, like spit."[115] It is present in Sara Ahmed's assertion that "race, like sex, is sticky; it sticks to us, or we become 'us' as an effect of how it sticks, even when we think we are beyond it."[116] In poetic language, "identity particles . . . hover like bees or clouds."[117] An atmosphere "thickens with racial matter."[118] Racial molecules.

We can think with Marquis Bey about the molecular in terms of sedimentation, desedimentation, and resedimentation "at the level of the micropolitical, the molecular, wherein small tinkerings yield micro-abrasions that dissolve the sedimented regimes structuring our horizons."[119] At the phase transition between sedimentation and desedimentation is where we find "molten genders" and also perhaps molten racializations.[120] We could begin to formulate the relationship between technique and identity, or knowledge and power, in terms of layers or speeds, but we will also need to recognize the radically differential qualities and effects of particular molecules, which are only revealed in relation to other substances and through experimentation. Thinking through a molecular chemistry of identity allows us to appreciate its mobility and fragmentation without underestimating its impact. The stickiness of whiteness is not the same as the stickiness of blackness or of brownness. The velocity of a microaggression, like a spark flying off one body and hitting another, depends on which chemical ignites and on the quality of the atmosphere. Chain reactions may be impossible to predict.

At this point the concept of the molecular should be put into conversation with those influenced by the writings of Gilles Deleuze and Félix Guattari. I chose not to begin this section from Deleuze and Guattari's molecular precisely because their usage emphasizes too strongly the knowledge side of the equation: experimentation, transgression, flight. Since my aim here is to counterbalance my previous work on identity as technique with a complementary focus on technique as identity, I began instead from examples that highlight the extent to which allegedly purely biochemical molecules are in fact heavily racialized and gendered, not only in their effects but also in their very constitution. A molecule in this sense is always "material-semiotic," as both TallBear and Chen assert, or what Deleuze and Guattari call a "particle-sign," here figured as a glob or chunk of "identity-technique" and analyzed in terms of both knowledge and power, interdisciplinarity and intersectionality.[121] Such an application of Deleuze and Guattari's work to race has been undertaken by a number of thinkers who, in the face of the widespread "deontologisation of race" (attempts to undercut racism by jettisoning or transcending racial categories) have called for a "reontologisation of race."

Most pointedly, Arun Saldanha argues that race must

> be conceived as a chain of contingency, in which the connections between its constituent components are not given, but are made viscous through local attractions. Whiteness, for example, is about the sticky connections between property, privilege, and a paler skin. There is no essence of whiteness, but there is a relative fixity that inheres in all the "local pulls" of its many elements in flux. Emergence and viscosity are complementary concepts, the first pertaining to the genesis of distinctions, the second to the modality of that genesis.
>
> Race's spatiality is emphatically *not* about discrete separations between "races." Nobody "has" a race, but bodies are racialised.[122]

Viscosity and emergence, sedimentation and desedimentation, are not simply metaphors, although they draw on chemical imagery. These terms describe the actual, material ways in which racial and other identities operate in moments and practices. Following Elizabeth Grosz's deleuzian feminist analysis of how sex is dichotomized into "the great binary aggregates" of male and female, which Deleuze and Guattari posit might be dismantled and recombined to proliferate "a thousand tiny sexes," Saldanha suggests that "the molecularization of race would consist in its breaking up into *a thousand tiny races*."[123] As I have argued, this cannot be a matter of pure desedimentation but must involve material experimentation with identity to produce new identities that fracture, disrupt, and transform older ones. Saldanha even suggests elsewhere that molecular race might be "irreducible," a kind of fundamental particle.[124] This of course does not mean that the racial identity of an individual is unchangeable—just the opposite, since a molecular or reontologizing approach to identity troubles the fixed assignment of identity to individuals. It means that race is substantial: a substance that demands to be treated as present and material in specific contexts and practices, even if its effects and dynamics are variable. This is also among the lessons that I draw from contemporary black studies: not that blackness cannot be analyzed in terms of factors that range from the phenotypic to the sociological and the historical—of course it can—but that disaggregating those components will not necessarily increase the practical grip of thought on the world and may in fact decrease it. The need for black studies itself indicates this irreducibility, this substantiality of blackness, which I suspect ought to be applied, crucially without symmetry, to other kinds of identity.

The chemical model is instructive in several ways. While molecules can theoretically be reduced to atoms and subatomic particles, physics on that level tells us very little about how actual molecules will behave. In Philip Ball's introductory account: "The Periodic Table really belongs to that realm where chemistry becomes physics, where we must wheel out the algebra and the cosines to explain why atoms of the elements form the particular unions called molecules." But the periodic table does not give us the molecular. "Many people believe that the nuclear bomb was itself the product of physics, but writing $E = mc^2$ does not give you Hiroshima—only separating isotopically distinct molecules of uranium compounds did that." To those technoscientific factors, we might add structures of orientialism, racism, whiteness, and fascism, which Ball cannot think alongside uranium but which other authors certainly would. Even without those kinds of forces, Ball's molecular chemistry is a much wilder zone than any table can grid. It is "a craft full of possibilities": "Wonderful, inspiring, inventive possibilities. Terrible, nightmarish possibilities. Mundane but useful things, bizarre things, hard-to-understand things."[125] This is the notion of the molecular on which I would call to think racial and other identities.

By way of comparison, Patrick Wolfe's definition of race as "traces of history" powerfully names the way in which lineages and legacies of violence and oppression continue to live and move in bodies, buildings, cities, and societies today. But even when focusing on "racialisation, race in action, which is prior to and not limited to racial doctrine," the phrase "traces of history" risks placing race primarily in the past.[126] What about the ways in which race operates today, not unrelated but irreducible to its history? Jasbir Puar's proposal to think identity as "assemblage," drawing on Saldanha's work among others, is closer to what I intend. For Puar, "racialization has become a more diffuse process, not only informed by the biological body, what it looks like and what it can do, but also disassembled into the subhuman and the human-as-information." This "subject is divided up into subhuman particles of knowledge that nevertheless exceed the boundaries of the body, yet it is also multiply splayed through, across, and between intersecting and overlapping populations." Yet I would not distinguish "identity politics" from "the politics of affect" as Puar does.[127] I think there is a risk, in deleuzian approaches to identity, of careening too far into the flexible, the moving, the porous, and the desedimented. What I want is a theory of molecular identity that can hold fast to both sedimentation and desedimentation, both power and knowledge, moving at different speeds. I don't think we can do this by getting past or moving beyond identity, but only by taking identity as real, material, and substantial, in order to work with it both above and below the level of the individual subject. As Amit Rai proposes: "Antiracism must become something else, experimenting with duration, sensation, resonance, and affect."[128] How can we think and work with race and identity across these scales and speeds? How can we prevent an investment in the creative capacities of the molecular (or, for that matter, of affect) from postponing an engagement with the weightier formations of power that often go by the name "history" but are in fact no more historical than a song or a slap in the present?

The risk of lightness, or too-easy excitement, in projects inspired by Deleuze and Guattari, may be traceable to a fascination with the discovery that identity is made of technique, which however fails to grapple sufficiently with the counterpoint that technique is made of identity. Hence I argue here not for molecularizing identity, as if the categories we call identities could simply be dissolved through sufficient will or ingenuity, but for *molecular identities*, meaning that what circulates at the molecular level remains irreducibly identitarian. There is no escape from identity in the molecular. Deleuze and Guattari do not account for this; if they offer a power analysis, it does not go very far into the details. As much as they attempt to attenuate such a reading, in their staging of an opposition between the molar and the molecular, the latter is the hero. In key passages on the molecular in *A Thousand Plateaus*, what comes through is the latter's power of flight, its capacity for excess, always in relation to a dominating molar force:

> You become animal only molecularly. You do not become a barking molar dog, but by barking, if it is done with enough feeling, with enough necessity and composition, you emit a molecular dog. . . . Yes, all becomings are molecular: the animal, flower, or stone one becomes are molecular collectivities, haecceities, not molar subjects, objects or form that we know from the outside and recognize from experience, through science, or by habit. If this is true, then we must say the same of things human: there is a becoming-woman, a becoming-child, that do not resemble the woman or the child as clearly distinct molar entities.[129]

The opposition between molar and molecular is compelling, but it easily falls into a romance of the latter. If oppressive power is simply "the molar," that is, the solidly aggregate, then where is the scope for the building of robust solidarities, let alone alternative societies and more just worlds? By the same token, if the molecular is imagined as inherently ethical, or "radical" in a political sense, then we have no way to work practically with violent or dangerous molecules. What shall we do then with molecular whiteness, or with particles of toxic masculinity? What if certain molecules form a tumor? Is it good to become a molecular dog? And how can a molecular "woman" or "child" appear, if they do not even resemble the molar entities out of which they have been desedimented? We have already seen how black studies in particular contests the claim that "bastard and mixed-blood are the true names of race."[130] To dissolve identity categories is not always desirable. Guattari writes: "It seems important to me to destroy such gross categories as 'woman,' 'homosexual' and so on. Nothing is ever as simple as that. When we reduce people to categories—black or white, male or female—it is because of our own preconceptions."[131] But what if, to avoid reducing people to categories, we need not or must not destroy the categories themselves? What if the categories themselves, both above and below the level of the individual, reveal a diversity of material effect that far exceeds the binary formulation of molar and molecular?

The terms "molar" and "molecular" have the same root: *moles*, meaning mass or barrier, indexing the heaviness or inertia of forces. "Molecule" adds the diminutive suffix *cule*.[132] This is not an ethical or political opposition but merely one of scale. What happens when the molar is rejected too easily? An early but prescient critique of Deleuze and Guattari by Christopher Miller is precisely concerned with the question of identity and the way in which the anti-identitarian or "nomadological" stance of *A Thousand Plateaus* conceals a profound reliance on unequivocally colonial sources of knowledge. Miller demonstrates how Deleuze and Guattari develop their conceptual worlds using ethnographic studies and then, in the same breath, reject those historical associations as reductive. Just as "becoming-woman" and "becoming-child" draw on specific politicized identity categories only to transcend them, Deleuze and Guattari make what Miller calls the potent but untenable claim that "there is no reason to identify a regime or a semiotic system," such as those they theorize at length, "with a people or historical moment"—in my terms, there would be "no reason" to link circulating technique with any given identity.[133]

Of particular relevance here is Miller's critique of what he calls "nomadological immunity": the way in which the process of molecularization itself, the dissolving and desedimenting of molar identities, can be operationalized as an escape from politics or from what I am calling a power analysis. Miller's critique of nomadological immunity can be read as a cogent critique of artistic privilege, or artistic immunity, which might be leveled at the (often white) artists who refuse to be held accountable for their artistic choices because, as quoted above, "cultures are not anyone's property." Miller's concerns can thus be applied directly to artistic research:

> How, then, does nomad thought deal with people and things that *are* stuck within the various interiorities of the world? Is there not a certain cosmopolitan arrogance at work here? If the question for

cultural studies must be of finding a way to think through constructed borders and identities, it will have to decide how to deal with the inscribed or projected reality of those borders.[134]

A related point is made by Jodi Byrd, who criticizes calls "for transformational new worlds of relation and relationship that move us toward a joyously cacophonic multiplicity and away from the lived colonial conditions of indigeneity within the postcolonizing settler society." Like Miller, Byrd reveals how the "Indian" or indigenous figure appears in Deleuze and Guattari's work as a "philosophical sign" and a "ghost in the system" that underwrites the radical line of flight while itself being erased in that transit.[135] It is not the joy itself that is a problem here but the erasure that enables and is enabled by that joy.

An even more sharply worded critique is offered by Jordy Rosenberg, who suggests that the molecular as posited by new materialisms might be defined by its exclusion of politics, "as particulate matter becomes a kind of sublime miniature and a point at which ontological wonder blooms." As Rosenberg suggests, the fetishization of technoscientifically produced molecules can be another kind of (white/male) fantasy in which the capacity to redesign bodies at a chemically molecular level allows for the jettisoning of cultural politics with a kind of "vicious, amnesiac joy."[136] Arguably, then, as Neel Ahuja contends, "Deleuzian writing on race" is

> incompatible with the trends towards racial exceptionalism and diagnoses of historically durable racial structure evident in some afro-pessimist and decolonial theories. . . . Unlike the majority of studies in the field, which centre on historical narratives about racial discourse, images and statecraft, Deleuzian approaches to race have thus far been more intimately concerned with the micropolitics of embodiment, technology and affect, connecting with feminist and queer theories that undermine the holism of the body.[137]

I hear in these critiques not a need to reject outright the molecularization of race and identity but a demand to restore to the material substance of race some of its heaviness and to put into dialogue what I am calling a knowledge analysis and a power analysis. In other words, we must read back into the molecularization of identity the full range of molecular and chemical interaction and complexity, including the heavy, the common, and the painfully stable. If a focus on molecularization as a process risks overemphasizing flow and flux, making cultural transformation appear too easy, this should be counterbalanced by an awareness of sedimentation and a willingness to look in more "unflinching" (but not structuralist, as in Wilderson) terms at racial violence, including anti-blackness and colonial genocide, as part of what is carried in the molecular.

This has immediate and practical implications, as Thomas DeFrantz suggests through the chemical metaphor of dangerous ignition:

> Again, and again, dances created in black environments are shared and then later used in contexts that have little reference to breathing black people. You drop the stanky leg or the nae nae into your contemporary performance project. It's supposed to feel hip and aware or funny and ironic. You vogue or j-sette to demonstrate your of-the-moment ability to get down with the kids. Just stop it. *You don't understand what those dances are for or how they operate or what they can do. It's like playing with fire.*[138]

We should recall here that very tiny things can be very dangerous and that molecules too small to see, if they are poisonous or viral, can bring down worlds. (A reference to the ongoing Covid pandemic hardly seems necessary.) There is nothing light or easy about molecules. There exist molecules of which half a gram will kill you on contact, while other molecules are so ubiquitous as to be confused with empty space. In the same way, we are constantly working with racial molecules because we are literally made of them. It is impossible to undertake embodied or artistic practice without engaging the racial. One therefore has no business talking about the body, materiality, or artistic research without engaging in some way with critical race theory, including radically interdisciplinary black studies. The body as archive, as memory, as sedimented technique—the postbiomedical body that has long been theorized by performance studies—is the racialized body. We misunderstand it on a material level if we do not recognize racial identities as part of its substance.

With these admonitions in mind, I would jettison any remaining attachment to "the molecular" as a good in itself. (As Miller demonstrates, Deleuze and Guattari themselves continually state that there is nothing ethically superior about the molecular over the molar, but their prose and examples do not bear this out.) Instead, what compels me about the molecular is its materiality and above all its radical asymmetry.[139] A molecule of whiteness behaves entirely differently than a molecule of blackness. Neither whiteness, nor manhood, nor any other category of hegemonic domination can be reduced to an abstract concept of the molar. It is not just that "white" and "black" as races are not mutually constituting principles but rather incommensurable histories and present substances. The further point is that, even in their incommensurability, they establish no larger container, and certainly no grid or axis, onto which other identities could be mapped. A "red" or indigenous being is not halfway between white and black. Indigenous identities bear complex relations to land and citizenship that contest the very constitution of the racial.[140] My own embodied and artistic research in jewishness has focused on the ways that particular identity cuts across race, nation, religion, and other categories, so that it emphatically cannot be mapped onto a black/white spectrum. Identities relate to one another without being the same; they interact through "difference without separability."[141] Nor is such radical asymmetry reducible to geometrical asymmetry. These differences are substantive, qualitative, chemical.

What is brownness, as José Esteban Muñoz thinks the "brown commons"?

> I mean "brown" as in brown people in a very immediate way, in this sense, people who are rendered brown by their personal and familial participations in South-to-North migration patterns. I am also thinking of people who are brown by way of accent and linguistic orientations that convey a certain difference. I mean a brownness that is conferred by the ways in which one's spatial coordinates are contested, and the ways in which one's right to residency is challenged by those who make false claims to nativity. Also, I think of brownness in relation to everyday customs and everyday styles of living that connote a sense of illegitimacy. Brown indexes a certain vulnerability to the violence of property, finance, and to capital's overarching mechanisms of domination.[142]

The slippage here from brown people to brown commons to brown customs and styles, like that from black bodies to black thought to black worlds, is not a mistake or a gap in logic. It is an innovation, a challenge, a demand for a kind of poetic thought that can see through the division of knowledge and power, technique and identity. Such a slippage is present in the yellowness of Anne Anlin Cheng's "yellow woman," which "is not meant to essentialize but to name the processes of racialization" and which therefore "denotes a person but connotes a style."[143] It is there also in Jean-François Lyotard's lowercasing of "jews" as a figural position, in principle open to anyone, rather than a demographic identity grounded in "real Jews."[144] As a slippage between knowledge and power, technique and identity, something like this characterizes all identity categories, including and beyond those indexed by an emerging decolonial grammar of colors: white, black, red, brown, yellow, jewish, muslim, queer, trans.[145] But this slippage does not apply in the same way to each. It does not apply symmetrically.

A molecular theory of identity therefore requires the sidestepping or at least downgrading of the middle categories by which identities are so often gridded and contained. The decolonial grammar of colors reclaims and redefines the racial categories of colonialism (black, white, red, yellow, brown), making room for a radical rethinking of religious, geographical, and gender categories. There is little place in this grammar for the metacategories of race and gender. "Blackness, thus, will outlast 'race'; transness will outlast 'gender'; feminism will outlast 'women.'"[146] As the grid explodes, each term that was positioned within it is revealed in its radical complexity and potential for activation, in the same way that experimental chemistry frees techno-scientific molecules from the grid of the periodic table. The term "identity" itself must also be questioned, although I retain it here as an inertial counterpart to technique. In this context, that term should be taken to suggest not a census or demographic model of identities as grids or axes but rather an experimentally oriented, historically grounded, politically engaged, and epistemologically provisional molecular mapping of material substances in the form of technique-identity compounds. To begin such a mapping, my primary reference points are blackness, whiteness, indigeneity, and jewishness. Even just these four materialities are already not griddable in relation to each other. On the contrary, they are entirely different kinds of things, radically asymmetrical phenomena, which demand the absolute rejection of any gridded model.

I cannot strictly avoid the term "race," as many of the sources I am working with use it. Moreover, sometimes it is necessary to foreground the racial so that the concept of identity does not slide back into a presumed whiteness. Identity is a very broad critical and theoretical term, whereas race carries with it the historical and world political violences of colonialism. Hence, we might want to affirm: *Race is made of technique; technique is made of race.* But I employ the racial here, like identity itself, only to summon a series of more urgent and evocative molecular beings to displace it. The same strategy can be applied to many other metacategories of identity that seem at first to be separate from race but which ultimately cannot sustain any such distinction: nation, language, citizenship, gender, sexuality, ability. Thinking race, especially in apprenticeship to radical black studies, compels us to push beyond the idea that race is a property of racialized bodies and to recognize instead how race transects bodies, floats in the air, gets lodged in buildings, becomes atmospheric, palpable. When we do that, race theorized from blackness may extend its slippages to other identities, causing the conceptual house of cards to collapse: Blackness is a gender.[147] Whiteness is a religion.[148] Islam, like judaism, is a race.[149] Disability, like africa, is a country.[150] Indigeneity is a sexuality.[151]

From the perspective of a critical hermeneutic methodology based in the arts and humanities, sociological and legal categories of race and gender are at best rough approximations, formalizations, or provisional quantifications of what is materially present in concrete moments, events, and practices. Such a perspective might even take the nation-state, major religious formations, and marxist formulations of class as subcategories of the racial, where the racial is broadly understood as the molecular materiality of technique/identity. Hence the materiality of blackness—and indeed of whiteness, brownness, and other identities beyond the grammar of color—is in no way limited to "race" as a census category. These materialities are transnational, in some cases perhaps planetary, and their recognition is bound up in a call that increasingly exceeds that of anti-racism: decolonization. This is how Robin D. G. Kelley describes "a Black studies epistemology that both critiques Western civilization and moves beyond the anti-racist framework of Western liberalism":

> Such a project must be committed to decolonization and revolution. Decolonization requires the abolition of all forms of oppression and violence, and thus is fundamentally anticapitalist. It means decolonizing the land, embracing a version of freedom not based on ownership or possession or anthropocentrism but stewardship and caretaking as expressed in indigenous thought. Dispossession is not just about property; it is spiritual theft, a disruption of history and our relationship with the ancestors who still occupy the land. It means disbanding the military/police, opening borders, opening the prisons, freeing the body from the constraints of inherited and imposed normativities of gender and sexuality.[152]

These are urgent and ambitious demands. As I have argued, artistic research can be a site at which racial and other identities are investigated and transformed through interventions into the forms of knowledge. Finally, then: What forms does knowledge take today?

Audiovisualizing Thought

The previous sections of this chapter have attempted to develop a molecular way of thinking about the embodied materiality of racial and other identities, neither dissolving this into flux nor fixing it as a static property of countable individuals. This theoretical framing is a prelude to forms of thought that exceed written theorization and cut across the media of communication through which identity and technique are constructed. To shift from casting to dramaturgy, and from a census or demographic epistemology toward radically interdisciplinary intersectionality, is also to lay groundwork for the decentering of writing itself. Such decentering then requires a further shift: from "thinking the molecular," a theoretical investigation of identity and technique, to *molecular thinking*, that is, to forms of thought—especially digital and audiovisual forms—in which identity and technique are brought forward as the means and methods of thought and not merely its objects.

I have proposed a critical framework in which racial and other identities are present in embodied encounters as molecular materialities. Such a reframing leaves everything still to be articulated and at the same time throws into question what it means to "articulate" such processes at all. I have argued that a representational analysis of the ways in which the identities of performers relate to those of roles and characters, no matter how sophisticated, is inadequate for this purpose, not least because it flattens an embodied research process into a static "work" circulating in an imaginary public sphere. Dorinne Kondo and Katherine Profeta offer a different type of analysis, resolutely dramaturgical, by examining the emergent development of theatrical form through embodied practice, including or even especially at moments of conflict and failure. But Profeta also draws attention to the limited capacities of both theatrical performance and dramaturgical writing to communicate what happens in such practices:

> Thus it is possible for intercorporeal work to be radical on a radically small scale. If the knowledge gained in the rehearsal room is not effectively disseminated, the collaboration will have been very meaningful for a very small number of people. Its impact could easily be limited to the owners of the bodies in question. And thus the dance dramaturg, spending her time thinking about intercorporeal exchange, still eventually shifts back to that old question of audience. How might other bodies, beyond those bodies in the room, feel the reverberations of this physical work? Could simply demonstrating the results ever be enough?[153]

It is in this context that Profeta refers, as quoted above, to her own "gut feeling that the dialogues, tensions, and provisional solutions of our process, all of which I was attempting to archive in my notebook, were always going to be more interesting than any scene we might stage inside a proscenium frame." Correspondingly, she highlights Lemon's "decision to publish his artists' journals on the *Trilogy*'s process and to publicly define the *Trilogy* not as a collection of three proscenium stage events but as the larger constellation of performance events, research events, visual art installations, journal writing, cast interviews, and the unruly work that wove them all together." With this "act of public redefinition—declaring that the larger process and all its many byproducts were, collectively, the product," we are challenged to rethink not only what happens in processes of artistic research but also the very forms of knowledge in which those happenings can be shared.

Returning for a moment to the documentary film *Bronx Gothic*, based on Okwui Okpokwasili's performance with the same title, the former "not only archives this Bessie Award winning solo performance of the same name, but also provides audiences access to Okpokwasili's reflection on the work, audience reactions, and Okpokwasili's intimate relationships with her family."[154] Yet the film shows almost nothing of the creative process that unfolds both prior to and alongside the public theatrical work. It reveals little of the kinds of dramaturgical flows and experiments with technique and identity that Kondo and Profeta describe. That absence is not a failure of the film but a feature of the documentary genre, which is neither designed nor intended to communicate the substance of embodied research. After all, the same could just as easily be said about the limits of documentary film in exposing techno-scientific research. The documentary form emphasizes the interpersonal and institutional dramas of the lab; it does not and in a sense cannot articulate the research findings that underpin those dramas.[155] Laboratory sciences have their own forms and languages, their own written and especially quantified discourses, their own styles and techniques of "engraving," through which the knowledge content of laboratory science is shared and archived.[156] To a great extent, the question of artistic research is then a question of form: What are the documents by which the knowledge generated in embodied and artistic processes and practices can be shared and archived? If both documentary film and dramaturgical analysis have an important part to play in the development of artistic research, so too might many other audio and audiovisual methods and forms. And if, as I have argued, identity is sedimented technique and technique is desedimented identity, what does that mean for the particles of writing, audio, and video that circulate within and ever more intensively constitute mediated networks, publics, cultures, societies, and worlds?

The phrase "molecular thinking" is intended to suggest a change in the meaning of both terms. It does not merely refer to a kind of thinking that, while unfolding through the conventional medium of writing, analyzes identity/technique or power/knowledge in terms of diverse and asymmetrical materialities. Instead it gestures toward other horizons, other ways of thinking: literally different forms, different technologies of thought. Another way to understand the imbrication of technique and identity that I have proposed in this chapter is as a strong claim for the inextricability of form and content in the transmission of knowledge. If identity and technique are not finally separable but continually involved in processes of mutual constitution, then there is no external position of written thought from which those processes might be objectively analyzed. It is a common conclusion of poststructuralist thinking that mind-body and theory-practice binaries are untenable, but that realization is rarely pushed into a serious reassessment of writing and a call to develop new technologies of thought. As noted in my critique of Eidsheim and Wilderson, the audio and audiovisual particles that circulate alongside writing in the digital milieu cannot be associated with either side of those binaries. The transmission of audio recordings changes the meaning of the voice, just as the circulation of video recordings changes the meaning of the audiovisual body. Such recordings are not translatable or convertible to written thought, but neither can they be treated as "the body" or "the world" about which writing "speaks" and in contrast to which (written) thought has conventionally been defined. Crucially, audiovisual recordings combine certain key features of writing—they can be copied, transmitted, and to a lesser but significant degree archived—with certain key features of "the body" and "the world," namely, the sonic and visual dimensions of appearance that define these media. Rather than call audiovisuality a kind of embodied writing, I would prefer to explore the extent to which the capacities of audiovisuality offer possibilities for thought and action that are unavailable to both embodied practice and written thought.[157]

There are then two layers of meaning that attach to the concept of the molecular as I am proposing it here: first, a philosophical proposal for a molecular model of knowledge-power and technique-identity relations, which has precedents both in black studies and critical race theory and in deleuzian new materialist thought; and, second, a proposal to radically expand the domain of what formally counts as thought and knowledge, which is really only found in the institutionally situated impulse of artistic research to reclassify that which was formerly contained within "the artistic" as forms of knowledge. In developing the latter, I will not be attempting to produce a comprehensive map of audiovisual forms or genres alongside embodied and written ones. (This would be just as oppressively totalizing a project as attempting to map racial, gender, and other identities comprehensively.) Instead, I want to investigate mediated forms of knowledge through a racial analysis of artistic research, which is also necessarily an examination of the racialization of knowledge. My intention is not only to "think" (write) identity as complex, processual, substantial, material, and in a sense irreducible, but also to point toward an expansion of thought itself that recognizes the saturation of all forms of knowledge by relations of power and vice versa.

Writing itself is both a material technology and a zone or area of technique. This means, as critical theory at least since Marx contends, that written words are part of the substance that constructs and sediments racial and other identities (identity is made of technique). Hence the act of writing has the potential to intervene in, and not merely document or describe, power relations. But it also means, as activist practices of anti-racism and decolonization contend, that writing itself is racial (technique is made of identity). The decision to formulate an argument in writing is already an identitarian act. In chapter 2, I will drill down into the epistemological and institutional entanglement of whiteness and writing through an interrogation of *white writing* as a technique-identity molecule. But first, a few words on the audiovisual.

Studies of audiovisual, internet, digital, and media technology from a critical race perspective provide grounds for understanding audiovisuality forms of thought. While such studies do not often cross over into the methodological terrain of artistic research, they do posit for artistic media practice a capacity to intervene in the material constitution of identity, linking identity to particular techniques and technologies of mediation. Under the rubric of "race as technology," Beth Coleman asks: "Is it possible to think of race as a disinterested object of our delight, as opposed to one that is overinscribed? Can race survive as something other than the remnant of a traumatic history?"[158] In my reading, this is not a case of falling into the too-easy celebration of the malleability of race but a critically aware intervention on behalf of the practitioner-researcher who must necessarily emphasize the technical side of identity in order to work with it experimentally and practically. Coleman's "disinterest" is not a lack of concern or seriousness but a proposal to make use of the specific capacities of various technologies to "dislocate race from its historically embedded status." Through the "prosthetic logic" implied by "rendering race a technology," the "historical weight of racism may be transmutated into a lightness (or speed) of being."[159] The example of Barack Obama returns here, but this time Obama appears neither as one who transcends race nor as one who is fixed or pinned down by its structural positioning. Instead, Coleman describes Obama's "magic trick" in the 2008 primary elections as that of using race as a "levered mechanism," a tool or technology, to position himself rather than being passively "framed" or racialized. Obama here is a skilled practitioner: neither a "charlatan," using technique to hide a structural real, nor a "chameleon," superficially changing while remaining essentially the same, but precisely a kind of practitioner-researcher, one who has "demonstrated excellent skills in the very old game of political mastery by remaining fluid."[160] These skills, in today's political world, substantially include those of audiovisual performance.

Following Coleman's proposal, Wendy Hui Kyong Chun asks:

> To what extent can race be considered a technology and mode of mediatization, that is, not only a mechanism, but also a practical or industrial art? Could "race" be not simply an object of representation and portrayal, of knowledge or truth, but also a technique that one uses, even as one is used by it—a carefully crafted, historically inflected system of tools, of mediation, or of "enframing" that builds history and identity?[161]

These are precisely the questions I have suggested must be faced by artistic research if it is to engage seriously with (racial) materialities. On a methodological level that has everything to do with the embodied practice of the researcher, the concept of race as technology "shifts the focus from the *what* of race to the *how* of race, from *knowing* race to *doing* race."[162] And while this *how* can and should be taken in many directions in the field of the digital, including "big data" and technologies of surveillance, I focus here on the politics of audiovisuality and the ways in which the audiovisual both resembles and represents embodiment, while simultaneously affording the characteristic transmissibility of writing.

Chun explains: "By linking outside to inside in an effort to make the body transparent, the body becomes a signifier: by creating a gap between what one sees and what one knows, racial markers are placed in an ever-shifting chain of signification."[163] I would push this even further by suggesting that the expansion of networked audiovisuality materially changes the meaning of "outside" and "inside" as dimensions of embodiment, a profound shift that cannot be associated simply with either the sedimentation or the desedimentation of race. Sometimes audiovisuality may help to desediment identity, breaking off molecules of racial and other matter and allowing them to circulate in unexpected ways. At other times, audiovisuality may resediment racial and other identities, an effect that might lead not only to the entrenchment of oppressive structures but also to the development and maintenance of solidarity. One thing is certain: When race is figured as technology—a term that already, in modern usage, combines knowledge and matter—in order to search for a "poiesis" or "agency" of racial practice, then we are close to the field of artistic research.

Kara Keeling develops these possibilities in relation to the politics of identity. As a result of the "complexity of the relationships between the digital regime of the image and global capitalism," she writes, digital media theorists increasingly perceive a "shift within the ways that the image functions vis-à-vis questions of indexicality and identity formation." This shift "does not jettison identification as a political strategy but introduces difference into the equation" in ways that are crucial to molecular thinking practices:

> In much contemporary thinking, digital media herald a transformation within the ways that visual data work on and through those sentient beings engaging them. At the same time, studies of practices emergent within digital culture are contending with the shifting ground of the body as a privileged mediator of and site for sociocultural identifications and are revealing the extent to which the body's textual or visual index in cyberspace opens onto new configurations, making possible different insights into processes of identity formation.[164]

Here again, it is the media form of audiovisuality that renders sensible what I have been tracking as the molecular substance or materiality of identity and technique. Keeling figures this "digital identity politics"—which is actually more specifically an *audiovisual identity politics*—through Audre Lorde's image of a "house of difference."[165] This is not a fantastical utopia or rainbow vision but a concrete proposal to grab hold of the image as a political technology because "the digital regime of the image is implicated in (at the same time as it offers a mode through which to challenge) global capitalist exploitation." According to Keeling, "digital films and other creative digital-media productions are in a position to belatedly fulfill aspects of the Third Cinema project."[166] This is because audiovisuality, as form and medium of thought, offers a particular kind of container, a virtual site that contains and holds—not in the sense of disciplining and controlling, but rather through caretaking and emplacement—modes and substances of asymmetrical difference that may not be able to appear through text-based processes and institutions.

The materiality of identity and technique are today increasingly audiovisual. Even the development of new materialisms and ontological turns in critical theory seems related to the rise of audiovisuality insofar as the diversity of phenomena that can enter the posttextual archive demands new ways of thinking about what is real and material. Keeling writes: "The challenge for the digital storyteller becomes one of excavating the collective history hidden in the often highly personal visual information."[167] But I want to suggest that the rise of audiovisuality actually changes what counts as the "personal," materially shifting the boundaries between individual and collective, local and global, by changing the form of the archive and hence what is transmissible.[168] We are used to understanding "embodied" interactions as micropolitics. This is the kind of politics, we assume, that takes place in many processes of artistic research, as well as perhaps in psychotherapeutic contexts or in local communities. It is "micropolitics" because it cannot directly engage with political discourse, which takes place on a different plane. To attain the level of abstraction needed to affect "macropolitics," we might then think, such interactions must be translated into words, whether as philosophy, ethnography, policy recommendations, or other forms of writing. But audiovisuality fundamentally changes the contours of the micro and the macro, so that what was previously understood as embodied, interpersonal, intercorporeal, or inherently "micro"—precisely because of its inaccessibility to writing—increasingly becomes the directly transmitted content of macro-level discourse and hence of politics.

This brings us back to Profeta's dramaturgical account of Lemon's choreographic process, in which topics like "the tensions between individual and group, the notion of 'freedom,' the residues of colonialism, or the connections between dance and spirituality . . . bubbled up easily from just below the surface of the daily work." Artistic research might be nothing less than the practical attempt to catch and articulate those bubblings through new, often digital and audiovisual, forms of thought and knowledge. One effect of audiovisual technologies, in other words, is to reveal that the apparent smallness of what happens in a room is *not* an effect of literal, physical size, but of its capacity to enter mediated discourse. The rise of audiovisuality changes the media of discourse. As a result, phenomena that were previously micro are now macro and the division between molecular and molar is scrambled. If discourse is the short-circuiting of the small to the large, via systems of technological reproduction, then the rise of audiovisual technologies materially changes what counts as small and large. Elements of embodied technique, such as gesture and timbre, as well as less malleable aspects of audiovisual identity (such as those that gender and racially mark bodies), may be too "small" or "micro" to register in a public sphere that is defined by the textual. But as discourse itself is increasingly audiovisualized, these same aspects and dimensions of embodiment are suddenly "writ" large, inscribed on the largest scales of the discursive and the public.

In staking a claim to knowledge and research, artistic research recognizes that certain kinds of thinking, which are not themselves new, can now be elevated and politicized in new ways, entering the public sphere and making a move from micro to macro that had previously been available primarily to what could be written. On an individual and community level, this can be understood as the development of new forms through which to share knowledge. But on a sociopolitical level, the sharing and assessing of such knowledge also constitutes a substantively new kind of thinking. We barely know at this point what such thinking might do, how it might combine with poetics and history, or with law and sociology, or what kinds of institutions it might afford. What could it mean, for example, to found an institution on an audiovisual document rather than a written one? What kinds of social movements or institutions (such as universities) might have as their founding document an audiovisual recording, rather than written declaration? On the one hand, live performance as an artistic medium cannot intervene directly in politics today, cannot appear publicly, without passing through digital mediation. The scales are simply too divergent, as even the largest physically gathered audience is tiny compared to the mediated one. Yet, at the same time as "live performance" itself can no longer be understood as a genre of art—because there is no special, marked zone between the performance of everyday life and the mediation of public discourse—the deep epistemic structures of thought and practice that we reductively call "performing arts" have never been more directly political. Artistic research, then, is a project to make thought catch up with politics: to render thought audiovisual, with all the (racial) implications of that rendering.

To accomplish this, we should stop comparing audiovisuality with liveness, or with its own prior history, and start comparing it with writing. Keeling writes:

> Representation is at work in digital identity politics, but the content of that representation is the relationships digital identity politics orchestrate, express, and make perceptible. The political challenge of the digital regime of the image is an ethical one that attends to representation more broadly, but the digital stages that question in terms of responsibility to and for others more clearly and more immediately than did prior regimes of the image.[169]

This call to reimagine ethics and politics in terms of the digital and audiovisual is salutary, but it is worth noting that Keeling still contrasts the digital primarily to "prior regimes of the image," rather than to writing and the textual. Of course, it is important to understand how contemporary audiovisuality synthesizes, transforms, and exceeds its own technological lineages: how drawing and painting, for example, interact with the development of the photograph, and then with the motion picture, which eventually combines with phonography and audio recording to become the audiovisual, first in cinema and film and then in television and online. But we cannot grasp the significance of this audiovisual trajectory unless we also examine its relationship to writing. Why does Keeling stop short of such a comparison?

Scholarly fields such as critical cultural studies and film studies are highly sensitive to the importance of the rise of digital and audiovisual media. But because of their own reliance on textuality as a medium of thought, they less often foreground their own methodological mediation in the technology of writing. This latter task falls to artistic research, which has the capacity to be critically situated in relation to both audiovisuality and textuality. Artistic research, in dialogue with critical textual fields of cultural studies, can extend Keeling's argument a step further: The digital stages the question of representation in terms of ethical and political entanglement ("responsibility to and for others") not only more clearly and more immediately than did prior regimes of the image, but also more clearly and more immediately than does the medium of writing. In chapter 2, I will argue that examining the rise of audiovisuality from the unmarked position of the textual critic is akin to studying comparative racialization without naming and acknowledging whiteness. A necessary further step, which I would nominate as the most radical proposal made by university-based artistic research, is to situate audiovisuality alongside writing and textuality as a medium of thought. It is this move that allows us to grasp, in a new way, how writing and text have been installed as the sole legitimate and transparent medium of thought, not only in critical theory, or in sociology and legal studies, but also in law, in and as the state, and as institutionality itself. Such comparisons put us in contact with media ontology and the racialization of knowledge, where artistic research makes its most important interventions.

We cannot avoid here the work of media theorists like Marshall McLuhan and Walter Ong, who have attempted comparative mappings between media, positing perhaps similar distinctions between written and audiovisual thought. But a racial analysis of contemporary media must avoid the linear and progressive trajectories onto which McLuhan and Ong map those technologies, relying as they do on colonial frameworks of history and development even in their attempts at anti-racism. In laying groundwork for a black media philosophy, Armond Towns offers a way to rethink the racialization of media, and therefore of knowledge, that rejects the progressive colonial narrative. As Towns explains: "McLuhan's early temporalization of media via cultures (tribal, detribal, retribal) all presupposed a state of nature (tribal), emergence from a state of nature into 'civilized society' (detribal), and a return to a drastically new, yet somewhat recurrent electric state, further from yet closer to the state of nature (retribal)."[170] McLuhan's "electric" state, imagined as a modulated return to natural or tribal forms of life, is related to what I am calling the audiovisual. Indeed, Towns draws on Rousseau, who criticized "civilization" on similar grounds, to highlight the social contract as the metaphorical technology that precedes the electric, the digital, and the audiovisual. It is the social contract that "ensures that there is a subset of people who cannot fully come out of a state of nature," dividing humanity into two groups. In this scheme, "white people sign contracts, Black bodies (state of nature) are what contracts are drawn up for and about."[171] Although Rousseau's social contract is not a literal document, the centrality of writing in its conception cannot be overestimated. The rise of the audiovisual therefore raises the question of how else, besides as a written contract, we might think the social.

McLuhan's arguments about the phonetic alphabet and the printing press are close to those I make here, insofar as these do mark a "break" in the formation of thought that is inextricable from McLuhan's "detribal" or "civilized" human.[172] Such claims about comparative media ontology have largely been left behind by critical theory because they have always reiterated the colonial timeline of technological and historical progression. This fault, as Towns observes, "renders McLuhan's attempt at anti-racism a form of racial fetishization."[173] But Towns also suggests that it may be time to revisit such comparisons from a different perspective: one that can think race and technology, identity and technique, power and knowledge, without and even against such a colonial timeline. Towns makes this possible by putting McLuhan into conversation with Sylvia Wynter:

> What McLuhan described was a materialist media theory read of what Wynter lays out throughout her important career: a nineteenth-century, modern, Western shift from mythic/religious knowledge to what she refers to as "degodded," objective, presumably secular knowledge. Yet, McLuhan lacked the care Wynter has, as he universalizes his raced media theory through his reliance on Western conceptions of time—media as empirically reflective of linear evolutionary capacity.[174]

Through a decolonial reading of racialized media, it becomes possible to think again, in broad yet materialist terms, about the relative onto-epistemological capacities of media in relation to each other and to embodiment and the world. As I have suggested, the shift in the form and media of thought proposed by artistic research has something to do with the decolonization of knowledge. But this connection cannot be figured as a return toward a prior state of nature, an escape from inherently corrupt civilization, or any other linear trajectory within a colonial timeline. Instead, the racialization of media and of knowledge must be reframed from a decolonial perspective, examining the specific ways in which, for example, writing and whiteness have worked together in support of white supremacy.[175] It is only in this context that the present and future of artistic research, both within and outside the university, can be recognized as an intervention in the racialization of knowledge and the mediatization of race. Will the growth of artistic research function as an expansion of whiteness and coloniality into yet more technological domains of thought? Or will it support pathways for the radical deconstruction of whiteness and the decolonization of knowledge? As both these possibilities are already underway, a more precise framing might be: How will colonial and decolonial impulses work through the media-technological innovations of artistic research? And how will new digital and audiovisual forms transform the substance of identity?

Citing media theorist Jussi Parikka, Towns makes the commonplace yet incisive point that "the majority of people walking around in the West right now carry around 'small pieces of Africa in our pockets.'" He refers to the presence of the metallic ore coltan in digital technologies such as mobile phones. Hence "the extraction of raw materials from Africa remains central to our mediated lives—carrying former colonial relations into our present."[176] We return here to the molecular, to the circulation of substances beyond sociological categories, and to the inextricability of identity and technique: DNA, testosterone, lead, indican, coltan. It matters that the domain of audiovisuality, as well as most contemporary textuality, is subtended and afforded by technological molecules like coltan. It matters that, according to Parikka, this coltan is likely african. But the way in which this matters cannot be described or accounted for in the language of technoscientific engineering. On the contrary, the technoscientific engineering discourse that controls the production of mobile phones precisely and rigorously excludes the african identity of the coltan it extracts and instrumentalizes. These same phones, which are made of molecules from around the world and constructed through extractive and neocolonial processes, are nevertheless among the most important media by which ideas of africa, europe, colonization, extraction, civilization, justice, and knowledge now circulate. On these phones and other devices, audiovisual markers of identity become exponentially more complex, materializing in unprecedented ways, growing in a sense more textual (more transmissible, more semiotic), even while they also carry into discourse aspects and dimensions of identity, embodiment, and emplacement that have historically been excluded from discourse. This transformation is happening through technology but it will also shape the future of technology. The more freely and quickly audiovisual data flows, the more audiovisual embodiment enters the zone of potential nonmeaning (an arbitrary relation between signifier and signified). But audiovisuality will never be identical to writing, because of its differing relationship to bodies and places.

I cannot end this chapter with a clear and simple definition of audiovisuality or audiovisual thought. To do so would be to reduce (or whiten) it to a flat technicity, distinct from race, gender, and identity. What I offer in this book is a rethinking of the racialization of audiovisuality, and the audiovisuality of race, in contrast and comparison to that of writing. As I will show in chapter 2, "writing" refers simultaneously to: (1) the technique of inscription of discrete symbols; (2) the practices of writing structured by that technique; (3) the zones of embodiment that articulate themselves through that technique, which we retroactively call "language"; and (4) the vast arenas of complex and distributed processes enabled by the interaction of those zones, which we might broadly call "thought." Audiovisuality, by the same token, is at once: (1) the technological layering of audio and video tracks, digitally analog tracings of particular aspects of the world; (2) the media practices, like film and television, made possible by that technology; (3) the zones of embodiment that are traced or captured by those techniques, such as the timbre of voice, the color of skin, or the shape of a gesture, which become technologically distinct because of their capacity to be captured audiovisually; and (4) the vast arenas of audiovisual thought, still very much in development, and the worlds they make thinkable. To understand the onto-epistemic implications of audiovisuality, it is crucial that we compare it not only to "prior regimes of the image" (and of sound) but also to the regime of writing and textuality, which continues to support so much institutional power.

"Molecular thinking" is a provisional response to the question, asked countless times in artistic research and cognate fields, of *what kind of knowledge* artistic practices can generate. Molecular thinking is not simply thought that takes place through the usual means but which theorizes and models the world as if it were composed of postscientific molecular substances, simultaneously sociocultural and material, technical and identitarian. Taking artistic research seriously as a claim to knowledge and thought beyond writing, molecular thinking necessarily refers also to new media, new *forms of thought*, in which the basic divisions that structure modern colonial institutionality and politics are transected by alternative onto-epistemologies. This is a radically broadened notion of thought, an expanded account of which acts constitute thinking and of the forms that knowledge can take. The keystone of my argument remains the foundational claim of performance studies, that knowledge is embodied and thus that embodied performance is a kind of thinking. But to grasp the implications of that claim in a mediatized world, where the very meaning of the "live" and the "embodied" are unstable, it is necessary to go beyond the concept of performance, into a comparative analysis of racialized forms of knowledge.

Chapter 2

Whiteness and the Racialization of Knowledge

White Writing

How to write whiteness after black studies? I mean "after" in the sense of following, both poetically and politically, through imitation and apprenticeship. How can one write whiteness in the manner that blackness has written itself—not with the same valence, of course, but with the same ferocity? How can one write this profound asymmetry, writing *against* whiteness, with the same dense vibration of poetry and blood that speaks through and from black theory, art, and philosophy? What kind of antifabulation or "unwhitely" performance can name and dismantle, call out, or even abolish that which continues to hold a deadly grip on thought itself?[1] How can whiteness be rewritten today?

> "Look, a white!" returns to white people the problem of whiteness. While I see it as a gift, I know that not all gifts are free of discomfort. Indeed, some are heavy laden with great responsibility. Yet it is a gift that ought to engender a sense of gratitude, a sense of humility, and an opportunity to give thanks—not the sort of attitude that reinscribes white entitlement. . . . Part of the function of tarrying is to create a space for whites to ask themselves the question: How does it feel to be a problem?[2]

One of the lessons I am learning from black studies is the need for writing that is rigorously poetic in its engagement with identity concepts. The recent work of scholars like Tiffany Lethabo King, Marquis Bey, Alexander Weheliye, and Christina Sharpe, which moves alongside and wrestles with the afropessimism of Frank Wilderson and Jared Sexton, calling upon and bringing forward earlier work by Hortense Spillers, Saidiya Hartman, Robin D. G. Kelley, Sylvia Wynter, Audre Lorde, the Combahee River Collective, and many others, is as far as possible from a cavalier play with signs and signifiers; but neither does it get bogged down in sociological conceptions of race as demographic or quantifiable. These poetic thinkers write and invent blackness in a way that constantly navigates the fault lines of technique and identity, refusing to define it either as entirely mobile or as permanently fixed. Powerful concepts like fugitivity and fungibility, which redefine blackness in postdemographic and postrepresentational modes, allow for slippage at the borders of identity—not to render the concept of blackness less substantial but to give it even greater bite.

I hear in these waves of critical practice an implicit challenge to rethink whiteness along lines that are methodologically parallel but functionally reversed: to rewrite whiteness through a poetics aimed at its deconstruction, or even its abolition, rather than its redemption or escape.[3] A different kind of theory of whiteness is called for. Although much has been written about whiteness, its theorization often remains stuck in a sociological mode, as if it were merely a ruse of capitalism with no substance of its own; or as if its very particular techniques of distancing and disembodiment, because they are not "culture" in an embodied sense, are therefore not technique at all, not substantive knowledge. But modern technocapitalism, with its economic theory of value and its extractive mode of relation, is part of whiteness. It arises from and reproduces whiteness. Class as economic stratification, economized via quantitative financialization, is founded on white ways of knowing, writing, and thinking. This is less a historical argument than an observation about the present: As radical black and indigenous analytics make clear, that which implicitly underpins the financialization of the world is whiteness as a way of being. We must therefore look again—unflinchingly, but without the guarantee of any structuralism—at what constitutes white worlding and why and how it is so dominant and damaging today. We must develop counterwhiteness in a nonheroic mode: counterwhiteness as everyday technique, a daily practice of disidentification.

Following the chemical language proposed in the previous chapter, we might say of whiteness that it can be as common as table salt and as deadly as radioactive waste. Touching whiteness can be compared to handling a volatile substance, such as an explosive or a virus, but also to being locked within caverns of concrete, as is physically the case for so many who are literally imprisoned by its terrible need to control. The naming of institutional whiteness must be done with care and seriousness but also with urgency, because this substance is all around us, exactly like concrete or plastic. We do not have the luxury of working slowly or of dealing only with small quantities of this whiteness. Whiteness in the form of militarized racism kills people daily in the united states and europe and many more across the globe. In the form of environmental racism, it is poised to kill billions. We are already drowning in whiteness, suffocating under it, struggling to comprehend a contagion that has saturated the air and water around us and dwells within our bodies, attaching differently to them depending on how we look and where we are from. An individual's relation to whiteness is determined not only by skin color but also by ancestry, genealogy, wealth, emplacement, and by crucial intersections with gender, class, religion, language, citizenship, and nation. My own whiteness is different in northern england than it is in new york city; different when I am perceived as nonbinary than when I am not.[4] Relations to whiteness are as complex and fractured as to any other identity and, while there is great political urgency to determine exactly how it is that whiteness must change—transformation, deconstruction, provincialization, abolition— there is also an ethical and political need to understand *how it works* as a field of power/knowledge and identity/technique.

A widely circulated anti-racist workbook enumerates several "character- istics of white supremacy culture" that show up in a variety of contexts. Following perfectionism, defensiveness, a sense of urgency, and an empha- sis on quantity over quality, the next item listed is "worship of the written word." (The first four items could be taken to define what "worship" means in the context of whiteness: perfectionism, defensiveness, urgency, quantity.) Worship of the written word is then broken down into elements, the first two of which are "if it's not in a memo, it doesn't exist" and "the organiza- tion does not take into account or value other ways in which information gets shared."[5] Additional characteristics mentioned include the hoarding of power, belief in objectivity, and individualism. This description of white supremacy culture is precise and perceptive, if simple. It is a distillation of experience, intended for practical use. But it also sums up many critical argu- ments about the ways in which western academic disciplines have failed to recognize, if not intentionally erased, nonwritten forms of knowledge.

Citing the work of Zora Neale Hurston, performance studies scholar- practitioner Dwight Conquergood has observed that the typical "white man researcher is a fool not because he values literacy, but because he valorized it to the exclusion of other media, other modes of knowing."[6] As Conquergood and others in the field of performance studies have long argued: "The root metaphor of the text underpins the supremacy of Western knowledge sys- tems by erasing the vast realm of human knowledge and meaningful action that is unlettered."[7] I begin this chapter by investigating the relationship between whiteness and writing. I do not wish to reduce whiteness to writing, or writing to whiteness, but to interrogate the racialization of knowledge as a keystone of large-scale power-knowledge dynamics, both historically and in the present. If writing is technique and whiteness is identity, then I am work- ing here with a technical-identitarian and cultural-material concept of *white writing*: a racial molecule, a particle of racialized knowledge.

Brigitte Fielder and Jonathan Senchyne have discussed the imbrication of writing and racialization, pointing out that "textual media and racial iden- tification rely on similar visual technologies to make meaning."[8] In their analysis, the whiteness of the conventional background for print (and now digital) writing becomes a metaphor for whiteness as the infrastructural and literal backdrop of written communication. In an edited volume focusing broadly on the need to think "technologies and techniques of racialization together," at least two of the contributors point to how the "book form itself . . . might actually be inextricable from the history of antiblack racism." Indeed, Fielder and Senchyne note: "If modernity and print are in some ways inextricable—and if modernity and antiblack racism are also in some ways inextricable—then we need to be more attentive in our thinking about what else books and print do."[9]

The meaning of the book form inheres in its linearity, its cohesion as a stable and reproducible object, but also in its very letters, its alphabet. Perhaps the strongest articulation of an anticolonial critique of writing was expressed by oglala lakota activist Russell Means, who does not mince words:

> *I detest writing.* The process itself epitomizes the European concept of "legitimate" thinking; what is written has an importance that is denied the spoken. My culture, the Lakota culture, has an oral tradition and so I ordinarily reject writing. It is one of the white world's ways of destroying the cultures of non-European peoples, the imposing of an abstraction over the spoken relationship of a people.[10]

Means criticizes not only the book form but writing itself, linking it to the destruction of cultures and peoples—that is, to material and cultural genocide. The fact that Means's speech, like my argument in this book, now circulates as a transcription in written form nuances but does not undermine his strong critique of writing.

Drawing on Aníbal Quijano, Maria Lugones also links eurocentric domination and the coloniality of power to a set of "cognitive" techniques and technologies that are inextricable from writing: "measurement, quantification, [and] externalization (or objectification) of what is knowable with respect to the knower."[11] A similar point is made by Tukufu Zuberi and Eduardo Bonilla-Silva, who trace white sociology to the colonial science of eugenics, arguing that "white methods" of knowledge production

> are the practical tools used to manufacture empirical data and analysis to support the racial stratification in society. White methods are the various practices that have been used to produce "racial knowledge" since the emergence of White supremacy in the fifteenth and sixteenth century and of the disciplines a few centuries later. These practices remain connected to White logic and, as such, cannot be easily divorced, no matter what their practitioners murmur or shout vociferously, from racial domination.[12]

Because they are working in the discipline of sociology, Zuberi and Bonilla-Silva aim their critique at quantitative, statistical, and demographic methods (also those mentioned by Quijano as the "cognitive" methods of capitalism). But the scope of writing is much broader than a narrowly sociological concept of method, hence a much wider range of methods must be examined to define white writing. As a technology, writing goes beyond quantitative or qualitative methods and beyond academic research.

The financial instrument or currency, the bureaucratic form to be filled out, the census or survey, the "logical" argument, and above all the law—including the written constitutions, legislations, and policies that found and structure governing states—are all unimaginable without the technology of writing. Writing is so fundamental to these social formations that we can legitimately ask what "the state" or "the law" refer to if not specific implementations of writing. Institutionality itself, at least in eurocolonial modernity, is a particular mode of regularization, stabilization, and standardization that relies fundamentally on the technology of writing. This technology is then reciprocally constitutive of colonialism itself, as Lisa Lowe suggests: It is "the tireless collection of tables, statistics, measurements, and numbers; the unending volumes of records and reports; the copied and recopied correspondences between offices; the production of legal classifications, cases, and typologies," that together "constitute the very media of colonial administration."[13] It is then not surprising to encounter Jared Sexton's comment that "the etymological roots of race link it to writing" or Frank Wilderson's statement that the "rule of law"—one type of "worship" of the written word—is a euphemism for anti-blackness.[14] Nor is it a coincidence that Denise Ferreira da Silva, whose work I read below alongside that of Jacques Derrida, repeatedly refers to european coloniality as enacted through writing, especially in those acts that establish the alleged transparency of the white self: "the writing of Europe in transparency."[15] In coining the term "white writing," I am not positing a technological determinism, as if writing itself were to blame for colonialism. Rather, white writing names the inextricability of the technology of writing from the construction of whiteness through colonialism.

In chapter 1, I drew on Armond Towns's discussion of Marshall McLuhan and Walter Ong to gesture toward a media ontology that would wrest the insights of media theory away from the colonial timeline. Following Towns, I suggested that, while we must reject an oversimplified progressive narrative according to which digital communication appears "after" writing, which in turn appears "after" something prior to writing, this should not lead us to underplay the critical, philosophical, and onto-epistemological implications of new media. The framework I am developing here does not arise primarily from a historical narrative, but from the concrete ways in which recent and current practices of artistic research actively decenter writing and intervene in the forms of knowledge. My thinking is especially informed by recent experiments in audiovisual thought. Although video is not the only medium by which (white) writing can be decentered, it does offer profoundly new ways of decentering writing because of how audiovisuality functions as a third modality that triangulates—and reveals the asymmetries of—a series of binaries that, I argue, are more or less artifacts of the technology of writing.

These include the apparent oppositions between *mind and body, theory and practice, thought and feeling, rationality and emotion, cognition and sensation, knowledge and experience*, and other such binaries, which continue to exert tremendous force despite decades of work aimed at their deconstruction. In each of these cases, I suggest, audiovisual recordings are characterized by some qualities of the first term and some qualities of the second: They are archival yet embodied; transmissible yet identifiably linked to individual bodies and places; digital signifiers that are analog in perception; inscriptive but not textual. By effectively breaking such hegemonic binaries, video reveals the extent to which they rely on the technology of writing and might even be considered an artifact of that technology.[16] Put simply, video is both "mind" and "body" in a way that strikingly reveals the limitations and narrow origins of the mind-body opposition. If we take video and audiovisuality seriously, we have no choice but to acknowledge that what we have come to call mind, thought, reason, theory, rationality, knowledge, and cognition are all defined retroactively by what can be written.

The technology of writing—especially after printing and later digital technologies render the act of copying trivial—produces a sharp cut between what can and cannot be transcribed. This cut then imbues certain aspects of lived practice or performance with heightened capacities of archivability and transmission. In fact, without reference to the technology of writing, no sharp distinction can be drawn between speech and song, words and gestures, or mind and body. As just noted, this is primarily a synchronic rather than diachronic argument, comparing writing to audiovisuality as media or forms of thought in the present. One has only to look at any audiovisual recording of a person speaking to see that there is no way to isolate "speech" or "language" as distinct from gesture, melody, and other "nonverbal" means of communication, except insofar as the former can be transcribed and the latter cannot. Ask yourself: What distinguishes, in an audiovisual recording, a spoken word from the *way* in which it is spoken, or the facial expression that comes along with it? Only the *writability* of the former, which produces a sharp cut between writable words and the rest of the audiovisual document.[17]

Writing itself implements a distinction between *transcription* and *description*, between what can be transcribed and what can only be described. And yet, even contemporary critical scholarship, foregrounding the radical reclamation of indigenous textual practices, continues to frame textuality and its others according to a binary "relationship between orality and textuality."[18] Let us be clear: There is no such thing as orality or "oral" culture without writing—not because people do not speak, but because speech is not severable from the rest of life except in the presence of a technology that can transcribe it and which, in doing so, retroactively defines it as separable. The very idea of "nonverbal" communication, by reifying the verbal as that which can be written, reduces to an accessory what is actually the far larger category. One need not historically excavate or ethnographically produce situations without writing to grasp this epistemic reversal. The technological specificity of written thought is evident as soon as we begin to perceive audiovisual recordings not as slices of life to be (textually) analyzed but as performances of thought that are inscribed without being written.

Related arguments have been made by postcolonial and decolonial theorists of writing, not necessarily by juxtaposing writing and video (I am not aware of this particular argument having been made elsewhere) but by comparing phonetic and alphabetic writing to other kinds. Chinese writing is among the most cited alternatives to "western" phonetic writing, with many european philosophers entranced by orientalist fantasies about the significance of its allegedly nonphonetic character. Whether or not chinese writing is as phonetic as european scripts or not is beyond the scope of this study, as would be an assessment of its relationship to chinese forms of colonialism.[19] More immediately relevant here are comparisons that have been drawn between european phonetic writing and precolonial indigenous writing systems of the americas. While chinese writing has often been set against european writing as a substantive alternative to it, Walter Mignolo notes that "Pre-Columbian writing systems in the New World have more often than not been left out of the picture" by colonial narratives in which the "invention of the letter" as the most effective "representation of speech" is assumed to enable rationality itself.[20] Following James Lockhart, Mignolo suggests that the concept of the word was unknown to nahuatl populations of the sixteenth century, who "transcribed sound, syllables, and sentences but not words."[21] In the multiple physical and cultural genocides that followed, "alphabetic writing, in complicity with the language of the state and the printing press, overpowered linguistic diversity and established a linguistic hierarchy largely supported by the power of national languages and their inscription in alphabetic scripts."[22] Colonialism as writing; writing as colonialism.

Birgit Brander Rasmussen further explains:

> As Europeans began to develop a sense of themselves as different from those they colonized, that difference became not only racialized but also linked to the possession of writing, defined narrowly as alphabeticism. The persistent use of the possessive in discourse on writing is notable. Eighteenth-century and nineteenth-century writers repeatedly stressed that Europe *had* history, writing, and literature, that others did not *possess* it. This possessive investment in writing eventually came to underpin white racial identity, particularly in North America, where it was elaborated through anti-literacy slave codes. As Europe and its descendants in the Americas claimed exclusive possession of writing and linked the possession of this technology to a hierarchy of humanity, "writing" became a maker and marker of racial difference.[23]

The fact of historical conquest and genocide should not lead us to miss the profound significance of the diversity of writing techniques and technologies. There is no singular technology of writing, but rather many different invented or discovered implementations of material inscription. This point should provoke a rethinking of the assumed transparency that attends alphabetic writing today. It also invites us to rethink the assumption that alphabetic or phonetic writing is distinct from other kinds, rather than being bordered on every side by its others: drawing, sketching, doodling, and ornamenting, as well as the creation of all manner of pictograms, ideograms, maps, diagrams, and other such inscriptions.

In this context, as Raúl Sánchez suggests, "the Western focus on alphabetic writing seems rather anomalous and, again, provincial."[24] The radical separation of alphabetic writing from other forms of material inscription and transmission does not simply result from its technical properties. It is generated by historical processes that are closely bound up in coloniality and the racialization of knowledge. The point is not exactly that phonetic alphabetic writing is white, or even that whiteness is constituted by phonetic writing, but that the qualities associated with this particular writing technology are inextricable from the materiality and institutionality of whiteness. Returning to the relation of technique and identity, it is simultaneously the case that whiteness is made of writing (the construction of white identity is historically and presently materialized through technologies of alphabetic writing and printing); and that writing is made of whiteness (that which is counted as writing and legitimized as constituting thought, knowledge, rationality, and indeed research, is determined by structures and institutions of eurocentric power).

The more precisely we can specify the technique of writing that is mutually constituted with white identity, the better we will be able to understand the racial implications and decolonial potential of alternative techniques and technologies, including new media forms. It is therefore worthwhile to dig deeper into the media ontology of alphabetic and phonetic writing in order to grasp how white writing is not merely the worship or reification of writing in general, but the colonizing dominance of a highly specific technique and technology that continues to structure institutionality in the present. By the same token, to avoid the reductive idea that technologies of phonetic or alphabetic writing can only be white and colonial, it is important to explore this connection not only in terms of the most obvious technical characteristics but also in less evident, underpinning layers of technique. For it is not only phoneticism and alphabeticism that make (some) writing white; whiteness is also to be found in the choice of words, the rhythm of sentences, the style of development, and other qualities.[25] Recognizing this allows us to invoke, alongside alternative scripts and literacies, alternative modes and styles of writing that may use the same alphabetic script to voice a different technique of thought.

Without collapsing an analytics of coloniality to one of patriarchy, it is worth mentioning Hélène Cixous's claim that "male writing" is "a locus where the repression of women has been perpetuated" and that "nearly the entire history of writing . . . has been one with the phallocentric tradition."[26] Contrasting the narrowly conceived "reason" of phallocentrism against a writing of the self and body that women must invent, Cixous's comment resonates with the incursion of poetic writing into scholarly text developed by women of color writers like Gloria Anzaldúa and Rosamond King. More recently, seeking an "other experience of language," J. Kameron Carter foregrounds the textual practice of poet M. NourbeSe Philip, who "*not-tells* or rather *un-tells*" the story of an eighteenth-century slave ship by "mutilating" extant court and other documents, literally erasing and deconstructing their textual fabric. Philip explains her practice in the poem *Zong!* as an assault on the textuality of these documents: "I murder the text, literally cut it into pieces, castrating verbs, suffocating adjectives, murdering nouns, throwing articles, prepositions, conjunctions overboard, jettisoning adverbs."[27] These examples demonstrate how generative attacks on white (and patriarchal) writing can be launched from within alphabetic writing, not only via literacies that make use of different technological substrates and types of sign.

Jacques Derrida's *Of Grammatology* may be the most influential book of the twentieth century about the relationship between whiteness and writing. Why then is it so difficult to piece together Derrida's position on phonetic, alphabetic writing as a historical phenomenon, or to derive any situated politics from his critique of western metaphysics? Derrida is clear from the start that his project attacks "the most original and powerful ethnocentrism," which is "in the process today of imposing itself upon the planet" by controlling three technologies that are actually one: writing, science, and metaphysics.[28] Yet Derrida's position, at least throughout that volume, is ambiguous regarding the possibility of a decolonial media ontology. He does not draw on philosophical or political frameworks outside the francophone european lineage, instead working from within it to deconstruct its foundational assumptions. Elsewhere, Derrida pointedly calls metaphysics "the white mythology," which "the white man" (mis)takes "for the universal form of that he must still wish to call Reason."[29] Thus, his deconstruction of metaphysics seems at least intentionally allied to a politicized decentering of writing. As Sánchez suggests, "Derrida's 'deconstruction' and Mignolo's 'decoloniality' can work together."[30] On the other hand, as Gayatri Spivak notes in her afterword to the 2016 edition of *Grammatology*, Derrida's critique of ethnocentrism, spanning forty years between the earliest and most recent translations of that book, remains backgrounded in his philosophical labor. "I have attempted to understand why he cannot claim it," Spivak writes, and "why it cannot end his book."[31]

Grammatology ends with an ambiguous, open-ended dream, not with any call to action. Why is this? Why does Derrida's critique of ethnocentrism tend to fade away and become lost behind his exhaustive efforts to root out the illusion of presence within a european philosophical tradition? Gil Hochberg offers a clue:

> Both Derrida and Cixous came to "Algeria" late in their lives and writing careers. Their upbringing in colonized Algeria was for the most part absent from their texts until they began to write semi-autobiographies; until, that is, they turned their personal memories and narratives into new modes of political intervention. Indeed, as long as the two prolific writers were engaged in deconstructing Western philosophical metaphysics (Derrida) and advocating "feminine writing" (*écriture féminine*) (Cixous), they were unquestionably recognized as "French": deconstruction was French; feminine writing was *very* French. But to continue to undo European hegemony without questioning "Europe" from its margins (and not only from "within," by means of deconstructing key European texts) had become by the mid 1990s truly impossible.[32]

Derrida in *Of Grammatology* remains largely within what I have called a knowledge analysis, closely examining the affordances of writing as the primary technology underpinning "western" metaphysics. Only secondarily, and mostly in passing remarks, does he begin to situate the "west" in a larger geopolitical field, suggesting a power analysis by linking writing to whiteness and the racialization of knowledge. Nevertheless, Derrida's critique of metaphysics and logocentrism stands as a valuable critique of white writing, one that offers a usefully deflationary account of european philosophy.

How exactly is it, after all, that—as Rasmussen says—a "possessive investment in writing eventually came to underpin white racial identity"? Guns and germs kill people. Fences and walls physically block movement. What does writing *do*? How does a specific technique and technology of writing both enable and produce the (white) philosophical lineage of metaphysics and the social framework of (white) technoscience? The answer to this question is crucial if one hopes not only to offer a compelling critique of philosophy and technoscience but also to continue to develop substantive alternatives to those lineages. If Derrida offers a crucial contribution to theorizing white writing, that is because he shows how the concrete and practical technology of writing can be used not only to announce its own dominance but also indirectly to reify and exalt something else, something that writing produces only by concealing itself as technique and technology. Writing in this sense has no direct material force, as a weapon or a wall might have, but instead works to create and install that which apparently precedes it, the subject or voice that appears to speak through it. Sometimes writing accomplishes this by acting as a transparent medium through which the threat of material force is communicated. These are the kinds of directly colonial situations treated by Mignolo and Rasmussen, in which writing is weaponized as the word of God, or as the incarnation of law itself, a bare-faced transmission of the threat of violent force. But the situations that interest Derrida are more ambiguous: They are those in which writing appears to attack, critique, and efface itself in order to shore up a different kind of power, which in fact has no independent existence apart from its appearance via the written word.

To understand this veiled operation of writing, it may help to read Derrida alongside Denise Ferreira da Silva's critique of some of the less obvious but perhaps more insidious dimensions of coloniality and racialization. Like Derrida, da Silva carefully reads canonical works of european philosophy. Like him, she is interested less in articulations of explicit white supremacy than in more subtle and indirect forms of racial thinking that continue to underpin dominant social theory and political formations today. "Though I recognize the relevance of statements by Hobbes, Locke, Hume, Kant, and Hegel that explicitly place non-Europeans outside the trajectory of european reason," writes da Silva, such overt exclusions are "insufficient to institute racial subjection." Therefore:

> I am interested in the most subtle and yet powerful tools of racial subjection, the ones that the sociologic of exclusion (and its resilient metaphors "double consciousness," the "veil," and "the color line") can never capture precisely because of its privileging of historicity—that which nurses projects of a "post-racial" future where the expansion of universality would finally include the others of Europe in the conception of being human that the transparency thesis produces.[33]

Da Silva's "transparency thesis," an "ontological assumption that still governs the critical arsenal," is a necessary extension of Derrida's critique of the role of presence in western metaphysics.[34] The transparency thesis is the assertion, explicit or implied, of a transparent, interior self underpinning worldly action. That self is none other than "Man, the subject, the ontological figure consolidated in post-Enlightenment European thought." Asserted and defined precisely in contrast to the "affectable" self of those who cannot act directly on the world (and upon whom the subject acts), it enables the "scientific" and objectifying "construction of non-European minds" as existing under the "condition of being subjected to both natural . . . conditions and to others' power."[35] In other words, the invention and sedimentation of race and racism have at their root the special capacity of writing to imply, and thereby invent, an allegedly "transparent" self or subject. Da Silva does not explicitly address the techniques and technologies of phonetic writing as Derrida does, but she uses the verb "to write" in a way that encompasses both the literal writing of texts and the implied material shaping of the world.[36] This usage underscores how writing is not simply a technology through which european thought happens to assert and display its transparency, in distinction from the affectability and exteriority of its racial and geographic others. Rather, phonetic writing and printing have a particular power to *appear to disappear*, to manifest in such a way as to augment something that seems to be behind them even though it could not exist without them. In becoming the privileged and even sole legitimate medium of thought, knowledge, and reason, writing is the technology that allows european power/identity to "write" itself—that is, to imagine and to violently construct itself—as uniquely transparent.

In a brief discussion of *Grammatology*, da Silva highlights Derrida's "decisive move . . . to reject the symbolic prerogative of *interiority*, the assumption of an immediate connection (transparency) between speech and truth." Derrida, she observes, "refuses" the "absolute referent, the transcendental I, that precedes and institutes signification."[37] In this respect, it makes no difference whether writing declares itself the unique transparent medium of thought or, by contrast, critiques itself as a flawed and secondary tool that only partially captures the thinking subject. In either case, the act of distributing written materials shores up and reifies the category of *that which is writable*. Derrida calls this writable thing "presence," or *logos*. da Silva calls the alleged link between that presence and the world "transparency." I would like to extend their incisive analyses further, to embrace an even broader set of terms, beginning with *speech* and moving quickly on to *mind, thought, reason, rationality, science, knowledge, research, theory, cognition*, and *law*. All these phenomena attain their contours and definitions by virtue of being writable. As Derrida says, "the problem of soul and body is no doubt derived from the problem of writing from which it seems—conversely—to borrow its metaphors."[38] Indeed, I am suggesting that there is no such thing as the mind (or "soul"), thought, reason, knowledge, or law, except in relation to the technology of writing. Writing is the cut that extracts what only afterward can be named by those terms.

Derrida does not go quite this far. He recognizes that the technology of writing poses problems for the analysis of speech, but he does not explicitly deny the existence of the category of speech prior to writing. (When he does argue that writing precedes both speech and self-present thought, this is already a very different sense of "writing.") Extending Derrida's argument beyond where it loses track of the political stakes, da Silva aims "to turn the transparency thesis on its head," that is, to reject the very categories by which transparency is attributed to those subjects who possess certain kinds of writing.[39] For both, the construction of whiteness as self-presence and transparency is perhaps even more powerful when the technological medium that makes this possible remains unacknowledged than when it is explicitly championed. If overt championing of writing as the great civilizing technology belongs to overt white supremacy, then the denigration of writing as incompletely capturing rational thought belongs to its subtler cousin, hegemonic white dominance. After all, if white thought is to be universal and unmarked—rather than explicitly marked as superior—then it cannot owe its existence to any particular technology. Thus, while one side of coloniality exalts writing as the great achievement of the western mind, the other, perhaps more insidious side presents writing as secondary to that which it transmits and reveals. While crucially constituting whiteness, writing is simultaneously degraded as less important than what it enables—just as the colonies are defined as secondary and external to the metropole, even though there can be no metropole without the colonies.

To break through the alleged transparency of writing, Derrida proposes to universalize it as a concept, defining "writing" in such a way as to sever any link with european thought and its phonetic alphabet. The political implications of this move are unclear. It is certainly the case that writing is not only *less than* speech, insofar as it can only capture certain aspects of any speech act, but also *more than* speech, insofar as the signification of writing also exceeds what can be spoken. (Derrida's examples include the blank spaces between words, written punctuation, and mathematical formulas.) In other words, although writing can only capture part of what is performed—that which is writable, which retroactively defines what we then call speech, language, and "oral" or verbal communication—it also creates its own webs of meaning that function independently from speech. It is also true that phonetic writing overlaps and is contiguous with other kinds of writing and that it necessarily develops gradually over time (both in its historical invention and in the training of each generation), rather than being a unique and sudden addition or supplement to the nonwritten world. It could perhaps make sense, then, to expand the meaning of the word "writing" to embrace a much wider array of techniques and technologies. Derrida goes further than this, however, with his concept of *arche-writing*, or "writing in general," which is intended to subsume not only the colonial concept of writing, premised on phonetic alphabets, but also the very premise of physical inscription.[40] "Writing" would then include not only chinese and other scripts, such as those described by Rasmussen, but also speech, music, dance, architecture—in short, everything that arises from *differentiation*, everything that differs and signifies. On the one hand, this seems a useful rejoinder to the colonial and white supremacist championing of (phonetic) writing as a crowning achievement of european genius, since it radically deflates the value and significance of that technology. But against the subtler, more indirect forms of logocentrism that Derrida and da Silva foreground, the effects of such a move are ambiguous. If "writing" henceforth refers to all modes of signification—and, as Derrida gradually suggests, to a kind of originary differentiation that subtends all meaning and perhaps even all materiality—then could a critique of writing still function as a critique of ethnocentrism?[41] Where does the *ethnos* go, and what is left to be critiqued, if distinctions are not drawn between divergent histories and technologies? And if we refer to originary differentiation as "writing," do we not also reinscribe the centrality of the particular technology that also goes by that name, perhaps falling into a new metaphysics that once again elevates to the level of universality what is specifically alphabetic, phonetic, and white?

To avoid such a depoliticization, which pulls Derrida's study of writing away from its intended critique of ethnocentrism and toward a critique of "presence" that inadvertently remains within eurocentric thought and scriptocentrism, I propose a different strategy of renaming. Instead of allowing the category of writing to dissolve into a general principle of *arche-writing*, my suggestion is to further specify the mode of writing that is at stake in coloniality by yoking identity and technique together in the phrase "white writing." Following both Derrida and da Silva, white writing is more than the specific technology of phonetic alphabetic writing. It is also the enactment and institutionalization of this technology as the unique legitimate and transparent medium of thought, whether through its explicit celebration or its disavowal. A decolonial media analysis of white writing must treat it as a specific historical technology alongside others, which however has played—and continues to play—a unique and central role in the colonization of the earth. The qualities of the *logos*, which western metaphysics has positioned as indivisible truth, presence, and transparency (often in contrast to writing as its inferior substitute) are then revealed as qualities intrinsic to the very *technique of whiteness* insofar as this is technologically defined by the capacities of white writing.

A core technique of whiteness is thus founded on the principle that truth, presence, transparency, thought, rationality, and other such phenomena must take the form of linear sequences of words, for no reason other than that this is what (white) writing can transcribe. As a technological fact, it is obvious and indeed tautological that writing can only transcribe what writing can transcribe. Yet, as da Silva ironically understates, "the transparency thesis has been rather powerful."[42] Not only do entire fields of analytic philosophy and logic continue to pursue truth and ethics through the formal manipulation of written statements, but institutionality itself, including that of nation-states, is almost universally understood to be necessarily founded on written statements of this kind. Writing in the narrow sense, as Derrida shows, is so pervasive and constitutive of the social today that it is difficult even to imagine how what we confusingly call "nonverbal" aspects of life could ever rise to the level of knowledge or thought. But while there may be no immediately obvious alternative to writing as a basis for institutionality, the rise of digital and especially audiovisual media allows us to decenter, in new ways, the core assumptions of linearity and transparency that define white writing. To see this destabilization in action, it is sufficient to undertake a deflationary reading practice in which every term associated with *logos*—thought, knowledge, reason, rationality, consciousness, mind, logic, cognition, law, philosophy, and many others—is replaced by the word "writing."

A similar deflationary move has been developed, to great effect, in the context of science and technology studies. For example, Andrew Pickering has explored the strict reliance of mathematical thought on mathematical notation.[43] Isabelle Stengers has demonstrated how the elegance of mechanical physics equations came to be interpreted as proof of the ontologically fundamental status of the phenomena they describe.[44] But to apply the same deflationary analysis to philosophy, knowledge, and thought more broadly is another matter.[45] What Pickering and Stengers reveal about mathematics and physics respectively, Derrida reveals about western metaphysics and da Silva reveals about (white) philosophy itself: that what writing captures, however powerful, is nothing more than that which can be written. There is no special unity or transparency of speech or language, no transcendent presence or coherence within the mind, nothing setting the verbal apart from the nonverbal, or the rational apart from the sensible, except insofar as the former benefit from the technological amplification afforded by writing. Hence, the power of writing is not that it captures something uniquely coherent, but that, as a technology bound up with the rise of european empires, that which it captures has been uniquely empowered and universalized.

The more reproducible writing becomes, the more powerful grows the reification of that which it transcribes. Yet even the iterability of writing is not a purely technological matter. Rasmussen explains technological iteration in a passage worth quoting at length:

> "Iterability" is usually cited as evidence of the unique nature of alphabetic writing. Separation of writers and written documents became increasingly common during the colonial era, as documents circulated between the metropole and distant colonies. In classic scholarship, the ability of a text to circulate independently of the writer and detached from its original context became a defining characteristic of "real writing," in distinction to mnemonic devices. However, as Mary Carruthers has shown, alphabetic writing in medieval Europe functioned mnemonically until the invention of print, the Age of Discovery, and other historical developments brought about dramatic changes in the use and function of writing, including greater circulation of texts detached from writers and authors. Yet such medieval texts are not now considered mnemonic because we still understand the code and context that make them "iterable." This is partially because *the context that gives alphabetic script . . . its iterability remains intact and has been extended across the globe as a consequence of the history of colonialism.* For many Western scholars, alphabetic script is so familiar and transparent as a code that it becomes naturalized and nearly invisible.[46]

The specific technological capacities of phonetic writing are inseparable, historically and in the pervasive constitution of every mainstream contemporary institution—state, law, financial currency—from the colonial metaphysics that define white writing. Perhaps, as Sánchez suggests, reading Derrida's critique of metaphysics as a critique of whiteness "allows us to witness Western

Modernity at the outer limits of what that system can imagine."[47] But what if something else is now becoming iterable? What if current changes in the fabric of technology reveal the extent to which the opposition of mind and body, theory and practice, knowledge and experience, was never more than an artifact of writing?

For Derrida and many of those whose work he examines, the pictogram is a tantalizing indication of what could potentially be a substantively alternative mode of thought. Even more than the diversity of sounds used in spoken languages, the signifier that visually resembles its signified seems to highlight, by contrast, the degree of abstraction that gives alphabetic writing its power. The pictogram or icon is like an alphabetic letter in its capacity to be copied and transmitted. But in this copying and transmission, it does not attain the same degree of abstraction or distance from its referent, because of an underpinning relationship of resemblance. Without overstating this distinction—the border between pictogram and letter is not sharply defined—there is a difference in quality and impact, and perhaps also in translatability, between the pictogram and the letter or word. Does this then suggest that there could be a "universal language," a language without distancing or abstraction, which transmits thought directly because it avoids even a scrap of alphabeticism? Of course not. As Derrida points out, the dream of a universal language remains fully logocentric: In failing to recognize how all kinds of writing, including the pictographic, are mediated and technological, the fantasy of a universal language is once again based on the assumption that there is something essential and coherent, prior to transmission, that either is or is not transmitted through a given medium.[48]

A formal and historical view of writing recognizes that the contents of knowledge and thought are not separable from the overall flux of life except retroactively, via the specific cut made by a given technology of transmission. Far from rendering the differences between technologies unimportant, this recognition raises those differences to the status of modes of thought, or even modes of being, hence the phrase "media ontology." What then might happen if pictographic or iconographic writing became as powerful and omnipresent as alphabetic writing? What if, instead of mere icons, symbols that resemble what they mean, a system of iconography were developed that were a thousand times more lifelike in its quality of resemblance? What if there were an iconographic technique that allowed the signifier to visually resemble the signified in tremendous detail? What if those signifiers could even move, depicting change over time? And what if this moving, visual iconography were to be accompanied by an unprecedented iconography of sound, according to which the signifier of speech and song, noises and grunts, also precisely resembled its signified? What if these astonishing new iconographies of the visual and the audible were combined to produce a new kind of document, one so graphic and *analogous* to life that the signified was perceived through the signifier in previously unimaginable ways? What if this perception were so compelling that those who encountered these new documents no longer said, "look at that image (or symbol) of a train," or "look at my name (or symbol)," but instead exclaimed: "Look at that train! And look, *that's me!*" What, in other words, does the rise of audiovisuality do to the institutional power of (white) writing?

It must be acknowledged that audiovisuality is no less complicit with whiteness or coloniality than is writing. As Rizvana Bradley writes:

> What can be rendered legible by the photograph comes to index the shape, boundaries, and directives of the political. Photography is deployed to ensure that the political is everywhere and all the time understood as that which can be rendered visible. The photograph is imagined simply as visual evidence of what must be made present, its universal accessibility and intelligibility presumed as ontological fact and ethical right.[49]

What may be surprising here is not Bradley's critique of the white supremacist underpinnings of photography as technology and medium but the fact that she does not name the equally white supremacist underpinnings of writing. Both writing and photography shape the boundaries of the political by determining what can rise to the level of thought and knowledge. Both are complicit in violence, but they operate in different ways. If photography "is one of the central means by which the modern world is made knowable," it follows and builds on the older and more fundamental production of modernity via writing. Photography has indeed "played a critical role in delineating the thresholds and limits of history, as well as of who can and cannot be among its proper subjects." But so has writing, perhaps even more profoundly. Quoting Ariella Azoulay, Bradley names two "fatal instruments": the camera and the gun. But what about the pen and the printing press? Can we find no perspective from which to critique both textual and audiovisual domination—white writing and also white photography, white imaging, white sound recording, white audiovisuality—without rendering either as a site of transparency from which the other can be objectively analyzed?

Perhaps the relative absence of a decolonial critique of writing in contemporary media analysis can be attributed to the fact that, while writing has had thousands of years to saturate society, politics, and thought, including hundreds of years since the advent of printing, the component and integrated elements of audiovisuality are much more recent. When it comes to combined audiovisuality, formerly the exclusive domain of cinema, these technologies have only become widely available within the past several decades. If technological development is not derailed by political and ecological catastrophe, we are surely still at the very beginning of the epoch of audiovisuality. The audiovisual has only just begun; if it seems as though it has already arrived, that is an illusion with significant consequences. Audiovisually transmitted form and content surrounds us constantly in marketing, entertainment, and social media, yes; but the boundaries of knowledge and institutionality have not been made porous to it. There are, as far as I know, no institutions founded on audiovisual documents, no laws passed in audiovisual form, no sciences constituted by audiovisuality itself (as opposed to analyzing audiovisual materials through writing).

In relation to this absence, artistic research makes its most significant intervention, throwing into relief the logocentric or scriptocentric assumptions that underpin (white) institutionality. As Samuel Ravengai states: "Arts research challenges the dictatorship of *logos* and privileges embodied ways of knowing—a major paradigm shift."[50] In light of the deflationary reading tactic proposed above, we can read the *logos* here as *that which can be transcribed in writing* and "embodied ways of knowing" as *everything else*. Thus, a crucial question is raised by the capacity of digital media to archive and transmit aspects of life and reality other than those which writing can transcribe. Today, to an unprecedented degree, a tripartite distinction can be made between: (1) highly transmissible forms of writing, especially alphabetic; (2) highly transmissible media that are not made of discrete symbols but rather of digital data at a resolution high enough to appear analog (sound, image, the audiovisual); and (3) everything else: weight, temperature, smell, physical presence, objects, architectures, infrastructures, life, worlds. The decentering of writing in relation to transmissibility amounts to a major onto-epistemological shift in the cultural and technological division between writing and life that underpins white institutionality. As noted in chapter 1, many aspects of life that were previously considered intrinsically micro and local—as indexed, for example, in the term "embodied"—have become transmissible to a degree that was previously unimaginable.

Can (or should) one do "philosophy" or "metaphysics" or "rationality" with pictograms, with hieroglyphics, with quipu, with wampum, with sand and rocks, with trees? Are philosophy, metaphysics, and rationality still valid reference points for such expanded forms of thought? If these are questions of decolonial knowledge production, they are also precisely the kinds of questions that artistic research brings to the university, on behalf of all that which has been marginalized as art and craft in distinction from knowledge.[51] Alphabetic writing itself offers many pathways and affordances beyond whiteness, some of which have already been mentioned here. Poetry and prophecy—and perhaps critique itself—might be considered alternative modes of writing that trouble the presumed whiteness of alphabeticism.[52] Can such nonalphabetic modes of inscription be recognized as thought or knowledge by institutionalities in which white writing is not only the dominant mode of communication but also assumed to be the only possible medium of thought? Like Derrida's deconstruction, much artistic research develops within predominantly white institutions as a particular margin of whiteness, neither wholly bound to white writing nor able to fully reject it.

It is, one might say, a kind of critical whiteness studies by other means. In contrast to black, indigenous, latinx, and even feminist/queer studies, each of which articulates a specific epistemic and political identity position opposing the white heteropatriarchy of the university, academic artistic research thus far has developed largely within eurocentric and politically conservative contexts and has tended to articulate its interventions in apolitical or even depoliticizing ways. It has extensively investigated questions of knowledge, method, and form, while much less often foregrounding the politics of even its own marginalization.[53] This might be considered a weakness, but it could also be taken as a tactic or strategy of engagement. Either way, the proposal to think by means other than writing cannot be overlooked or dismissed as a radical challenge to the dominance of white writing.

By treating artistic research as an alternative mode of critical whiteness studies, I perform and further extend the deflationary move proposed in this section. Where artistic research claims to be investigating, expanding, and deconstructing things like *knowledge, expertise, science, thought, rationality,* and *research*, I would provincialize those terms by reframing them, in the context of european colonialism and the ongoing global hegemony of european and eurocentric modes of thought, as artifacts of white writing. White artistic research is then a potentially radical critique of white ways of knowing, white expertise, white science, and white thought. By framing artistic research in this deflationary way, I hope to avoid, on the one hand, dismissing artistic research as if it were merely another iteration of colonizing whiteness and nothing more; and, on the other hand, universalizing or overly valuing it, as if it were a general experiment in universal "knowledge" rather than a specific intervention into white thought and white institutionality.

Critical Whiteness Practice

It should not be controversial to link the critical theoretical work of poststructuralist philosophers like Derrida to the embodied need of white people to deconstruct whiteness. As Patricia Hill Collins writes, offering a black feminist analysis of postmodernism:

> Postmodernism may be more grounded in the needs of contemporary colonizers who refuse than is typically realized. Antiracist Whites grappling with their position in institutionalized racism, antisexist males coming to terms with patriarchy, White women who treated their domestic workers like "one of the family," and highly educated, affluent individuals from diverse backgrounds who must justify their own privileges in the face of the stark realities of chronic global poverty—all experience a "crisis" of identity of the loss of authority vested in old centers.[54]

Spivak, in her well-known essay "Can the Subaltern Speak?," also explores the connection between postmodernism or poststructuralism and critical whiteness when she highlights the difference between framing Derrida's deconstruction as "a program for the Subject as such" and framing it as "a program for the benevolent *Western* intellectual."[55] Spivak explains why she prefers Derrida over Foucault and Deleuze in this respect:

> As a postcolonial intellectual, I am not troubled that [Derrida] does not *lead* me (as Europeans inevitably seem to do) to the specific path that such a critique makes necessary. It is more important to me that, as a European philosopher, he articulates the *European* Subject's tendency to constitute the Other as marginal to ethnocentrism and locates *that* as the problem with all logocentric and therefore also all grammatological endeavors . . . *Not* a general problem, but a *European* problem.[56]

The crucial deflationary move here is to provincialize that which european colonialism has elevated as universally applicable: not thought, but *writing*; not all writing, but *white writing*; not the problem of the subject or thinker in general, but the problem of whiteness. I do not necessarily agree that Derrida is more useful to postcolonial or decolonial thought than Foucault or Deleuze, but I am convinced that Spivak's reframing of the scope and relevance of poststructuralism is necessary. Deconstruction and other poststructuralist developments in critical and philosophical thought are best understood as attempts to decenter and dismantle whiteness from its margins. They are written statements that attempt to practice writing differently. I propose here to expand on this deflation by analyzing white philosophy in relation to critical whiteness studies, with the hope that this can contribute to a reframing of artistic research as a complementary mode of critical whiteness practice.

Derrida shows, in *Grammatology*, how a nascent critical whiteness begins with Rousseau's romantic desire for the pure presence that he claims existed before writing. Following Deleuze we could add many other writers, from Friedrich Nietzsche to Franz Kafka, to such a lineage at the borders and margins of dominating, colonial whiteness. The texts of french critical philosophy, including Derrida and Cixous as well as Deleuze, Foucault, Luce Irigaray, and others, may to a large extent be produced within and generative of whiteness. But they are also written from and on behalf of specific margins of whiteness: jewish, feminist, queer, disabled, poor . . . These writers are not outside coloniality, but neither are they fully or simply aligned with it. Derrida's "margins of philosophy" are also the margins of whiteness.[57] The question always to be asked, when reading Marx or Lacan or Derrida: Is this just more white writing, the technique of eurocentric colonial empire? Or is there something else here—a madness, a queerness, a disability, a femininity, a kink—that takes the writing in another direction, along another path, toward another technique?

Other analysts of whiteness, from Fanon to Du Bois to Ahmed and bell hooks, constitute a crucial "counter-gaze, a gaze that recognizes the ways of whiteness, sees beyond its 'invisibility,' from the perspective of a form of raced positional knowledge."[58] Yet as much as this counter-gaze is defined by its position outside whiteness, it also finds its purchase on whiteness through an intimate engagement that makes it another kind of margin or border zone. Following the claims I made in the previous chapter, I have no choice here but to define the margins of whiteness—those locations from which critical whiteness studies (and practice) can be articulated—in terms that defy the neat categorization of individuals into racial categories. In fact, my argument emphasizes the fundamental ambiguity and ambivalence of both those margins and those positionalities. To criticize whiteness is at the same time to acknowledge one's entanglement with it. Whether one comes from inside whiteness and attempts to leave behind the ignorance of its assumed transparency, or comes from outside whiteness and is compelled to relinquish its simple condemnation, the margins of whiteness are messy. Critical whiteness studies "has the goal of complicating white identity. It has the goal of fissuring white identity, not stabilizing it according to racist myths and legends."[59] White writing is a case in point: To reject it entirely is impossible, even from a position like that of Russell Means. To critique, unmake, deconstruct, and develop alternatives to it is essential.

The fundamental ambiguity of critical whiteness studies is then not simply a result of the identities of its practitioners but part of what constitutes those identities in complex (interdisciplinary, intersectional, dramaturgical) ways. As Robyn Wiegman demonstrates in her study of identity-based academic disciplines, this ambiguity may be inherent to the relationship between critical practice and its object of study. How does one "study" something that one wishes not to elevate or promote but to deconstruct, dismantle, or even abolish? In contrast to other "identity knowledges," which are "more typically understood as crafting epistemic authority for their minoritized objects of study—women, queers, racially subordinated ethnics, and the minor forms of citizen that collate around each—critical practice" organized around the study of whiteness (or around the idea of "America" in Wiegman's other example, american studies) is "oriented toward undoing the epistemological and geopolitical privileges that accrue to the object's overdetermined worldly value."[60] This orientation raises fundamental problems:

> Whiteness Studies, some of us remember, emerged in the 1990s with the hope of differentiating, in the name of antiracism, the relationships among bodies, identities, and subjectivities that have constituted the universalist privilege of white racial formation in modernity. From the outset, it was greeted with skepticism. Did whiteness need *more* attention; did white people really need to devote more time to studying themselves? For many feminist scholars the anxieties it

raised recalled the turn toward the study of masculinity that had marked the end of the 1980s, but the critical difficulties that faced it were far more challenging, in part because the goal of masculinity studies had never been calibrated to the destruction of masculinity altogether. Indeed, the force of discerning the difference between men and masculinity had been crucial to opening the door to female masculinity and to forms of masculinity incongruent with the biogenetic determinations that had accompanied the earliest feminist depictions of patriarchal sex. Whiteness Studies, on the other hand, arrived fully clothed in abolitionist rhetoric. Its promise was to destroy not only white supremacy but white identity and identification, if not the white race itself.[61]

I take this point to be crucial in understanding both poststructuralism and artistic research as modes of critical whiteness. The fundamentally ambiguous relationship to an object of study like whiteness is not something that can be finally avoided. Just as Derrida's critique of eurocentrism is limited by its extensive engagement with european philosophy, without which it could not exist, the project of critically studying whiteness is intrinsically entangled with the privileges and powers of whiteness itself. This entanglement is what led Richard Dyer, whom Wiegman glosses as a "major contributor to the project of deconstructing whiteness," to declare: "My blood runs cold at the thought that talking about whiteness could lead to the development of something called 'White Studies.' "[62] The danger of such a development, however, is not generated by the naming of whiteness, nor can it be resolved by avoiding that term. To study Derrida, Foucault, Deleuze, or even Spivak—to study at all, if by that we mean engaging with the canonical texts of university-based and more broadly white institutional thought—is to encounter this problem. To state that poststructuralist philosophy is a mode of critical whiteness studies is a necessary deflationary step, one that makes explicit a preexisting problem, namely ongoing white supremacy. To use a term proposed by Michael Rothberg, the critique of whiteness, whether or not it names whiteness as its object, is continually implicated in the reproduction of whiteness.[63]

"What [then] is to be done?" This is the question that Frank Wilderson refuses to answer, as discussed in chapter 1.[64] It is also a question that seems to be on the lips of every white-identifying individual attending their first anti-racism seminar, and increasingly also posted on the website of every white institution suddenly awakening to contemporary anti-racist politics.[65] The problem with this question is not that it is too easy or obvious to be worth answering but that it is extraordinarily difficult, while often being asked *as if* it were relatively simple. The white person at an anti-racist seminar who asks "What can I do?" implies that the leader of the seminar should be able to offer a concise and coherent set of instructions, when what is actually being proposed is a revolution, an overturning of fundamental assumptions that will require change on a level that is likely impossible to imagine for the person asking that question. In the language I am proposing here, we might say that the inquirer poses this question at the level of technique, while the antiracist leader knows that it can only be answered by plunging down through (white) technique to upset (white) identity itself.[66] As Wiegman observes, facing the paradox of critical whiteness studies: "The larger questions . . . concern the academic project itself."[67] But the stakes are even higher than this: They concern writing itself, institutionality itself. To answer "what is to be done" regarding the constitutive ambiguity of critical whiteness studies is as difficult as unmaking writing, transforming thought, altering what counts as an institution, redefining the social. I am not suggesting that this ambiguity leads to a dead end. On the contrary, it leads to a consideration of method that suggests possible ways forward, not by answering or resolving the question of what is to be done but by changing the level on which it is asked. For that which is stuck and blocked in critical whiteness studies has not only to do with whiteness but also with the limits of critical methologies and with the onto-epistemological assumptions that burden the concept of "studies." Are there not alternatives to critique and "studies" by which the problem of whiteness might be approached?[68]

In the following extended passage, Wiegman describes the limitations of critical whiteness studies in terms that resonate with my discussion of white writing above and which could suggest a move from critical whiteness *studies* to critical whiteness *practice*.

> Whiteness Studies thus hoped to bring *consciousness* and *knowledge* to bear on the historical problem of white racial supremacy and, in this, it was a social constructionist project that sought to counter the massive problem of white racial ambivalence that structured the public sphere. But to the extent that its antiracist agenda was drawn repeatedly to a white subject now hyperconscious of itself, Whiteness Studies was founded on an inescapable contradiction: its project to particularize whiteness was indebted to the very structure of the universal that particularization sought to undo. This was the case because particularization required an emphasis on the body and on reconstituting the linkage between embodiment and identity that universalism had so powerfully disavowed for the white subject. To particularize was to refuse the universal's disembodied effect. And yet the destination of the dominant theoretical trajectories in Whiteness Studies were never toward the white body but away from it, and away from it in such a way that consciousness emerged as the methodological fix to the white body's universal authority—the very means to forge an antiracist white subject. One *saw* whiteness by *knowing* what whiteness had come to mean. But how did one come to know? And in what ways did such knowing challenge the universal

authority of whiteness, especially given the fact that for everyone except the white subject, whiteness was never "invisible" to begin with? Or to put this another way, how was the fantasy of mastering the meaning of the body by subordinating it to conscious intentions *not* a replication of certain aspects of the universal power of whiteness, which had long produced a seemingly self-authorized subject able to determine the meaning of his subjectivity in the world?[69]

It is easy to recognize here the key terms of Derrida's critique of presence and da Silva's critique of transparency: "consciousness" and "knowledge" enable a "self-authorized" and "hyperconscious" subject who fantasizes about "mastering the meaning of the body by subordinating it to conscious intentions." But what is also interesting here is the way in which the body and embodiment appear in relation to those (white) tropes of presence, transparency, and knowledge. Whiteness studies moves "away from" the "white body," toward a "consciousness" that would be the "methodological fix" to the white body's materialization of racism. The white body is mastered and subordinated by a "hyperconscious" mind, a mind so fully saturated with positive knowledge that it becomes able to transcend its (white) embodiment and thus, in a sense, its whiteness. In attempting to critique whiteness as a harmful identity, critical whiteness studies arguably proposes a technique that is no less white than the white embodiment it seeks to master, subordinate, and escape. After all, what could be whiter than moving from "talking about whiteness" to the declaration of "Whiteness Studies" as a new field of knowledge? What could be whiter than developing a new class of (predominantly white) experts to write authoritatively about whiteness, as if critical whiteness studies were "a new and uncharted theoretical turn" rather than a modest development building on the older fields of black and indigenous studies, with their profoundly critical analyses of whiteness?[70]

Critical whiteness studies dreams of developing countertechniques that might eventually sediment down into an identity other than that of harmful whiteness. According to my thinking around race and the dramaturgy of the body, it is not an impossible dream to imagine that people racialized as white, along with those racialized in other ways, can change their relationship to whiteness and/or the meaning of whiteness itself. To suggest that it is impossible for white people (or anyone else) to enact such change would be to radically sever the link between technique and identity and to posit whiteness as unchanging and unchangeable. But what kind of technique has the potential to alter identity in this way? For the "race traitor" school of whiteness studies, such a change aims for "the abolition of whiteness," perhaps by "mapping a history of white disaffiliation from race privilege."[71] For others, like Linda Martin Alcoff, the aim is rather to "help whites to become more positively embodied as white within a multipolar landscape," for example by "coming to understand whiteness as a mere particular among other particulars." In this way, "living whiteness mindfully as a particular would have a deflationary effect."[72] These two perspectives are not as far apart as they may seem. They take different approaches to the possibility of semiotically repurposing the term "white"—one abandoning it, the other transforming it—but both emphasize anti-racist action as the way forward, whether to abolish the category of whiteness or to redeem it. On a certain level, this is obvious: How could whiteness, the central category of racial supremacy in posteuropean worlds, be deconstructed or dismantled without actively working against racism? But this approach also risks prioritizing a kind of heroic and worldly (political) action that may rely on the same underlying technique of knowledge, mastery, and transcendent consciousness as the coloniality of the white subject. It is then just as important to consider another approach, which we might call intentional disappearance or nonaction. This pathway is risky in a different way, avoiding both the costs and benefits of linking critical whiteness to worldly and political action. But in the context of my argument that the rise of audiovisuality changes what counts as worldly or political, the complementarity I am setting up between critical whiteness studies and critical whiteness practice may be recognized as necessary a step along the way toward a different understanding of their reciprocal relations.

While those who focus on the performance of worldly or explicitly political anti-racist actions may take strong positions on whether the concept of racial whiteness should be abolished or redeemed, a different set of thinkers sidestep that question and shift focus from positive action to embodied practices of unmaking and desedimentation. This line of inquiry may draw on psychoanalysis via Fanon or on phenomenology via Ahmed to explain how whiteness is deeply sedimented in and as the body, so that it cannot simply be dislodged through conscious action. In this sense, as George Yancy observes,

> whiteness is *not* simply the successful result of a *superimposed* superstructural grid of racist ideology. Rather, the white boy's performance points to fundamental ways in which many white children are oriented, at the level of everyday practices, within the world, where their bodily orientations are unreflected expressions of the background *lived* orientations of whiteness, white ways of being, white modes of racial and racist practice.[73]

To dislodge whiteness on this level can never only be a matter of knowledge or consciousness, still less of escaping or subordinating the (white) body. Instead what is needed is a kind of unmaking, an undoing of the self, which might then open the door to more or less radical transformations: operations of technique that become changes in identity.

Techniques of unmaking have been explored in relation to the felt experience of shame, developing a practice of acknowledging or perhaps even dwelling with that shame. Alexis Shotwell suggests that it might sometimes "be a good thing for white people to be (a)shamed in racial situations."[74] Alison Bailey similarly suggests that the cultivation of meaningful rather than paralyzing shame and vulnerability could be a kind of "practical wisdom" in the sense of the ancient greek *phronesis*, which is close to my own concept of technique. Bailey writes: "Conscientious whites must work towards a non-whitely practical wisdom (*phronesis*) in order [to] have a sense of when silence is appropriate, and when a few choice public words of support would be meaningful."[75] Here Bailey cites a passage by James Baldwin, who calls on whites to return to their beginnings to unmake the historically sedimented dishonesty that is integral to the white self: "Go back to where you started, or as far back as you can, examine all of it, travel your road again and tell the truth about it. Sing, shout, testify or keep it to yourself: but *know whence you came*."[76] Taken together, these embodied and somatic approaches to critical whiteness aim to surmount the critical contradiction to which Wiegman points. They do not attempt to take control of the racial situation or to master their own bodies or identities in a self-dominating way. Instead, they accept and plunge into, or even seek to intensify the ambiguities, tensions, and contradictions that accrue to whiteness as lived practice.

Writing in relation to performance practices, Esther Neff suggests that, although "we may not currently be able to behave *non whitely*," this "does not mean we shouldn't try to behave *less whitely*."[77] Neff cites Kevin Rigby Jr. and Hari Ziyad, who argue that

> white people should move comfortably in neither Black spaces nor white spaces. Even those who are well-meaning should drive themselves into the ground trying to figure out how to occupy a positive whiteness—because it is impossible. Only in this frenzy, when the sense of order that is critical to whiteness turns to chaos in every place, can the motivation to destroy it overcome the compulsion to reform it.[78]

The call here is for a practice of discomfort, self-negation, frenzy, disappearance, shame, and vulnerability; a practice of turning inward that is not about self-acceptance but rather aims at unmaking the self, even violently. Popular concepts like white privilege and white fragility, which invite white people to recognize some of the sedimented embodied technique that constitutes their whiteness, begin to move in this direction. But as numerous critiques of those concepts have suggested, they are easily rendered superficial, stopping at the level of what can be taught in short workshops and training sessions without ever provoking the kind of "frenzy" that Rigby Jr. and Ziyad suggest could initiate more radical change. Such concepts also center white experience, rather than demanding of white people that they do the work to imagine and learn outside the bubble of whiteness. Ahmed, in an essay on the ineffectiveness or "nonperformativity" of white anti-racist declarations, proposes that "the task for white subjects would be to stay implicated in what they critique, but in turning towards their role and responsibility in these histories of racism, as histories of this present, *to turn away from themselves, and towards others*."[79] Yet Ahmed acknowledges that even this "double turn" is "not sufficient," although it "clears some ground." The clearing of ground is precisely a practice, something that one does without knowing what the result will be, because without doing it nothing can be achieved. To clear such a space, critical whiteness studies is necessary but not sufficient. It must be augmented, I suggest, by the kinds of critical whiteness practice that can be developed through embodied and artistic research.

Precisely because of the ways in which the methodology of "studies" is linked to the mastery of life and embodiment through (white) writing, critical whiteness studies must be complemented by practices that work through situated embodiment and through technologies of thought that are not limited to writing. And precisely because of the predominant whiteness of the university institution, critical whiteness *practice* has not yet found a home in academia as has critical whiteness studies; while, on the other hand, scholarship on the rise of embodied practices like postural yoga and "mindfulness" has only recently begun to grapple with the whitewashing and white supremacy that such cultural translations and appropriations often carry.[80] It therefore remains to be considered what critical whiteness practice might look like if it were better informed by critical whiteness studies. What I hope to make clear at this point is that the enactment of anti-racist actions and behaviors by people with variously unquestioned and/or marginal relations to whiteness cannot be only a matter of knowledge and conscious action but must also be cultivated in an ongoing way through forms of embodied practice. This is not to detract from the need for white people to get politically involved in anti-racism and decolonization; it is rather to question, first of all, the apparent obviousness of the category of "white people," and second, the forms that such involvement might take. Even the most explicit acts of material disinvestment, such as returning land to indigenous nations or resigning from a compromised institutional position, arise and take their meaning from broader and deeper processes of unlearning. Such practices must involve reexamining individual and cultural histories, but this will be futile if the methods of that reexamination are not also questioned. What does it mean to reexamine a particular lineage or cultural history? What counts as research into the past or present of the world? What kinds of practices and relations support critical unlearning? What do anti-racism and decolonization look like at the level of embodiment? Questions like these can only be answered by drawing on resources outside the range of conventional interdisciplinarity.

In the introduction to this book, I referred to what Kesha Fikes calls "racial transparency" or "extimacy": not the direct resolution or fixing of racism—"we're not there yet"—but an "embodied awareness of our ongoing unresolved historical material realities" and "a mutual and reciprocal reckoning with the unspoken."[81] Fikes is one of a growing number of black and asian practitioners of bodywork, somatics, and embodied therapies, as well as those who are white and otherwise identified, who have begun to undertake an analysis of whiteness that is not only critical but also embodied or somatic, focusing on the ways in which racial identity and whiteness are sedimented in and as the body. I encountered Fikes through an online event called the Embodied Social Justice Summit, which seemed to reply to and implicitly critique a prior event called the Embodiment Conference. While the earlier event had positioned "Trauma & Social Change" as one channel among others, the later one, by shifting from "embodiment" alone to "embodied social justice," located matters of justice and identity at the core of embodied and somatic practice, rendering technique inseparable from identity.[82] In doing so, it acknowledged that there is no pure or neutral embodiment and that claims to avoid race and social justice in embodied practice are nearly always reinscriptions of whiteness as an implicit default.

This point is made more explicitly in an open letter to the Embodiment Conference and its founder, Mark Walsh, written by cultural somatics practitioner Tada Hozumi. In the letter, Hozumi states that embodiment itself, as a concept and set of practices, is primarily a practice of white appropriation of noneuropean techniques. That is,

> "embodiment" as a modern idea and industry has been directly born out of collective disembodiment, a result of historical traumas from inter-European imperialism (which also includes invasions from and of so-called Asia), followed by what we now recognize as modern colonialism, which can be mostly attributed to pale-skinned European descendants who we now refer to as "white" people.
>
> This history of white disembodiment is why the current embodiment industry is dominated by white people, and especially white men, who have acted as founder-discoverers, while the bulk of their actual practice has and continues to come from marginalized communities of color. Somatic Experiencing, Hakomi Method, Continuum, Strozzi Institute & Generative Somatics, Dance Movement Therapy . . . you name it, the core inspiration of these modalities comes from cultural practices such as yoga, qigong/energy work, indigenous ritual, internal martial arts, Afro-diasporic dance, and so on—all of which arise from communities that have been in opposition to Western/white Imperialism.[83]

Hozumi subsequently edited his letter to acknowledge greater complexity in the gender and class identities of white somatics practitioners. (Many somatics and related dance practices in the twentieth century were developed and led by white women.) The underlying point remains: It is not possible to understand whiteness as a social or institutional force, a history of colonial violence, or a set of onto-epistemological assumptions, without also under-standing it as an embodied identity that is composed of sedimented technique and can be thoroughly unmade by changing that technique. As Arran Gare puts it, today's "quest for re-embodiments is a reaction against a culture that has deluded itself into believing that it has become progressively dis-embodied," one that follows an "entrenched, powerful grand narrative of disembodiment" that enables its ruthlessly extractive colonial and capitalist politics.[84] In the previous section I showed how the illusion of disembodiment or transparency relies on and weaponizes a specific technique of writing. But the desire for a return to embodiment, or to escape from the apparent disembodiment of white culture, is necessarily routed through knowledges held and stewarded by those outside whiteness. Hence the moment in which people close to whiteness turn toward the cultivation of black or asian body techniques can involve, without contradiction, both an act of cultural appro-priation and a much-needed revalorization of marginalized and subjugated knowledges.[85]

My thinking here is influenced by Hozumi's arguments regarding the cul-tural dimension of somatics, which resonate with my understanding of the inextricable and constitutive relationship between technique and identity. Hozumi claims, for example, that somatics "is an Asian practice."[86] I accept this, but I lowercase the word asian to acknowledge that, while Hozumi's analysis makes it incumbent on somatics practitioners to trace and name the asian roots of their knowledge, it also troubles the whiteness of somatics as a field and thereby perhaps also of some practitioners who might oth-erwise be classified as white. Similarly, when Hozumi describes whiteness as a kind of "complex cultural trauma" generated by "being disconnected from ancestry," I do not necessarily read this as a sidestepping of the more recent and ongoing trauma of black, indigenous, asian, and other people of color at the hands of white violence.[87] Perhaps most significant in this con-text is a point Hozumi makes about the substance or even material agency of transmissible body techniques. Reflecting on situations of obvious cultural appropriation, such as corporate mindfulness retreats, Hozumi nevertheless maintains that it would be a mistake to treat that which is appropriated as entirely passive in relation to its appropriators. Instead, he claims, the "actual practices themselves are their own beings, with their own intentions."[88] While I have not tended to theorize practices as living beings in Hozumi's avowedly mythopoetic sense, the underlying point is crucial if we are to take culture or technique seriously as knowledge and not simply habits, norms, or rules. Even when appropriated, with all the epistemic and economic injustice that may entail, transmissible knowledge in the form of bodily technique is not inert but has its own capacity to transform those who practice it. Of course, in this context, everything depends on the depth of that knowledge and on exactly which knowledges are transmitted. I differ from Hozumi in his appar-ent confidence that somatic practices unilaterally determine sociopolitical ones. On the contrary, critical (whiteness) practices also cannot do without critical (whiteness) studies.

Another practitioner who has used the term "cultural somatics," Resmaa Menakem, also develops an analysis of historical trauma that reframes the origins of colonialism, linking the enactment of colonialism on black and indigenous people in the americas to prior intraeuropean violence. In this narrative, trauma "was passed from one European body to another during the Middle Ages, then imported to the New World by colonists, and then passed down by many generations of their descendants" in the form of "white-body supremacy."[89] Menakem articulates the limits of belief and ideology as concepts for understanding whiteness:

> If you see white supremacy as a belief system or ideology, in this book you will discover only a fraction of it exists in our cognitive brains. For the most part, white supremacy lives in our bodies. In fact, white supremacy would be better termed *white-body supremacy*, because every white-skinned body, no matter who inhabits it—and no matter what they think, believe, do, or say—automatically benefits from it.[90]

By incorporating intraeuropean violence and trauma into his narrative, Menakem extends the timeline of coloniality to a point even earlier than that emphasized in contemporary black studies and, most challengingly, incorporates whiteness and white people into a decolonial framework of history.[91] Such an approach makes it possible to organize explicitly political somatic practice groups, such as one organized in 2021, "for white-bodied community workers and activists who are actively organizing groups of people towards social change and are ready to transform their internalized white-body supremacy towards embodying racial justice."[92] Similar initiatives to integrate critical racial and social justice analysis with somatic and embodied practice are increasingly found throughout contemporary yoga and mindfulness networks. In my understanding these constitute an important layer of critical whiteness practice that must be understood in relation both to critical whiteness studies, as a textual or written mode, and to artistic research. What Menakem calls "white supremacy as a belief system or ideology" is a layer of technique—grounded in the written texts of european colonial hegemony, as Derrida and da Silva show—that rests on many further layers of unwritten technique, sedimented over centuries into embodied identity.

The development of critical political approaches in somatics, yoga, mindfulness, martial arts, and other embodied practice networks deserves more attention than I can devote to it in this book. What is most important here is that the presence and appreciation of embodiment and embodied practice in social and racial justice contexts requires a deepening of the demand for racial justice that necessarily operates according to a dramaturgical rather than a demographic understanding of identity. Staci Haines, another practitioner working at the intersections of social justice and somatic healing, observes that whiteness is "profoundly somaticized." It is a "somaticized identity that has to be transformed" and "uprooted." White people, Haines says, "have embodied and inherited this profound misperception that, as white people, our safety, belonging, and dignity is dependent upon racial domination." To move beyond this misperception will require "a very deep redefinition, re-perception of safety, belonging, and dignity, that is not based on [the] disappearing of indigenous people," on the "domination and ownership" of black people, or on "separation from the earth, separation from the planet, dominion over."[93] Such an articulation of anti-racist and decolonial politics in somatic terms could be perceived as a weakening or depoliticization of the potential for revolutionary action, insofar as the lines drawn between sedimented identities are blurred. But it also enables a more profound questioning of the substance of identity than is possible within a sociological or demographic frame.

Focusing on embodiment can be seen as a kind of slowing down of political rhythm, which might be deemed inappropriate given the urgency of ongoing violence, incarceration, and extraction along racist and colonial lines. On the other hand, given the equally ongoing dominance of whiteness in posteuropean contexts, it is difficult to deny the need for an embodied or somatic approach to decoloniality that complements and underpins the sociopolitical. Perhaps, at least for people working within and close to whiteness, a kind of slowing down of the pace of individual action, to incorporate deeper change, need not slow down the overall project of political transformation. On the contrary, by deepening the level of the work undertaken, a slowing down of individual practice might support a speeding up of social movement. In my view, practitioners of cultural somatics, political somatics, and somatic abolitionism do not necessarily underplay the material reality of racial and cultural identities by acknowledging that those identities are subject to transformation. Instead, precisely through the integration of political and somatic perspectives (or what I have called "studies" and "practice" in the context of critical whiteness), such practitioners conduct research into the meaning of justice at the level of embodiment and identity as well as technique and culture.

Many of the issues of critical whiteness practice identified here are addressed by Arun Saldanha in his detailed ethnographic, but also highly theorized, account of the genre of electronic dance music developed in goa, india. Saldanha was mentioned in the previous chapter as one of the theorists proposing to "reontologize" racial identity.[94] Because he develops a materialist account of race following Deleuze and Guattari, rather than an account based on knowledge, belief, or consciousness, Saldanha's analysis of whiteness provides an important complement and extension to those developed in critical whiteness studies. As an ethnographer practicing participant observation and thinking across highly divergent geographical contexts, it would not be possible for Saldanha to rely on a narrow definition of whiteness as a set of beliefs or an empty signifier of racism. Instead, he develops a molecular and materialist account of whiteness, in part by recognizing the core ambiguities that I have been exploring. This account provides additional historical context for reframing poststructuralism as a form of critical whiteness studies and embodied or artistic research as contributing to a complementary form of critical whiteness practice.

Saldanha acknowledges the extent to which white countercultural practices, even when they do not explicitly align themselves with anti-racist politics, are often motivated by an embodied desire to escape or transform whiteness.

> It is a commonplace assumption that whites have for a long time been fascinated and transformed by drawing on other people's cultures and landscapes. These fascinations and transformations have been notably given systematic attention in Edward Said's *Orientalism*. Yet the fact that white appropriations of otherness were fueled by a conscious effort to transcend the constraints of white society—that European exoticism and primitivism, though intertwined with colonial subjugation, also tell of the self-critique and self-transformation of whites—has seldom been put at the center of theorization.[95]

Saldanha redefines "psychedelics" as a "commitment certain whites have to transforming themselves through drugs, music, travel, and spiritualities borrowed from other populations."[96] The psychedelic and hippy movements, parallels and precursors to the growth of white institutionalized yoga, somatics, and mindfulness, were thus an earlier "culmination of white modernity's deeper engagement with its geographic and racial beyonds—with what Deleuze and Guattari would call the 'lines of flight' of white modernity."[97] This point should not be taken as undermining the critique of cultural appropriation or as claiming for white embodied practitioners an anti-racist badge they do not deserve. The point is rather to emphasize the inescapable ambiguity of critical whiteness, both studies and practice, insofar as positions at the margins of whiteness can just as easily effect a recentering and reinscription of white supremacy as undertake the work of its deconstruction.

Saldanha continues: "The love of India of Jack Kerouac, Allen Ginsberg, George Harrison, and millions of their fans said as much about their own whiteness as about India. Sixties exoticist imaginations of India are but one instance of a wider yearning of adventurous whites to taste, know, pin down, and/or attain otherness."[98] But the economic and political fact of cultural appropriation across deeply unequal power dynamics, as Hozumi argues, does not mean that whiteness and white people are unaffected by the process. Rather, it "begs the question what happens to actual white bodies once they engage with nonwhite spaces and cultures." In the gradual development of electronic dance music, Saldanha explains, white consumers and tourists gradually "started to comprehend what musical repetition was about."[99] I would argue that learning about embodied repetition from people of color is not a trivial transmission of knowledge. Indeed, if we are to take rhythm seriously as a vast and profound field of knowledge, it could be argued that repetition as a mode of temporality is rigorously opposed to the demands for unending growth and innovation posed by capitalism. In the context of european high-art lineages that distinguished themselves from factory and military discipline by their resistance to repetition—and, in music, the extreme elevation of melody over rhythm—the transmission of knowledge about repetition has had a definitive effect on mainstream white popular music and culture in the twentieth century.[100] In such cases, we might conclude, a real transmission of knowledge takes place, but its epistemic and political significance is denied and disavowed, the circulating technique detached from its roots in particular identities and places. As Saldanha admits, "the Goa freaks of Anjuna do not follow the lines of flight of whiteness to critique their own position as whites."[101] If they engage in critical whiteness practice, it is detached from any critical whiteness studies perspective that could make its anti-racist potential explicit.

Lacking a critical perspective on the role of whiteness in their own capacity for embodied experimentation—which may include various forms of economic and citizenship privilege, as well as those that continue to accrue to light skin even as they travel across the globe—the "freaks" of Goa trance are "hardly 'freaking' the racial assemblage" of whiteness in the sense of contributing to anti-racism or decoloniality.[102] On the contrary, when white embodied experimentation is delinked from critical whiteness, it can tend instead toward an entrenchment of white supremacy:

> Yes, freaks did experiment and go molecular, to use Guattari's word for a loose, centrifugal, and open-ended kind of organization. And there is no doubt that [Timothy] Leary, Ken Kesey, Abbie Hoffman, and their entourage were creative and revolutionary. However, as this study suggested, freaking or molecularizing whiteness has a strong liability to microfascism if it happens carelessly.[103]

The ambiguity and ambivalence pointed out by this quotation cannot easily be avoided. Positionality at the margins of whiteness is no guarantee that one's actions are anti-racist or even critical, nor can any degree of "white self-criticality" produce such complete knowledge of the white self that embodied and material whiteness would be fully transcended.[104] By the same token, no depth of practice, no matter how far one travels along a line of flight from white modernity, can arrive to a point of externality at which whiteness has been fully abolished. What might be possible, however, is a dramaturgical or molecular synthesis of, on the one hand, the conscious embrace of anti-racist technique and knowledge, and, on the other, the slower and more ambiguous cultivation of unwhitely embodied practice.

I have tried to show in this section how a line of flight via critical whiteness studies might be complemented by embodied and somatic practices of critical whiteness that trouble the very identities of "white people." In applying the concept of critical whiteness to certain fields of knowledge—such as white critical theory and poststructuralist philosophy, white somatics, and white artistic research—my aim is to productively deflate these fields (bringing them down from an assumed universality to a situated relation to whiteness) without collapsing them (implying that they therefore have little value). Critical whiteness in this understanding is valuable and important, but only to the extent that it is not positioned as universal or transcendent of racial histories and politics. In this sense, critical whiteness practice seeks to rejoin the world, which it imagined—in part through the technology of writing—it could transcend, but instead merely violated. Those operating from and within whiteness cannot rejoin the world through that whiteness, but neither can they fully escape it. From an embodied or somatic perspective, critical whiteness aches and yearns to draw near to others (to its own specific others and to "the" other), but it also knows that it must not and cannot do so in ways that colonize and devour—for example, by ignoring the wishes of those others who proclaim an ethical need and desire for separation and distance.

In practice, there is no necessary contradiction between the desire for closeness and intimacy that critical whiteness practice reveals and the need for distance and separation that, for example, both the black radical tradition and indigenous politics at times powerfully express. A contradiction arises when the felt need for connection that animates critical whiteness practice is raised to the status of a universal claim: oneness, unity, universality. Then this claim devours, engulfs, and displaces difference. Critical whiteness practice makes no such claim. Its focus on embodying ethics makes it ambiguous with respect to the political, so that it cannot on its own articulate anti-racism. The question of what somatic abolitionism could mean therefore must remain open and in ongoing dialogue with critical modes of thought and study, including critical whiteness studies as well as critical black and indigenous lineages of thought and practice.

Grotowski's White Exit

Why am I writing about Jerzy Grotowski again?[105] I engaged with Derrida at some length above because his influential critique of writing exemplifies the ambiguous yet unavoidable perspective of critical whiteness studies beyond the relatively narrow confines of the field that goes by that name. But why Grotowski? Why another white father? Can it be that for me Grotowski exemplifies a certain limit of the movement toward an embodied practice of critical whiteness? One could make a similar claim about Anna Halprin, Steve Paxton, Deborah Hay, Pina Bausch, and many others: The work of predominantly white experimental performing arts in the twentieth century, like the work of predominantly white poststructuralist philosophy and predominantly white somatic bodywork, can be productively deflated and resituated as a search for critical whiteness.[106] But Grotowski's legacy in particular has had a transformative impact on my own embodied and artistic research practice. Without it I would not have been asking the questions that led to this book. I therefore accept my embarrassment as the kind of white shame to which Alexis Shotwell and Alison Bailey refer in the quotations above. In resituating and deflating Grotowski, by reframing him as a practitioner of critical whiteness rather than of transcendent presence, I also resituate and deflate myself as one influenced and inspired by his work.

As Kris Salata explains, in his book on the "unwritten" dimensions of Grotowski's work and legacy, theater scholarship in the united states has largely left Grotowski behind.

> To most, Grotowski remains a dictionary entry or a chapter in a theatre history book: an avant-garde director famous for a few productions, remarkable actor training, experiments with the actor/spectator environment, and the concepts of "holy actor," and "poor" and "autonomous" theatre. All of these markers come from a ten-year period (1959–1969), during which Grotowski, with his Laboratory Theatre, created groundbreaking performances and creative processes. His consequent withdrawal from theatre productions for the sake of audience-less research focused on the performer and his or her craft has resulted in a complex silence among theatre scholars, for whom the lack of spectatorship in the work became a central theme and an impassible obstacle.[107]

I want to suggest here that the substance of Grotowski's "withdrawal" or exit, the structure and detail of his retreat, and the epistemic location to which he retreated are the most important aspects of his legacy. I recognize the "myth of uniqueness and genius" that continues to cloud interpretations of Grotowski's work.[108] I also recognize the value of queer and feminist critiques of Grotowski, many of which I have embraced and developed in my own thought and practice.[109] Yet my encounters with Grotowski's complex legacy, including but not only via the italian Workcenter of Jerzy Grotowski and Thomas Richards, lead me to trace and value certain perhaps surprising connections with other lines of contemporary artistic research.[110] As Harry J. Elam writes: "While Richards's and the Workcenter's use of Afro-Caribbean song may broaden definitions of race, it also evokes some ethical problematics of cultural engagement. Certainly, their application of folk materials should not easily be considered cultural appropriation, but are Richards and the Workcenter self-reflective on how culture operates in their practice?"[111] Although my focus here is on Grotowski's exit from theater rather than on the Workcenter's practice after his death in 1999, Elam's question about self-reflexivity is highly relevant.

Grotowski and his Laboratory Theatre were part of the countercultural movements that Saldanha describes as psychedelic whiteness. In particular, Grotowski's "paratheatrical" work of the 1970s resonates with a broader countercultural movement and desire to escape from the restrictions of modernity, which Saldanha rightly links to whiteness.[112] Yet what is most interesting about these open-ended and participatory experiments is how dissatisfied they left Grotowski. Retrospectively describing his life's work, Grotowski characterized both paratheater and the later "Theatre of Sources" as steps along a trajectory: from "Art as presentation," the productions of the Laboratory Theatre, to "Art as vehicle" at the Workcenter in Italy. Grotowski's published texts from each of these steps or periods are dense with uncited or incompletely cited references. Usually edited transcripts of his talks and conversations, rather than written prose, the selection of four such pieces republished in *The Grotowski Sourcebook* offers a starting point for understanding Grotowski's move away from theatrical production and its relationship to knowledge, technique, and identity.

In "Holiday," the first essay, Grotowski declares a series of words linked to theatrical production ("show, spectacle, theatre, audience, etc.") to be "dead" and initiates a search for "*our own kind*," those who can share in the event of "holiday."[113] The framework for this exit from theater is a strong opposition that Grotowski presumes between the culture of modernity, understood as a false and superficial shell, and an authentic form of life that lies hidden beneath, behind, or before it. Reading this 1972 text alongside the more recent work of Saldanha, Hozumi, Fikes, Menakem, and other critical and somatic thinkers of white embodiment, it is clear that Grotowski was searching for a kind of embodied healing process that might serve as an antidote to (white) modernity:

> This shell, this sheath under which we fossilize, becomes our very existence—we set and become hardened, and we begin to hate everyone in whom a little spark of life is still flickering. It envelops all our tissues and the fear of someone's touch, or of exposing oneself, is ever greater. Shame of naked skin, of naked life, of ourselves, and at the same time, often, complete shamelessness when it comes to putting it all on the market, selling it all. We do not love ourselves, our own selves anymore; hating others we try to cure that lack of love.[114]

While Grotowski did not frame his search in racial terms, the same deflationary repositioning should be applied here as to Derrida and other poststructuralist philosophers. If we take the "shell" or "sheath" of inauthentic social existence to be a general problem for all humanity, then we posit a universalist teleology according to which personal ethics is the only meaningful domain of action and there is no possibility of authentic political action or sociality. The political is then evacuated as such, becoming equivalent to falseness. But we might instead undertake a decolonial reframing of this opposition, wherein the inauthenticity and falseness of society is not posited as a universal problem but instead is historicized and grounded as a problem specific to the culture of whiteness. It is then a problem of colonialism, of modern extractive capitalism and the resulting individualist consumerism; not a universal human problem but a problem arising from the political ascent of the "human" as a white supremacist category, understood in contradistinction to indigeneity and blackness as nature and animality. We thereby once again deflate the alleged universality of Grotowski's search while at the same time expanding the meaning of critical whiteness practice, so that the latter can be used to reframe the work of practitioners for whom the whiteness of modernity remains implicit or incompletely recognized.

During Grotowski's paratheatrical period, the turn away from society and toward natural human being or essence was closely linked to natural physical environments: "And what remains, what lives? The forest. We have a saying in Poland: *We were not there—the forest was there; we shan't be there—the forest will be there.* And so, how to be, how to live, how to give birth as the forest does?"[115] Some of the keywords developed in the practices of that time included "games, frolics, life, our kind, ducking, flight; man-bird, man-colt, man-wind, man-brother," with a sense of brotherhood or fraternity being "most essential": "the brother of earth, the brother of senses, the brother of sun, the brother of touch, the brother of Milky Way, the brother of grass, the brother of river."[116] It is impossible today to read these poetic evocations of ecological technique without asking to what extent they are related to, inspired by, and appropriative of indigenous cultures (including what is called the folk culture of poland). Indeed, the implicit sources of such knowledge during the paratheatrical period became explicit during the next phase of Grotowski's work, which came to be known as "Theatre of Sources."

Previously, Grotowski recalls, he had "dedicated a thread of life" to seeking out and learning from individuals whom he considered to be living especially significant lives; but this had been done privately, apart from his theatrical directing.[117] Now he used the cultural capital accrued by the Laboratory Theatre to found a "transcultural group" that included "representatives of different Asiatic traditions, of traditions in origin African, American Indian, European, and Judaic."[118] What Grotowski understood as "tradition" in this sense differs from contemporary concepts of indigeneity, not least in the absence of any political articulation that would link traditional knowledge to a national or tribal polity through land relations of stewardship and sovereignty.[119] Yet it is not the case that Grotowski had no concerns about cultural appropriation. While he did not engage with the critical politics of somatics in the sense explored above, one of the most consistent aspects of Grotowski's embodied and artistic research was his commitment to interpersonal modes of knowledge transmission that are not appropriative. In this respect it is significant that the essay called "Theatre of Sources" begins with a discussion of personal need, which Grotowski links to his own wartime childhood in rural poland and his sense of physical disability.[120] From such a perspective, emphasizing relations of ethical kinship and personal need, rather than of mastery and transcendence, the transmission of knowledge is a starting point by which one—especially one who has been shaped by whiteness, whether or not one identifies as white in a demographic sense—might become capable of better ethical relations and perhaps eventually a more integrated politics.

Within the shifting, transcultural Theatre of Sources ensemble, many of the participants were "allied to a technique of sources close to them, traditional for them. But a very important fact is that this is not shared." The word transcultural, as opposed to intercultural, indicates an emphasis on what, according to Grotowski, precedes differences between cultures rather than synthesizing them:

> Though a colleague of mine is a Japanese Buddhist priest, he is nevertheless not doing something that is of his religion. . . . We don't "share" the techniques of sources. There is a Latin American Indian who has been with us for a long time. We began working with him long before the name Theatre of Sources was used. There is also a Hindu Bhakta. He is deeply rooted in his own tradition but is also keenly aware of the contemporary world. The three of them, the Latin American Indian, the Bhakta, and the Japanese priest work together but they do nothing that belongs to only one tradition. They look for some action, evident in its consequences for all three. That means it works for all three despite the differences of cultural context. The Project is oriented toward the kind of actions which "precede the differences," and for this reason englobe persons from traditions and techniques far from one another.[121]

One can point to gaps in this methodology. One can ask whether the fact that a technique "works" for diverse expert practitioners really means that it precedes their differences, rather than emerging newly from their collaborative research. One can question Grotowski's position of authority as the convener and in a sense still the director of this group, likely the one who in a sense finally decides what "works" and what does not; as well as his choice, in published texts, to refer only to lineages and cultural or national contexts and not to individual practitioners by name. (I return to this point below). Yet it is significant that Grotowski's approach to intercultural or transcultural exchange was based on a principled rejection of cultural tourism and cultural appropriation, albeit one that foregrounded bodily or somatic interactions over the concerns of representation and economics that are most often prioritized in current debates. In Theatre of Sources, "practical phenomena of traditions are approached directly, but . . . the members of the small nucleus group are consistently keeping just the first step of contact, careful to avoid becoming fascinated, as for example tourists could be fascinated, or pretending to get some illusory competence; the approach is modest, receptive, based on recognition of everyone's cultural and practical boundaries."[122] Grotowski's emphasis on avoiding cultural tourism through an embodied practice based in modesty, receptivity, and boundaries is markedly different from that of many more obviously extractive approaches. While there can be no final inoculation against harmful appropriation, these ethics take us close to the work on cultural and political somatics discussed above and may hint at the ongoing relevance of Grotowski's work.

Rustom Bharucha's important critique of Grotowski resonates differently when we shift and deflate the framing of Grotowski's research from a universal search for transcendent essence to a situated need for embodied healing that is launched from a particular margin of whiteness. In fact, Bharucha's argument is precisely that Grotowski's project is less universal than he claims. Questioning the value of Grotowski's visit to west bengal during Theatre of Sources (an institutionally supported and hence somewhat public-facing visit, distinct from his private travels), Bharucha emphasizes the economic disparities at play between europe and india, asking pointedly: "What could [Grotowski] really teach" the participant actors "about their inner selves that they didn't already know?"[123] According to Bharucha, what Grotowski sought through laborious effort is scarce and lacking only within whiteness.

> I am thinking specifically of Calcutta, my home, where people live in the closest proximity to one another, sharing whatever they have, at times on the city's pavements where they live in one sprawling, turmoiled, united family. On our crowded streets, where one can never walk without brushing against other people's bodies, we can't really avoid touching each other in our everyday encounters. We don't have to keep saying "Excuse me" as people do in the West, even when they don't touch one another accidentally in a subway or elevator. We are still in touch with our bodies without making an issue out of it. Alienation may be creeping into the more sophisticated areas of Bombay and New Delhi, but it is still possible to look into another person's eyes, without feeling embarrassed or "afraid." It is still possible to meet a stranger and make him your friend. We don't necessarily think about these things, but I have a strong feeling that what you're talking about with so much (perhaps unintended) mysticism, is actually a very normal part of our everyday lives in India.[124]

Bharucha treads a fine line here, as do Hozumi, Menakem, and others who analyze whiteness in terms of cultural somatics. How is it possible to acknowledge the cultural and bodily impoverishment of white culture and the profound undervaluation of marginalized and colonized knowledges, without reinscribing exotic characterizations of the latter? What, after all, is the relationship between the rich traditional knowledge that Grotowski sought in yogic and other "source" traditions and the economic poverty that Bharucha romantically links to the shared embodiment of his "sprawling, turmoiled, united" cultural family? A recent reconsideration of Bharucha's work highlights the ongoing relevance of such questions today and points to some of the ways in which "intercultural flows" have been theorized more recently: as interculturalism from below, rhizomatic interculturalism, asian interculturalism, intersectional interculturalism, social interculturalism, reflexive interculturalism, and interweaving.[125] Yet an important distinction can be drawn between Grotowski and the rest of the cohort of european "intercultural" theater-makers with whom he is often grouped.

Alongside Grotowski, Bharucha critiques Antonin Artaud, Eugenio Barba, Richard Schechner, and Peter Brook. To this list we could add Ariane Mnouchkine, whose controversial performance of north american indigeneity launched my discussion of cultural appropriation in the previous chapter, as well as Włodzimierz Staniewski, a former associate of Grotowski and director of the Gardzienice Centre for Theatre Practices. With the exception of Artaud, who never generated much in the way of theater productions, each of these individuals enacted both an exit from (white, european) theater, or a series of exits, and a kind of return. To be sure, the modality of their returns greatly expanded and enriched the meaning of theater, from Barba's "barters" and Staniewski's "gatherings" and "expeditions" to Schechner's influence on the development of performance studies.[126] Grotowski himself also initially worked in such an integrative mode, incorporating yoga and other "eastern" techniques into the Laboratory Theatre's actor training.[127] But while Barba, Brook, Staniewski, and Mnouchkine always remained theater directors, Grotowski's gradual exit was permanent. While he eventually shifted back from outdoor work based on explicit cultural exchange to indoor work with a less frequently changing team, Grotowski never returned to the creation of theatrical works.

After Theatre of Sources, during the period of "Objective Drama" at University of California, Irvine, Grotowski returned to many structural aspects of european theatrical ensemble practice: score, montage, repeatability, and even Konstantin Stanislavski's technique of physical actions.[128] But one crucial aspect of the european theater form did not return: the definition of the process in relation to an external audience. I have previously suggested that Grotowski's turn away from audience-focused production exemplifies the possibility of "blue skies" embodied or artistic research. Here I am interested in a different angle: the resonances between Grotowski's exit and critical whiteness practice.[129] If Grotowski "left the theater"—the white theater world—"a domain roughly bounded by the Wooster Group, Robert Lepage, and Pina Bausch on one side, Peter Brook, Robert Wilson, and Ariane Mnouchkine in the middle, and Broadway, the Boulevard, and the West End on the other," then it is crucial to recognize that his exit was also a white one.[130] Following one of the more complex prescriptions for critical whiteness, Grotowski did not go on to generate an explicitly political theater, nor a liberally inclusive intercultural one, but rather a kind of intentional and intensive practice of disappearance.

Grotowski's exit was not recuperated or returned into written, institutional, white culture by the time of his death. Between the founding of the Workcenter of Jerzy Grotowski in 1986, its renaming to acknowledge the coleadership of Thomas Richards in 1996, and Grotowski's death in 1999, Grotowski led in the development of a mode of intensive embodied research that resonates with what I am calling critical whiteness practice. (Richards's own experience of biracial embodiment further supports this connection, although I would not analyze that aspect further without his input.[131]) Equally important is Grotowski's cultural context and in particular his strong connections with polish romanticism. As Salata observes, Grotowski's poland was not a center of whiteness but another of its margins, subject to violent erasure through a kind of internal colonialism, even if this did not involve genocide or enslavement.[132] Dominika Laster further underscores the importance of gnostic christianity and prechristian polish ritual practices, which might be recognized today as indigenous knowledges of europe.[133] Taking these influences into account, how might we reread Grotowski's orientation toward intensive embodiment and luminosity of presence? How can we understand his relation to indigenous and traditional knowledges, given that his attitude was always that of an artisan researcher rather than an ethnographer? In my view, what sets Grotowski's interest in "traditional" knowledge cultures apart from more obvious cultural appropriations is his openness to transformation, which comes with a particular, paradoxical understanding of mastery: mastery as wholeness or self-integration that includes rather than excluding animality, receptivity, and vulnerability.

Openness to the divine is part of mysticism, but these qualities also resonate with Bailey's idea of a practical wisdom or *phronesis* grounded in the acknowledgment and acceptance of (white) shame and disembodiment. Recall that Bailey here cites James Baldwin's exhortation to white folks: "Go back to where you started, or as far back as you can, examine all of it, travel your road again and tell the truth about it. Sing, shout, testify or keep it to yourself: but *know whence you came*."[134] White people here are called to come back into their bodies, into relationality, into vulnerability and receptivity, which requires an engagement with the shame and disavowed trauma that founds and defines white embodiment. When Grotowski speaks of "*standing* in the beginning," could this be the same "where you started" as that to which Baldwin refers?[135] "The beginning," says Grotowski, "is all of your original nature, present now, here," which nevertheless "gives a contradictory and mysterious plenitude." Philip Auslander has criticized Grotowski's concept of presence as romantic and pretheoretical, naive in how it "grounds self-presence in physical presence," but I think Bharucha's criticism is more accurate.[136] Everything depends on how we read the "contradictory and mysterious plenitude" that exists at "the beginning": Is it a romantic and transcendent presence that spiritually bypasses real-world politics? Or is it the profound yet in some way mundane plenitude that arises out of ethical kinship and mutual interdependence with others and with the earth? As a program for universal humanity, Grotowski's project would be irredeemably eurocentric and colonial, not least in how it relies on indigeneity to support its own search for presence. Yet the same project appears in a different light when it is reframed more modestly as a program for healing and dissolving whiteness through lifelong and even multigenerational engagement with indigenous knowledges.

Like many european romantics before him (including Rousseau, at least as described by Derrida), Grotowski's historical narrative locates indigenous knowledge in an essential past that remains ontologically prior even when it becomes present and hence makes contemporary indigenous politics impossible. But this problem is not avoidable through a shift to a general indigenous identity as a foundation for contemporary politics, as such an identity can only be defined by reference to colonialism—which means, in a posteuropean context, in relation to whiteness. While political coalitions between and among indigenous nations can build on local and perhaps even global or planetary histories of colonization, the concept of indigeneity itself remains slippery in its relation to politics. Grotowski's posttheatrical research is impossible to understand apart from his engagement with indigenous embodied knowledges. Yet, unlike many of those who are routinely considered his peers, Grotowski did not recuperate that engagement back into a (european) theatrical frame. He did not instrumentalize his relationships to practitioners of diverse traditions, did not bring these back into a framework of public performance, but instead guarded them closely, so that even after his death many of his encounters and relationships remain obscure.[137] Instead of prioritizing a european theatrical frame, Grotowski emphasized the impact of particular kinds of embodied technique on individual practitioners, locating them in a context that is both cultural and, in a very specific sense, beyond the merely cultural.

"Who is the person who sings?" Grotowski asks the performer:

> Is it you? But if it is a song from your grandmother, is it still you? But if you are discovering in you your grandmother, through your body's impulses, then it's neither "you" nor "your grandmother who had sung": it's you exploring your grandmother who sings. Yet it can be that you go further back, toward some place, toward some time difficult to imagine, when for the first time someone sang that song.[138]

The aim here is explicitly to rediscover ancestral connection. "If you refind this, you are someone's son. If you do not refind it, you are not someone's son; you are cut off, sterile, barren."[139] In rereading this passage I am reminded of Resmaa Menakem's evocation of his grandmother's hands and of the embodied situatedness that practitioners of cultural and politicized somatics would offer even to those whose ancestors were on the colonizing side of the colonial divide.[140] Many of the exercises proposed in Menakem's book resemble both Grotowski's work specifically and the basic exercises of contemporary somatic bodywork and performer training more generally. For example, Menakem asks the reader to "invite the presence of an ancestor" and to practice humming, singing ("pick a song with a simple melody"), and chanting as techniques for working with the vagus nerve, which he calls the soul nerve.[141] He uses the term "source" to name that which sustained embodied practice and cultivation is able to realize.[142] Like Grotowski, Menakem would no doubt describe these exercises and their underlying physiology as universal attributes of the human species. Yet, unlike Grotowski, Menakem also situates the contemporary need for such cultivation within a decolonially framed history of ancestral trauma, white supremacy, enslavement, and genocide. In a text not yet published in english, Grotowski states: "It is not that the body remembers. The body itself is memory."[143] This is perhaps the central premise of cultural somatics. What then would be a somatic antidote to whiteness? What kind of embodied practice could directly combat the technical, material, and habitual ways in which white supremacy, complicity, and privilege structure white embodiment?

Grotowski's work must be reframed in relation to critical whiteness in order to avoid a universalism that could only be neocolonial. In this reframing, we could perhaps compare Grotowski's engagements with "source traditions" to that of any other (white) person who culturally appropriates a song or dance in private, as part of a personal process or ritual practice, in response to personal need. Such appropriation cannot be deemed violent, but neither is it heroic. This "Performer" may be "a doer, a priest, a warrior"—as Grotowski writes in one of his last texts—within their personal journey, but in a wider public and political context they are merely someone who has ceased to be violent, an abuser who has, at least in that moment, ceased to abuse.[144] While undertaking such work is indeed ethical and may contribute to political change, it is also fundamentally therapeutic and must be practiced humbly to be effective. In the creatively deflationary language of contemporary social media, we might say that a person undertaking such work does not deserve a "cookie." The cookie is a playful way to name the public recognition or kudos that can instantly attach to critical whiteness practice as soon as it begins to return to a (white) public sphere. What is interesting about Grotowski is that, while he was no political hero—he was not John Brown, becoming "a paraontological Negro" in martyrdom—he was prepared to follow his own investigations out of the public sphere, giving up social recognition and the many cookies he might have been awarded had he chosen to reintegrate and instrumentalize his cultural appropriations within a theatrical frame.[145] This distinguishes him from many other european directors of his time and foregrounds the question of the return, on which everything depends in the move from an ethics of practice back to politics and the social.

For there to be a return, there must have been an exit. If we disallow Grotowski his framing of "Performer" as transcendent achievement, instead reframing the rigorous ascetic and aesthetic practice developed at the Workcenter as a mode of critical whiteness practice, then how do we understand the substance of his exit? More pointedly, why is presence for Grotowski linked to "source traditions," that is, to indigenous embodied technique, especially songs and ways of singing (in combination with Stanislavski's method of physical actions)?[146] Grotowski sought indigeneity not as a political identity but as embodied technique. He was careful to reject the appropriation of specific indigenous cultures as a means of becoming indigenous, instead always redirecting questions of identity back to matters of technique. Philip Deloria describes how american identity, since the revolutionary war with the british empire and the founding of the united states as a settler colonial state in north america, "has used Indian play to encounter the authentic amidst the anxiety of urban industrial and postindustrial life." What Deloria calls "playing Indian" continues, in various forms, to the present day:

> At the turn of the twentieth century, the thoroughly modern children of angst-ridden upper- and middle-class parents wore feathers and slept in tipis and wigwams at camps with multisyllabic Indian names. Their equally nervous post–World War II descendants made Indian dress and powwow-going into a hobby, with formal newsletters and regular monthly meetings. Over the past thirty years, the counterculture, the New Age, the men's movement, and a host of other Indian performance options have given meaning to Americans lost in a (post)modern freefall. In each of these historical moments, Americans have returned to the Indian, reinterpreting the intuitive dilemmas surrounding Indianness to meet the circumstances of their times.[147]

What distinguishes Grotowski's work from these modes of claiming and appropriating indigeneity is its depth of engagement, which is to say, the rigor of its exit. While Deloria emphasizes the role of "disguise and costume" in american "identity play," with its "bad imitations of native dress, language, and custom," Grotowski—from a position in whiteness very different from that of euro-americans—sought a different kind of transformation. Those who "play Indian" appropriate the label superficially, in discourse and public appearance, without deeply engaging knowledge or technique, let alone power and identity. Grotowski, in contrast, approached indigenous and other noneuropean technique in the context of a lifelong process that aimed to profoundly transform an individual's identity. Furthermore, he did so without recuperating that transformation back into european theatrical structures. This distinction may clarify why and how indigenous technique and in particular songs "of tradition" came to have such importance at Grotowski's Workcenter.

The locus of indigeneity for Grotowski at the Workcenter was, crucially, embodiment rather than emplacement. Following his paratheatrical experiments, Grotowski returned to the containment of the studio. The physical place in which he guided and mentored Richards in the development of repeatable performative scores called "Actions" was reduced at this point to a square of wooden flooring in a repurposed building in the italian countryside.[148] This reduction, I believe, is part of his exit strategy. To expand beyond that tiny place, to develop a relation to land and emplacement as part of the practice, would require a political reckoning, a more explicit accounting of "sources," and a questioning of whiteness on an entirely different level: that of sovereignty, the state, and the appropriation of land rather than culture. This does not mean that the exit is a fantasy, a defensive "move to innocence" in the sense defined by Janet Mawhinney.[149] But it does limit the scope of his work to the body as distinct from the land; embodiment rather than emplacement. Grotowski repeatedly underscored the *reality* of what he sought, distinguishing it from language and representation: "A man of knowledge [człowiek poznania] has at his disposal *the doing* and not ideas or theories."[150] But this "real" is not the real of sociopolitical struggle, of relations between state and land or sovereignty and nation. All that Grotowski abandoned early on.[151] The real, for Grotowski, as the manifestation of presence, could exist only at the level of embodied encounter: people in a room together, where "room" implies abstraction from place.

Drawing on the work of scholar and chickasaw citizen Jodi Byrd, we might then recognize in Grotowski's work a particular kind of *racialization of indigeneity*: a separation of embodiment from emplacement that allows questions of political sovereignty to be suspended in favor of "work on the self." According to Byrd, "indigeneity collapses into race at the beginning of empire."[152] That collapse produces not only whiteness but race itself, as a theory of embodiment that severs identity from place. Even in critical race studies, Byrd argues, the transformation of diverse

> indigenous nations into a single racial minority within the national borders of the United States is folded a priori into postcolonial and racial critiques of what Patrick Wolfe has identified as "regimes of difference" within deep settler societies. This presumed self-evidentiary process of minoritization, of making racial what is international, continues to infect competing understandings of citizenship, identity, inclusion, and exclusion with, among, and outside the intersections of sovereignty, race, land, and labor. The processes by which citizens of

American Indian nations become minorities within the United States, with no prior claim to nation or territory that exceeds the U.S.'s will, further inform current struggles over citizenship and historical reconciliation within the indigenous nations colonized by the United States.[153]

Grotowski invokes place and emplacement only in the past, or in relation to specific microsites of embodied practice—never as a defining context or mutually constituting reality for embodiment. This does not invalidate his project, but it signals the limits of any critical whiteness practice insofar as even the term "practice" tends already to depoliticize by severing embodiment from emplacement.[154]

While drawing ethically rather than extractively on indigenous knowledges, a critical whiteness practice like that developed by Grotowski concentrates the transformative force of those knowledges on individual bodies as distinct from nations, cultures, and lineages. It foregrounds, in the language I have been developing, the transformation of identity through technique, rather than the way in which technique is also molecular identity or even *molecular place*. There is a sense in which emplacement can be accessed through technique because both whiteness and indigeneity are materially racialized. This is Grotowski's white exit, his search for indigeneity: not by appropriating another identity but through a rediscovery of the (white, partially white, or formerly white) self as grounded, situated, and emplaced. It is undeniable that white (and other) colonial societies need urgently to learn from indigenous ones about kinship and justice, as well as about ecological sustainability. Scholars across the humanities now write about the more than human, often citing white feminist scholars like Jane Bennett and Karen Barad but less often acknowledging the ways in which black and indigenous philosophy and theory, and even some critical anthropologies, propose alternative worlds and ways of being.[155]

An ethics of naming and attribution can only accomplish so much here, as they rely on logics of writing and property that may undercut the more subtle politics at work. For his part, Grotowski consistently favored the interpersonal sharing of written fragments, like that of embodied technique, over an ethics of citation. Kris Salata explains:

> Always a ferocious reader, Grotowski has been known for unequivocal, irreverent "essentialism" in his treatment of books. He would often tear out "important pages" and pass them to his friends and collaborators, disregarding the rest of the book. In his talks, he would acknowledge quotations, but not necessarily their source,

stating that "the text speaks for itself." In the same way, the "insistently 'oral attitude' toward writing in the practice of the Workcenter" suggests not a desire to appropriate written sources, but a stance of strict opposition to the institutionalization of (white) writing.[156] Such a strategy raises problems, but it is not clear that these problems can be resolved through the naming of individual authors and tradition-bearers. Grotowski's white exit was a particular project to escape logocentric institutionality and the white writing that founds it. As Salata describes it, Grotowski cultivated a "distrust of writing" and even "forbade any note-taking and audio/video recording" during his public meetings and talks.[157] Like others, Salata frames the opposition of writing and embodiment in universal terms:

> The "knowledge-through-doing" at the heart of Grotowski's work remains vulnerable to textual capturing, which decontextualizes and then objectifies it in order to turn it into a "true" knowledge. In oral transmission, objective knowledge plays itself out within a subjectively impenetrable fact, the result of an *event* in which an ineffable transmission occurs. Clearly, something in that transmission moves beyond its specific context, but stays un-captured, and un-capturable due to its transitory quality. The "knowable-by-doing" remains in motion. The employment of the written word captures that motion, like photography captures life, as an "agent of Death."[158]

Given the argument made at the beginning of this chapter, I cannot accept any inherent link between writing and death, or even a strict opposition between written knowledge and "knowledge-through-doing." Instead, both that opposition and the equation of writing with objectification and death must be attributed to whiteness and its logocentrism.

What is violent about writing is not the way in which it technologically traces or captures an otherwise ineffable event but the colonial structures and histories of domination that sediment the hegemonic worship of a particular kind of writing. If that is the case, then we do not need to subscribe to a Rousseauian depiction of indigeneity as pure presence to understand why Grotowski, along with many other (white) leaders of (white) ensemble theater projects, might wish to learn from indigenous embodied knowledge in attempting to form microcommunities outside the dominant logics of white modernity.[159] Such projects cannot achieve the romantic "image of a community immediately present to itself, without difference," but they do investigate the actual, material potential of a contemporary social formation in which "all the members are within earshot."[160] They do not avoid or transcend difference in general, but they do have substantively different relationships to the technology of writing and hence to (white) institutionality. It is no wonder that such projects should seek out and attempt to learn indigenous embodied technique, not necessarily as a fetishized image of pure presence or an identity to appropriate but as practical knowledge, a repertoire of alternative ways of structuring life and practice. I take issue with Salata's simplistic characterization of both the Workcenter's practice and "performance in traditional cultures" as transcendently authentic and free of nostalgia. But I cannot deny that the cultivation of embodied technique within a sustained microculture has the potential to offer radically different ways of relating to writing and to institutionality, even to the extent of enacting an embodied exit—real and meaningful, even if partial—from whiteness.

Ultimately, this same rejection or postponement of white writing and logocentrism is what accounts for the central emphasis on singing in the later practices led by Grotowski.

> Because the Occidentals are productions of notation systems, both in the sense of writing (musical notes) and of tape recordings, and because they are not related to oral transmission, the Occidentals therefore confuse song with melody. Anything that is possible to "notate" they are more or less able to sing. But anything belonging to the quality of the vibration, the resonance of the space, the resonating chambers in the body, the way in which exhalation carries the voice, all this they are not even able to grasp in the beginning.[161]

If again we reverse the framing of this passage, so that it emphasizes the value of song beyond melody for white people ("Occidentals") specifically and not for humanity in general, then it becomes clear that the *presence* Grotowski sought is not a universal or transcendental principle but a specific articulation of that which is not enfolded by white logocentric institutionality. In other words: The vibratory qualities of a song are not inherently more present, sacred, transcendent, ethical, innocent, or universal than its melody or its lyrics. But in the context of hegemonic whiteness, with its massive reification and weaponization of the technology of writing, precisely that which is not captured by white forms of inscription may become valuable as an instrument to seek alternative modes of being.

Presence does not inhere more in vibration than in melody or in words, just as innocence is not a bodily attribute of indigenous people or communities. But given the historical reality of colonization, there is every reason to turn toward indigenous knowledges in the search for ways out of whiteness. This is the double-edged meaning and force of indigeneity, which is both essential for critical whiteness practice and always out of its reach:

> The Indian—as a threshold of past and future, regimes of signs, *alea,* becoming, and death—combats mechanisms of interpretation through an asignifying disruption that stops, alters, and redirects flow. This stopping of the world of signification is the same as Derrida's "tattooed savage" at the beginning of deconstruction. The Indian sign is the field through which poststructuralism makes its intervention, and as a result, this paradigmatic and pathological Indianness

> cannot be circumvented as a colonialist trace. In fact, this colonialist
> trace is exactly why "the Indian" is so disruptive to flow and to exper-
> imentation. Every time flow or a line of flight approaches, touches,
> or encounters Indianness, it also confronts the colonialist project that
> has made that flow possible.[162]

We return here to the problem of writing and knowledge. Grotowski looked
for techniques that could transform or even transcend identity. In this way,
he also racialized indigeneity and severed embodiment from emplacement,
ethics from politics. It would be wrong to foreground such depth of epistemic and practical engagement over the politics of indigenous identity, a
move that could only be violent in its erasure of indigenous sovereignties and
alternative politics. On the other hand, such a practice may do important
work at the level of knowledge transmission and embodied research, where
what is at stake is not cultural authenticity so much as the invention of new
ways of being.[163] It is not yet possible to say what exactly it could mean to
develop a large-scale politics of place and emplacement outside white logics
of logocentric institutionality. Any substantive answers to that question will
surely depend on both the politics of indigenous nations and the epistemic
and technical transmission and adaptation of indigenous ways of knowing.
And if those answers are to be implemented at scale, many others will need
to find ways to exit from where they are.

If the work of Grotowski and other twentieth-century theater ensembles
remains incomplete, this is not because their exit from whiteness is illusory
but because it does not go far enough. Like many other "floating islands" of
theatrical and paratheatrical practice, the Laboratory Theatre and the Workcenter emphasized disciplined and virtuosic practice in a way that makes it
difficult to incorporate techniques of kinship and community, such as those
that attach technique and identity to place and without which the exit from
whiteness can never go beyond embodiment and toward emplacement. The
Odin Teatret in Denmark and Double Edge Theatre in Massachusetts offer
different approaches, which in some ways may be more conducive to the widening of communal contexts and an engagement with place that ultimately
leads back toward politics and the social.[164] In relation to Grotowski's own
legacy, the question of politics and a return to the social could be addressed
to the work led by Thomas Richards and his colleagues after Grotowski's
death. Just a few years after Grotowski died, the Workcenter began to open
its doors to places and situations far beyond its previous enclosure. In the following decades, codirector Mario Biagini put down roots in brazil, new york
city, and elsewhere, while the composition of the Workcenter's two teams
became more visibly diverse. From outside it seemed that the geopolitics of
racialization and indigeneity had become more explicit themes of the Workcenter's practice, especially in the work led by Biagini. Yet the return of the
Workcenter to the public sphere always remained cautious and partial, still

reliant on a valorization of exclusively embodied practice that untenably somaticizes and racializes the political.[165] In my view, this tension—between the narrowly corporeal ethics of "Performer" and the geopolitics of identity and place—cannot be resolved without a radical transformation of institutional form.

As I was in the process of revising this manuscript, the institutional journey of the Workcenter of Jerzy Grotowski and Thomas Richards came to an end. In January 2022 Biagini announced that he was leaving the Workcenter; a few days later, Richards announced its closure.[166] These developments are not entirely surprising, given the nature and substance of Grotowski's "exit" as I have described it. The calling of the Workcenter—to develop an ethical and perhaps germinally political healing process through an epistemic racialization of indigeneity via embodied technique—cannot return to the (white) world without losing its purpose. But neither can it break radically from that world to create a new one, as an emplaced and politicized indigenous nation might do. With the closure of the Workcenter, one of the most rigorous and determined lines of flight, exiting with the countercultures of the 1970s, has come to an end. It was one that adamantly refused to return to whiteness via the reorientation to individual self-help and neoliberal certification that now organizes many other postcountercultural practices, like yoga and mindfulness, where appropriated embodied technique is deracialized for the sake of popularization and commercialization. Yet neither could it establish a truly public institutional face, nor open itself up to radical institutional change.

There can be no direct return to the world following an exit like that of Grotowski. His path leads into a forest, where it disappears among the trees, much as is suggested by today's calls for white people to ethically decenter themselves in the public sphere. The politics suggested by Grotowski's texts were dissolved into ethics by his own practices. His legacy, for better or worse, can be tracked now only through countless individuals, rather than standing as a model of alternative institutionality. To further confront matters of institutionality, I therefore now turn to a different set of practices, which may also be experiments in critical whiteness but which carry a very different relation to the problematics of institutionality, because they locate artistic research within the university.

White Experiments

In this chapter and the previous one, I have tried to expand the concept of artistic research, opening it beyond an encounter between predominantly white artistic worlds and predominantly white universities in order to consider its more radical onto-epistemological and perhaps decolonial potential. Approaching artistic research as a contestation of the primacy of (white) writing—which is hegemonically installed as the sole legitimate form of thought and knowledge—I have foregrounded the relationship between technique and identity in the racialization of knowledge. I will now consider three models or approaches by which artistic research is currently being developed in european and north american universities. Each of these approaches deserves to be treated at greater length and could have been the focus of this whole chapter. However, given the intentions of this book I felt it was important first to devote most of the chapter to a broader examination of whiteness as the cultural and institutional context for academic artistic research. The three approaches I consider here all constitute, in different ways, both experiments "in" whiteness—attempts to question, deconstruct, transform, escape, or exceed white institutionality in the form of the university—and "white experiments": experiments conducted by and within predominantly white institutions. In this sense they are continuous with the work of critical whiteness studies and practice outlined above, including its inherent ambiguity as both a deconstruction of whiteness from its margins and a more or less self-aware reinscription of whiteness. They each undertake, in varying ways and perhaps to differing degrees, a kind of escape or exit from logocentrism, theorized in the previous section through the work of Grotowski. At the same time, as academic projects, they deal more directly and thoroughly than Grotowski did with the problem of the return to sociality and politics through matters of institutionality, documentation, and the archive.

Not unlike somatics as described by Tada Hozumi, artistic research "proper" has developed within predominantly white institutional contexts and has, by emphasizing its formal and technical elements over its cultural lineages, downplayed the extent to which it is made possible and informed by the unacknowledged flow of marginalized knowledges developed prior to and outside whiteness. These hidden sources may include somatics itself, which Hozumi identifies as predominantly asian; black diasporic forms of dance and music; indigenous knowledges of land and story; and also lineages from within europe, including those that are marginalized geographically, economically, religiously, and through gender and sexuality, all of which have complex relations to whiteness. Some recent artistic research, perhaps especially in canada, has begun to acknowledge these connections and to seek more explicitly respectful relations with marginalized and subjugated communities both inside and outside academia.[167] To do so without reinscribing a colonial epistemic relation, the acknowledgment of such lineages and the development of such connections must be understood as a kind of critical whiteness practice. In other words, artistic research, as an intervention in the form of the modern university, must frame its projects of unmaking and deconstruction as responses to, in Spivak's words, "*Not* a general problem, but a *European* problem": a problem for white people and for people who operate within and on the margins of whiteness; a problem generated by whiteness. This distinction amounts to a substantive deflation of the scope and focus of artistic research as a developing field within predominantly white universities. Rather than presenting artistic research as a further addition to or enhancement of a generally valuable and honorable institution, it might be reframed as a necessary corrective or even healing of a profoundly wounded and violent, damaged and damaging, white supremacist epistemic culture.[168] Alongside critical theory and identity-based interdisciplines, artistic research could then be seen as part of a movement in the arts and humanities—which may find both allies and enemies across the rest of the onto-epistemic map of academic disciplines—to overturn the dominant extractive episteme of capitalist colonialism and advance other ways of knowing, living, and being.

The three approaches to artistic research I consider here can be roughly glossed as those of inclusion, escape, and experimentation. To elucidate them, I will draw on particular examples, case studies, and publications, which are based primarily in the united states, canada, and europe. This should not be taken to imply a simply national or geographical mapping as all three approaches are active at various scales across the geographies of artistic research. Schematically, the three models could be compared respectively to liberal, radical, and pragmatist political positions. Given the complexity of the world and the urgency of change, I see a place for all three models in the development of artistic research and try to avoid describing them in a hierarchical way. But it is only honest to admit that I find myself personally in closest alignment with pragmatist and experimental approaches: those that neither take prevailing institutions for granted nor seek to disappear from them but instead grapple with them through a kind of technics that is deeply engaged with matters of form.[169] As much as I have tried to formulate these three approaches on equal footing, acknowledging the validity and strengths of each, I have found it difficult not to imply a kind of synthesis in the passage from inclusion through escape to experimentation. Such a passage could be described in various ways: from too little anxiety (implying satisfaction with the status quo) through too much anxiety (rendering mobilization impossible) toward just the right degree of anxiety; from defending the institution through calling for its abolishment toward a radical transformation of its form; or, perhaps most to my taste, from an approach that assumes method as unproblematic, through one that explicitly rejects method, into one that makes the question of method its primary focus.

The first model of artistic research described here is based on integrating artistic practices into the (neo)liberal university. This approach may be illustrated by the launch of the Alliance for the Arts in Research Universities (a2ru), a consortium founded by the University of Michigan in 2012 that "advances the full range of arts-integrative research, curricula, programs, and creative practice to acknowledge, articulate, and expand the vital role of higher education in our global society."[170] The inclusive or liberal approach of a2ru is implied in its name, which suggests not a methodological intervention but merely the integration of "the arts" into an existing framework defined by the category of research universities. According to its mission statement, a2ru "fosters and champions the role of the arts and design in research universities." It thus takes "the arts" for granted as a category, extends them in a particular direction through the addition of "design," and installs them "in" an existing set of elite academic institutions.[171] By framing its project this way, a2ru declares that it has no stake in art that might be developed at other kinds of universities or outside academia. This narrative is confirmed by the organization's history:

> Responding to the growing number of arts-integrative collaborations and programs that exist across the landscape of higher education in the U.S., in May 2011 The University of Michigan's ArtsEngine—a body that drives arts-integrative collaborations among the arts, architecture, and engineering units—convened deans and other academic leaders from top research universities across the country to identify and begin addressing institutional barriers to arts-integrative efforts.

The term "arts-integrative" foregrounds an inclusion-based approach, while the rest of the passage uses the corporate language of leadership and success to explain how "deans and other academic leaders from top research universities" convened to launch a2ru. The drawing of boundaries around "top" universities here already indicates that this version of artistic research will not be one that radically challenges hierarchies of knowledge.

I do not wish to paint a superficial picture of a2ru as disengaged with the political, even in terms of the racialization of knowledge. On the contrary, a2ru is in some ways more explicitly engaged with anti-racist politics than many of the other predominantly white artistic research projects I address in this section. In June 2020, during the Black Lives Matter uprisings following the murder of George Floyd, executive director Maryrose Flanigan published on the a2ru website a "Statement on Dismantling Racist Practices in our Work" with the subtitle "Black Lives Matter."[172] Similar statements were made by many elite white institutions at the time and do not necessarily indicate serious or long-term commitments. But the topics and content of annual a2ru conferences have also been more politically engaged than the consortium's founding statements suggest. The 2019 conference included a keynote by Nicholas Mirzoeff titled "Whiteness: What Is to Be Done?"[173] The 2020 conference had a keynote from Adrienne Keene called "Native Appropriations, Indigenous Social Media, and Responding to Racism."[174] To my knowledge, no european artistic research conference has named and grappled with the whiteness of its own institutional context in this way. These points suggest that a2ru may be moving toward becoming a site at which anti-racism and decoloniality can be foregrounded and considered at the level of identity. But it is also significant that these interventions have not necessarily come along with any substantive questioning of the methods or techniques by which research in general is conducted.[175] Following a logic of inclusion, anti-racist jewish and decolonial indigenous perspectives have been included within a2ru institutional space. But it is not clear to what extent those inclusions might escape the demographic and quantifying logics by which the university has always included its others, unless they are put into a more far-reaching dialogue with the radical methodological and onto-epistemological questions posed by artistic research.

One is hard-pressed to find any mention of artistic research or research-creation, let alone performance or practice as research, in a2ru's organizational documents and reports prior to 2019.[176] By foregrounding the integration and inclusion of the arts within a preexisting research landscape, these documents effectively sidestep the more radical epistemological claims of artistic research in its multiple lineages. It appears that, from the perspective of "deans and other academic leaders from top research universities," there is no need to engage with epistemological or methodological considerations when integrating the arts into research universities. This is presumably because the existing methods of those universities are already sufficient and need only to be enriched and enhanced by the additional presence of artists and the arts. Further, as might be guessed from such a framing, those presumed robust and already validated methods are primarily those of the sciences.

In a 2015 "Review of Best Practices and Challenges for Arts Integration in Higher Education," Bruce Mackh notes that the "majority of research collaborations observed . . . take place between the arts and STEM disciplines," although "partnerships with humanities and social sciences exist as well." In the section "Research Best Practices," three individual projects are described, all of which involve cognitive studies and/or healthcare and medicine.[177] Such projects tend to integrate art either as an object of study within existing quantitative (or perhaps qualitative) methods or as a means of dissemination of knowledge that has been legitimated by another discipline. By locating the value of arts research in relation to health outcomes and cognitivist understandings of the human, they sidestep the decolonial potentials I have been foregrounding. The same study defines arts integration as that which "pairs one or more disciplines of the arts (e.g., visual art and design, music, theater, dance, creative writing, or poetry) with one or more curricular areas," uncritically implying that the arts are inherently extracurricular. Moreover, it offers a familiar corporate defense of the arts as contributing to students' "career success by fostering the skills necessary in the 21st-century workplace."[178] Arts integration here is pedagogical, career oriented, and dependent upon the sciences for its epistemic legitimacy.

It is no coincidence that Sara Ahmed's incisive critique of the modality of inclusion is simultaneously a critique of white institutionality. Her book on this topic, *On Being Included: Racism and Diversity in Institutional Life*, reveals how fundamentally the whiteness of white institutions is based on the primacy they accord to writing. As I have argued, this primacy is so deeply ingrained and hegemonic that it is barely possible today to imagine anything deserving to be called an institution that does not have a founding set of written documents or for which debates over policy and practice do not constantly return to the apparent stability of meaning attributed to written language. It is notable in this context that Ahmed consistently refers to "diversity and equality *practitioners*" who navigate the contemporary university in a variety of ways.[179] Her emphasis on practice in the context of diversity work contrasts with the nonperformative or unreliably performative circulation of written documents like mission statements, diversity statements, and anti-racism statements. Practitioners are those who navigate the university from a position that is both critical and embodied, or rather, whose embodied practice and experience places them in a marginal and often critical relation to the institution. Thus, for Ahmed, "diversity work is institutional work in the sense that it is an experience of encountering resistance and countering that resistance. Each new strategy or tactic for getting through the wall generates knowledge of what does or does not get across."[180] If we understand artistic research as a call for radical diversity of method—for the expansion of method far beyond what can be imagined as long as writing is equated with thought, an expansion into what Rosamond King calls "radical interdisciplinarity"—then there may be some resonance between the practitioner of diversity work and that of artistic research. I am not equating these fields or suggesting that artistic research is inherently justice oriented. But I do want to elucidate the ways in which the whiteness of white institutions, following Ahmed, operates through technical, formal, and methodological registers, alongside and in addition to the skin tone and demographic racial categorization of bodies and people.

As Ahmed suggests: "Whiteness is not reducible to white skin or even to something we can have or be, even if we pass through whiteness. When we talk about a 'sea of whiteness' or 'white space,' we talk about the repetition of the passing by of some bodies and not others."[181] But skin color alone is not the only marker that determines which bodies can pass or pass by in white institutions: "If whiteness is what the institution is oriented around, then even bodies that do not appear white still have to inhabit whiteness." Moreover, "whiteness is an effect of what coheres rather than the origin of coherence. The effect of repetition is not then simply about a body count: it is not simply a matter of how many bodies are in. Rather, what is repeated is a very style of embodiment, a way of inhabiting space *by the accumulation of gestures of 'sinking' into that space*."[182] In the predominantly white universities of european and north american academia, what I have called "white writing" is built deeply into the style of embodiment and the accumulation of gestures that cohere the institution itself. To ask "What is [a white] institution?" therefore involves asking about the ways in which practitioners work with and through writing in the form of documents.[183] "An institution gives form to its aims in a mission statement," Ahmed writes, but "documents, once written, acquire lives of their own."[184] Furthermore, "documents are not simply objects; they are means of doing or not doing something" and might even be considered the "paradigmatic artefacts of modern knowledge practices."[185]

By tracing the ways in which diversity practitioners work strategically with and through the circulation of documents through institutions, Ahmed offers another important analysis of white writing: one grounded in the daily navigations of those who work with documents but who, for reasons of ethical and political commitment, as well as individual positioning and identity, refuse to define their work only in terms of those documents. "Practitioners spoke with a sense of caution about whether the documents, even if they are what practitioners are doing, are themselves doing anything. There is a kind of tiredness around them," which is associated with the risk that the diversity worker may become merely "a document machine, one that churns documents out."[186] There are significant points of overlap here between Ahmed's diversity practitioners and practitioners of artistic research, as well as all practitioners based in universities today, who are increasingly burdened by extractive forms of quantification that dominate and displace other practices through techniques of white writing, especially assessment, that have been imported from business contexts.

An inclusive approach to artistic research, as exemplified by a2ru—at least in its origins—risks defusing and defanging "the arts" of their capacity to embody and transmit alternative and marginalized knowledges. On the other hand, arts integration may open doors into the university through which such knowledges can pass, as the keynote interventions of Mirzoeff and Keene during recent annual conferences suggest. Ahmed highlights this double-edged nature of inclusion in the context of diversity work: "If diversity becomes something that is added to organizations, like color, then it confirms the whiteness of what is already in place. Alternatively, as a sign of the proximity of those who 'look different,' diversity can expose the whiteness of those who are already in place."[187] To advocate for the inclusion of the arts in research universities may leave both the category of "research" and the ranking taxonomy of "research universities" intact, as the addition of the arts confirms their supplementary role in relation to STEM fields. In the same way that diversity can become "about *changing perceptions of whiteness rather than changing the whiteness of organizations*," arts integration can allow the research university to expand, incorporating more and more sectors and industries, without questioning its core assumptions.[188] Integrating arts could then be a way of integrating epistemic diversity that keeps it in its proper place, as a secondary addition to the university's core business; or it might work to dilute the concept of diversity itself, producing "the arts" as an alternative and less threatening form of diversity than those attached to more explicitly political identities. Just as the "discourse of diversity is one of respectable differences," the arts themselves can be instrumentalized as modes of respectable difference or even as ways of rendering difference respectable by separating it from the production of knowledge.[189]

The inclusion or integration of the arts will be epistemically and politically conservative as long as the "structural position of being the guest, or the stranger, the one who receives hospitality, allows an act of inclusion to maintain the form of exclusion."[190] Who is it that takes on the role of host in welcoming the arts into research universities? Who are the "deans and other academic leaders" who are empowered to make this invitation? What happens to the research university when it includes the arts? Does this initiate a process of questioning, a critical analysis, a grappling with history? Or is it simply a matter of continued liberal expansion, an ever-growing inclusivity in which nothing substantially changes? Ahmed notes: "The creation of an idea of the university as diverse might modify the idea of the university slightly. Indeed, a slight modification of the idea of the university might be a way of protecting what goes on by obscuring what is ongoing."[191] This would be artistic research at its most diluted and inconsequential.

a2ru's early documents and reports are examples of what Ahmed calls "mission talk" or "happy talk": "a way of telling a happy story of the institution that is at once a story of the institution as happy."[192] They posit an exciting, boundlessly energetic, and inclusive future in which everyone will be able to participate. Issues of power and the unequal distribution of harm and exploitation, to say nothing of the exhaustion of earthly resources, are left unaddressed and framed as external to the conversation. At its most deceptive, this happy narrative is simply that of colonialism.[193] Diversity practitioners and others who steward lineages of alternative and marginalized knowledge within the white university are aware of these narrative styles and may indeed cultivate them as skills, while maintaining strategic distance and an awareness of alternative historical perspectives. In nearly all academic institutions today, corporate administration and executive power are increasingly separated from practices of teaching, studying, and making. For Ahmed, this does not mean that inclusive approaches should be rejected outright. The moment of inclusion can "be viewed not only as one of co-option but of opportunity."[194] Indeed, to be a practitioner in the university is necessarily to accept at least some of the terms of predominant institutionality. Diversity workers, no matter how tired or jaded in the face of institutional white supremacy, may still imagine a radical future: "For diversity workers to reach the heart and mind of an institution would mean becoming an institutional insider; it would mean that diversity becomes part of how the institution feels and thinks."[195] I wonder then what it could mean for "the arts"—understood not as creative industries or platforms for individual merit but as alternative lineages of knowledge—to become part of how academic institutions feel and think? What could make artistic research sticky in this way, interrupting the happy narrative of arts integration? Which terms and pressure points highlight the radical epistemic potential of these developments? And what about those for whom the aim is not to integrate the arts into the university and its mission, but instead to call the university's mission, history, and assumptions into question from a position that is radically external to it?

The second approach considered here is diametrically opposed to that of inclusion. It is one that positions artistic research as always in excess of the university, constantly fleeing and escaping its expectations and in this way radically unavailable to capture and co-optation. Precedents to such claims include Peggy Phelan's influential theorization of performance as inherently ephemeral, unavailable to documentary capture, and proponents of what Jon McKenzie has called the "liminal norm" in performance studies.[196] This approach has been memorably articulated by Simon Jones, who draws on Phelan, Deleuze and Guattari, and others to characterize "Practice-as-Research" (then the prevailing term in the united kingdom) as

> that which flees textual practices. Furthermore, and most outrageously, if it does so, ontologically it is also *outside of judgment*. Since the laws, rules and standards by which one judges the discipline's "outputs" must themselves have been phrased out of some textual practice that attempted to come *to know* performance. So, in fleeing the known, performance will inevitably evade judgment, since any phrasing of judgement, even—as in this writing itself—of performance *as evanescent event*, will fail to recognize those very aspects that make performance worthwhile; that is, those that escape phrasing.[197]

The alignment of writing and textuality with law and judgment in this passage resonates with the arguments I have been making about white writing. But in the absence of a decolonial historical framework that situates the technology of writing in relation to european colonialism, such an opposition between writing and performance risks its universalization and the loss of any grip on the specificities of media and the racialization of knowledge. In the slippage here between textuality, law, and judgment, are we to understand that the technology of writing itself is inherently violent? In the equation of writing with knowledge ("flees textual practices" becomes "fleeing the known"), do we surrender any claim to knowledge that might be made on behalf of nonwritten forms? And can we really assume that "those very aspects that make performance worthwhile" are just precisely those that escape textuality? This last question gets to the heart of the issue: the idea that ephemerality itself, uncapturability, that which evades judgment and flees the textual (or perhaps mediation in general), might be the ultimate good toward which artistic research aims.[198] To what do we commit ourselves when we prize the remainder or excess of writing and knowledge as the desired focus and most important value of artistic research?

The trope of excess or escape evoked by Jones is echoed in many chapters across numerous edited volumes on practice as research, performance as research, artistic research, and research-creation.[199] But the most thorough and influential account of artistic research in terms of excess is that developed by Erin Manning, whose work is increasingly cited as a reference point across the geographies of artistic research. Manning is based in canada and writes in response to that country's formulation of research-creation, drawing especially on her experience as founder of SenseLab, "a laboratory for thinking and making that works at the intersection of art, philosophy, and activism."[200] But Manning's writing is primarily philosophical rather than descriptive and her accounts of specific SenseLab events and projects most often serve as jumping off points for the development of a philosophical analysis of the capacity of research-creation to go beyond conventional ways of knowing. In two recent books, *The Minor Gesture* and *For a Pragmatics of the Useless*, Manning elaborates a complex poetics of the excess, the "minor" and the "useless," the "anarchic" or "speculative" share, the "infrathin": that which remains outside, uncounted, uncatalogued. In this poetics, nouns are dropped so that adjectives and prepositions can take their place, becoming nouns that invoke their own insufficiency: the *more than*, the *between*. Manning describes this as an intentional "abeyance of the substantive."[201] Influenced as much by the philosophies of William James and Alfred North Whitehead as by Deleuze and Fred Moten, Manning's analysis has a clear ethics in that it proclaims a need to stay with the specificity of emergent events rather than pinning them down through writing or other forms of capture. Yet precisely because this ethics so often works through abstraction and avoids the pinning down of particular techniques, its political potential is not as clear as Manning seems to suggest. As with my analysis of Grotowski, I find it necessary to ask in more detail about the positionality from which a given exit or escape is made, the ripple effects it leaves behind, and the way in which it does or does not effect a return to the social and the political.

I understand the allure of approaches that emphasize and even reify the uncapturable and the ungovernable, especially as a response to the rapid neoliberalization of the university. I am less convinced by Manning's philosophical elaboration of such approaches, which at times risks implying that escape itself is the important point rather than *what* escapes, *how* escape is managed, and what might happen in the return. What remains frustrating in Manning's account of SenseLab's work, and of experimental practice in general, is her intense rejection of situatedness. The desire for that which exceeds capture is so urgently felt in her writing that it displaces any possibility of orientation, any account of situatedness that might allow one to understand just what is being escaped and hence what kind of escape it is. Neither *The Minor Gesture* nor *For a Pragmatics* offers much detail regarding the actual techniques and processes that have developed within SenseLab since its launch in 2004. Perhaps most conspicuously absent is an account of structure and leadership, not only in Manning's explicit disavowals of authority but also in a repeated use of the passive voice that risks mystifying rather than clarifying process. Every action and idea developed by SenseLab seems to arrive through the passive voice, as if from nowhere: organic, emergent. Nothing is ever attributed to the power or desire of Manning herself or of any other individuals holding institutional power or authority. This is a delicate line to tread. One might read it as a model of humility and self-effacement, honoring the collective agency of a network that has intentionally never had an official list of members.[202] Yet such an approach also risks concealing the actual workings of SenseLab, including the extent of implicit authority wielded by Manning and other individuals. In trying to imagine what SenseLab activities might actually feel like, I find the closest parallels in my own experiences with the Performance as Research and Embodied Research Working Groups of the International Federation for Theatre Research.[203] We too have struggled with questions of membership, intellectual property, collective creation, and responsibility. But I have never believed that simply refusing to name individual contributions is an adequate solution to such problems. Concealing authority can be as much of a trap as overstating it.

A related tendency to romanticize the trope of excess attends Manning's account of method. For Manning, to be "against method" is "not simply an academic stance. Much more is at stake."[204] That is because method, for Manning, "is aligned to a making-reasonable of experience. At its worst, it is a static organization of preformed categories. At its best, it is an inquiry into the formation of categories that will, in the future, stand in as organizational strategies for academic thought."[205] Manning's alignment of method with reason follows the same logic as that of Simon Jones, here developed in greater detail:

> In working as an apparatus of capture, method gives reason its place in the sun: it diagnoses, it situates, it organizes, and ultimately it surveys and judges. Methods, we hear, are ever-changing, and this is surely the case. But any ordering agenda that organizes from without is still active in the exclusion of processes too unintelligible within current understandings of knowledge to be recognized, let alone studied or valued. Despite its best intentions, method works as the safeguard against the ineffable: if something cannot be categorized, it cannot be made to account for itself and is cast aside as irrelevant.[206]

Method in this passage is not only associated with reason and judgment but is also defined as "any ordering agenda that organizes from without." Yet again this suggests a universalizing dichotomy that can slide easily from a specific contextual debate, such as that over the status of method and methodology in artistic research, to an apparently universal critique of reason, judgment, and order. Where I have enumerated such dichotomies above— linking reason, rationality, and the mind to the technology of alphabetic writing—I have done so not to produce a transcendent dichotomy but with the opposite intention: to deflate the categories of reason and rationality by revealing the extent to which they are linked to historical materialities of coloniality, whiteness, and writing.

Interestingly, Manning does not reject technique as she rejects method. While methods for her are external to event and process, technique is emergent and processual:

> Technique touches on how a process reveals itself as such. Dance technique involves the honing of repetitive movements, but it also encourages the experimentation of what else those movements can do. Painting involves techniques for mixing color, for composition and form, but it also generates techniques of exhibition invested in mobile reorientations of what painting can do. This is not method: it is more dynamic than method, open to the shift caused by repetition, engaged by the ways in which bodies change, environments are modulated and modulating, and ecologies are composed.[207]

What strikes me here is how Manning's poetics, in its commitment to its own unacknowledged method of philosophical abstraction, continually reiterates binary dichotomies rather than proposing third-way alternatives or detailing experimental practices. At times, this dichotomization leads Manning to produce a caricature of academic research, as if it generally proceeds in a dull and mechanized way ("Most academic questions are of the solvable, unproblematic sort") and then, as a counterbalance, to offer a romanticized and transcendent account of subaltern experience as that which "directly perceives the complexity before (and between) the parsings" of methodological capture.[208]

Already in *The Minor Gesture* and more frequently in *Pragmatics*, Manning draws on concepts rooted in black studies, for example comparing research-creation to the "undercommons" and to "study" as influentially formulated by Fred Moten and Stefano Harney.[209] In *Pragmatics*, Manning also cites Hortense Spillers, Saidiya Hartman, Sylvia Wynter, and Denise Ferreira da Silva. There is indeed a resonance between the trope of excess or escape as it has developed in predominantly white critical theory (notably as Deleuze and Guattari's "lines of flight") and the concept of fugitivity in black studies. Yet I am reluctant to equate them as easily as Manning does. The fugitive is one form that the political can take, when it is pushed to its limits. But there are other modes: active resistance, daily subversion, large-scale transformation, revolution, alternative sovereignty. Each has its own rhythms and techniques. "Like the colonial police force," write Harney and Moten, "university labor may harbor refugees, fugitives, renegades, and castaways."[210] Tiffany Lethabo King adds: "Black fugitivity morphs and changes according to the vicissitudes of power."[211] But there is a difference between a fugitivity that flees literal and social death and an escape or exit that claims to reject an institution even while accepting its support. I qualified Grotowski's exit as a white one because the point and manner of exit matters. The meaning of any given exit and its capacity to generate force toward a later return, or even a radically distinct alternative, depends profoundly on the point from which it launches.

Manning's stated point of exit is less that of whiteness than of neurotypicality and, while I recognize the value of linking blackness and neurodiversity—"all black life is neurodiverse life," Moten commented on a draft manuscript of *The Minor Gesture*—it also seems crucial not to collapse them.[212] Whiteness is more explicitly acknowledged in *Pragmatics*, along lines similar to those I have explored here: whiteness "in its colonial imperative," which is "always about hierarchies of meaning and categories of sense"; whiteness as "the executive, the deep-seated belief in the truth of the one-after-the-other elocutions of an impoverished linearity of time charted."[213] Yet again there is a risk here that whiteness and neurotypicality blur into one another as pure structure and domination, losing their grounding in specific technical and historical formations. Put coarsely (and contra Frank Wilderson), the fugitivity of a slave is not that of a professor. A (white) academic may exit or even flee the university, but this does not make them fugitive in the sense developed in black studies. Indeed, I question the extent to which this particular imaginary applies to the white experiments of white artistic research unfolding in predominantly white institutions. The dichotomizations of structure and emergence, form and force, containment and excess make more sense to me in the context of black studies, where whiteness and blackness, even when they are taken to their ontological limits, are never reducible to a pure opposition of structure and excess but always also derived from empirical and affective histories of political violence and resistance.[214] I recognize the force sustained by ideas of fugitivity, flight, nonbeing, escape, and excess in contemporary thought, within and beyond black studies, but I am not certain how well these concepts fit with artistic research.

Both *The Minor Gesture* and *For a Pragmatics of the Useless* demonstrate a certain tension: between the desire to reify the unknown and the necessity to position it in relation to the known; or perhaps between an account of pure exit and an acknowledgment of (white and academic) positionality.[215] Yet a significant shift also seems to occur between the two volumes, unfolding on at least two registers. First, in its overall structure, the later book moves toward a "practical" or "technical" mode through the inclusion of a series of "pocket practices" interlaced throughout the volume.[216] Second, *Pragmatics* narrates a significant structural shift taking place within SenseLab itself, as the organization spawns—or perhaps is replaced by—the 3Ecologies Institute (3E), which is imagined as "a parainstitutional practice in excess of the university where the question of living and learning can be practiced otherwise."[217] I take the shift from "lab" to "institute" as signifying a different relation to institutionality. It suggests, perhaps, that the mobile and diffuse laboratory of SenseLab has now generated sufficient techniques and momentum to crystallize a more solid and strategic engagement with its own institutional contexts, enacting what I have been calling a "return" to a more direct engagement with dominant modes and structures—not in the sense of being absorbed or included, but armed with concrete alternatives that might now perhaps be implemented on a larger scale.

In the case of 3E, this shift seems to encompass a significant and provocative shift in the question of *which* dominant institutions are to be engaged: no longer just the neoliberal university, but also neoliberal finance. It is difficult to understand from outside exactly what kinds of technique are being developed through this new engagement with finance and value. But what emerges most concretely from Manning's discussion of "finance at the limit" is an attempt to reconceive or even reinvent the digital as resistant to quantification.[218] With this, SenseLab and 3Ecologies seem poised to enact a return that is both surprising and exciting. As Manning suggests: "To end the book on finance at the limit is to carry the schizoanalytic gesture from the artistic, political, and philosophical environments into the world of capital."[219] What might be activated by such a passage? Having previously exited from the university, Manning and the undefined network of SenseLab now undertake a critical return toward a different institution, one that is no less socially dominant and hegemonic but which has historically foregrounded very different technique: finance, money, the quantification of value. Digital finance and coding, including cryptocurrencies, are built on technologies of writing but, like digital audiovisuality, they also amplify and/or diverge from the history of white writing in significant ways.[220] If anything, finance would appear to be even less amenable to contestation than the university. But is it? I do not know. I only know that the movement of a loosely organized collective like SenseLab toward an explicit and practical engagement with a major social institution other than the university is worth following. This move also takes us from the second to the third artistic research model described here.

Change happens, when it does, on multiple levels simultaneously. Politically, I accept the need for liberal and radical projects to work alongside each other, if not always together. When it comes to artistic research, I acknowledge the value of both inclusion and escape as strategies. But the approaches that resonate most with my own practices and positionalities are of a third kind, which I call pragmatic or experimental: those that seek to *propose alternative forms*.[221] Recognizing that one's offerings will no doubt be limited in scope, such an approach nevertheless moves forward at the edge between the known and the unknown, refusing to romanticize that edge through abstraction and instead concretizing or even deflating it in relation to a particular place and moment. A pragmatic or experimental approach follows Deleuze and Guattari's memorable instruction: "Lodge yourself on a stratum, experiment with the opportunities it offers, find an advantageous place on it, find potential movements of deterritorialization, possible lines of flight, experience them, produce flow conjunctions here and there, try out continuums of intensities segment by segment"; for it is only "through a meticulous relation with the strata that one succeeds in freeing lines of flight."[222] A meticulous relation with existing stratification is the premise of experimentation.

The meaning of a technique is relative to the context of its enactment, hence there can never be a universal technique. Romancing the excess is a form of disavowal that, like other strategic essentialisms, may reify oppositionality at the expense of the capacity to generate substantive alternatives. My interest in social epistemology has always been in how it is able to diagram knowledge-making practices as processes of onto-epistemic change. When a technique for attuning to a given excess is discovered or invented, it brings that zone of (former) excess into the realm of the known and the technical. This does not kill that excess unless we have prematurely defined it in terms of its own excessiveness; in other words, if we have disavowed our own working contexts. Instead, as a given excess moves into the technical—as the unknown becomes known—new worlds become possible and new excesses appear: that which was previously beyond the horizon of the imaginable now becomes marginally or liminally present at the edges of experience.[223]

It seems to me that an entity like SenseLab is more interesting rather than less when it is situated in relation to the university, just as Grotowski's exit must be understood in relation to european theater for its trajectory to have meaning; or, to reference one of Manning's key examples, just as Guattari's radical interventions into institutional psychotherapy at La Borde made use of techniques that might not have been radical or even noteworthy in other contexts.[224] While also deeply influenced by black studies, I would align my vision of artistic research less with Harney and Moten's undercommons than with Katherine McKittrick's black methodologies and black "method-making":

> This story is not meant to eschew academic institutions. As I note below, black methodology and method-making (which are academic and extra-academic), offer rebellious and disobedient and promising ways of undoing discipline. And those of us who work in these places that weigh us down can carve out surprising and generous spaces that challenge existing political visions, allow us to fight against inequity and racism, work against racial violence, and collaborate . . .—freedom spaces (that are sometimes right there within and in excess of the mess of the academy).[225]

Mess and excess are important here, but they are not the endpoint or goal. On the contrary, the opposition between structure and excess is always moving, changing, and transforming as what was once excess gradually becomes structure, displacing prior structure and bringing new horizons of excess into view.

For many scholar-artists and practitioner-researchers, the university is more than just a structural location and site within which to undertake covert epistemic operations. Instead the university becomes the actual site of battle, the form that is to be transformed. Thus Thulile Gamedze, with a nod to Harney and Moten, writes:

> I'm not quite sure what the importance is of the university itself. I don't know if I believe in the university, but there are certainly people at the university; people will go wherever has potential. . . . What is the university classroom space? How can we acknowledge it? Where do we see the violence? Where do we see the potential for something? I guess that the emphasis is always on what people are doing in that space, and how we can together identify the way and the style and the texture of the coloniality in that space. It always tends more to do with us—us being split and trying to do something else—as opposed to *questioning what the space is. We must look at the space.*[226]

To look at the space, to question the space rather than only ourselves, is to engage with the institution in a pragmatic way, seeking out leverage or pressure points at which one might take hold of it, gripping or twisting it into a different form. To foreground and thematize the structure of particular spaces is to ask how their structure might be changed, how spaces themselves have forms, and how changes in this form might generate different kinds of space. Could we not recognize this as the mission of artistic research? Such a definition is articulated by Esa Kirkkopelto in a short but incisive essay. Applying the art world concept of institutional critique to the university, Kirkkopelto imagines

> artistic research as institutional research: *artistic research not only takes place in institutions, but it should also conduct research on them*, take institutions as its object. By this, I mean not only the particular institution where the research happens to take place but also institutions in a broader sense: from the aesthetic institutions of perception and affect to current political institutions, through showing how the latter are connected to the former or even based on them. Hence, the inventiveness of an invention is to be assessed in relation to institutions that surround and sustain it: we should ask to which extent an invention has the potential to change these institutions and, finally, why they should be changed.[227]

This claim marks a dramatic shift in perspective, away from an artistic research that is included and co-opted by the institution, or one that ontologically flees institutionality itself, toward one that takes the form of the institution as its working material.

Kirkkopelto concludes:

> Whereas the neo-liberal market economy destroys institutions, or rather, maintains them only in order to exploit them, the people in charge of the development of the institutions of higher education in the arts should defend institutions by deconstructing them. . . . In order to make their struggle more active and to put an end to the constant withdrawing, to the disputes over the diminishing resources, they could adopt a wider, more affirmative and active idea of what institution and instituting may mean. Institutions define the fundamental forms of our experience and action. Instituting always implies *re-institution*, the changing of those fundamental forms. Particularly in the case of artistic research practice we should take into account its simultaneously inventive and institutional nature, consider its results as *media of invention with significant institutional consequences*.[228]

The idea that artistic research is primarily engaged with innovating forms (institutional and mediated) opens the door to a study of pressure points and points of leverage. Which forms and structures might be shifted, in which specific ways, to enable or provoke "significant institutional consequences"? To avoid overstating the impact of such interventions, it must be acknowledged that local innovations in form are not enough on their own. Without links to wider social and political movements these will be ripples in a pond, quickly stilled. But there can also be no meaningful politics without innovation of form; thus, the question of form and media, archive and mediation, must be central to imagining change. This is perhaps to take a perspective closer to that of cultural and performance studies than of philosophy, zooming into particular mediated enactments rather than general schema.[229] Theories of exit and escape, energizing as they can be, will never provide concrete alternatives to the way things are. At best they can offer strategic cover for what happens outside and beyond the institution. Such cover is needed at times, especially when the dominating force of an institution is so violent that direct experimentation is precluded. But at other times, when a window opens, there can be a dialogue between approaches that emphasize escape and those that tackle existing forms and structures of institutionality more directly.

What are the pressure points of academia? My argument in this chapter has been that the technology of writing is a crucial pressure point not only for academia but also for white institutionality in general. The displacement of writing as the sole legitimate and transparent medium of thought and knowledge might then be the primary intervention made by university-based artistic research. Artistic research in this sense examines and experiments not only with the form of the event but also with the form of the document. It takes the question of the document (not documentation, which presumes the primacy of the event, but a much wider ontology of documentality) seriously as a challenge and a responsibility. As Ahmed shows, documents alone do not constitute agency or commitment, but they can be used as tools or levers in the shifting and reimagining of institutions: "A working document is one that multiple actors work over. To work over a document is to become involved in its political life. The body of the document becomes part of the body of the institution."[230] This book's introduction mentioned a PhD dissertation, produced in south carolina, that took the form of a recorded album and was followed by the release of a peer-reviewed album.[231] That project is significant, but as far as I know it has not been linked to any wider discussions about the form of the PhD dissertation in the united states, where a book-length written document is still almost always expected. In contrast, digital and multimedia PhD dissertations began to appear in the 1990s in the united kingdom, although the question of form as it pertains to doctoral-level artistic research remains open and contested.[232] The doctorate, as a crucial form of knowledge and institutional gateway, is just one of the pressure points at which artistic research can intervene in the structure of the university and the racialization of knowledge.[233] In chapter 3, I address other leverage points through an examination of my own artistic research.

Chapter 3

✦

Audiovisual Ethnotechnics

The Judaica Project

July 31, August 18, November 9, 2012. I enter the performance space barefoot and begin to sing. I am wearing a moroccan kaftan, black steampunk goggles, and biker gloves, carrying an army camouflage backpack. Sometimes the kaftan is white with gold stripes, other times it is purple. The song is "Avinu Malkeinu," a jewish prayer that is traditionally recited on the holiest of days. After singing, I place the backpack on the floor and look around the space, speaking softly to myself. From the pack I remove a medium-sized carpet, which I unroll onto the floor. Sometimes this is a thick, black-and-white mexican blanket; other times, a red persian wall hanging. The unrolling reveals a single volume of talmud, tucked away inside the material. I begin to sing again, this time a wordless hasidic melody or *nigun*. I kneel beside the book, remove my goggles, page through it, bow to it. From the backpack I pull a manila envelope full of woven yarmulkes, jewish religious skullcaps, which I may or may not distribute in a pattern across the floor. Sometimes I am alone; sometimes I am joined by another performer and a story is told about a werewolf and a magical child. Another song is introduced: "Ale Brider" ("All Brothers"), a well-known yiddish folk song but performed here as a lament. What is the meaning of this strange ritual?[1]

Throughout the previous chapters I have attempted to develop an ontology (or perhaps what Marquis Bey would call a "paraontology") of molecular identity to support a mode of practice that I provisionally call molecular thinking.[2] I have attempted to learn from black studies in extending the theorization of identities as both intersectional fields of power and interdisciplinary fields of knowledge, ontologizing such fields both above and below the level of individuals and emphasizing their radical asymmetry. I have rejected a structuralist paradigm according to which positions like "Black" and "White" can be taken for granted as static and wholly incommensurable, while at the same time building on a more complex grammar of colors to think whiteness, blackness, indigeneity, and other categories of identity in relation to each other. Advancing the dramaturgical to conceptualize the material workings of embodied identity beyond a census epistemology, I have explored how identity and technique are inextricably interwoven and mutually constitute each other through processes of sedimentation and desedimentation in practice. These ideas derive not only from sustained reading but also from my own life experience and in particular from an extended line of artistic research called the Judaica project. Throughout this project I have attempted to concretize and render practical certain questions about contemporary identity via a focus on jewishness. Evolving alongside my scholarship on embodied technique, the Judaica project has centered an embodied practice of singing or songwork in which jewishness is treated as molecular. In this way, the Judaica project has been a literal if unconventional laboratory in which to develop a theory and practice of molecular (jewish) identity. The creative theory articulated in the previous chapters both emerged from the Judaica project and drives my ongoing attempts to understand what I am doing in that laboratory.

Much older as a category than whiteness, blackness, or indigeneity in its modern sense, judaism and jewishness have at various times and places named a religion, a nation, a race, an ethnicity, a language, an ethics, a gendering, and more.[3] If, in parts of the united states and europe today, jewishness is too often imagined to be unproblematically aligned with whiteness, this is due to a radical but historically recent transformation in its meaning, prior to which jewishness might have been more closely associated with islam, with blackness, or even with indigeneity, precisely in racialized opposition to an emerging whiteness defined in large part by christianity.[4] As a result of this shift, jewishness can serve as a limit case that reveals the flaws in oversimplified accounts of identity. As Jonathan Boyarin writes, "Jewishness remains an inspiring or irritating exemplum" of the complex and perhaps irresolvable politics of identity across diverse contexts.[5] Yet there is a substantial gap between most contemporary theories and practices of jewishness and those that engage with critical race theory and the decolonial grammar of colors I have been exploring up to this point. This gap is caused by the major obstacle to understanding jewishness in a contemporary geopolitical landscape: its entanglement with whiteness. Jewishness is emphatically not synonymous with whiteness, nor a variety of it, but that does not mean it is easy to define jewishness outside this entanglement. Whether considering the neocolonial whiteness of the state of israel, the racism of many white jewish institutions, or the reflex on the part of some white jews to deny their own complicity with anti-blackness and other racisms on account of being jewish, the entanglement of whiteness and jewishness is complex, with deep historical roots and profound contemporary effects.[6]

There are at least three levels at which the disentangling of jewishness and whiteness must take place. In the first place, jewishness is simply and factually not synonymous with or containable within whiteness insofar as there are, and always have been, many jews and jewish communities that are in no sense white. "The influx to Britain and Israel of Jews from Baghdad, Calcutta, Cochin, and Mumbai; the presence of African American and Caribbean Jews in the United States; and the growing number of racially mixed marriages in America should all alert us to the fallacies of speaking of Jews as if they were 'White' or European."[7] Furthermore, a variety of communities and lineages of black jews "have played pivotal roles in the transformation of the Jewish world's self-consciousness," despite antiblack racism in white jewish communities and the latter's frequent refusal to accept black jewish communities as kin.[8] For jewish communities in subsaharan africa, the categories of jewishness, blackness, and indigeneity may entirely overlap.[9] Highlighting and centering nonwhite jewish identities is a crucial part of disentangling jewishness from whiteness. But equally necessary is a second mode of disentanglement, which grapples with the historical racialization of european jews and their profoundly contested relationship to whiteness.

In a recent talk on jewishness and whiteness, J. Kameron Carter asks: "How does a certain imagination of 'the Jews' figure within or in relationship to that western, civilizing humanism that organizes the planet? What's the relationship between Jews and the religion of whiteness?"[10] Responding to Carter's talk, Shaul Magid recognizes that the "structural and theological" connection between jewishness and whiteness must be addressed beyond pointing out the fact that not all jews are white: "all Jews may not be white, but 'the Jews' (the figural Jew) have become part of Whiteness."[11] Jewishness in this sense is a particular margin of whiteness. Like other margins of whiteness mentioned in the previous chapter (feminist, queer, disabled, polish), it has the potential to counteract or deconstruct whiteness from its specific marginal position but it may also risk falling into complicity. This is the positionality of posteuropean "non-Jewish Jews": those who have historically exited jewish religious orthodoxy, seeking to develop a broader conception of jewish identity and knowledge and to dwell "on the borderlines of various national cultures."[12] Such a positionality might well apply to many contemporary scholars who, while not based in the discipline of jewish studies, nevertheless develop critical analyses out of and in relation to their own jewishness, as in Judith Butler's critique of zionism and Michael Rothberg's concepts of multidirectional memory and implicated subjectivity.[13] Nicholas Mirzoeff, as a starting point for a critical analysis of whiteness, invokes the complex status of his jewish identity and the way it has changed across time and geographies.[14] Even the work of Mark Rifkin, whose recent book on black and indigenous imaginaries does not mention jews or jewishness, might benefit from being understood as a kind of jewish critique.[15]

Building on the analysis of white writing I conducted in chapter 2, it seems important to pause here and situate critical theory itself as an alternative mode of writing—a different way of working with the same alphabet and often the same languages—that is in many respects specifically jewish. Modern critical theory is substantially jewish in both its german and french lineages and in a deeper sense as well. The jewishness of Derrida has been thoroughly explored as an essential resource in the development of deconstruction.[16] The Frankfurt School, which developed critical theory as we know it between pre- and postholocaust germany and the united states, was staffed and directed mostly by german jews.[17] Jewishness is what allows Emmanuel Levinas and Hannah Arendt to stand alongside Frantz Fanon as part of what Fred Moten calls a "dissident strain in modern phenomenology," together asking "a question concerning the humanity they cannot assume."[18] Adding Marx and Freud to this list of major european thinkers emphasizes the extent to which jewishness and whiteness are profoundly entangled in everything that today is called philosophy, theory, and knowledge. As with white writing, it would be fruitless to attempt to specify the exact borders of jewish critical reading and writing practices in either technical or identitarian terms. But it is possible to link the twentieth-century development of critical theory with jewishness in a broadly technical way, by conceptualizing *talmud* as an archaic jewish countercurrent within and against philosophy as white writing.

Sergey Dolgopolski explains:

> At the margins of different scenarios of poststructuralism's disengagement with Heidegger, Talmudic (or more broadly, Jewish) tradition keeps emerging. In the case of Derrida, it arrives via Levinas. In the case of Deleuze, it arrives via Spinoza. In the case of Lyotard, it arrives via Freud's connection to Jewish tradition. In all these cases, the Talmud has become involved in poststructuralism's discussion of metaphysics.[19]

This is talmud, with no definite article, not in the sense of a particular set of texts but as an "art or *techne*," a "scholarly discipline" or "type of rationality," that sustains an interdisciplinary (and intersectional) relationship to philosophy proper, rather than being merely its object.[20] According to Dolgopolski, talmud is the "art of disagreement" in contrast to philosophy, which has "always hoped to reach agreement." As I suggested in the previous chapter, philosophy's desire for agreement or consensus has profoundly political and colonial stakes: "In their scarier, but perhaps also more intellectually honest, practice, philosophers have sought to eradicate disagreement as a place of mistake, error, deviation, or, in religious terms, heresy."[21] Talmud, in contrast, exemplifies "an approach in which, unlike false disagreements, true disagreements should be preserved and even developed further." According to Dolgopolski's radical interpretation of the aims of thought and writing, "true disagreements are very hard to achieve" and are "even harder to maintain, for the ghost of agreement constantly haunts and dissipates them."[22] In a passage that carefully teases out a specifically jewish "materialist approach to language," Jonathan Boyarin similarly juxtaposes jewish textual interpretation or *midrash* with the state-oriented ontology of language as logos.[23]

While it is beyond the scope of this project to develop a full analysis of the jewishness of critical theory, any decolonial media ontology will benefit from acknowledging the specific jewishness of certain alternative reading and writing techniques.

In marking the jewishness of critical theory, I am of course not attempting to limit the latter to demographically jewish bodies, still less to police its boundaries. On the contrary, while european jewishness is surely constituted in large part by a marginal and deeply textual relation to dominant white christian power (identity is made of technique), it is also the case that this relation, and the mode of writing/thinking to which it gave rise, are and remain jewish even when they are no longer demographically so (technique is made of identity). If critical theory is jewish, then a kind of deracialized jewishness haunts the full range of "critical humanities" today. Critical race theory, critical black studies, and critical native or indigenous studies are all jewish—not in any sense that would claim or appropriate them for jewishness, or which in any way undercuts or overwrites their identities as black and indigenous, but rather on a level of epistemic technique and potential solidarity. We might in this sense say that they are *cryptojewish*.[24] The question then becomes why jewishness, which as critical theory underpins so much of today's vital counterhegemonic thought, no longer sits at the table as an identity alongside the other radical modes of critical production I have been discussing. Why, over a period when critical theory has been profoundly advanced by feminist theory, black studies, indigenous studies, and other interdisciplines, is jewish studies itself not properly critical in this sense? Put bluntly: Why is it so provocative to name the jewishness of critical theory? To account for this, we must look again at how the racial position of jewishness changed during the twentieth century, examining the forced assimiliations and voluntary complicities with whiteness that have led to the gradual separation of jewish studies from critical theory.[25]

There may be good reasons to reject the idea that critical theory is jewish, including that it plays into conspiracy theories. It is indeed both risky and ironic that a reclaiming of critical theory as jewish echoes the most antisemitic tropes: those that position critical theory as a jewish/leftist corruption of the academy and of knowledge.[26] On the other hand, refusing to name critical theory as jewish only conceals the roots of its counterhegemonic thinking, allowing the dominant narrative of white philosophy to prevail.[27] The delinking and relinking of technique and identity is always political. As current work in black studies rigorously demonstrates, no escape from racism is to be found by recourse to a neutrally human subject or a universal rationality as those concepts are themselves founded on the abjection of racialized others. I therefore take up the talmudic roots of critical theory as a project of reclamation, highlighting its potential to counter white writing in solidarity with techniques of black, indigenous, queer, and feminist writing that also displace logocentrism. Most importantly, I am not proposing a one-way relationship, from technique to identity, whereby critical theory would be reduced to its connection with demographically jewish people or peoples. I am equally suggesting that jewishness is present, on a molecular level, wherever reading and writing are practiced in talmudic ways. From such a radically judaizing perspective, all of critical theory might be said to be contiguous with talmud—not with "the Talmud" as a set of ancient texts, but with a talmudic "way of thinking" that can never be completed and "has no bounds."[28] This talmud, as a technique of counterthought deeply entangled with the dominant history of philosophy, offers a mode of reading, writing, and thinking that precedes and continually counters european logocentrism. It is literally a technique for working with letters, even and especially an *alphabet*, that foregrounds their materiality (including their mystical and magical capacities, as in kabbalah) without installing behind them an illusion of pure thought, coherent rationality, or logos.[29]

The jewish *word*, as in the famous story of the golem, is not a transparent utterance voicing an inner subjectivity but rather a tool, a technology, a chip or fragment that activates events and possibilities. Critical theory as talmud continually works and reworks textuality, worrying text like a piece of cloth—wrestling with, dwelling in, embodying textuality—from the mystic force of letters to the form and shape of books, without ever arriving at a coherent edifice or a complete system. Talmudic thought is written but not systematic; it is iterative rather than linear, offering a different textual practice and a different practical relation between writing and life. As such, it is a crucial part of the artistic research methodology developed in the Judaica project, one of the ways in which jewishness is both method and object of study. But this is not enough. Talmudic thinking, understood as the technique of critical theory, is insufficient on its own to develop new ways of being jewish in the larger field of molecular identities that I have been describing. There are several reasons for this, which are once again entangled with whiteness and with writing.

The problem is not quite the same as that which Robyn Wiegman applies to critical whiteness studies: It is not that critical theory attempts to master the body and therefore imagines itself to be impossibly complete. Precisely in its jewishness, critical theory retains a certain textual materiality that goes along with its argumentative style. The assumption in critical theory, unlike the positivism of classical white writing, is that there will always be more to say. Yet, for all that, critical theory remains a technique of reading and writing. Moreover, the study of talmud and torah, at least traditionally, is a masculine and masculinist endeavor. While the binary gender formation produced in jewish orthodoxy may not be the same as that of whiteness proper, it is a form of patriarchy and heterosexism.[30] Additionally, the entanglement of jewishness and whiteness has meant that much of the jewish critical tradition is mired in antiblack racism.[31] In my own experience, it has not been easy to disentangle the critique of (white) writing from internalized antisemitism.

My desire to go "beyond" writing seems uncomfortably to combine both a substantive critique of logocentrism and a more personal need to escape from a stereotype of jewish masculinity as excessively textual. This is not an individual problem, I suspect, but an effect of the generational entanglement of jewishness, masculinity, and whiteness, which has enabled a long line of white male jewish thinkers and artists to theorize and perform their own marginalization in ways that reinscribe patriarchy and anti-blackness. The Judaica project has sought embodied and eventually also audiovisual alternatives to that lineage. This is the third level at which jewishness can and must be disentangled from whiteness.

Alongside a demographic acknowledgment or political centering of jewishness outside whiteness, as well as a technique/identity analysis of critical theory as jewish counterknowledge, exists the possibility of inventing new modes and forms of jewishness that operate in previously unimagined ways, cutting across racial, religious, and national forms of identification in solidarity with anti-racist and decolonial practice. In attempting to move toward the development of such forms, the Judaica project—and my understanding of the politics of contemporary jewish identity more generally—has been most decisively influenced by Santiago Slabodsky's *Decolonial Judaism: Triumphal Failures of Barbaric Thinking*. This extraordinary volume reframes the matter of jewish identity as an epistemic challenge within which both the overdetermination of jewishness by whiteness and its potential to develop decolonial alternatives are explicitly at stake. Slabodsky does not directly engage the fields of black and indigenous critical theory to which I have been referring, but he does situate jewishness within a decolonial historical framework (via Walter Mignolo and Aníbal Quijano) that provincializes europe and refuses to separate european modernity from european colonialism.[32] While critical jewish thinkers like Judith Butler and Atalia Omer also seek to develop jewish resources in solidarity with palestinians, and jewish studies scholars like Daniel and Jonathan Boyarin theorize the "powers of diaspora" over and against the state of israel, Slabodsky goes further by resituating jewishness in the context of global south decolonial theory.[33] Slabodsky's notion of decolonial judaism integrates and further extends the other two strategies of disentanglement. It begins by decentering jewish whiteness, but it does not end with a merely demographic project. It recognizes critical theory as a possible jewish contribution to decoloniality, while acknowledging the failure of the most prominent jewish critical projects to retain their radical orientations following the global repositioning and reracialization of jewishness since 1948.

For Slabodsky, decolonial judaism—"the positive adoption of barbarism and the desire to create a barbaric space inserting Jews within decolonial struggles"—has failed, not only in the global north, but also in the global south.[34] As a result, what Slabodsky offers is neither a method nor a manifesto but more like a caution, a warning, or a challenge:

Today, more than ever, there are protests against the consequences
of Jewish re-positionality. The normative portrayal of Jews, however,
has left little space for a geopolitical challenge that can emerge from
the barbaric instead of the civilized features of Judaism. The historical reality ultimately challenges the location from which Jewish
discourses are allowed to emerge.[35]

Slabodsky observes how, within the united states, his own jewishness actually whitens him, counteracting other ways in which he is marginalized or
racialized by his precarious immigration status, spanish accent, and visible
brownness.[36] His account underscores the sense in which jewishness today is
normatively white even though many jews are not white. Yet what is particularly compelling for me in Slabodsky's formulation is not only its decolonial
historical framing but also its refusal to cede the grounds of a possibly decolonial judaism to the ongoing absorption of jewishness into whiteness.

Slabodsky describes the challenge of a decolonial judaism as "the interrela-
tion between existential conditions and epistemological creativity," arguably
another way of naming the interplay between identity and technique, or
power and knowledge. He asks: "If it is true that Jews have undergone a
racial re-classification, can they still represent a challenge to the same structure that now welcomes them? In other words, can Jews still be a compelling
source of decolonial proposals?"[37] Such questions are precisely the kind that
must be answered not only via ethnographic studies but also by the interventions of creative and artistic research.

What are the conditions according to which one could undertake a
Jewish decolonial reading of the geopolitical scene? What is clear is
that there is no single answer. Some Jewish discourses will need to
deconstruct the narratives that establish the peoplehood in order to
show the perversity of a model that has achieved a normative positionality. Other Jewish discourses will re-appropriate old narratives
to re-claim a forgotten or overlooked normative core that shows
the historical betrayal of the new positionality. Only a critical dialogue between such strategies, perhaps one that exceeds the limits
of academia, can show the possibilities and limitations of such a
project.[38]

When Slabodsky suggests that critical dialogue toward decolonial judaism
necessarily "exceeds the limits of academia," I suppose that he is thinking
primarily of direct forms of political activism. Yet, invoking an expanded and
decolonial sense of artmaking and given the limitations of my own positionality, I have taken up Slabodsky's challenge as an invitation to ask how such
a "critical dialogue" could move beyond the textual through an engagement
with nontextual forms of thought and knowledge.[39]

Taking Slabodsky's challenge seriously, as a research question, crystallized the relatively inchoate desires and interests that had led me to begin the Judaica project. By what method could a project of embodied artistic research seek to develop answers to the problem of decolonial judaism in the twenty-first century? With what materials and which researchers, in what configurations, and with what outcomes might such a project take form? It is easy enough for a scholar-artist in the global north to source and cite thinkers and practitioners in the global south. But how to configure a methodology so that this would be an instance of ethical apprenticeship, or even solidarity, rather than mere appropriation? The risks of positing a decolonial (or "barbaric" as Slabodsky also calls it) judaism are great, not least because the appropriation of indigeneity is a key strategy of coloniality and specifically of zionism, leading to what Gil Hochberg calls "brownwashing" or what Michael Zalta calls "hallucinatory ethnicization."[40] Beneath such maneuverings are complex, long-standing questions about the place of jewishness in relation to european colonization and anticolonial resistance.[41] Given that context, the "hallucinatory ethnicization" of jewishness cannot be so easily dismissed.

To be sure, a simple equation of jewishness with indigeneity, particularly in relation to palestine, is part of a colonial narrative that leverages jewish victimization within europe to support neocolonialism and white supremacy elsewhere. On the other hand, nothing is resolved by an equally simple equation of jewishness with whiteness, which forgets the complex racialization of jews throughout european colonialism. If anything, jewishness is a particularly rich point of intervention precisely because it cannot check any of those census boxes. (When jewishness does appear on the census form today, it is as a religion, alongside christian and muslim, following the demographic separation of race and religion that hides their entangled histories.) Hence, jewishness needs to be thought and reinvented dramaturgically, through modes of critical fabulation and speculation like those that have been developed in black studies. As much of that work powerfully reveals, all ethnicization is in a sense hallucinatory. There is no formulation of contemporary jewishness that is not, at least in part, a hallucination. This does not make jewishness meaningless or simply plastic; rather, it means that formulating, fabulating, or indeed hallucinating the meaning of jewishness today is task that requires movement beyond the critical, perhaps even beyond the textual, into further modes of radical interdisciplinarity. Ethnographic and theoretical studies of jewishness might search for the seeds of radical diasporic or decolonial judaism within subaltern jewish communities and critical lineages. For artistic research, on the other hand, what is needed is not ethnography but *ethnotechnics*: a technical investigation of the contemporary limits and potentialities of a given category of identity.

There are parallels, as well as differences, between what artistic research proposes and the epistemological shift in ethnographic method that aims "to take seriously the knowledge practices" of its objects, those "people who are more often understood as vulnerable subjects than as political actors."[42] While artistic research is sometimes framed as a kind of autoethnography, I prefer to move from the writing of "graphos" to the more broadly applicable knowledge implied by technique, coining the term "ethnotechnics."[43] This would be the practical working and reworking of identity as that which ethnographic texts increasingly recognize as knowledge practices undertaken by those whom ethnographers study. I do not exclude ethnography itself from the category of ethnotechnics—certainly, writing about culture also produces culture—but ethnotechnics emphasizes the creative methods, speculative orientation, and posttextual forms of embodied and artistic research. Perhaps ethnotechnics is a form of experimental (auto)ethnography, one that explicitly prioritizes invention rather than description. The idea that embodied and performative acts can be substantive interventions in the construction of identity is nothing new. Yet it remains controversial to suggest that the aims of artistic research might embrace not only a better understanding or articulation of existing identities but also the transformation of identity and perhaps even the invention of new identities. Autoethnography can certainly contribute to such a methodology, insofar as the existing identities of the researcher-practitioner are the sedimented grounds of future research. Thus my own identity is necessarily the starting point for the Judaica project. Yet the aim of the project was never only to situate or contextualize my own identity, but always also to develop new fragments or molecules of jewishness that could embody and formalize, on a small scale, some of its alternative potentialities.

The Judaica project has explored how a project of embodied artistic research could organize itself around a critical decolonial theory of identity and technique.[44] When I began the Judaica project in 2012, I was following an impulse to reconnect the embodied technique of postgrotowskian songwork with a cultural politics of jewishness. In the earliest performances of the Judaica project, such as those described at the beginning of this section, everything was thrown together: talmud and steampunk; hebrew, yiddish, and nonlexical vocables; skullcaps purchased online and a robe given to me by my iranian grandfather-in-law. In later versions I would remove all these props and strip down to a pair of white thai fisherman pants, projecting the letters of the hebrew alphabet in gold onto my skin and the floor around me; clothe myself in plain black pants and a T-shirt to retell the famous story of the dybbuk; wrap myself in paper towels and a keffiyeh, my song pierced by the sound of an israeli siren, under the direction of a palestinian colleague; and, finally, unfold the aesthetics of the process through a new approach to the audiovisual embodied research laboratory based within a university. Across these different iterations of the Judaica project, song and singing remained constant, as did the question of what jewishness can mean and be—a question that I framed as not merely ethnographic but also ethnotechnic, exploring and reworking jewishness on a molecular level. The aim of the Judaica project has always been to feel my way into an embodied practice and performance of jewishness that could not be accessed through textual means alone. The rest of this chapter explores both the problem of locating jewishness within a molecular geopolitics of identity and the formal means I have developed to grapple with that problem. By analogy with chapter 2, the central question here might be how to think jewishness "after" black studies; except that I can no longer allow writing to stand as the sole or even primary medium of thought.

What Is a Song?

The Judaica project was preceded by almost a decade of artistic research in which I explored a variety of approaches to song. Having participated in musical theater as a child, I gradually abandoned that genre in favor of apparently more serious (experimental) genres. I did not reconnect with the act of singing in performance until a brief encounter with a north american indigenous practitioner in 2003, which led me to search for a way to reactivate embodied song in my artistic practice.[45] Shortly after that experience I moved to poland, where I worked with a number of artists and teachers who can loosely be called postgrotowskian. I have written elsewhere about this experience and in the present context only want to acknowledge that many of those practitioners worked for extended periods, often decades, with selected groups of traditional indigenous or "folk" songs from around the world. These included lineages of song from poland, ukraine, bulgaria, and caucasus georgia, as well as european early music, music of the north american shakers, southern american blues, and other traditions from haiti, cuba, western and southern africa, and china.[46]

During and after these encounters, I searched for ways to integrate what I had learned from them, which amounted to much more than extended vocal techniques and melodies. From these experiences, I arrived at a question: *What is a song?*[47] This work is the prehistory of the Judaica project, a period in which I created, adapted, and worked with a wide range of songs, searching for my own pathway through what I now call songwork: embodied practice that is cultivated around the act of singing but which is more than musical in its scope.[48] At first I created ensemble vocal adaptations of short extracts from a diverse selection of audio tracks.[49] Later, I led the creation of english-language songs using texts by Mikhail Bulgakov and Edward Bond, as well as my own. But the most important discoveries I made during this period took place through the creation of several nonlexical song cycles. In these I attempted to "smuggle" musical qualities that I had encountered in various song traditions—rhythms, harmonies, intervals, timbres, and more—into new songs with nonsense lyrics. My approach to the smuggling of musical qualities ranged from the intuitive to the compositional.[50] In this way I explored a wide range of vocal technique, while to a large extent deferring the politics and problematics of cultural identity.

Nonlexicality, in the narrow sense of vocal music that eschews recognizable words, need not imply a lack of engagement with particular cultural sources and identities. From yodeling to jazz scat to hasidic nigunum—the last of which later became central to the Judaica project—many traditions of nonlexical song are culturally identifiable despite not involving words. Yet I did approach nonlexicality, in this period, as a way to separate technique from identity. To some extent this approach now appears to me as an example of what Marie Thompson calls "white aurality": a "bifurcation of materiality and meaning, sonic nature and culture," which "obscures the co-constitution" of sound and the social.[51] From this perspective, pure nonlexicality is an illusion of whiteness; or, we might say, whiteness is the (un)marking of some sounds as "nonlexical," essentially a disavowal of sociopolitical and historical context. The upshot of Thompson's critical analysis of white aurality is that there is no such thing as absolute nonlexicality. My "nonsense" is anglophone nonsense, made mostly of anglophone phonemes, which sounds very different from turkish or polish nonsense. The crafting of nonlexical songs, including the careful separation of melody and words from other aspects of vocal technique, requires so much effort precisely because these are all bound together in the act of singing.

On the other hand, following my previous analysis of Grotowski's critical whiteness practice, the separation of technique and identity in my earlier approach to nonlexicality can also be seen as a temporary strategy that allowed me to postpone critical modes of identity-based analysis in order to begin to reopen my own identity on a different level, through embodied practice. The theory of technique and identity developed in this book allows both perspectives to coexist without contradiction: Sound does have a nonlexical edge (or many nonlexical edges), interfaces with emergent materiality that may express the uniqueness of particular moments; but it is always also grounded in implicit lexicality, as each molecule of technique emerges from the sediment of identity. There is then no pure or absolute nonlexicality, as each moment or edge of nonlexicality emerges from its particular location in the lexical. The nonverbal and nonmelodic qualities of song may be no less culturally grounded than melody and lyrics, even if they are not lexically defined. Hence, as my idea of "smuggling" suggests, cultural reference was covert rather than absent in these nonlexical songs. After several years of working in this way, the tension that concealment generated was no longer satisfying and a further step began to feel necessary: to approach a new set of songs, this time explicitly culturally marked, so that I could begin to integrate critical cultural analysis with what I had learned from attempting to work nonlexically.[52]

The term "Judaica" conventionally refers to physical objects, often antiques, associated with jewish culture and ritual. In my usage, jewish songs are also judaica: fragments of history, knowledge, and identity. Just as I had often referred to my nonlexical song cycles as comprising song "fragments" rather than whole songs, the Judaica project has focused on fragments, scraps, or molecules of jewish song. These fragments of song might be encountered as shards or sparks of light to be collected, as in the jewish ethical practice of *tikkun olam*. They are what Albert Memmi called "micro-judeities," which I have theorized as molecules or particles of technique-identity.[53] (One series of Judaica project concerts was presented under the polish title *Okruchy Pieśni*, or "Crumbs of Song.") Emphasizing the potentially fragmentary nature of songs as embodied knowledge—their capacity to be disassembled and reassembled, stretched and repurposed—counters a prevailing, overly holistic account of songs, reopening them as epistemic objects. This approach to fragmentation is different from the way in which a musicological analysis might separate melody from lyrics. My interest is in how song fragments remain connected to their social, cultural, and political contexts, including those I am calling identities, so that even a single note or syllable carries some of the force and materiality of those larger phenomena.

At stake here are multiple ontologies of song, which are inextricable from the technologies that afford them. In the Judaica project and in this chapter, five such technologies/ontologies are especially relevant: five modes in which song can exist or five answers to the question of what song might be. These are: *embodied, textual, notational, audio* (this could also be called aural or sonic, but the reference is to audio recording technologies), and *audiovisual*.[54] Each of these modes is defined by a different inscriptive technology, the first being the absence of any such inscription. Without suggesting that the four technologies deterministically produce corresponding ontologies, I want to propose that the way in which one encounters and works with a song profoundly shapes how one learns from it and what can be done with it. Moreover, in the larger context for which the Judaica project serves as a case study, these technologies are interwoven with indigenous, precolonial, colonial, postcolonial, and neocolonial forms of knowledge and power.

The Judaica project began from an *embodied ontology of song* that prioritized the presence and materiality of songs as embodied actions, enacted by living human bodies and transmitted from one body to another through the act of singing together. A song in the body can in this sense be understood as a fractional bit of habitus: a chunk of embodiment that is separable not anatomically but in practice, precisely insofar as it may be repeated across space, time, and bodies.[55] My embodied approach to songwork grew directly out of my experiences with postgrotowskian theatrical and paratheatrical practices. To place the postgrotowskian in a wider context we can refer to Caroline Bithell's study of the natural voice movement, which is similar in its prioritization of "oral" (embodied) transmission over written notation and of ensemble vocal practice over the solo voice or instrumental music.[56] More significant in this context are the considerable resonances (as well as important differences) between postgrotowskian songwork and what Dylan Robinson identifies as indigenous ontologies of song. Given the complex connections between postgrotowskian practice and indigenous lineages of knowledge, discussed in chapter 2, it is not surprising to find commonalities here. In fact, Robinson's is the first musicological text I have read that sheds light (indirectly) on Grotowski's work.

The way in which the Judaica project has worked with songs is much closer to Robinson's description of indigenous song than to his contrasting account of western art music. For example, one of Robinson's central points is that indigenous ontologies accord songs a kind of agency, or even subjectivity, which white or western music refuses.[57] Songs in this sense demand ethical and not only aesthetic engagement: There is a "need to be responsible to sound as we would another life." Unlike the european notion of fidelity to an artistic work, this notion of ethical responsibility does not imply a demand for exact repetition. On the contrary, improvisation, adaptation, and transformation are very much part of the life of a song, which follows a rhythm that is linked to breath and heartbeat rather than the "unvarying meter" of white time.[58] As Robinson shows, classical european musical education produces not only specific capacities for listening but also specific *incapacities*, what he calls the "tin ear" of settler colonialism.[59] Even Robinson's choice to prioritize "song" over "music" has decolonial implications that resonate with Grotowski's work and with my approach to artistic research. Of course, one must carefully distinguish between indigenous songwork that is embedded within indigenous communities and nations and postgrotowskian or other approaches to songwork that learn in substantive ways from indigenous knowledges without being embedded in corresponding political formations. I am not suggesting any kind of equivalence between these very different contexts of songwork. But the Judaica project, like some other postgrotowskian practices, shares with Robinson's approach to indigenous sound studies an ethical investment of life in songs and a principled rejection of logocentric ontologies.

A logocentric ontology of song defines it as a "dual form" that combines words and music: "a text wedded to a musical structure."[60] Such an overtly philosophical definition (recalling that philosophy in the european tradition is a bastion of logocentrism) produces a dualism where none exists by defining song in terms of two dominant european technologies of inscription, two forms of *white writing*: alphabetic and musical.[61] European music notation is not alphabetic, but I refer to it as a form of white writing because it is interwoven with colonial whiteness, although not in the same ways or to the same degree as alphabetic writing.[62] Moreover, to the extent that musical scores are understood as transcriptions of an ontologically primary musical "work," the implementation of such scores in white modernity is not only scriptocentric— reliant on the technology of written notation—but also logocentric as defined in the previous chapter: producing a textual ontology that elevates and reifies an imagined prior object that is understood to exist above and behind the notation that more or less transparently reveals it.[63] As ethnomusicologists have long argued, such a definition leaves out many crucial dimensions of song, from variations in rhythm and vocal timbre to nonverbal or nonlexical voicings, which are rendered invisible (and even inaudible) because they are not amenable to these forms of white writing.[64]

According to Robinson, some indigenous songs "have their primary significance as law, history, teachings, or function as forms of doing. This is to say *they are history, teaching, law, that take the form of song*, just as Western forms of law and history take the form of writing."[65] To define song as words plus melody is thus to whiten it, to reduce its ontology to forms of writing. The violence of this reduction should not be underestimated: Robinson quotes Marius Barbeau's unforgettable description of the european musical stave as "a rack upon which to pin down sounds and rhythms."[66] But as I have argued throughout this book, the relationship between embodied and textual ontologies must not be conceived as a binary dichotomy. To position scored european music and indigenous song as schematic opposites—I am not suggesting that Robinson does this—would be to accept the framework of the colonial encounter, including the elevation of textuality to the transcendent status of "mind" or "knowledge." We then remain trapped in the colonial binary of mind and body, even if we attempt to reverse their valuation by championing indigenous and embodied ontologies of song. In fact, while the opposition between white colonial or settler auralities and indigenous ones remains relevant today, the technological status of writing and notation has changed. Simply put, writing is no longer the only inscriptive technology that produces a distinct ontology of song. Newer technologies, still informed by coloniality but perhaps also offering ways to think beyond it, afford other ontologies of song, which are neither embodied nor textual and which can help to denaturalize that hegemonic opposition.

Audio and audiovisual recording technologies developed late in the period of historical colonization in the americas. While they are still constrained by the neocolonial realities of the present day, they offer possibilities that cannot be realized as long as we remain preoccupied by the apparent binary dichotomy of the textual and the embodied (with all the other binaries that one supports). The Judaica project, while rejecting textual and logocentric ontologies of song, also progressively moved away from a strictly embodied approach that would focus narrowly on embodied practice, perhaps risking its fetishization. Instead, I gradually developed a methodology that moved intentionally across and between two other technologies and ontologies of song, the *audio* and the *audiovisual*, positioning embodied practice as a link or nexus between them. In this way, I began to understand songs as complex things that move between multiple ontologies including the embodied, the alphabetic, the music notational, the audio, and the audiovisual.

The movement of songs between technologies is common. For example, a musical concert often stages the interpretation or performance of a written song in embodied form. In contrast, the recording of a studio album might follow a three-step process whereby a written song is embodied and performed in order to capture that performance as an audio track. The methodology developed in the Judaica project is structurally similar to this latter process, but the movement is between different technologies: Instead of written songs passing through embodied performance to become audio recordings, audio recordings pass through embodied performance to become audiovisual (video) recordings. In the rest of this section I address the first part of this methodology—the *audio ontology of song*—to explain how and why I eventually decided to base the Judaica project's experimental practice on it. In the following two sections I examine the *audiovisual ontology of song* that emerged out of this process.

Perhaps the most significant link between the Judaica project and Robinson's account of contemporary indigenous songwork is found in the problems and questions faced by younger generations who seek to reconnect with ancestral knowledge from which they have been severed through processes of genocide and assimilation. As Robinson explains, a profound set of issues is raised by the existence of ethnographic archives containing not only textually transcribed but also audio recorded songs:

> A new generation of Indigenous artists has begun the challenging task of singing these songs anew, of reconnecting severed ties between songs and their lineages, as they reconfigure their work as a form of dialogue with ancestors. In this re-sounding, choices are sometimes made to break protocol, or move forward where knowledge of protocol is absent or only partially known.[67]

For Robinson, these important practices of reconnection "understand song not as an object but as a form of affirming kinship."[68] In this regard, the Judaica project's investigation of jewish songs through diverse technologies overlaps considerably with Robinson's account:

> In returning to this song-knowledge and song-life, it is not only important to consider what functions these songs served but to what extent we need to uphold these functions, either in part or exclusively. Questions surrounding the ontological significance of songs prompt further questions about whether ontological shifts occur through the physical transfiguration of song into an object [such as] a wax cylinder. Does this material shift result in a similar level of toxicity to the shift in museological "preservation" of our material culture where masks were treated with chemicals such as arsenic?[69]

The Judaica project began from a desire to reconnect with song as an agentic force, gradually relinking the embodied ethics of intercorporeal performance practice with a broader politics of situated identity. It shares with Robinson's account of contemporary indigenous songwork a profound need to return to "song-knowledge" and "song-life" as part of a process that is at once personal, artistic, aesthetic, and spiritual. Yet crucial distinctions must be drawn between the Judaica project's postgrotowskian approach and that described by Robinson. Most importantly, the positionality from which I have approached jewish songs is neither indigenous nor settler colonial but diasporic.

As a "diaspore," and taking into account the particular entanglements of jewishness and whiteness described in the previous section, it has not been possible for me to encounter jewish songs with any simple intention of "affirming kinship."[70] Jewish kinship, for me and for many others, is complex and contested. The entanglement of jewishness with whiteness is reflected both in my individual positionality and in the artistic and academic form of the Judaica project. Borrowing Robinson's terms, I find myself to be simultaneously a postgenocide descendant reclaiming lost connections to ancestors and, *at the same time*, a postmodern scholar-practitioner working through citational pastiche. The stark distinction between indigenous and settler positions, on which Robinson's account relies, does not apply to my understanding of diasporic judaism. Nor is there any given location of jewish sovereignty or national community to which I could subscribe; hence, no clearly definable boundary between proper and improper uses of cultural material. This major difference in positionality and the geopolitics of culture—between diasporic european jewishness and north american indigeneity—plays out in my songwork practice at every level. In engaging with the question of jewish song, in choosing which archives to explore, in asking what makes a song jewish, and in practicing and working with particular songs, I am always also discovering and cultivating (my own) jewish identity. Robinson writes that "it would be unthinkable for anthropologists and curators to give Indigenous masks to settler artists so that they might repurpose these in the creation of new artistic works," since such repurposing can only be undertaken by indigenous artists working in relation to indigenous community.[71] In contrast, I can accept no such givenness of a jewish sovereign community, which could only be grounded in either religious orthodoxy or zionist nationalism. Indeed, having located a crucial aspect of jewish ancestral knowledge in critical theory—and thus in the university as a social institution—my relationship to ethnomusicological archives and to anthropology itself is much more ambivalent than those Robinson describes.

At the start of the Judaica project, I followed the conventional assumption of postgrotowskian songwork: that my desired encounter with jewish songs would be richest and most authentic if it were based on direct, interpersonal, "oral" transmission. As Bithell writes of the natural voice movement, "emphasis on oral transmission is of central significance," not only because of the value of the interpersonal pedagogical process but also because of the authenticity a "native teacher" is understood to carry.[72] Because of the privileging of such an embodied ontology of song, I undertook to learn songs from people who have specific and grounded expertise linked to particular communities and performances of jewishness. First I asked Rebecca Joy Fletcher, an ordained professional cantor (jewish liturgical singer) who also works professionally as an actor and theater-maker and who happens to be an old family friend, to meet me in a dance studio and teach me a jewish song of her choosing.[73] Later I attended a session for the singing of original nigunim, wordless jewish tunes, led by Joey Weisenberg, an innovator in the form of jewish prayer service.[74] The songs I learned from Fletcher and Weisenberg remained with me throughout the Judaica project, even as I came to feel that an "oral" or embodied form of transmission was actually less appropriate for my intentions than I had initially assumed.

I have never rejected the particular value of interpersonal transmission, but I came to feel that the attendant ontology of song was preventing me from formulating the kinds of questions I wanted to ask. Even before encountering Slabodsky's idea of decolonial judaism, I felt strongly that my engagement with jewish songs must decenter prevailing assumptions about jewishness and that my own background as white, european, and ashkenazi should not limit my learning to those lineages of songs any more than my academic scholarship should be limited to citing european sources. At the same time, I was highly aware of the risk of cultural appropriation and wanted to avoid a flattening multicultural approach.[75] Gradually, I came to feel that the process of embodied transmission was paradoxically both too limiting and too freeing. On the one hand, given the contested nature of jewish identity, it was important for me to hold space for the possibility that I might disagree, perhaps radically, with an individual who "gave" me a song. The process of interpersonal gifting risked creating a sense of personal obligation that could interfere with my artistic process. On the other hand, such gifting could perhaps also lead me to feel too much freedom, too much permission, as if the fact of "direct" transmission carried with it an unrestricted authority over a song's usage. Whether freeing or restrictive, the sense of close interpersonal proximity in such transmission seemed to hold me back from the matters of cultural politics that I increasingly wanted to face, overdetermining questions about the circulation of song fragments by referring them back to specific moments and interpersonal relationships. Eventually these concerns led me to shift from an approach that prioritized "direct" and "oral" or embodied transmission to one based on audio recordings sourced from digital archives.

Numerous studies of black diasporic musical production, while building on canonical discussions of (embodied) slave songs and spirituals, have similarly shifted focus to an audio ontology of song and music.[76] For example,

Katherine McKittrick refers to "waveforms" as sonic interventions. Writings on black music, she explains, often

> draw attention to the tensions between the materiality of black music (the racial economies and racial histories that underpin the production and distribution of black creative works), lyrical content (if the tune indeed has lyrics), and the *waveforms that underpin and sonically frame song* (beats, rhythms, acoustics, notational moods, frequencies).[77]

For McKittrick, following Sylvia Wynter, black music is not simply a form of aesthetic enjoyment, separable from embodiment and politics. On the contrary, black waveforms "affirm, through cognitive schemas" (what I call technique), "modes of being human that refuse racism just as they restructure our existing system of knowledge."[78] In this account, black music is similar to indigenous song, as described by Robinson, in its resolutely political and decolonial force; but it differs from indigenous ontologies through its deep and multigenerational symbiosis with audio technologies. In black music as described by McKittrick, identity and community are reinvented in a postembodied and posttextual context, through the revolutionary use of such technologies. Thus, for McKittrick (and in contrast to the separation of technique and identity proposed by Nina Sun Eidsheim), songs and sounds do not cease to be black when they become waveforms.[79] On the contrary, audio technologies function as a powerful substrate for molecular blackness.

It was to "waveforms" in this sense that I gradually turned in the Judaica project, looking for molecules, fragments, shards, or crumbs of jewishness in the ethnomusicological record. In this way I hoped to experiment dramaturgically with the possibilities afforded by various configurations of identity and technique. Taking recorded songs as a starting point ensured that such issues could not be reductively referred back to an ethics of interpersonal relation, as if the potential meaning of a given song were fully owned and transferable by each authentic teacher. Instead, the question of what it meant to sing a given song would have to be resolved on other terms, with the technological break of audio recording as its premise. I explored several online archives of jewish song before deciding to base the project's 2017 laboratory phase on eighteen albums selected from the Smithsonian Folkways Recordings digital archive.[80] This choice offered several advantages, including an unconventional way to circumscribe the category of jewish song: the online Folkways archive has a metadata tag, the genre classification "Judaica," which as of this writing is attached to eighty-two albums. These albums vary tremendously in terms of when and where they were recorded, as well as their languages, functions, and cultural contexts. Many of them include liner notes. As a major institutional repository, the Folkways archive has the advantage of providing a reliable back end to the project's experimental research, allowing our Judaica project outcomes to be compared with their source recordings.[81] Taking the Folkways archive as our starting point allowed me to distinguish between ethnomusicological research (the acts of recording that generated the archive) and song-based embodied research (new experimental performances leading to a different kind of archive)—putting the latter, emerging field into dialogue with the former, more established one.

With this digital archive as our starting point, the project's core questions came into focus: In what ways might I and the other practitioner-researchers in the lab team explore and practice these songs? What might happen in the experimental, dramaturgical relations between the technique of the songs and the identities of the practitioners? Simplistically, one could imagine a spectrum along which various audio tracks could be arranged in relation to the identities of a practitioner such as myself. At one end of the spectrum would be songs that are "mine," or close to me, and with which I feel relatively free to play. At the other end would be songs that are "not mine" and which I must therefore be careful with, or perhaps not touch at all. In practice, the situation is more complex. There is no single spectrum running between "mine" and "not mine," but a variety of dimensions in which a given song might be close to or distant from me. A song that seems culturally close to me might be one that I barely feel able to approach, while one that seems culturally distant might invite me to sing it with surprising ease. Two songs from the same album, despite their apparently similar provenance, might turn out in practice to be more different from each other than two songs recorded decades and many miles apart. Amid such complexity, the materiality or substance of songs is dynamically revealed through the intersectionality of power and the interdisciplinarity of knowledge in practice. When I say that a song does or does not invite me to sing it, I am not suggesting that I have some final or objective knowledge of its truth. The point is rather that, following my discussion of identity and technique, it will not be possible to resolve such questions solely through distanced critical analysis, whether of knowledge or power, song as transmissible technique or song as incarnated social dynamics. Instead, the complexity of what a song is—and the resulting necessity to employ multiple forms of thought, extending beyond the critical—demands an experimental and dramaturgical approach in which the interdisciplinary and the intersectional come together in the context of specific bodies, moments, and encounters.

I cannot attempt here to discuss or analyze all the songs that were explored or practiced in the Judaica project. Even if I could offer a richly interdisciplinary and intersectional analysis of all the songs, one by one, this would be counterproductive, since my aim is to move beyond the textual, into posttextual modes of audiovisual thought.[82] But it may be worth briefly tracing the trajectory of a handful of songs across the dramaturgy of the Judaica project, if only to indicate the breadth of songs used and the variety of transformations they underwent.[83] To begin with, consider the three songs mentioned in the vignette at the start of this chapter. These were the earliest songs incorporated into the Judaica project, when I was still exploring a range of sources and media. "Avinu Malkeinu" was taught to me by the cantor, theater performer, and friend mentioned above, in a dance studio in brooklyn where I had worked for many years. Given that context of transmission, I might have expected to feel very free in developing this song—but I did not. The song's religiosity and my awareness of its deeply formal context, linked to the high holy days, seemed to weigh it down. This contextual knowledge is inextricable, in my experience, from the song's melody and hebrew lyrics. Although it is ripe for reinterpretation in relation to contemporary jewish identity, this was not a song through which I felt able to develop a research practice.[84] It rarely returned in later phases of the Judaica project.

The second song mentioned, in contrast, the "wordless hasidic melody or nigun," became central to the Judaica project, a pillar that scaffolded numerous experiences and moments over the years. This song is "Nigun Simcha," the "tune of joy," which I learned from a music album that I found on the Chabad website.[85] Such a commercial album is surely the kind that ethnomusicologist Abigail Wood is thinking of when she describes contemporary jewish orthodox popular music as "kitschy":

> These recordings are often well produced; nevertheless, while the use of synthesisers and beats derived from pop music reflects the influence of wider American music culture, to an outsider to the Hasidic world, they sound kitschy at best, far from the historicist or contemporary musical aesthetics which have largely been adopted by world music artists including klezmer revivalists.[86]

The orthodox hasidic life from which this recording comes is worlds apart from the Judaica project's concept of jewishness. It is ironic, she writes, that "the two American Jewish groups most committed to the preservation of the Yiddish language stand at opposite poles of the modern Jewish spectrum: leftist, secularist, Yiddishism versus strict ultra-Orthodoxy."[87] Culturally, conceptually, and politically, I am much more aligned with the former. Although the Judaica project began in new york, I never seriously considered trying to participate in a hasidic community event, exactly because of this political and cultural divide. On the one hand, I am aware of my privilege as an academic researcher and would not wish to take an extractive ethnographic approach to hasidic worlds. On the other hand, where I encounter political conservatism, heteropatriarchy, and white supremacy, I also see myself as productively contesting those meanings. Hence, for example, I took special pleasure in teaching "Nigun Simcha" to people of all genders.[88]

Like Wood's klezmer revivalists, but with a very different method, I approach hasidic music and the vast tradition of nigunim with a mix of humility and iconoclasm:

The musicians discussed here reconfigure musical symbols to reflect their own search for a meaningful balance between East European Jewish and modern American culture. They place themselves neither as insiders nor outsiders: none are practising Hasidim, but all approach Hasidic music as part of their own heritage, whether through direct family connections or as insider performers of cognate Ashkenazi musics. Further, in challenging the premise that authentic spiritual and musical expression within this repertory must necessarily lie within the strictly Orthodox Hasidic community, these musicians also question the bifurcation of secular and religious culture implicit in popular and scholarly literature, also challenging the frequently aggressively secular voice of the ethnographic outsider.[89]

Kitschy as this recording of "Nigun Simcha" may be, I could not deny its power. Over the years, I have found it possible to return to this melody over and over, to lean on it, to speak and chant it, to summon great energy from it, and to build moments and events around it. Early on, I invented an imaginary "folkdance," which I performed and taught in workshops, following the song's three-part structure. Later, this song became the spine around which some of the Judaica lab's most important sessions (and resulting audiovisual works) were organized. The song's nonlexicality allows it to behave in many different ways and to bridge between diverse energetic states. While it has no words, it is not "purely" nonlexical in the sense imagined by white aurality: Its melody, rhythm, and nonlexical vocables are all undeniably jewish. The rhythmic force of "Nigun Simcha" is such that, when I sing it slowly, I can feel it pulling me toward greater speed and dynamism, creating a sense of momentum as it builds. Within this trajectory, I can also feel the subtle impulses of the dance I built around it, even when I am not dancing. For all these reasons, in which technique and identity are inextricable on a molecular level, no song has been more central to the Judaica project.

The third song mentioned, "Ale Brider" ("All Brothers"), was perhaps the first song of the Judaica project. It is also the song after which Wood's study of contemporary yiddish music is named. As Wood explains, this popular yiddish song is based on a poem by Morris Winchevsky that "invokes close familial relations as a metaphor for a Jewish romantic nationalism," while an updated text by the Klezmatics band, "evoking feminism and gay rights, simultaneously evokes fluency with and distance from the author's cultural context."[90] But it first arrived to me through a close family connection: I heard it on an album produced by my aunt and uncle's band and I asked them to play it at my wedding in 2011.[91] I do not know whether I had heard this song before, but the melody resonated with me in a way I can only call ancestral. As I began to integrate it into the Judaica project, I first imagined it as a very old tune—perhaps one of those sung by the founder of hasidism when he was a child in the early 1700s, as in Martin Buber's retelling of that life.[92] Later an israeli musical archivist informed me, somewhat sharply, that "Ale Brider" is a modern socialist song; but I have never been certain whether this pertains to the melody as well as the words. Wood does not attribute the tune, which itself is in two parts, of which the second remains nonlexical even in contemporary versions and which I imagine to be far older than the first.

In any case, and for all these reasons, I felt this song to be mine in a different way or even to a different degree. Socialist, familiar, and pre- or neo-hasidic, it belongs to me and I belong to it. Between 2012 and 2016, I taught several workshops around "Ale Brider," breaking it apart, layering it, repeating short fragments on their own, and sometimes interweaving it with stories from Buber. I became interested in what happens when I sing just the first syllable: *un* ("and" in yiddish). This syllable, or vocable particle, became for me a paradigmatic example of the inextricability of technique and identity at a molecular level. From a strictly (white) analytic or musicological perspective, a single vocable on a single pitch has no harmonic context, let alone a cultural meaning. Yet it was clear to me experientially that when I sang this vocable, *un*, even if I immediately stopped and proceeded no further, I was singing this song and no other. This tiny fragment did not lose its cultural meaning, did not cease to be yiddish (or jewish), when it was isolated. Instead I felt it hanging in the air as a molecule of meaning, a fragment of a whole cultural lineage and identity. This was an objective fact: Even if there were no other jews in the room and no one recognized this song, I *had begun* to sing "Ale Brider" and in this way had introduced that song, with its vast cultural context, into the space. Following this discovery, I developed further exercises around "Ale Brider" and produced some videographic studies. Later, another version of the song appeared, growing out of some experiments with irregular canon: taking the song out of phase, so that multiple voices were singing the same melody but without any regular meter. Gradually, in this process, what initially appeared to me as a happy children's melody became yearning, mournful, almost a kind of dirge.[93]

These are three relatively simple and well-known songs. They are not rare or difficult to find, not especially melodically complex, not exotic. Yet even these songs have revealed profound depths, over years of practice, in which the technical details of melody, rhythm, and vocables cannot be separated from cultural contexts and identities. The 2017 laboratory phase of the Judaica project introduced many more complex navigations, through the eighteen Folkways albums and through the addition of two full-time embodied/artistic researchers for a period of six months. The Folkways albums brought with them a much wider range of cultural, geographical, and historical reference points. At the same time the knowledge, skill, and commitment of my lab colleagues, Nazlıhan Eda Erçin and Agnieszka Mendel, opened many questions that I could not have asked or answered on my own. I became interested in the ways in which our different positionalities sometimes led us to relate to the same songs in very different ways. For example, the traditional passover song

"Chad Gadya," a comically violent song for children, might suggest community and celebration to one person while evoking feelings of alienation and
discomfort in another. Or a pastorale, describing love in a rural landscape,
might cause one of us to imagine peace and tranquility while another, having
read in the liner notes that this song was "popular among early pioneers in
Palestine," might hear in that same melody the cruel displacements of zionist
colonialism.[94]

During this period I found myself drawn to the album *Abayudaya: Music
from the Jewish People of Uganda*, which seemed to raise particularly thorny
questions about the global scope of categories such as whiteness, blackness,
and jewishness. This album was created by a jewish ugandan community, the
abayudaya, in collaboration with north american white jewish ethnomusicologist and rabbi Jeffrey Summit.[95] This is already a complex collaboration
involving a significant amount of institutional and financial reciprocity as
part of Summit's anthropological ethics, which is rendered even more complicated by his status as a rabbi. Rather than asking the simplistic question
of whether I may or may not sing a given song (as if, in a binary and quite
colonial model of property and ownership, being able or allowed to sing
a song means following no restrictions or protocol in doing so), I became
interested in the complex dramaturgy that an album like *Abayudaya* presents
to me. The factors at play, it seemed to me, include at least the following:
the lyrics of the song and their contemporary meaning; the way in which
the song calls to me personally and musically; the ethics of the relationship
between Summit and members of the abayudaya community, as well as their
joint relationship to the Smithsonian Folkways label; the abayudaya's relationship to judaism and jewishness, including their desire to join a global
jewish community and the antiblack racism they have experienced from the
israeli state; the north-south relationships between uganda, the united states,
and the united kingdom; and, particularly in the context of performed or
videographic work, the signification of skin color as it circulates audiovisually.[96] All these factors were present, on some level, whenever I would sing the
abayudaya version of "Hinei Ma Tov." This is a song whose lyrics are biblical
(from Psalm 133: "Behold how good it is for brothers to dwell together") and
identical to those of a well-known version, which my aunt and uncle also play
and which I assume is european; but the abayudaya melody is different.[97]

Many different versions of this song developed in my songwork practice.
The european version could be sung in the standard way, in unison, or in canons; the canons could be broken apart to produce a lament. The abayudaya
version could be sung in english or in luganda. There were many smaller fluc-
tuations in rhythm, speed, and timbre. These apparently sonic and musical
differences also made a difference in how and when I practiced the song. For
example, I found that I was often not comfortable teaching the abayudaya
version in the context of Judaica project workshops, where participants were
predominantly white and, I worried, might too easily absorb it as part of an

easy multiculturalism of the kind that Bithell describes in the natural voice movement and which Robinson sharply critiques. Instead I would teach the more common, european version of "Hinei Ma Tov," which I feel is more mine to share, and then introduce a small fragment of the abayudaya version, only to stop and explain that this version was created by a ugandan community of jews. In such moments, it felt more important to me to highlight the existence of ugandan jews and their music while suggesting that a degree of thought or caution might be in order before simply absorbing their songs into an implicitly white cultural milieu. On the other hand, in contexts where a firmly diasporic and anticolonial (antizionist) jewishness has been established, I have found it possible to sing not only "Hinei Ma Tov" but also a ugandan lullaby from the same album, which may be jewish only in that it is sung by jews.[98]

These are a handful of songs that have been particularly significant to me during the Judaica project. Other practitioners working in the project have been touched by different songs, asking different questions from their own interests and positions and making different connections between technique and identity. Eda Erçin, a core member of the project since 2017, has written elsewhere about her experience with a turkish song that appears on one of the Smithsonian Folkways albums.[99] Like the ugandan lullaby just mentioned, this is a turkish song that may just happen to be marked as "Judaica" in the Folkways archive because of the context in which it appears. I found no contradiction in Eda exploring her own turkish identity, and the exoticization of turkey and islam in relation to whiteness and the idea of europe, by working with a turkish song as part of the Judaica project. On the contrary, this is precisely the point: The identification of the song as jewish, through its circulation to us from the Feenjon Group ("America's most exciting near eastern ensemble") via the Folkways label, invited Eda to reexamine her own identities in a context where identity was understood as both weighted and malleable, material and signifying.

Another song to which Eda drew our attention has an even more complex and layered identity. The Folkways version has lyrics in five different languages (french, spanish, italian, arabic, and english), spliced together word by word.[100] This unusually multilingual construction—words as verbal molecules, mixing multiple languages together within a single sentence— resonated with the multilingual scope of the Folkways archive and with the 2017 Judaica project lab team, whose native languages were english, polish, and turkish. Moreover, as the liner notes point out, the melody is that of the turkish song "Uskadara," a song whose richly contested lineage is the subject of an independent documentary film.[101] The Judaica project team often taught this song in workshops, as it seemed to bring together some of the key concepts of the project in a contained and tangible form.

Agnieszka Mendel, the third core member of the 2017 Judaica project lab team, brought a very different set of questions to the research. In addition to many years as a performer with the Gardzienice Centre for Theatre Practices in poland, she has a long-term interest in eastern european jewish culture from a polish perspective. As Wood writes, the "revival of public interest in Yiddish music occurred in both north America—primarily among Jews—and Europe—primarily among non-Jews—at a similar time."[102] Having a very different relationship to the idea and process of jewish cultural revival, as well as a strong desire for a certain kind of musical rigor, Agnieszka introduced a further set of songs to our research practice. These included the songs of Mordechai Gebirtig, who was killed in kraków during the holocaust, which were explored in the Judaica project lab at various points. But there was a significant difference, sometimes resulting in aesthetic tension, between Agnieszka's approach to cultural revival—which more closely resembles that described by Wood—and my own interest in radical experimentation.

For Agnieszka, the primary meaning of jewishness was in the context of the european holocaust and the disappearance of jews from poland—especially given a contemporary polish political landscape that increasingly combines repressive antifeminism with virulent racism and antisemitism. As she wrote to Erçin and me a few months before the lab project began:

> I speak now as an average citizen of Poland, not as someone who has studied this topic. These are my subjective feelings. During this tiny expedition [to a number of rural synagogues, described below], following the preserved traces of a nation and finding them every step here, suddenly I profoundly realised that Jews—in Poland—they lived everywhere. And now they are gone. Vanished. They are completely not present in the consciousness of the young generation. They rather belong to a mythical, semi-fairy-tale sphere of long bygone era of heroes and ancestors, together with the kings and saints. Today most Polish people imagine Poland as a land of homogenous society since forever. That is such a miseducation. I was truly overwhelmed. Following these traces and pieces I realised this truth: that Poland has pushed the Jewish nation out of memory.[103]

Not being academically affiliated, Agnieszka's perspective on the Judaica project is underrepresented in its publications, yet her embodied and artistic impact on its aural and videographic practices is ubiquitous and profound throughout the 2017 lab recordings. In 2020, Agnieszka's Yaron Trio released an album called *Carmina Judaica*, which thanks the Judaica project in its liner notes "for a magical journey made together—through the wilderness of archives and for the priceless perspective of diving in to the inner worlds of individual songs thanks to appropriately posed research questions."[104] In this way the Judaica project's experimental approach to jewish identity has fed into a separate artistic process, which is now unfolding elsewhere and outside the university.

What then is a song? Is it the pattern of notes on a page, which a singer performs by remaining within an implied field of interpretive technique? Is it a reproducible audio track that captures the sonic details of a moment at a given density of samples? Is a song something that lives inside me, a piece of fractional habitus that structures my embodied self? Or is it an intersubjective passage between bodies, a pathway defined by its repeatability, a cut of transmissible knowledge? Who owns a song?[105] Can a song be owned? Can a song be summoned, broken, appropriated, violated, protected, or honored? What happens when an academically embedded theater laboratory works experimentally with songs as potentially volatile cultural materials? How do the identities and backgrounds of the practitioner-researchers in such a milieu interact with the meanings and connotations of those materials and with their cultural and institutional contexts? What ethical and political guidelines can be called on when culturally unmarked experimentalism is confronted by a cultural politics of identity, which asserts that no such process can be innocent of the power dynamics that configure the relationship between laboratory and world? I have only a few provisional answers to such questions.

A song is not one but many things: an audio recording, but also a video recording; memory, but also present action; individual, but also interpersonal; ethical responsibility, but also political intervention; a chunk of habitus, but also a strategy for change; technique, but also identity; identity, but also technique. As José Estaban Muñoz proposed, song—like fiction—is a technology of the self.[106] A book can be read like a song, but a song can also be sung like a book.[107] Artistic researchers must take seriously the idea that songs and other cultural materials bring political meanings with them into the studio laboratory. There can be no escape from or exclusion of politics from that space. At the same time, we must acknowledge that the formalization and fragmentation of songs and other materials likewise formalizes and fragments their social, cultural, and political meanings. Even a small amount of material, such as a few words or notes, may be highly volatile. By the same token, a small enough quantity of even the most toxic material may be safe to handle. A tiny fragment of melody, a tonal quality, a vocal color, a rhythmic pattern, or a handful of lyrics may not carry the same risk, or the same potential energy, as a whole song. The meanings and capacities of each aspect of a song must be tested in practice. And there are unlimited, unfolding potentialities to be discovered within even the tiniest of fragments.

For songwork research, a decade is very little. The above descriptions of songwork are intended to offer a glimpse into the Judaica project's artistic research since 2012. This span of time is small when compared to the longer-lasting postgrotowskian ensembles, let alone to the vastly older indigenous lineages that Robinson invokes. Yet perhaps the framing of such research, at the border between academic and artistic practice, has something to offer when it comes to matters of identity and technique. How much of the power and efficacy of a given song comes from its melody, rhythm, and lyrics and how much comes from the contextual knowledge of those present regarding its history? Does it matter whether older or more traditional songs are *really* older and more traditional, or only believed to be so?[108] My research suggests that these are, in many situations, the wrong questions to be asking, based on false oppositions and particular types of epistemic reduction owing to the dominance of certain (white) methods and logics. The archival tracing and historical and cultural positioning of song need not be divorced from embodied and embedded experimentation through songwork. If we do not accept the reification of white writing as half of an overarching binary model (mind vs. body; theory vs. practice)—if instead we see writing *and* audio *and* video as technologies of knowledge that can be implemented in divergent ways, in relation to each other and to living practice—then that which might previously have been called "body" or "practice" opens up radically.

Grotowski explored some of these possibilities, within the limitations of his context. I take it that various forms of (white) "new materialism" also move toward such an expansion of the nontextual, albeit most often in textual form. Robinson's account of indigenous ontologies of song indicates how much further such a radical reopening can go: Song can be history, law, ethics, philosophy. Artistic research, in my account, must centrally explore this transformation in the ontology of song and other "embodied" knowledges, radically expanding the forms and media through which knowledge can be shared and archived. In the Judaica project, what surprisingly became more and more central was yet another form of knowledge, thus far only mentioned: an audiovisual or video ontology of song.

Video Ways of Thinking

May 4, 2017. I am in an empty theater studio with white walls. It is the second day of work on a new laboratory phase of the Judaica project and I am singing a traditional children's song from the jewish holiday of pesach or passover. The director invites me to sing along with an imaginary community and I freeze. I realize that she expects this song to evoke a sense of belonging in me, associations of connection and uninterrupted kinship with the past. Instead, her suggestions bring up feelings of isolation and fear. I stop singing and sit motionless. "Why are you denying them?" the director asks, referring to those nameless others. "I don't trust them," I reply.[109]

August 3, 2017. My mother has come to visit me for a week and I invite her into the Judaica project studio laboratory. The same empty theater studio with white walls is now transformed into a multidisciplinary space in which artistic disciplines and lines of kinship intersect. We bring drawing papers, pencils, and charcoal into the space, so that my mother's own very established craft as a visual artist can be present alongside our embodied songwork. After several hours of improvised singing and drawing, a colleague and I find ourselves locked in a wordless, rhythmic melody, its intensity building through repetition. My mother's pencil dances across the page, following our spiral vocal rhythms, no longer composing images but embodying the rhythm of our voices.[110]

September 8, 2017. I stand with my two colleagues in an abandoned, ruined synagogue in rural poland. The roofless walls are stark against a bright blue sky. A line of gray pigeons perch above. The ground is covered in their feces, bones, and broken eggs. I am singing another wordless melody and holding a recent academic book that links contemporary racism and islamophobia to the climate crisis. Slowly, I begin to sing the words of the book, following the melody of the tune, as if casting a spell to link the memory of the european holocaust with the ongoing violences of the present.[111]

The three moments just described are similar in some respects to those evoked at the start of this chapter, but also crucially different. Bookending five years of the Judaica project, between 2012 and 2017, they are all structured by the circulation of jewish embodied knowledge, especially songs, through a broader dramaturgy of performance, with the aim of learning something about contemporary (jewish) identity or even inventing new molecules of identity in the lab. The choice of songs and the depth of collaborative practice evolved over those five years, but even more significant is the difference in techno-ontological status between these events. The 2012 account describes a series of live performances, presented a handful of times across multiple venues and defined as an artistic work by its evolving yet always repeatable structure. Video recordings of those performances exist, but they are marked by all the problematics and limitations of performance documentation.[112] The three 2017 accounts, in contrast, describe unrepeatable moments of audiovisual embodied research, which are crystallized and archived through the technology of video recording.

Unlike the performances of 2012, no audience attended these videographic lab sessions, only the participants. Indeed, being present would have turned any spectator into a participant because there was no physical or epistemic fourth wall. The three 2017 moments are now accessible to viewers through a series of video essays and peer-reviewed video articles. Those video works are critical interpretations of what happened, but their form is neither that of live performance nor a written account. While the core intention to explore jewish identity through songwork did not change from 2012 to 2017, the nature and meaning of the events through which this exploration took place was transformed. If the 2012 events were based on a relatively well-established genre of performance-based artistic research, the latter propose something different: a *video way of thinking* in which the videographic outputs of an experimental practice are contextualized and published as academic research.

As Natalie Loveless observes, "the academic scholarly history that suggests that the 'objective voice' is a 'neutral' voice, a transparent container for the research, is racist and sexist."[113] Moreover, recognizing the racism and sexism of what I have called *white writing* makes the question of form central to the politics of artistic research. At the end of chapter 2, I suggested that artistic research must understand itself as making specific interventions into the structure of the university via particular leverage points such as the form of its transmissible documents. Loveless describes such a process eloquently: "Research-creation mobilizes the artistic as a sensibility and approach attentive to how *form* makes *worlds*, and does so specifically within the university-as-site. Research-creation lends itself to formal reshaping practices within university knowledge-making spaces."[114] If this is the case, then the relatively new availability of videographic recording and editing is a crucial leverage point that has only just begun to be explored. How might the university be remade, its knowledge practices disrupted and transformed, by the development of transmissible and archivable forms that are no longer only or even primarily textual but which instead activate the onto-epistemological capacities of the audiovisual?

It is hardly uncommon to conceive of filmmaking or videography as a mode of thinking, at least outside academia. Since the invention of cinematic technology, it has been possible to claim that "epistemological inquiry and the project of a revolutionary cinema converge in that world of truth seen by the cinematic eye."[115] Of course film is a kind of thought—but *whose*? Most often it has been the person holding the camera, or the one directing that person, who has been imagined as doing the thinking of cinema. I am interested here in how the audiovisually embodied subject, the person or being whose *audiovisual body* is traced by the camera, can be recognized as a thinker and theorist rather than merely the object of another's gaze. This entails postponing (or, better, redistributing) the roles that have been most often associated with videographic thought—the filmmaker, the documentarian, the video essayist, the ethnographer—in order to focus on the embodied research of the audiovisual performer or practitioner. What could it mean for a performer or other expert practitioner, who has always worked through embodied practice, to articulate their knowledge in audiovisual form? What happens, for example, in the shift from an audio ontology of songs—songs as waveforms or audio tracks, aural phenomena defined by the capacity of audio recording technologies—to a video ontology of song? And what are the implications of recognizing video works as forms of critical scholarship?

What I mean by a video ontology of song is the foregrounding of those aspects of embodied songwork that are traced by audiovisual recording. A helpful comparison could be drawn with the form of the music video, in which the embodied skill of a singer is conventionally placed at the center of a complex, often quasi-narrative world. As Katariina Kyrölä suggests, the resulting audiovisual composition can be understood as a mode of thought, a nontextual form of knowledge.[116] There is considerable overlap between music videos and the kind of videographic songwork I am describing and proposing here, insofar as the medium of video allows song to interact with visuality, narrative, embodiment, and other "non-songish things" in ways that go far beyond the aural or audio.[117] And there is no question that the music video form is one of the most powerful manifestations of songwork in the contemporary world and a compelling genre through which to examine the mutual construction of technique and identity. Yet with few exceptions music videos still rely upon a primarily audio ontology of song, insofar as the visual component is produced after and in response to a separate recording of the song "itself." The primary audio song, which circulates independently through radio and other channels, is then attached, often via lip-synching, to a separately produced image-only track, combining two very different moments of songwork in audiovisual montage. In contrast, the video ontology of song that I am exploring here arises when the act of singing itself is documented, so that what is traced or captured on video is the actual, material entanglement of song and world, rather than a cinematic montage of the two that technologically produces a division between the (audio) song and the (video or visual) body and world.

At the other end of the spectrum of digital culture, the present explosion of social media networking platforms suggests a much wilder and more complex ontology of song—a truly multifaceted *digital ontology of song* and an associated *digital way of thinking*—which lies beyond the scope of my investigation here. I am not trying, at least here, to think beyond video into any of the more recent developments of networked platform culture. I am not investigating code, surveillance, or finance as ways of knowing; not considering what Facebook or Twitter might mean as algorithmically structured forms of thought; not attempting to analyze the *data ways of thinking, platform ways of thinking, drone ways of thinking*, or other modes of artificial intelligence that are rapidly expanding alongside and through the audiovisual.[118] Although such investigations are urgent, I appreciate Bernard Dionysius Geoghegan's claim that the screen, or (audio)visuality, "can't be radically excluded as nonessential to the digital."[119] In other words, it will not be possible to think "the digital" in general without paying serious attention to audiovisuality.

To posit a sharp distinction between the digital and the analog is merely to reproduce the mind-body and theory-practice binaries, exactly those frameworks I am hoping to break open through triangulation with the audiovisual. I am exploring the thesis that audiovisuality radically displaces writing from its logocentric position of transcendence, thereby revealing the way in which categories like "mind" and "knowledge" are structured by logocentrism. Artistic research can and does work through postaudiovisual forms of digital media. In fact, the best-known journal for artistic research publishes not video articles but web-based multimedia expositions that make use of the nonlinear capacities of the web.[120] Some artistic research projects intervene through code or finance.[121] Yet despite the speed with which the internet hurtles us into ever more complicated layers of form and content, important questions remain to be answered about video as a form of thought. If white writing is all around us, so is white audiovisuality. But just as there are alternative lineages of writing, there are decolonial potentialities of the audiovisual.[122]

To recognize these potentialities, we need to return to certain basic questions about *what video records*—questions that may seem to have already been answered, because of the economic and hierarchical production methods that have until recently been attached to the audiovisual. I have suggested that the neat and tidy separation of "speech" and "language" from a much wider category of embodied practice and performance is only made possible by the technology of writing. In the medium of video, no such easy distinction exists. And yet, amazingly, those aspects of embodiment that appear on video but are not transcribable into alphabetic writing—eye movement, gesture, vocal timbre and rhythm, accent, and much more—continue to be described very often as "nonverbal," as if they were a supplementary or secondary layer augmenting speech. But this is backward: If we take video not as a supplement to writing but as a form of thought in its own right, these "nonverbal" aspects of practice and performance are no less central to communication than speech. Speech itself then becomes recognizable as a zone or tendency of technique, rather than a clearly defined medium. As noted above, there is no such thing as pure nonlexicality, no bodily gesture or rhythm that does not potentially signify, no molecule of technique that is not at the same time a molecule of identity. What video traces of practice, then, is not speech "plus" some kind of nonverbal supplement, but an entirely different mode of appearance, what we might call the audiovisual body.

Consider the question whether video adequately captures the act of singing (or dancing). This is an impossible question because, at the present historical moment, the very definition of song and dance is undergoing transformation through reference to the audiovisual. Does "singing" include how a performer smells? Does "dance" include the heat generated by moving bodies? Video does not simply fail to capture these aspects of embodiment; it actively intervenes to redefine song and dance in terms of audiovisuality. Audiovisuality, in other words, retroactively defines an audiovisual self in the same way that writing retroactively defines a writing or speaking self (or subject). Just as literacy produces a cut between words and not-words, audiovisuality produces a cut between the audiovisual body and all those aspects of life and practice that are not traced by the audiovisual (such as smell and heat). Yet it would be foolish to call this a failure on the part of audiovisuality. To compare audiovisuality to embodiment, faulting the former for inadequately capturing the latter, only reinstalls writing as the assumed medium of transparent thought. On the contrary, audiovisuality should not be compared with embodiment; it should be compared with writing. The question at hand is *what the audiovisual body can do*, how it appears, and how it produces meaning *in contrast to the written and writing body*.

Since long before the audiovisual body of the researcher could appear within a research document—with the exception of some ethnographic films—feminist thinkers have attempted to situate the knower or thinker by verbal means. This occurs most clearly through what became, in the 1970s, a particular use of the word "as" to declare one's identifications as a premise for an argument. For example: "I write this as a woman."[123] Nancy Miller traces this evocation of the personal in a range of feminist texts that "mark the body's presence, or personalize it; speak autobiographically or representatively."[124] She asks:

> If according to the current protocols, every "I" must be located as an "as a" (as, for instance, a middle-aged, white, East Coast feminist), where does what's left over get placed in a singular critical act? Does what's left over get left out because it doesn't fit the categories: too personal, too embarrassing to be taken seriously?[125]

The written "as" formulation remains in use today. It is common enough that it can become a target for those who would like to sever knowledge from technique according to a colorblind logic. Thus, Kwame Anthony Appiah asserts in the *New York Times*: "Because members of an identity group won't be identical, your 'as a' doesn't settle anything."[126] But Appiah gets it wrong when he takes the "as" statement as merely descriptive (intended to "settle" things), rather than as a performative intervention and a substantive aspect of what is being said. The person who accompanies their sharing of knowledge, perspective, or opinion with an "as" statement does not merely describe their positionality. On such a reductively individualizing account, Appiah is right: We can't know anything conclusively about an individual based on their identifications alone. But the "as" statement does more than check a census box. It is a substantive claim about the relationship between technique, or knowledge, and identity. The person who speaks "as" an X (woman, queer, indigene, diaspore) actively claims a connection between what they know and who they are. They say, in effect, that their knowledge arises from or is grounded in their identity and, just as importantly, that this knowledge is part of what constitutes that identity.

Taking myself as an example: When I say that I am invested in critical theory "as" a jew, I am not only situating myself, giving you more information about myself as an individual. I am also claiming that critical theory is part of my jewishness and hence making an intervention into the construction of that identity. This second statement is a claim not about myself as an individual but about the identity of which I am part: If jewishness is the basis of my investment in critical theory, then there must be something jewish about critical theory and something critically theoretical about jewishness. There comes a moment when descriptions of technique are not enough, precisely because they individualize. For me, it is no longer enough to say that I am passionate about reading and writing, or that I possess skill or talent in those areas, as if this were an individual matter. I need to assert that I am jewish and I need that to *mean* something about a profound and life-giving relationship to writing and textuality. This is not to suggest that all jewish people are good writers any more than all black people are good dancers; those are racist caricatures that conscript individuals into colonial models of group identity. On the contrary, such statements aim to break open those restrictive models of grouping, opening jewishness and blackness away from racial biologisms (or nationalisms) and toward the rich dynamics of knowledge and embodied technique, ways of living, or culture. If we accept this entanglement of knowledge and identity, then "as" statements become creative staging grounds on which emerging categories of identification are rehearsed and performed, constructed and established.

Sara Ahmed states: "I write as a lesbian. I write as a feminist."[127] With greater detail, G Patterson declares: "Positionality matters. I write this essay as a nonbinary, trans, queer, dfab, gender-nonconforming, multi-ethnic, neurodivergent, first-generation academic with white-skin privilege."[128] At stake in this usage of "as" are the identities of the researcher as a relevant source and context for their knowledge. The writer must collate a set of descriptors through which to identify, ranging from the mundane to the explicitly politicized and from those that indicate pride to those that acknowledge privilege. A crucial question for audiovisual thought is then: What happens when the researcher's body is aurally and visually traced, not instead of but in addition to and alongside such verbal identifications? What happens to the "as" when thought takes audiovisual form? How might these verbal or textual "as" statements be transformed by the presence of audiovisual embodiment and vice versa? In other words, what is the content of audiovisual appearance in relation to the mutual constitution of identity and technique?

One of the points made mostly clearly in recent scholarship about and from queer, trans, and racialized identities is precisely that audiovisual embodiment is as real an expression of the self as is the written word. Hence Madison Moore proposes to reject "negative theories of appearance" that dismiss appearance as merely superficial, instead acknowledging the content and meaning of visible "fabulousness," for example, as "creative labor, a type of 'self-couture,' where our bodies become the site of artistic expression and creativity."[129] Whereas it is often said that how one looks or sounds ought not to matter, an epistemic perspective on audiovisuality makes such a politics untenable. The prevailing assumption is that foregrounding audiovisual embodiment will automatically reinscribe patriarchal, racist, and ableist norms, but a predominantly textual politics can never substantively counteract such norms. A very different approach to audiovisual politics and the politics of audiovisuality is therefore needed. If it emphatically *does* matter how one looks and sounds, then the politics of that mattering will depend on how audiovisuality and textuality mutually construct each other in relation to what underpins them both: embodiment, practice, life, worlds. Since it is no longer possible to ignore or dismiss the audiovisual body, that body must become a central point of analysis, debate, and intervention.

Taking up Arendt's concept of the "space of appearance," Nicholas Mirzoeff describes the rise of the Black Lives Matter movement as follows:

> Here I will call *the interface of what was done and what was seen and how it was described* as "appearance," especially as the space of appearance, where you and I can appear to each other and create a politics. *What is to appear?* It is first to claim the right to exist, to own one's body, as campaigns from antislavery to reproductive rights have insisted, and are now being taken forward by debates over gender and sexual identity. To appear is to matter, in the sense of Black Lives Matter, to be grievable, to be a person that counts for something. And it is to claim the right to look, in the sense that I see you and you see me, and together we decide what there is to say as a result. It's about seeing what there is to be seen, in defiance of the police who say "move on, there's nothing to see here," and then *giving the visible a sayable name.*[130]

In this passage Mirzoeff articulates the three-part model that I have been developing throughout this book, whereby the binary separation of mind and body, which is uniquely afforded by the technology of writing, is triangulated by a third term, the audiovisual. "Appearance" is then the tripartite "interface" of "what was done" (action, life, practice, embodiment) *and* "what was seen" (the visual, which I extend to the audiovisual) *and* "how it was described" (the textual, here deflated from its logocentric transcendence).

Appearance in this sense is not fundamentally textual or audiovisual but political; a political that is constituted by the interaction of multiple media or forms of knowledge in relation to life and action. Indeed, if we understand media as racialized forms of thought, then there is no space or arena of politics except as produced through media. To formulate a contemporary politics, it is essential to understand the differences and relations between audiovisual and textual appearance. What if writing is not only thought but also appearance? And what if video is not only appearance but also thought? In that case, the work undertaken by artistic research—to explore the relations between writing, video, and other forms of thought—is much more than an abstract debate over what constitutes knowledge. It is a practice of laying technological and onto-epistemological foundations and developing practical tools that may become the foundations of future institutions and worlds.

It is no coincidence that queer, trans, and racialized artists and practitioners offer the most profound theories and practices of audiovisual appearance today. As I have argued throughout this book, the rise of audiovisual media demands that knowledge and technique be considered alongside identity and power, requiring interdisciplinary and intersectional research of the kind that marginalized communities are most often compelled to undertake. Hence, while taking care to avoid romanticizing online streaming video platforms as utopian spaces, Laura Horak points to the specific, multimedia strategies that have been developed there through "attempts to use audiovisual and network technologies to grapple with the gaps between the felt body and the body as seen and heard by others."[131] Through techniques of montage and the placement of on-screen text that frames audiovisually evidenced processes, video blogs (vlogs) can "position trans youth as experts, implicitly contesting the expertise over trans bodies claimed by medical professionals, educators, and parents."[132] Here again it is the juxtaposition of spoken and written textuality with audiovisuality, rather than any capacity (or opacity) of textuality or audiovisuality on their own, that affords new modes of articulation. This suggests a type of authority, a type of power/knowledge, that can only be grasped through simultaneously textual and audiovisual appearance.

Alongside these examples of politicized videographic appearance, academic research in film criticism and performance studies are also experimenting with video ways of thinking. Building on prior scholarly work that theorizes cinema as embodied and affective, haptic, and fundamentally trans/queer, videographic film critics have taken up video editing as a new way of interacting with film that is simultaneously critical and creative.[133] Meanwhile, performance journals like *Liminalities* have been publishing multimedia scholarship for many years, while the more recent *Journal for Artistic Research* offers a uniquely coded platform for publication.[134] My own interventions in the field of artistic research include not only the video works produced by the Judaica project but also the *Journal of Embodied Research* (*JER*), the first exclusively videographic journal based in performing and embodied arts.[135] *JER* has an intentionally narrow formal scope in that it publishes only peer-reviewed video articles, with no accompanying written statements. All text associated with a *JER* article, including its required metadata—title, author(s), abstract, and keywords—must be contained within a single video file. Topologically reversing the dominant hierarchy of knowledge, whereby video is necessarily situated within a framing text, *JER* publishes text only within video. This approach could be seen as formally and methodologically conservative insofar as it sidesteps much of what is made possible through more recent, internet-born digital technologies. Yet I am convinced that it remains worthwhile to devote further attention to the form of the video article and to the many ways in which textuality and audiovisuality can be composed and juxtaposed within that container.

With these political, theoretical, and logistical contexts in mind, I return to the Judaica project and its audiovisual outputs. Participants in the 2017 Judaica lab, including but not limited to the core lab team, brought with them a wide variety of national, religious, ethnic, linguistic, age, gender, and other backgrounds. If unknown formations of jewishness or judaism emerged from our practice, so too did fragments of christianity, islam, and buddhism; molecules of queer and trans and cis gendering; and sometimes pointed shards of whiteness that sparked up from across our different relationships to the history and idea of europe. Within this laboratory, the apparently simple act of learning and singing a song was revealed as involving innumerable layers of intersecting technique and identity. As a result, even the simplest video recordings of studio practice offered abundant possibilities for critical analysis and reflection, inviting us to pore over the audiovisual material for hours as we tried to articulate the complex entanglements between what we knew about the song being sung and what we perceived and remembered to have been happening in a given recorded moment.

At first my approach to the layering of textuality and audiovisuality in research-oriented video publications was rigidly structured and attempted to establish a kind of analytical authority over the audiovisual material.[136] Gradually, however, a different approach to audiovisuality emerged, culminating in the development of a new audiovisual research method. This method is based on several transformations in both the configuration of laboratory sessions and the iterative analysis and editing of videos generated through that process. On the one hand, the presence of a video camera at the heart of the practice freed the team from the need to produce a repeatable performance score and hence from some of the problems of authorial vision and directorship that can put intense pressure on theatrical performance processes. By prioritizing the experimental rigor of each session and letting go of the desire to create performance "works" in the classical (white or european) sense, it became possible to disaggregate a variety of roles and powers among the team, allowing them to circulate across bodies rather than being stuck to particular individuals over extended periods of time. Moreover, this same integration of the video camera into the space of practice automatically produced, without the need for an external videographer, an increasingly wide variety of audiovisual material: a new kind of data for which we had at the time little context and no method of analysis. Through the process of discussing and editing these videos, a new understanding of video editing as a mode of analysis emerged, gradually suggesting the need for a video way of thinking.[137]

The initial site for the development of this "video way of thinking" was the editing and publication of the "Songwork Catalogue," a web page collecting videos that were initially generated and uploaded alongside the lab sessions. Completed in 2019, the Songwork Catalogue contains more than three hundred videos, ranging in duration from less than one minute to nearly twelve minutes, from recordings produced during the 2017 laboratory period. These videos are presented chronologically and organized into three sections: Songwork I, "Technique" (98 videos), documents a period (May 3–June 15) that involved only the three core practitioner-researchers (me, Eda, and

Agnieszka); Songwork II, "Identity" (80 videos), documents a period (June 26–August 15) during which a number of guest practitioners joined us in the lab; and Songwork III, "Place" (130 videos), documents a period (August 31–October 31) in which the core lab trio traveled to a variety of sites and venues.[138] Extracted from approximately five hundred hours of recordings, the Songwork Catalogue offers a careful selection of audiovisual moments. Each moment was chosen and given a title by one of the researchers and then approved, sometimes after lengthy discussion, by everyone who had been present in that session.

The most important feature of the Songwork Catalogue is the way it constructs a simple but fundamental relationship between textual and audiovisual elements: All the titles for the video selections were chosen and agreed on *after* the recording was complete. This may seem an obvious way to do things in the context of videographic research methods, where video is treated as data and subsequently analyzed.[139] But such an approach overturns the presumptions of nearly all practices of performance documentation and filmmaking, where it goes without saying that the topic and title of a videographic work will be predetermined. (The name of a work of performance documentation is nearly always the same as that of the performance it documents.) By inviting the researchers to name what was happening in a given selection from a retrospective perspective—a technique I started using just before the 2017 lab phase began—the Songwork Catalogue opened the door to a different way of thinking through video, in which recordings were understood not as documenting a preexisting work but rather as revealing a unique audiovisual tracing of an experimental event, the content of which could only be interpreted with hindsight.

The titles of video selections in the Songwork Catalogue include specifications of physical and vocal technique ("four songs, four directions"; "somaticizing the camera"), problems and issues in the process of embodied collaboration ("conflicting associations"; "mutuality"), poetic or narrative evocations that effectively reframe the content of the video ("lucky jew"; "lepidoptera"), and concrete descriptions of place ("by the river"; "lullaby for a dead synagogue"). In all cases the presence of a title operates as an interpretive claim, if not about *what happened* in the lab session overall then at least about *what happens* in a particular audiovisual tracing of it. The selection itself becomes a form of "appearance": an "interface of what was done and what was seen and how it was described." Many but not all the selections engage explicitly with the problematic of contemporary jewish identity, or with questions of identity more broadly. Some of them center a repeatable element of performance technique while others are less repeatable, their content arising from particular configurations of people, times, places, objects, and songs that could not happen again. In the Songwork Catalogue these different types of moments—different in both their audiovisual content and in the textual framing offered by their titles—are placed alongside each other, offering a transversal view or "catalogue" of embodied research that responds to the obligation to contribute to the archive while resisting conventional forms of artistic and scholarly publication.[140] While the three sections of the Songwork Catalogue are named for what is most salient in each—Songwork I foregrounds differences in technique among the same three people, working together consistently for several weeks; Songwork II foregrounds differences in identity, as guest practitioners enter that space for shorter periods; and Songwork III reveals the crucial dimension of place by following the lab across a variety of locations—it goes without saying that technique, identity, and place are operative and entangled in every video.

The process that led to the Songwork Catalogue soon evolved into the generation of more complex edited video works, such as the three that are cited at the beginning of this section. Like the selections in the Songwork Catalogue, these video essays and articles are not very usefully compared to works of live performance. Instead they should be compared and contrasted with written essays and articles, to investigate the onto-epistemic difference that videographic thought can make. While the videos in the Songwork Catalogue are unedited except for the selection of their in and out points, the Judaica project's more complex publications explore the hermeneutics of video editing as a way of analyzing and interpreting audiovisual material, most significantly via the inclusion of textual annotations within the video itself. Such annotations allow the performer, practitioner, embodied researcher, or artist-scholar to intervene textually upon their own audiovisual body in an unprecedented way that is quite distinct from modes of textuality in live performance (e.g., by projecting text onto one's body). In my experience, the act of making a videographic cut, or of inserting critical texts within a video that includes my own audiovisual body, answers one set of questions and immediately poses another. This action and practice break radically with scholarly convention insofar as my textual self, the scholarly "voice" in which I am writing this book, works alongside and in relation to my audiovisual self. The subject-object split is not transcended but is approached in a different way, since I occupy both positions at once. That situation becomes even more complicated when the video I am editing includes another researcher's audiovisual body, or when another researcher is editing my audiovisual body. All of this complexity is ideally held within a cyclical and iterative relationship between the temporality of the lab sessions, which produces video material, and that of ongoing discussion, editing, publishing, and lab design.

Each of the three videos cited at the start of this section attempts to draw out the more or less deeply sedimented layers of knowledge that reside within complex moments of practice. The first, "ancestors," carefully analyzes a very short moment, just three minutes, during which a minor conflict of associations between myself and another researcher (who was directing me) led to a freeze or failure of songwork that nevertheless raised several interesting questions about power and identity. The second, "Diaspora," is considerably longer and more complex, exploring my personal relationships to identity and technique, not only through songwork but also by virtue of the presence of my mother in the lab, which introduced into the space both her distinct embodied knowledge as a visual artist and our actual kinship relations as diaspora. The third video, "Działoszyce," differs from the other two most significantly in that it was not edited by me. Composed by Eda Erçin, this video offers a different perspective of the Judaica project. It is also site-specific, taking place in a ruined synagogue in poland rather than a theater studio in northern england. None of these three videos documents a theatrical performance, not only because of the absence of an audience but also because of the way in which we as a team approached each session.

About two-thirds of the way through the video essay "Działoszyce," Eda looks around the synagogue ruins and asks herself: "Which song?"[141] As the video's editor, she has not only selected this moment for the essay but also provided subtitles for it, emphasizing and reiterating these english words. It is a crucial moment, one that speaks to the methodological and epistemic capacities of the video essay as a form of knowledge. Eda's choice of which song to sing is informed by many different kinds of knowledge, all embodied by the practitioner in that moment: ethnomusicological knowledge about the source and history of various songs; linguistic knowledge about their lexical and nonlexical meanings; practical musical knowledge about the rhythmic, melodic, and tonal qualities of a given song; personal and ethical knowledge about who she is, to whom she is connected, where she comes from, what she carries; as well as situated, perceptual, and historical knowledge about *where* she is and about the beings that come together in that place. Eda sees the crumbling brick walls, the dead and living pigeons, the broken glass, the pebbles, me, Agnieszka. She hears the sounds of the birds, my footsteps, my reading aloud. She listens, she looks. She appears to smell her own hand, as if grounding herself in an intimate somatic reflexivity. And then, out of all this, she answers the question—*Which song?*—by starting to sing.

This is what we usually call "embodied knowledge." But in this case, Eda's actions are made substantially less ontologically ephemeral—or the ephemerality of her actions is configured or bounded in a different way—by the presence of an audiovisual recording device. The song appears uniquely and ephemerally in that moment but it is also recorded, audiovisually traced, by a Nikon D750 DSLR camera, which at that moment is held by Agnieszka. Later the three of us, and others as well, can watch this video recording and ask: Why did she choose that specific song? Why did she begin to sing in that particular way? Eda herself can also do this—and she does, composing a whole video essay around the kinds of embodied, intuitive, and poetic, but also deeply informed and knowledgeable choices that the three of us made on that day, along with the choices made by the pigeons, by people outside the synagogue, by the stone, by the sky.

The 2017 Judaica project lab team traveled to about thirty different sites and venues in england, poland, and the northeastern united states. These included theater venues, dance studios, universities, jewish community centers, and synagogues both ruined and restored. Across these different kinds of borders—geographical, national, disciplinary, aesthetic, cultural, political—we offered workshops, performances, video screenings, talkbacks, and lab sessions. In each location we asked, together and individually: *Which song?* Which songs are appropriate, necessary, or useful for this moment, location, audience, and context? Looking back on this period of work, I now ask myself: What precisely are we doing—what kind of research are we practicing—each time we pose this question? In a sense, we are researching the songs as epistemic objects. For each song that we have learned, whether through embodied transmission, written score, or audio recording, we are discovering what it can do, how it can work, which functions and actions it can serve. In another sense, through this research practice we are exploring our own relationships to those songs: who we are, the three of us, as embodied creatures; our identities. In the vocabulary I have been developing, we are investigating not just the songs as technique and knowledge, but also the relationship between that technique and our own identities.

But there is a third layer, which comes through much more strikingly in "Działoszyce" than in "ancestors" or "Diaspora": the meaning and substance and agency of place. For there is a strong sense in which the video essay "Działoszyce" is most importantly an articulation of our research into that particular place. If we imagine, by way of comparison, the kind of video that a documentary filmmaker might produce about such a site—similarly showing the bricks and stones and pigeons, perhaps alongside interviews with local residents, with descendants of jews who lived in that region, and perhaps a historical voiceover—then it is clear that we are undertaking a related but quite different kind of research into place. For the Judaica team, our bodies and identities (as well as the bodies and identities and melodies and rhythms and vocables and lexical meanings of the songs we practice) are epistemic tools through which we encounter and expose the site, the specific location or place, in a particularly embodied and affective way. Through our bodies and practices, and through the songs, the place speaks—audiovisually.

There is then a kind of plumb line in this research: from songs, through bodies, into the synagogue; or, more abstractly, from technique, through identity, into place. I understand this now as a specific approach to the *earthing* of research practice. At the same time, in the opposite direction, there is a rising up, or *unearthing*, of knowledge: from place, up through identity, into technique; from the synagogue, up through our bodies, into the songs. I think here of Robinson's account of tahltan scholar-artist Peter Morin's songwork practice in anthropological museums in canada and at a range of "British landmarks, many of [which] support structures of colonial power and monarchy," as well as several "lesser-known Indigenous monuments and sites of

Indigenous presence in London."[142] In each place the songwork practice must be enacted differently, beginning with the question of *which song*.

But I also notice how the embodied practice methodology of the 2017 Judaica project lab interacts with and is ultimately transformed by its videographic form. Already in an audio recording, words are not separable from vocal utterances, or even from broader soundscapes, except by reference to what is writable. Video takes this further, creating an audiovisual field in which body is not separate from place. One can watch the Judaica project video essays and attempt to separate the songs from the singers and the singers from the places, but this is only possible by reference to other forms of media. In reading or writing the lyrics of a song, those words become separable from the audiovisual field. In the same way, one might listen to the recording from which a song was learned and thereby attempt to extract that song from the rest of the video recording. But video itself, as a medium, recognizes no such differences. The audiovisual field encodes no borders or boundaries between the songs, the bodies, and the time and place in which those bodies sang. Only retrospectively, by way of other media, can one analyze the video and divide it into such component elements. Is there then something about video, in comparison to other forms of knowledge (such as writing), that is especially or fundamentally *emplaced* as well as embodied?

Earthing the Laboratory

The 2017 Judaica project lab was originally designed to investigate "song-action" through the interactive and collaborative practice research of its three core researchers: me, Eda, and Agnieszka. This changed when we began to invite guest practitioner-researchers to visit the lab and again when we left our university theater studios and took the lab on the road. Our first guest visitor was Caroline Gatt, an anthropologist and theater practitioner, who at the time was working both with senior anthropologist Tim Ingold and with master teacher of postgrotowskian songwork Gey Pin Ang.[143] Caroline's own research explores the living and material agency of books and it was she who first brought scholarly texts into the Judaica project lab.[144] The presence of books alongside songs and bodies in the lab had a massive impact on the future of the project and on my own understanding of songwork and videographic embodied research. But Caroline also questioned my theoretical reliance on the concept of embodiment and invited the Judaica project team to pay more attention to the agency and impact of other elements in the lab, from the video camera to the studios where we were working. Gradually, I understood that the impulse to better recognize *emplacement* in research was coming to us, through Caroline, from anthropology's own long and ethically fraught engagement with indigenous cultures, peoples, and knowledges. I had previously encountered arguments for the importance of place in research, but now this idea struck me in a different way, because of the videographic medium in which our research was being inscribed. Suddenly I understood, with the force of revelation, that songwork as traced audiovisually is literally inextricable both from the audiovisual bodies of its practitioners and from the audiovisuality of place.

The videographic mechanism traces not only audiovisual song but also audiovisual embodiment and audiovisual emplacement. If white techniques of writing effectively conceal and deny the identities and embodiment of an author, how much more effectively do they deny and dismiss emplacement! In this final section of the book, I wish to consider how the Judaica project's dual commitments to embodiment and to videography work together to foreground the agency of place; or, rather, to refuse the denial of emplacement that is enacted by white ways of knowing. I will first reflect on the absence of place in my previous thinking about technique and identity, which I attribute not only to the denial of place in white methods but also to the diasporic positioning of the main resources by which I have thus far attempted to counteract white epistemologies and to decolonize my research practice. I will then carefully draw on some recent theories of place and emplacement, including from critical indigenous studies, to rethink the embodied audiovisual laboratory as a site that could foreground the inextricability of technique, identity, and place.

Conventionally the scientific laboratory is defined by acts of displacement. Karin Knorr Cetina, with others working on critical laboratory studies in the 1990s, observed that "laboratories rarely work with objects as they occur in nature." Instead, "laboratory sciences bring objects *home* and manipulate them on their own terms in the laboratory."[145] Thinking with and from indigenous critiques of extractive knowledge production, we might say that white laboratories are definitionally *antiplace*, much as they are *anti-identity*. The displacement and denial of place go along with the disembodiment and denial of identity in constituting the whiteness of the conventional technoscientific laboratory. There is today a veritable explosion of "labs" and "laboratories" across the arts, humanities, and social sciences.[146] To what extent do these labs reproduce and/or counteract the displacement and disembodiment established as the foundation of white laboratory science?

While social science research may not aim to achieve the absolute transcendence of locality claimed by technoscience, a similar disavowal of place has been observed in social and ethnographic methods. Responding to this, Eve Tuck and Marcia McKenzie suggest that "social science research that better addresses place is one part of what is needed to redress the consequences of colonialism and enable the sustainability of (human) life on the planet."[147] Developing an argument for "critical place inquiry" and "methodologies of place," they observe that "in much social science research, place is just the surface upon which life happens (and from which data are collected). If mentioned at all, it is usually as the backdrop of the inquiry, described briefly beneath headings like 'the research site,' or 'the research context.' "[148] Tuck and McKenzie survey a wide range of research methods, including several that incorporate audiovisual recording. In a table comparing methods, they suggest that photographic and videographic methods are especially helpful in revealing place via its "concrete aspects (appearance, sounds, smells)," while "written explanations behind photos revealed use of places, information about friends and favorite places," and "narration of video revealed emotions, personal meanings, use of place."[149] The Judaica project video essays resonate with these approaches while extending them through a more specific engagement with videographic form that, I have argued, is a key task for artistic research. It treats video recordings not only as "embodied and emplaced data" for analysis but also as the material out of which to compose, through video editing, new forms of transmissible knowledge. Moreover, because the Judaica project's methodology is ethnotechnic rather than ethnographic, there is no strict subject/object divide separating researcher from researched or analyst from analyzed. Instead, the role of artist-scholar or practitioner-researcher is shared by members of a team, who explore their differences and similarities through an iterative practice of lab sessions, discussion, and video editing.

The postgrotowskian theater laboratory, and the european model of theatrical production in general, often replicates many of the same techniques of displacement as found in the hegemonically white laboratories of technoscience. As Frank Camilleri points out, laboratory theater has done significant and important work in demonstrating the capacity of embodied practice to generate transmissible embodied knowledge. He proposes "to extend the embodied materiality, or the physicality of technique, to include the materiality of the environment (hence also of technology) that situates, impinges upon, and conditions that same technique."[150] While Camilleri does not cite indigenous scholarship, I would argue that the emplacement of the theater laboratory is a necessarily decolonial undertaking that should engage and wrestle with indigenous approaches to land, place, and sovereignty. As I see it, the placelessness of the twentieth-century theater laboratory might be attributed not only to hegemonic whiteness but also to its notably diasporic positionality. Through metaphors like Barba's "floating islands," theater ensembles working outside mainstream and commercial theater have attempted to develop microcultures through alternative modes of living together, constituting small intentional communities that are neither colonial nor indigenous. Such ensembles and companies may be strongly linked to the places in which they make their homes, yet they are always also intentionally delinked from emplacement through their engagement with transnational networks of artistic and embodied practice.[151]

To think more rigorously about the emplacement of such laboratories is to ask the question of the "return" (as I called it in chapter 2), which always involves both the specifics of relational emplacement and the broader politics of land and governance. In Tuck and McKenzie's terms, this requires a shift from "embodiment," which "implies the integration of mind and body," toward an "emerging paradigm of emplacement" that links mind, body, and environment.[152] This tripartite formulation is very close to what I am calling the inextricability of technique, identity, and place. The salient difference, as I see it, is that the latter trio of terms suggests a deeper engagement with critical theory and an unwillingness to accept the language of universalizing science and philosophy: Instead of a universalist idea of "mind," which I associate with the coloniality of white writing, a materialist and poststructuralist concept of *technique* as knowledge; instead of a universal human "body," the more controversial and politicized notion of *identity*, necessarily entangled with theories of race and gender; and instead of a generic or universal "environment," the specificity of *place*. To *earth the laboratory* would then mean to reconnect technique, identity, and place—or, rather, to understand that every "molecule" of technique-identity is actually a molecule of technique-identity-place.

I want briefly now to rethink the category and positionality of diaspora in the context of my larger argument. The Judaica project is an experimental investigation of diasporic jewish identity. It found its richest and most resonant theoretical resources in studies of black diaspora. Yet although this book contains the word "race" in its title, its core commitment is to epistemic decoloniality. There is then a gap or elision between my political intentions and my methodology, which I attribute to my central reliance on diasporic black and jewish sources. As a result of this gap, the question of how the *diasporic* relates to the *decolonial* has gone largely unasked thus far. I turn to this question now, not to resolve it but once again to resituate jewishness in a larger framework of historical and contemporary decoloniality by noting some of the ways in which diaspora appears problematic for decolonial thinking at the crossroads of black and indigenous studies.

Eve Tuck and K. Wayne Yang's much-cited article, "Decolonization Is Not a Metaphor," has become a focal point for debate around this topic, because of its strict focus on the politics of land transfer as fundamental to any claim for decolonization.[153] This article has had a significant impact across multiple fields and is now cited even in europe, where the idea of decolonization operates very differently than in north america. But important criticisms have also appeared.[154] Tapji Garba and Sara-Maria Sorentino notably critique Tuck and Yang on two related grounds: First, the latter's "positivist affirmation of land" leaves no room for an ontology of blackness that is based in the forced diaspora of enslavement. "Slavery," they write, "is resistant to the project of recovery—there is no hidden material, neither land nor identity, to be recovered."[155] Even more relevant here is their second critique, which is that distinctively indigenous approaches to land and sovereignty are rendered immaterial by Tuck and Yang's attempt to make land transfer a strictly literal rather than metaphorical act. As Garba and Sorentino write:

"Tuck and Yang *cannot* positively address what Indigenous approaches to land are, without complicating how land is the ground upon which decolonization hinges."[156] In other words, Tuck and Yang's emphasis on what lies "below" the categories of race—perhaps necessary, to avoid the absorption of indigenous sovereignty into the racial categories of today's neoliberal multicultural state—effectively severs place from identity and technique. This makes it impossible to foreground the ways in which indigenous approaches to sovereignty, and to the very definition and ontology of land, differ from the colonial legal frameworks of property and ownership that will, unless carefully avoided, define what counts as the nonmetaphorical transfer of land.

The issue of how to connect racialization and land, or identity and place, arises throughout critical indigenous studies.[157] On the one hand, the strategic political claim to land may often be necessarily dependent on a reductive definition of indigeneity and a presumption that historical precedent demands legal recognition. On the other hand, indigenous land claims do not and should not have the same ontological or epistemological status as claims made by one colonial state against another. Part of what is important about indigenous claims to land, and the reason why these claims are becoming more central in planetary-scale debates, is that they do not simply aim to transfer land from one nation-state to another while keeping the terms of ownership and statehood intact. If indigenous nations only proposed to wrest power from the colonial state, without redefining the meaning of that power, then the conflict would be purely agonistic and of less concern to those not directly involved. On the contrary, the indigenous demand for land transfer is simultaneously a demand to change the way land is understood and to reconfigure the meaning of ownership, shifting it toward indigenous concepts and practices of stewardship, relationality, and collective responsibility that directly oppose those of private property and resource extraction. To articulate such claims, land must be thought together with race/identity and technique/knowledge. What is land? What is a nation or a people? Only if the answers to such questions are presumed and rendered static can the act of land transfer become nonmetaphorical in a simple way. In practice, the ontology of land, the act of transfer, and the identities of those between whom land might be transferred are all mutually constituted. Hence, at the same time as one militates for the legal and political act of land transfer, one must also question the equation of law with writing, and of writing with institutionality, on which that act and its material effects depend.

The category of diaspora is essential to untangling these threads, for diaspora detaches identity from place, unfixing people, but not in the same way as colonialism. If decoloniality cannot be reduced to land transfer insofar as the latter must presume a set of stable identity categories that "the law" in fact also constructs, then neither can it be grasped through a politics of technique and identity alone. Rather, identity itself must be understood, beyond racialization, as making and made of place. This is not to devalue what I have thus far developed as a radical critique of whiteness from a diasporic perspective. It is instead to emphasize, again, the asymmetrical qualities of molecular blackness, whiteness, jewishness, and indigeneity. To understand the relationship between identity and place, we must examine that between diaspora and indigeneity. This is, again, to attempt to *earth* my own concepts of technique, knowledge, research, and the laboratory, which are fundamentally linked to the mobility of technique and require further ethical and political grounding.

As the editors of the volume *Otherwise Worlds: Against Settler Colonialism and Anti-Blackness* attest: "A more sufficiently *diasporic* approach to Black studies can provide a more nuanced assessment of the asymmetries and contingencies that exist between Black and Native appeals to liberal humanist forms of recognition," as well as to those "otherwise ontologies" that must be rediscovered and reinvented outside the bounds of liberal humanism.[158] Elsewhere, Tiffany Lethabo King theorizes diasporic blackness as "perpetually out of place," an experience of "placelessness" and "permanent exile," in contrast to the emplacement and even nationhood proposed by theories of indigeneity.[159] Such diasporic blackness, as conceived in radical black study, does not seek racialized absorption into the multicultural state any more than does radical indigeneity. Both equally contest the validity of the settler colonial nation-state and the terms of such absorption via "recognition."[160] Yet there are crucial differences between the ways that figural blackness and figural indigeneity resist and counteract the process of colonial absorption or engulfment.

Mark Rifkin, focusing his analysis on black and indigenous science fiction, offers a useful gloss on the difference between these politics and figurations as a relation between land and flesh.[161] Land, as we have seen, is a concept that necessarily grounds indigeneity without being sufficient to account for its politics. Indigenous politics are indeed a politics of land, but their approach to land must be distinguished from that of the colonial state, a distinction that can only be drawn through reference to the separable identities and techniques of indigenous people and cultures. Flesh, in the same way, is a central term in the critical theorization of blackness, linked to the fungibility produced by enslavement.[162] Flesh is a particular mode of the body: the body made transferable, detached from any connection with place or knowledge. The central position of black thought and practice in theorizing the flesh accounts for its pivotal role in the development of what I have been calling an emergent decolonial grammar of color. This grammar of color names the detachment of identity from place—the process of racialization—in both its colonial and decolonial iterations. Coloniality detaches whiteness from europe, rendering europe molecular, so that it can spread and construct new europes across the planet. By the same token, the decolonial reclaiming of that racist grammar of colors can only begin from blackness, because of the work that black study has done to articulate the position of those who are reduced to the purely embodied, the flesh. Without black power there can be no red power, as "redness" has a much more ambiguous relation to indigenous sovereignties, which operate not as races but as political alterna-tives to embodied racialization. From blackness and the work of black study it is possible to learn how knowledge and place can be molecularized, how identity can separate itself from place and become mobile, without evaporat-ing into technique.

Where does this leave the relation of identity and place? Marquis Bey:

> There is no origin, we know. No bedrock foundation, no Aristotelian prime mover or first cause to which we can point, no Motherland housing our totality prior to some kind of corruption, no Eden. We are not in search of a totalizing whole, for which beingness is indexi-cal. Our aim is the paraontological, a sort of originary impurity, which is no origin at all if origin is definitionally a pure, unperturbed beginning state. We are, and must be, impure from the start. Desedi-mentation . . . revokes the sediment's license to stay here, grounded, as the ground.[163]

It must be emphasized that the "bedrock foundation" or "Aristotelian prime mover" to which Bey refers is in no way equivalent to the land or place invoked by indigenous sovereignty. What radical black study rejects is the white construction of a prior totality, a "totality prior to some kind of corrup-tion," which I have argued, following Derrida and others, is inextricable from logocentrism and the particular use that white institutionality has made of the technology of writing. A confusion must therefore be avoided between Bey's "ground" as the dominating first principles of white writing—exemplified, perhaps, by the Cartesian cogito, the *Principia Mathematica*, or even the (markedly non-talmudic) Ten Commandments—and an indigenous sense of ground or land as the material affordances underpinning life.[164] The universal ground deconstructed by poststructuralism is the enemy of land and place as conceived by indigenous thought and practice. On the difference between these two versions of ground or bedrock now hangs the survival of many worlds. To unmake the first principles of white thought need not—indeed, cannot—involve further alienation from the earth. Just the opposite: Logo-centrism cannot be unmade except in relation to the earth. The earth is an alternative ground of being and a politics of earthing must be against logo-centrism. If whiteness is a domination and violation of the earth based on logocentrism, in which writing is reified in place of living ecologies (recalling here that "white writing" includes the entire apparatus of global finance), then the development of alternatives must be sought through an earthing of thought. Such an earthing may begin with processes of embodiment but it can-not end there because, just as thought and writing are made of embodiment, embodiment is made of the earth. To repurpose my earlier phrasing: Identity is made of place and place is made of identity. Their mutual constitution is analogous to that of technique and identity, but on a deeper and slower level.

Katherine McKittrick has emphasized that the historical fact of forced diaspora through enslavement never finally severs blackness from emplacement. Quoting Ruth Wilson Gilmore, she declares: "There is no life that is not geographic."[165] McKittrick therefore proposes a counterconcept of black geography in which, following Édouard Glissant, "the naming of place—regardless of expressive method and technique—is also a process of self-assertion and humanization."[166] Through the material linking of technique, identity, and place, which McKittrick grounds in black feminism and the subaltern spatial practices of black women, we can grasp certain "reconceptualizations of space and place" by which geographies themselves are "made alterable" as embodied and expressive acts work through identity to reconfigure place itself.[167] Thus diasporic identity, for all its unfixity, remains entangled with place—not only because we diaspores retain our connections to the places our ancestors have left or were forced out of, but also because of how we transform the world through acts of diasporic placemaking.

Because of the radical work of black studies, McKittrick can approach black geographies without being tied down to the demographic logics that characterize, by contrast, most studies of jewish diaspora. The latter have tended to focus on the conditions and practices of particular jewish populations, which are assumed to occupy preexisting spaces and places. While jewish diaspora studies has often been at pains to reject racialization in favor of the supposed concreteness of particular communities that are assumed to be jewish, black diaspora studies has tapped into a very different kind of speculative power through the reclamation and radical reimagination of the racial term. Hence Gilroy's "Black Atlantic" does not only locate black people in the Atlantic but also blackens the ocean itself; and McKittrick writes that "blackness is integral to the production of space," citing Rinaldo Walcott to confirm that "questions of blackness far exceed the categories of the biological and the ethnic."[168] Blackness is an "identity" not in the sense of a demographic label but as a force that is mutually generative of both technique and place. To think more creatively about jewish diasporic geographies along these lines would require a radically alternative and avowedly oppositional reracialization of jewishness, along the lines suggested by Slabodsky's "barbaric," so that its meaning and materiality can depart somewhat (though never completely) from demographics. This is what I have attempted to do by tracking judaism beyond jews, both as critical theory and in the experimental songwork practices of the Judaica project.

In chapter 1 I suggested that we living beings are made of molecules. These may be the organic molecules we call DNA or testosterone, or those like lead or indican that enter our bodies and become part of us in another way. But the biological and technoscientific disciplines do not exhaust, or even really begin to survey, the riot of molecules comprising *technique-identity-place*. Just as technique is an upsurge, loosening, desedimentation, or molecularization of identity, so identity might be conceived as an upsurge, loosening, desedimentation, or molecularization of place. Place surges and bubbles into beings and those beings, bubbling themselves, uncover and transmit knowledge, techniques, ways of doing. As Max Liboiron writes: "Place-based relations are not properties of things so much as what make things."[169] Nor does the movement of molecules flow in just one direction. Technique sediments downward, over time, becoming identity; and identity sediments downward, over time, becoming place. Identity, then, is not only sedimented technique, but also desedimented place. We living creatures are elutriated earth, clarified earth, our bodies and identities temporarily rising up and separating from the denser matter of place, only to dissolve and return back into land.

This flow of matter across levels or speeds does not privilege flux over fixity. It suggests not a universalism but perhaps an "earthism": positing earth and its ecologies as the temporal and situated source of all power and knowledge, identity and technique. Nor should this talk of "up" and "down" movements be taken to imply a literally vertical line. If it sometimes feels as if knowledge moves above us while the earth lies below, this is not a rigorous model and may indeed collude with extractive and colonial relations. A better way to think the relations between technique, identity, and place, as Deleuze and Guattari picked up in their geophilosophy, is in terms of differential speeds or temporalities. When we say that technique sediments down into identity while identity sediments down into place, or that identity is generated by the upward flow of place while technique is generated by the upward flow of identity, we do not really mean "up" and "down." We are talking about bits and pieces, fragments, crumbs, molecules, more or less stable and sedimented; how things come together and come apart.

This is what I perceive, now, when I watch the Judaica project videos. Not only because I was there but also because of the particular way in which those sessions were orchestrated, with the camera intimately entering a mobile and configurable space of practice defined by a set of fluid but precise embodied and emplaced relations. The output from the camera device has a certain flatness: In the image, all elements appear together, inseparable except through analysis. Place, identity, and technique are entangled: the site of practice, the bodies moving, the songs. Since 2017, I have returned again and again to these recordings, searching for new ways not only to analyze and understand them but also to share that analysis through new types of publication, new forms of knowledge.

The inextricability of technique, identity, and place is one rubric that might be used to unpack the density of these audiovisual documents. In this way a viewer or video editor might ask, as I have done, how the particularities of time and place interact, in a particular recorded moment, with the embodied histories and identities of the practitioners and with the songs we choose to sing. I offer this as a simple yet powerful rubric to concretize and render practical certain movements in contemporary thought, especially those developed in critical black and indigenous studies. A quite different analysis might

follow Ian Baucom's enumeration of seven "layers or scales" of time: cosmological, geological, zoological, biological, nomological, biographical, and
finally messianic or theological time.[170] Baucom aims to bridge the deep time
of colonialism and slavery with the even deeper time of ecological change. I
can see how such multiple temporalities might be excavated from a video like
"Działoszyce": there is the sky, overhead, a cosmological constant; the geology of rock and mortar, materials mined for construction, now ruined and
returning to the earth; the zoological interaction of humans and pigeons; the
latter's biological cycles of life and death, feeding and shitting, into which we
momentarily enter; the nomological ghosts of patriarchal religion and fascist
demolition; the biographical journeys that led us to that place; and the messianic force summoned by the power of song to crystallize these layers in a
single moment.

Yet another mode of analysis might eschew the framework of time and
temporality in favor of an epistemological layering. Elsewhere I have sketched
a possible framework for an epistemic trajectory that rejects flattening ontologies of "objects" in favor of a phenomenological account of epistemic depth.
In this model there are not so much multiple layers of time as a variety of
phenomena that are differently experienced because of our differing epistemic
relations to them: objects, thresholds, techniques, principles, fields.[171] With
this rubric in mind, we could return to the same video and find still different
things: objects, like the book we carry and from which we read; thresholds,
like the songs we enter and explore; techniques, like the distribution of roles
(practitioner, director, videographer) that structures the laboratory practice;
principles, like the camera that frames the event; and fields, like holocaust
memory, which in that particular place becomes inescapable.

My point here is not to compare these different frameworks of analysis but to evoke the density of videographic material by touching upon a
handful of the countless ways in which one could attempt to draw out the
richness of what is captured audiovisually. Whether one uses the five elements
of my proposed "epistemic trajectory," the seven timescales or temporalities
enumerated by Baucom, the much simpler three-part model of technique-
identity-place, or another analytical scheme, it is undeniable that audiovisual
recordings, particularly when they document experimental or unpredictable
moments, offer an unprecedented richness that absorbs and exceeds the hermeneutic complexity of the textual, photographic, aural, and temporal. If we
are not to approach such documents as yet another substrate for white ways
of thinking—if instead we aim to wrest audiovisuality away from coloniality and logocentrism—then we must be prepared to face, enjoy, and grapple
with their richness. How to unearth audiovisual complexity? For decolonial
artistic research, I have argued, this is most essentially a question of form:
What form of audiovisual work or publication can embrace and articulate
both the embodied experience of practitioners and its saturation by diverse
temporalities, knowledges, and emplacements?

Since 2017 a certain form of work has arisen from the Judaica project, a discussion of which concludes this chapter. That form is what I call "illuminated video." It is on the one hand entirely specific to the Judaica project, answering a particular set of questions about contemporary jewish identity and the racialization of knowledge, and, on the other hand, a general proposal for artistic research.[172] This form, more than any other outcome of the Judaica project, convinces me that artistic research can intervene in the racial ontology of media by developing new forms of knowledge, out of which which new forms of institutionality and worlding might be imagined and constructed.

The basic form of illuminated video is textual annotation overlaid onto an audiovisual recording. Reversing the epistemic hierarchy of the illuminated manuscript, in which a primarily textual work is enhanced with visual imagery, illuminated video uses textual annotation to expand and augment—and perhaps also to critique and interrogate—a primarily audiovisual work. This epistemic reversal is, as I have suggested, profoundly talmudic in the power it accords to the word: not a power of domination and containment, as in white writing, but that of annotation and illumination, in the mode of critical theory. The content of such textual illuminations may be analytical or poetic, tending toward coherent argument or associative imagery. Personally, I find the annotation process and its results most intriguing when they operate through that most talmudic of textual moves, the citation. And while textual illuminations can of course be layered onto an edited videographic montage, I am particularly drawn to video works that textually illuminate otherwise unedited and uncut video. Uncut video invites viewers to sink down into the temporality of practice, slowing thought in a way that is unfamiliar to the conventions of mainstream audiovisuality. At the same time, the potential density of textual illumination can enrich a video document—even one that is low resolution or framed by a stationary camera—with a kind of epistemic depth that is uniquely textual and, in my reading of racial media ecologies, archaically jewish.

Illuminated video is analogous to approaches that might be found in video art or visual ethnography, but it does not arise from those lineages. Its inner structure—the processes that generate the performance-based video to be illuminated—are homologous with those of experimental performance and laboratory theater, but it does not share their form. To further explore and give voice to this new form, I edited a special issue of the *Journal of Embodied Research* dedicated to illuminated video. Included in this issue are thirteen contributions, ranging in duration from less than three minutes to more than thirty, all of which explore the timing and placement of textual annotation layered upon uncut video material. The last of these contributions is my own video article, "He Almost Forgets That There Is a Maker of the World," in which I surround my own audiovisual body and those of my colleagues with about fifty textual citations.[173]

"He Almost Forgets . . ." asks a central question of the Judaica project—what (else) can jewishness be?—not only textually, in its written abstract, but also through a precise configuration of songs, books, practitioners, and relational techniques that contour but do not determine how the moment unfolds. What is jewish here, in my understanding, is not only the songs, the books, and my body, but also something about the way the question is posed: through an iterative process that links audiovisual embodiment and emplacement to critical textual annotation. On the one hand, I am happy to call this a jewish research method, an extension of critical theory that reconnects talmudic textuality with a quasi-mystical, very loosely hasidic, audiovisual tracing of embodied song and movement. On the other hand, nothing in the jewishness of this method limits the potential scope of its content. The crystallization of illuminated video, as a practical experiment in the relationship between textuality and audiovisuality, resonates on a molecular level with questions about diasporic and decolonial judaism. But it has nothing like a proprietary relation to jewish identity, let alone to "Jewish Studies."[174] Rather, its formal intervention is a concrete, methodological proposal for new epistemic solidarities. This is most obvious through the focal point of my own dual-authorship positions, as both embodied songwork practitioner and video editor. Layering numerous textual quotations onto the video allows me to destabilize my own embodied identities and to give an account of myself that does not require me to speak in a coherent narrative voice. I appear in multiple ways in this video, but I never speak words of my own. Beyond the fragmentation of my individuality, "He Almost Forgets . . ." swarms with material and agentic presences: songs, bodies, objects (including books)—all grounded in time and place to a degree that is not possible in any textual form.

I do not believe it is a coincidence that I find myself staging the problem of disentangling jewishness from whiteness as a formal and methodological battle over the relative epistemic status of audiovisuality and textuality. This is the way that I have found to ask, following Slabodsky, whether jewishness can rejoin the world—not the white world, but the other world, the rest of the world, the world beyond whiteness, which is also the only world, since whiteness was never really a world but only a logocentric extraction and domination of the world. Can writing support land and flesh, rather than exploiting them? Can writing be practiced in a way that acknowledges how the word arises from and is rooted in land and flesh? Likewise I do not believe it is too wild or too fabulative to sketch a historical narrative whereby today's radical black and indigenous theory draws on a prior generation of differently racialized jewish thought precisely because, as Slabodsky shows, jewishness—as trope, figure, substance, and geopolitical position—has largely failed to perservere against its complicity with and absorption into whiteness. The current critical effervescence at the edges of blackness and indigeneity relies on jewish thought, even as the politics of jewishness have profoundly failed to join this eruption of "positive barbarism" or decoloniality. Might it not then be the task of today's jewish thinkers, artists, and practitioners—white and not—to reorient figural jewishness, on a molecular level, back toward the positive barbarism of decoloniality? Perhaps by inventing or revealing some newly barbaric cryptojudaism? As Houria Bouteldja writes, speaking to "the Jews" in the voice of "a new political identity that we will have to invent together, the We of a decolonizing majority": "Between us, everything is still possible."[175] Through what forms of knowledge might such new political identities think themselves into appearance?

According to Fred Moten, the rejection of "song and dance, of cinema and theatre," is epistemologically central to white ways of knowing.[176] The failure of jewish decoloniality is then found precisely in the rejection of song by a thinker like Levinas, as Moten carefully traces. "To speak truly," Levinas says, is to speak "not as one sings." Here Levinas equates logocentric speech with philosophical rigor and "the audiovisual domain" with "distraction." Yet if this is the point at which decolonial judaism has failed, then perhaps that failure need not be final. "At issue is the possibility of avoiding song, which is associated with intoxication, sleep, lack of seriousness, the technoprimitivity that attends modern audiovisual distraction [and] accompanies the ongoing inability to escape being."[177] In Levinas, according to Moten, as everywhere throughout hegemonic forms of white writing, the eruption of audiovisuality is linked to primitivity and severed from the power of thought, knowledge, and law. With this onto-technological severing in mind, I close by invoking again the apparent paradoxes of *audiovisual thought* and *molecular thought*, perhaps even pushing these further, toward *audiovisual law*. This would not be a form of law that rejects the textual but one that repositions (white) writing within a broader horizon, passing through audiovisuality and its "primitivity" toward the horizons of embodiment and emplacement. Such mediated law can never be the kind of embodied and emplaced gathering through which, as Dylan Robinson explains, living song (and dance) may come to function "as law, medicine, or primary historical documentation."[178] But neither is it reducible to the forms of white law, white writing, and white institutionality.

What if, instead of a set of laws or principles, formalized in written words, the founding document of an institution were an audiovisual recording? What would be a university, or a state, founded on an audiovisual constitution? What kind of recording would that be, produced and edited according to which techniques? Would it show people, speaking words? But people never only speak words on video; that is not possible. In their audiovisual tracing, words have timbre, voices have faces, utterances have bodies, and bodies are always in places. What then could such a founding video document show? People singing and dancing? People caring for each other, going for walks, making love, gardening? Or just trees? Or just the ocean? What would be an institution founded on such a document? What would be a polity with an audiovisual constitution? What might be audiovisual law?

Afterword

♦

On Death and Ceremony

In this book I have tried to understand the implications of thinking technique and identity, knowledge and power, media and race, as inseparable. I have endeavored to understand how the apparent flux of technique, the apparent stability of identity, and the apparent solidity of place are nevertheless interwoven and intermeshed, each constituting the others in real and material ways that are neither infinitely fluid nor permanently fixed. I have argued that racial and other identities are malleable precisely through transformations in technique, where technique is understood not as a dichotomy of oppression and resistance but as the very stuff of the world: the reliabilities, never more than relative, that structure each moment of practice. For this reason there can be no such thing as pure technique or pure knowledge, because everything that we might fancifully call "mind" or "thought" is materially constituted by that which we must call identity and place.

By thinking identity (especially the racial) together with technique (especially the audiovisual), I have tried to render today's rapid technological transformations less separable from the materialities of racial injustice, extractive capitalism, and climate catastrophe that are their emplaced grounds. There is, I have argued, no single public sphere of discourse, or any neutral or fundamental institutional structure, on or through which we can take action to reduce inequality, save ecologies, or make human society more sustainable. Instead, the very construction of any large-scale sense of "we" takes place through mediated forms of knowledge—the same ones that are undergoing rapid change. This has led me to foreground interventions that are manifestly both discursive and material because of how they act on and through specific *forms of knowledge,* which are always both mediated and racialized, both technical and cultural. Such interventions include (but are in no way limited to) those undertaken by university-based artistic research, especially when they recognize themselves as actively formulating critiques of and alternatives to whiteness.

whiteness

I have been reading aloud from a book. Now I stand across from my partner, my chant swiveled into melody, our voices spiraling together in a kind
of nonsong. The book rises in my hand and I began to move it around my
partner's body. She responds, our gestures mingling, the book cutting through
the space like a ritual prop, as our nonsong swells. Her voice cascades into
a rhythmic pulse. I give the book to her and move quickly away. She takes
the book and continues the pulse, becoming harsher, wilder. The camera
comes close to her face and she looks back at it, half-smiling as her own
voice continues to break through her like a wave. Slowly that voice changes,
lightening, softening, cresting, and as her song becomes gentler she seems to
rediscover the book that she has been holding against her chest. Holding it
away from her body with a tight grip, she turns her focus to the object as if
to coax or threaten it. She raises the book above her head, balancing it on her
fingertips, then thrusts it to the ground where she paws it, pushes it, and flips
it over as if to test its dangers. Picking it up again, she balances the book on
one hand, moving quickly yet attempting to keep control of it, until it flies off
her fingers as if of its own accord.

We hear the book hit the floor but we do not see it. The sound continues,
but the image is replaced by a dark gray screen. Upon this darkness, white
words fade in. At first we see only a series of poetic declarations and questions: *Words are not things that can be written down. Freedom is not a kind
of speech. How do we* call in *philosophy? How do we* call in *the act of writing? Only by abandoning the* logos, *the illusion of transparency: not writing,
but the tyranny of writing.* The final question is provocative: *Can the white
body be decolonized without killing it?* Gradually this text is joined by a
series of references to theorists of black studies, indigenous studies, and critical whiteness studies: Leanne Betasamosake Simpson, Robin D. G. Kelley,
Katherine McKittrick, la paperson, Erin Manning, Dylan Robinson, Giorgio Agamben, Denise Ferreira da Silva, Tiffany Lethabo King, Marquis Bey,
Kevin Rigby Jr., and Hari Ziyad, and finally my own name. (Agamben's name
may be unexpected in this list, but it is his book that stars in the video alongside two human practitioners, an unseen videographer, and a fourth witness
who remains silent.) The video is called "whiteness."[1] It runs about twelve
minutes, during which the visual image is broken three times by a black
screen overlaid with white text. The latter brutally cuts into the visual flow of
practice, literally writing over it. But the sound, or song, or nonsong, remains
continuous even through the closing credits.

The video essay "whiteness" combines a largely nonverbal exploration of
embodied voice, in which a philosophical work about human-animal relations
is both verbally and physically examined, with a textual layer that critically
interrogates whiteness. Perhaps the editorial juxtaposition of these two components suggests a possible counterwhiteness practice, yet that synthesis is

riven: the two parts never integrate. If this is an attempt to portray counter-whiteness, it is split down the middle by a division between audiovisuality and textuality that is much sharper and harsher than in any of my other video works. Reading that montage allegorically, the whiteness of the mind/body split—noting again that "mind" here means textual and "body" means audiovisual—is further mirrored by the structure of the journal in which the essay is published, which places it in a section called "Margins" despite its explicit engagement with philosophical questions and a robust process of peer review. The textuality of the article is insufficient to move it from margin to center because the center is reserved for articles in textual form. Meanwhile, the video's critical textual content, no matter whom it references or how close a brush it has with a call for ethical death, can never do more than frame or intervene in the video, which retains its own flow through the continuity of its sound. Even as the audiovisual track depicts apparent whiteness, the life that comes through the voices demonstrates the incompleteness of white racialization as disembodiment (another kind of death). And even as the text raises the possibility of a necessary death, it asks whether that death could be a pathway to another life.

As I wrote in an earlier essay:

> White bodies pose a specific problem for decoloniality. For revolutionary decolonization, outright war against whiteness in the form of the colonial state seems justified. But for more thorough processes of decoloniality, the complexity of embodiment demands an engagement with the impossibility of neatly categorizing bodies. The problem of whiteness cannot be solved through military or political action alone. On the one hand, white bodies incarnate coloniality. Their constructed whiteness is the fortress around which other bodies are subjugated and oppressed. On the other hand, white bodies are also *bodies*, and . . . processes of racialization cannot account for the fullness of lived embodiment. No bodies are entirely white; there is no body that has been fully saturated (drained? bleached?) by whiteness. . . . It follows that there are differing degrees, levels, and qualities of whiteness, and this raises the question of how to unearth the nonwhiteness of bodies that have been racialized as white.[2]

This problem lingers over the songwork traced in the video.

Shortly after publishing "whiteness," I came across Hadar Kotef's incisive discussion of Lorraine Hansberry's play *Les Blancs*.[3] In this brief meditation, Kotef responds to Lorenzo Veracini's proposal to reverse a horrific colonial slogan with the following recipe: "Kill the Settler in Him and Save the Man."[4] Kotef is not convinced by Veracini's neat formulation, according to which "an indigenous-led type of settler decolonization" will "help decolonization," so that "the metaphorical resurgence of the settler" can "follow his metaphorical death."[5] For Kotef, despite Veracini's mention of (metaphorical) death, this solution is too sanguine. Instead, Kotef meditates on the figure of a settler who must literally die to enact her own ethics. In the play *Les Blancs*, Kotef writes, "Madame Nielsen has to die."[6] Kotef is not necessarily placing herself on the side of political violence here or eschewing the possibility of radical structural transformation. Rather, she finds Veracini's solution lacking because it does not sufficiently attend to how deeply whiteness is written into bodies: "Although undoubtedly necessary, institutional change consisting of the democratization of the settler state is not sufficient, because it leaves intact the deep structures of racialized hierarchies, violent desires, and attachments to dispossession."[7] Transformation is incomplete if it does not tackle and change the "deep structures" of whiteness, those sedimented forms of technique and knowledge that produce white identity, making whiteness both embodied and emplaced.

Faced with this question, Kotef shifts from the registers of the analytical and the political to that of her own imaginative capacity:

> To kill the settler in the man is to kill so much of the man himself that the distinction becomes questionable. This is not just because it is analytically messy, but also because, politically, *I cannot imagine it taking place*: it is to demand that he give up his property (or at least some of it), his language, his cultural references; but also, if I am correct, that he change his "structures of feeling," modes of desire, and attachments—to places, to people.[8]

Kotef is caught here between two kinds of white death: one that accomplishes little through its sacrifice and another that sacrifices too little. She knows that literal, biological death can only be a small part of any solution, but she "cannot imagine" a metaphorical or epistemic death profound enough to bring whitened people into the fold of decolonization. Instead of pushing through this impasse, Kotef stops, leaving the question to linger: "Here I stop writing. I do not know how one writes dead ends or how one writes themselves out of history."[9] The israeli colonial self remains a burden that Kotef cannot imagine escaping; a form of memory so deeply embedded, embodied, and emplaced that it cannot be shaken off.

Postmemory

I am standing in a doorway that is too small for me. The camera captures the top half of my body, my arms and hands pressed against the cold stone of the passage. The right side of the screen shows part of a restored wall painting; the left side, a ruined plaster surface where nothing has yet been restored. Above me are hebrew letters, which a colleague later translates for me: *There stand the thrones for judgment* (Psalm 122).[10] I am singing. The song is "Ale Brider" but it is not sung as usual, joyfully. Every word comes slowly—a lament. The camera pans to show the extraordinary paintings on the ceiling: hebrew writing, magic animals, multicolored vines—and then nothing. The painting stops, is broken, simply ends, where it has not been restored. The edge reminds me of my mother's paintings, which ceaselessly depict the edge of the painted surface as the edge of representation itself.[11] It also reminds me of the way in which a dark gray screen cuts into the image in the video essay "whiteness." But here the cut is not neat and the emptiness of the bare ceiling is not filled by any explanation. My song continues, lamenting a lost world that has been lamented so many times before. What makes this moment any different? Only perhaps the presence of my colleagues, our specific way of directing the audiovisual power of the camera, and the context of a critical project aimed to resituate and reimagine jewishness in a decolonial frame. I place my back against one side of the doorway, my hands and feet against the other. As the image fades, I am held by the walls, my hands caressing their surfaces, literally suspended in space. I remember the feeling of my head pressing against the top of the door.

This video, *Postmemory: Crypt*, was shown alongside another, *Postmemory: Fragments*, in a three-channel version that was specially edited for the small auditorium of a local holocaust memorial center.[12] Each video runs about forty-five minutes and was composed from video recordings taken at one of two ruined and partially restored synagogues in rural poland. From the program booklet accompanying the exhibition:

> The videos presented in this exhibition follow the encounters of the 2017 Judaica project lab team with ruined and partially restored synagogues in the rural *świętokrzyskie* region of poland, where we undertook a kind of *research on place* as well as memory. In these unique places, we encountered the relics of genocide alongside museum exhibitions, archival traces, and objects ranging from the mundane and the kitschy to the downright racist.
>
> In these practice sessions, we lay our songs and our bodies against the particularities of each site. We did not plan what would happen or draw explicit distinctions between memory and imagination, tradition and invention, the proper and the improper. We worked with care, supporting each other in our practices. As each of us takes the role of performer in turn, we perceive different aspects of the place and respond in different ways.

If "whiteness" is a meditation on whiteness and death, the *Postmemory* videos together explore the potentiality of jewish postdiasporic ceremony to move toward life.

Ceremony is a kind of event that touches on and transforms the materiality of the world. As Shawn Wilson has argued, academic research has never been apart from the world, a pure observation that avoids changing what it touches. To think otherwise would be to allow writing to float apart from the world that affords it—the illusion of logocentrism or white writing. Hence, in a sense, all research is ceremony.[13] But to extend the preceding conversation, if white research is ceremony then it can only be a ceremony of death: either a ceremony that continues the living death of whiteness through techniques of disembodiment and displacement or else another kind of death, literal or epistemic, that seeks to transform whiteness by passing beyond the limits of its imagination. The *Postmemory* videos come at this problem from another angle, another identity. Rather than directly interrogating whiteness and seeking its unnameable alternatives through death, the *Postmemory* videos cleave to an alternative lineage of diasporic experience, another experience of death, and a form of thought beyond writing. Through the inscription of these particular moments in audiovisual form, followed by a multilayered editing process, I attempted to bring forward layers of meaning that might otherwise remain hidden within the songs, bodies, and places that came together during these particular sessions of practice.[14]

Tiffany Lethabo King names ceremony as a site at which black and indigenous worlds can meet and mingle to imagine and create new worlds. Ceremonies, King says, "reorganize space-time."[15] Perhaps ceremony is the orchestration or coming together of technique, identity, and place in mutually transforming ways. On the one hand, form is unimportant to this process. Ceremony can take place through poetry, sculpture, film, live performance, or a scholarly monograph. On the other hand, form is everything in the sense that only a poem, only a sculpture, only a monograph can do particular kinds of work, enact or transmit particular kinds of ceremony. King's reading of Charmaine Lurch's sculptures, undertaken through an iterative and collaborative relationship, is an example of artistic research despite their separate authorship of the textual and sculptural components.[16] And this reading returns again and again to the matter of form, with Lynch's wire Sycorax an "antimodern" form that reveals the "form of flesh": the "fleshy and liberated materiality of Black and Native peoples that conquest disavowed."[17] Political protest—as when "Black people and members of the Six Nations blocked off a section" of a street in front of toronto's city hall in 2006—is another form of ceremony, one in which "the violence in the land," that of coloniality, can in a sudden moment "surge up through the concrete and permeate every molecule of air/space."[18] In such moments, through a precise form of action, all the blood and power that is gathered in that place suddenly "surges up," through differentially racialized and emplaced bodies, to affect the very air, to change the very space.

It is increasingly recognized that part of the work of dismantling whiteness must involve bringing forward the precolonial and noncolonial roots of those bodies and identities that have been racialized as white. As one of the most recently absorbed identities, whose hairpin turn from racialized victim of genocide to white supremacist colonial power is a hinge of twentieth-century history, the role of jewishness in decoloniality requires much further investigation. In saying that, I do not mean to dismiss the substantial histories of radical jewish politics that others have traced. My aim is rather to expand the frame so that it might include, alongside jewish politics, techniques and strategies of political jewishness that have yet to be imagined. Perhaps more than other posteuropean identities, diasporic jewishness has the potential to disentangle itself from whiteness and to demonstrate what that means. To do so, it will need to commit to a radically interdisciplinary intersectionality, learning deeply from black and indigenous approaches to knowledge and power.

This book, *Race and the Forms of Knowledge*, is in considerable part a response to King's work, inspired by her radical writing on form and ceremony and by her courage in thinking black and indigenous onto-epistemologies together. I have tried to show here that the development of networked audiovisuality affords unprecedented potential for ceremony, which is itself already a mode of research. Audiovisuality, as Kara Keeling suggests, can be a "house of difference" more capacious than even the most poetic or deconstructive textual forms.[19] But there is no easy refuge in audiovisuality. The moment that audiovisuality is treated as mere technology, it is made implicitly white and can then join with white writing to solidify and extend white institutionality, further colonizing life and earth. What is urgently necessary, therefore, is to extract audiovisuality, writing, and institutionality itself from whiteness, restoring to them their histories and materialities of racialization. Only in this way can the forms of knowledge be reopened.

ACKNOWLEDGMENTS

This book is deeply rooted in questions about race, gender, identity, knowledge, and embodiment that I have been asking my whole life. But its origins as a specific project might be traced to 2016, when I received a UK Arts and Humanities Research Council Fellowship to investigate contemporary jewish identity through a "laboratory of song-action." This grant supported a period of work with Nazlıhan Eda Erçin, Agnieszka Mendel, Caroline Gatt, and others. Before the laboratory phrase began, I dove into literature at the crossroads of jewish studies and contemporary critical theory, searching for a way to understand the materialization of jewishness in my artistic research practice. It was then that I encountered Santiago Slabodsky's *Decolonial Judaism*, a volume that, more than any other, challenged me to resituate judaism and jewishness within a broadly decolonial view of history. I thank Santiago for his work and ongoing engagement, including putting me in touch with the brilliant Lxo Cohen, in conversation with whom my ideas about jewishness continue to evolve.

I am very grateful to Faith Wilson Stein for taking this project on and for the encouraging and generative comments of two peer reviewers. Thanks to so many others whose questions, invitations, dialogue, and inspirational work have informed the writing of this book on a molecular level. These include Maiada Aboud, 'Funmi Adewole, Hadar Ahuvia, Tamara Ashley, Rowan Bailey, Celia Weiss Bambara, Meghan Moe Beitiks, Mira Benjamin, Nicole Bindler, Johannes Binotto, Ben Blum-Smith, Alex Boyd, Eric Burkart, Franc Chamberlain, Rosa Cisneros, Guy Cools, Diana Damian, Sarah Davey-Hull, Elizabeth de Roza, Scott Delahunta, Lindsey Dodd, Lindsey Drury, Nathalie Fari, Michele Feder-Nadoff, Sophie Fetokaki, Giovanni Sabelli Fioretti, Manola Gayatri, Craig Gingrich-Philbrook, Yelena Gluzman, Cara Hagan, Rachel Hann, Cara Herbitter, Tai Howard, Cathy Johnson, Thomas Kampe, Esa Kirkkopelto, Michael Kliën, Linda Knight, Paula Kolar, Ilona Krawczyk, Adriana La Selva, Jennifer Lee, Natalie Loveless, D. Soyini Madison, Matej Matejka, Scott McLaughlin, Anna-Helena McLean, Henry McPherson, Deb Middleton, Royona Mitra, Daniel Mroz, Alan O'Leary, Shanti Suki Osman, Jonathan Pitches, Francesca Placanica, Katherine Profeta, Duska Radosavljevic, Dylan Robinson, Jon Rossini, Morwenna Rowe, SAJ, Arun Saldanha, Chelsea Sambells, Melina Scialom, Peter Sciscioli, Greg Seigworth, Kiki Selioni, Dani Snyder-Young, Tatyana Tenenbaum, Julia Ulehla, melissandre varin, Freya Vass, VestAndPage, Tobaron Waxman, Jed Wentz, Ni'Ja Whitson,

Xine Yao, and Phillip Zarrilli; Christopher Breu and the Comparative Theory Facebook group; and the John Brown group (Henry Bial, Michelle Liu Carriger, Eero Laine, and SAJ). I also want to thank Bidston Observatory Artistic Research Centre, where the final copyediting for this book was done. I keep thanking Pedro Alejandro and Hope Weissman (z"l) again and again, but it's true: much of this work started with them. My deepest gratitude goes to my parents, Elaine and Morris, and to my sister, Rebecca, for teaching me everything. My father also proofread this manuscript. Annalise Friend produced the index. Infinite love to my two amazing kids.

Some of the material in this book was previously published, in more or less differing versions, as part of the following articles and book chapters: "Molecular Identities: Digital Archives and Decolonial Judaism in a Laboratory of Song," *Performance Research* 24, no. 1 (2019): 66–79; "Earthing the Laboratory: Speculations for Doctoral Training," *Performance Research* 25, no. 8 (2020): 33–41; "Artistic Research and the Queer Prophetic," *Text and Performance Quarterly* 41, no. 1–2 (2021): 81–105; "Between Death and Ceremony: The Judaica Project 2012–2022," *Public: Art, Culture, Ideas* 67 (2023): 62–80; "Thinking the Molecular," in *Interpreting the Body: Between Meaning and Materiality*, edited by Anne Marie Champagne and Asia Friedman (Bristol University Press, 2023), 44–66; and "Race and the Dramaturgy of the Body," in *A Companion to the Body in Performance*, edited by Victor Ladron de Guevara, Roberta Mock, and Hershini Young (Routledge, forthcoming). Over the past several years I have had the opportunity to present my research in numerous venues and contexts. I will not list them here, but recorded versions of many of those talks can be found on the Urban Research Theater website.

Author's Note

1. See Sarah Hammerschlag, *The Figural Jew: Politics and Identity in Postwar French Thought* (Chicago: University of Chicago Press, 2010), 89. Precedents for the lowercasing of jewishness and judaism include Rosza Daniel Lang/Levitsky, "Spilling Out Juice and Brightness," in *There Is Nothing So Whole as a Broken Heart: Mending the World as Jewish Anarchists*, ed. Cindy Milstein (Chico, CA: AK Press, 2021), 261n3; Jean François Lyotard, *Heidegger and "the jews"* (Minneapolis: University of Minnesota Press, 1990); and Albert Memmi, "Negritude and Judeity," *European Judaism: A Journal for the New Europe* 3, no. 2 (1968): 4–12. My practice of lowercasing jewishness began with Ben Spatz, "Molecular Identities: Digital Archives and Decolonial Judaism in a Laboratory of Song," *Performance Research* 24, no. 1 (2019): 66–79. Nicholas Mirzoeff, following the coinage of *latinx*, imagines the possible writing of *jewish* as *jewxsh*, the "x" implying "a crossing out, a cancellation, an erasure in the middle of a mode of identification." Nicholas Mirzoeff, "Whiteness: What Is to Be Done?," 2019 a2ru National Conference, Lawrence, University of Kansas, November 7–9, 2019, https://vimeo.com/378612639 (1:14:10–1:15:00).

2. Frank Wilderson uppercases racial categories as part of his racially structuralist project, which I critique in chapter 1. Tyrone Palmer follows Wilderson in uppercasing "Black," as well as "World," while lowercasing "white." Tiffany Lethabo King and Christina Sharpe, whose approaches resonate more closely with mine, also uppercase Black and Blackness. See Frank B. Wilderson, *Red, White & Black, Cinema and the Structure of U.S. Antagonisms* (Durham, NC: Duke University Press, 2010), 6; Tyrone S. Palmer, "Otherwise than Blackness: Feeling, World, Sublimation," *Qui Parle* 29, no. 2 (2020): 273n1; Christina Sharpe, *In the Wake: On Blackness and Being* (Durham, NC: Duke University Press, 2016); and Tiffany Lethabo King, *The Black Shoals: Offshore Formations of Black and Native Studies* (Durham, NC: Duke University Press, 2019). For a journalistic argument, see Lori L. Tharps, "The Case for Black With a Capital B," *New York Times*, November 18, 2014, https://www.nytimes.com/2014/11/19/opinion/the-case-for-black-with-a-capital-b.html.

3. One particularly resonant explanation reads as follows: "I do not typically capitalize *black* because I do not regard it as a *proper* noun. Grammatically, the proper noun corresponds to a formal name or title assigned to an individual, closed, fixed entity. I use a lowercase *b* because I want to emphasize an *improper* blackness: a blackness that is a 'critique of the proper'; a blackness that is collectivist rather than individualistic; a blackness that is 'never closed and always under contestation'; a blackness that is ever-unfurling rather than rigidly fixed; a blackness that is neither capitalized nor propertized via the protocols of Western

grammar; a blackness that centers those who are typically regarded as lesser and *lower cases*, as it were; a blackness that amplifies those who are treated as 'minor figures,' in Western modernity." La Marr Jurelle Bruce, *How to Go Mad without Losing Your Mind: Madness and Black Radical Creativity* (Durham, NC: Duke University Press, 2020), 6, italics original. See also Marquis Bey, *The Problem of the Negro as a Problem for Gender* (Minneapolis: University of Minnesota Press, 2020); Katherine McKittrick, *Dear Science and Other Stories* (Durham, NC: Duke University Press, 2021); and Alexander G. Weheliye, *Habeas Viscus: Racializing Assemblages, Biopolitics, and Black Feminist Theories of the Human* (Durham, NC: Duke University Press, 2014). Nicholas Whittaker responds to Tharps, cited in the previous note, in "Case Sensitive: Why We Shouldn't Capitalize 'Black,'" *The Drift*, no. 5, September 17, 2021, https://www.thedriftmag.com/case-sensitive/. See also Emma Dabiri, *What White People Can Do Next: From Allyship to Coalition* (London: Penguin, 2021), 65–66; and Alessandra Raengo and Lauren McLeod Cramer, "Editors' Notes," *Liquid Blackness* 5, no. 1 (2021): 1–3, https://doi.org/10.1215/26923874-8932545.

4. On lowercasing whiteness, see Robyn Wiegman's tracing of the transition from "Whiteness Studies" to "critical whiteness studies" in *Object Lessons* (Durham, NC: Duke University Press, 2012), 193; and Esther Neff, "Performing Unwhitely / Becoming Imaginary I: Theory 07/12/2016," *Medium*, November 9, 2017, https://medium.com/@esthermneff/performing-unwhitely-becoming-imaginary-part-i-theory-07-12-2016-48b04830f77d. I discuss both in chapter 2.

5. An alternative approach would be to lowercase geographical territories (the united states, also known as turtle island; israel/palestine) while uppercasing institutionalized entities (the United States and Israel as colonial and governmental institutions). This would not be out of respect for the latter, but to separate their textual institutionality from the ungovernable materialities of land and place. On the other hand, see Max Liboiron, *Pollution Is Colonialism* (Durham, NC: Duke University Press, 2021), 6–7n19.

Introduction

1. Text by Okwui Okpokwasili, transcribed from Okpokwasili and Andrew Rossi, *Bronx Gothic* (New York: Grasshopper Film, 2017), 01:07.

2. A "quintessential anti-Semite" of the 1920s, quoted in Sander L. Gilman, *The Jew's Body* (New York: Routledge, 1991), 175.

3. Melissa Blanco Borelli and Raquel Monroe, eds., "Screening the Skin: Issues of Race and Nation in Screendance," *International Journal of Screendance* 9 (2018): 1–2.

4. Diana Taylor, *The Archive and the Repertoire: Performing Cultural Memory in the Americas* (Durham, NC: Duke University Press, 2003); Tim Ingold, *The Perception of the Environment: Essays on Livelihood, Dwelling and Skill* (London: Routledge, 2000).

5. Cedric J. Robinson quoted in Robin D. G. Kelley, "'Western Civilization Is Neither': Black Studies' Epistemic Revolution," *Black Scholar* 50, no. 3 (2020): 4.

6. McKittrick, *Dear Science and Other Stories*, 71, 74.

7. McKittrick, *Dear Science and Other Stories*, 41.

8. For a conversation about the risks of nonblack people making use of black studies and black thought, see Tiffany Lethabo King's conversation with Frank

Wilderson: "Staying Ready for Black Study," in Tiffany Lethabo King, Jenell Navarro, and Andrea Smith, eds., *Otherwise Worlds: Against Settler Colonialism and Anti-Blackness* (Durham, NC: Duke University Press, 2020), 55–58.

9. Stefano Harney and Fred Moten, *The Undercommons: Fugitive Planning and Black Study* (Wivenhoe, UK: Minor Compositions, 2013); José Esteban Muñoz, *The Sense of Brown*, ed. Tavia Amolo Ochieng' Nyongó and Joshua Takano Chambers-Letson (Durham, NC: Duke University Press, 2020).

10. McKittrick, *Dear Science and Other Stories*, 65.

11. Omise'eke Natasha Tinsley, *Ezili's Mirrors: Imagining Black Queer Genders* (Durham, NC: Duke University Press, 2018), 1.

12. A. D. Carson, "Owning My Masters: The Rhetorics of Rhymes & Revolutions" (PhD diss., Clemson University, 2017), https://tigerprints.clemson.edu/all_dissertations/1885/; and *I Used to Love to Dream* (Ann Arbor: University of Michigan Press, 2020), https://doi.org/10.3998/mpub.11738372. For a discussion of the musical album in comparison to the book form, see Brigitte Fielder and Jonathan Senchyne, eds., *Against a Sharp White Background: Infrastructures of African American Print* (Madison: University of Wisconsin Press, 2019), 22–23.

13. Manning Marable, *Beyond Black and White: From Civil Rights to Barack Obama* (London: Verso Books, 2016), 111.

14. Keisha-Khan Y. Perry and Tasneem Siddiqui, "Contours, Continuities, and Evolutions in Africana Radical Thought: A Conversation with Keeanga-Yamahtta Taylor," *Black Scholar* 50, no. 3 (2020): 66, https://doi.org/10.1080/00064246.2020.1780864. Influenced by Harney and Moten's *Undercommons*, a recent petition to create a Black Study department at the University of California Riverside distinguishes Black Study from Black Studies as follows: "The UCR difference, signaled by our title Black Study, emphasizes the verb 'study' and stresses the engaged and embodied practice of this ever-morphing transformative project. The project name invokes Black Studies, UCR's short-lived department, but is a departure from it as the singular, Black Study, signifies profound shifts. Black Study is the insurgent practice (that is inevitably a theory) of curriculum, teaching, and research that is simultaneously local, communal, planetary, historical, contemporary, and futurity oriented, straddling various disciplines in the Social Sciences, Humanities, STEM, and the Arts" (petition circulated via Facebook, October 13, 2021). For a historical perspective on the radical interdisciplinarity of african american studies, see Reiland Rabaka, "24th Annual W. E. B. Du Bois Lecture," UMass Amherst Libraries, February 20, 2018, https://www.youtube.com/watch?v=6SEJoRCWLCk. With reference to Du Bois, Rabaka asserts that african american studies has never drawn sharp distinctions between the arts, humanities, and social sciences (30:30–31:00).

15. On artistic research in continental Europe, see Henk Borgdorff, *The Conflict of the Faculties: Perspectives on Artistic Research and Academia* (Leiden, Netherlands: Leiden University Press, 2012); and Michael Schwab, ed., *Experimental Systems: Future Knowledge in Artistic Research* (Leuven, Belgium: Leuven University Press, 2013). On research-creation in Canada, see Erin Manning and Brian Massumi, *Thought in the Act: Passages in the Ecology of Experience* (Minneapolis: University of Minnesota Press, 2014); and Natalie Loveless, *How to Make Art at the End of the World: A Manifesto for Research-Creation*

(Durham, NC: Duke University Press, 2019), On practice as research, increasingly called practice research, in the United Kingdom, see Ludivine Allegue et al., eds., *Practice-as-Research in Performance and Screen* (New York: Palgrave Macmillan, 2009); and Robin Nelson, *Practice as Research in the Arts: Principles, Protocols, Pedagogies, Resistances* (Basingstoke, UK: Palgrave Macmillan, 2013). On performance as research, see Shannon Rose Riley and Lynette Hunter, *Mapping Landscapes for Performance as Research: Scholarly Acts and Creative Cartographies* (Basingstoke, UK: Palgrave Macmillan, 2009); and Annette Arlander et al., eds., *Performance as Research: Knowledge, Methods, Impact* (New York: Routledge, 2017). Una Chaudhuri and Shonni Enelow, *Research Theatre, Climate Change, and the Ecocide Project* (Basingstoke, UK: Palgrave Macmillan, 2016), also describes a form of artistic research, but without reference to the above contexts. They use the term "research theatre," which I have only otherwise encountered in my own work, where I have been using it since 2004 (see chap. 3).

16. On the modern european development of the idea of the artistic work, see Lydia Goehr, *The Imaginary Museum of Musical Works: An Essay in the Philosophy of Music* (Oxford: Oxford University Press, 1992). For my previous thinking about embodied research and embodied arts, see Ben Spatz, *Blue Sky Body: Thresholds for Embodied Research* (New York: Routledge, 2020). The phrase "performing, martial, and healing arts" was suggested to me by Daniel Mroz, a theater scholar and practitioner who is also skilled in chinese martial arts. "Ritual arts" was a term used by Jerzy Grotowski; see Richard Schechner and Lisa Wolford, eds., *The Grotowski Sourcebook* (London: Routledge, 1997), 368. Sexual or erotic arts could be linked to Foucault's distinction between *ars erotica* and *scientia sexualis*.

17. Throughout this book, I use the term "culture" in the various ways that it continues to circulate across arts and humanities discourse. But when it comes to my own theorizations of the relations between knowledge and power, or technique and identity, I prefer to work with terms that emphasize the ontology and materiality of acts and practices that might otherwise be dismissed as "merely" cultural. For an anthropological perspective on the weakness of the culture concept in comparison to political ontology, see Mario Blaser, "Ontology and Indigeneity: On the Political Ontology of Heterogeneous Assemblages," *Cultural Geographies* 21, no. 1 (January 2014): 49–58, https://doi.org/10.1177/1474474012462534, and the rest of that special issue.

18. I use logocentric here to refer to the hegemony of writing, which could be seen as misuse of the term as proposed by Jacques Derrida. I explain my thinking around this intentional slippage in chapter 2.

19. Nelson, *Practice as Research in the Arts*, 106.

20. Roderick A. Ferguson, *The Reorder of Things: The University and Its Pedagogies of Minority Difference* (Minneapolis: University of Minnesota Press, 2012), 232.

21. Estelle Barrett and Barbara Bolt, eds., *Carnal Knowledge: Towards a "New Materialism" through the Arts* (London: I. B. Tauris, 2013), 4–5.

22. Henk Borgdorff, Peter Peters, and Trevor Pinch, eds., *Dialogues between Artistic Research and Science and Technology Studies* (New York: Routledge, 2020), 1.

23. Borgdorff, Peters, and Pinch, *Dialogues*, 2.

24. In this sense, the artistic research experiments I consider here should be understood in the context of debates about the future of the university; see Keri Facer and Christopher Newfield, eds., "Special Section: Global Higher Education in 2050: Building Universities for Sustainable Societies," *Critical Times* 5, no. 1 (2022).

25. On whiteness in the netherlands, see Gloria Wekker, *White Innocence: Paradoxes of Colonialism and Race* (Durham, NC: Duke University Press, 2016). On the late development of black studies in europe, see Kehinde Andrews, "The Radical 'Possibilities' of Black Studies," *Black Scholar* 50, no. 3 (2020): 17–28. On the not unrelated status of trans studies in the united kingdom, see Ezra Horbury and Christine "Xine" Yao, "Empire and Eugenics: Trans Studies in the United Kingdom," *TSQ: Transgender Studies Quarterly* 7, no. 3 (2020): 445–54, https://doi.org/10.1215/23289252-8553104.

26. Bolt in *Carnal Knowledge*, 13.

27. I want to acknowledge the relevance of feminist science studies here, including the much-cited work of Donna Haraway and Karen Barad, as well as earlier work by Sandra Harding and others. I take race rather than gender as my starting point in this book, partly as a corrective to my earlier focus on gender in *What a Body Can Do: Technique as Knowledge, Practice as Research* (London: Routledge, 2015), which I discuss further in chapter 1. For a brief discussion of how feminist epistemologies might sit "at one table" with decolonizing epistemologies, see Kimberly TallBear, *Native American DNA: Tribal Belonging and the False Promise of Genetic Science* (Minneapolis: University of Minnesota Press, 2013), 22–25; and see also McKittrick, *Dear Science and Other Stories*, 129–35.

28. Diana H. Coole and Samantha Frost in *New Materialisms: Ontology, Agency, and Politics* (Durham, NC: Duke University Press, 2010), 9.

29. For example, see Rick Dolphijn and Iris van der Tuin, *New Materialism: Interviews and Cartographies* (Ann Arbor, MI: Open Humanities Press, 2012), 16. On the other hand, see José Muñoz's discussion of Jane Bennett, Graham Harman, and Timothy Morton in Muñoz, *Sense of Brown*, 4–7.

30. Wilderson and King, "Staying Ready for Black Study: A Conversation," in King, Navarro, and Smith, *Otherwise Worlds*, 58. For a more extended consideration of related critiques of postdeleuzian theory, see the third section of chapter 1: "Thinking the Molecular."

31. Borgdorff, *Conflict of the Faculties*, 161, 179.

32. Aruna D'Souza, *Whitewalling: Art, Race & Protest in 3 Acts* (New York: Badlands Unlimited, 2018), 9.

33. D'Souza, *Whitewalling*, 35.

34. I consider the mechanism of "inclusion" further in chapter 2, via Sara Ahmed's work.

35. Janelle G. Reinelt, "Is Performance Studies Imperialist? Part 2," *TDR: The Drama Review* 51, no. 3 (2007): 8, italics original. See also Stephanie Nohelani Teves, "The Theorist and the Theorized: Indigenous Critiques of Performance Studies," *TDR: The Drama Review* 62, no. 4 (2018): 131–40. For a related discussion about the more recent development of "performance philosophy," see Laura Cull Ó Maoilearca and Alice Lagaay, eds., *The Routledge Companion to Performance Philosophy* (Abingdon, UK: Routledge, 2020), 12–13.

36. Paula Kramer and Stephanie Misa, "Artistic Research as a Tool of Critique," *Nivel–Artistic Research in the Performing Arts* 10 (2019), https://nivel.teak.fi/adie/artistic-research-as-a-tool-of-critique/.

37. Sarah E. Truman, "The Intimacies of Doing Research-Creation: Sarah E. Truman in Conversation with Natalie Loveless, Erin Manning, Natasha Myers, and Stephanie Springgay," in *Knowings and Knots: Methodologies and Ecologies in Research-Creation*, ed. Nathalie Loveless (Edmonton: University of Alberta Press, 2019): 221–49.

38. Loveless in Truman, "Intimacies of Doing Research-Creation," 225–26. See also Loveless, *How to Make Art at the End of the World*.

39. Ferguson, *Reorder of Things*, 18.

40. Zakiyyah Iman Jackson, *Becoming Human: Matter and Meaning in an Antiblack World* (New York: New York University Press, 2020), 4, 35.

41. Manola K. Gayatri, "PAR and decolonization: Notemakings from an Indian and South African context," in Annette Arlander et al., *Performance as Research*, 170–84. My own contribution to this book, "Mad Lab: Or Why We Can't Do Practice as Research" (209–23) challenges practitioner-researchers to grapple with a definition of "practice" that embraces longer durations and deeper kinships than the university in its present form can recognize.

42. Juan Manuel Aldape Muñoz, "Violence and Performance Research Methods: Direct-action, 'Die-ins,' and Allyship in a Black Lives Matter Era," in Arlander et al., *Performance as Research*, 317. See also Muñoz's careful critique of "practice as research" and of my own proposal for "embodied research" (314–16).

43. Muñoz, "Violence and Performance Research Methods," 331.

44. Initial call: https://www.facebook.com/artsresearchafrica/posts/66293960 7555107 (July 11, 2019). Conference proceedings: Arts Research Africa, *How Does Artistic Research Decolonise Knowledge and Practice in Africa?* (Johannesburg: University of the Witwatersrand, 2020), http://wiredspace.wits.ac.za/handle/10539/29181.

45. Christo Doherty, introduction to Arts Research Africa, *How Does Artistic Research Decolonise*, iii.

46. Brett Pyper, "Artistic Research and African Musical Performance: Listening Beyond Euro-American Canons," in Arts Research Africa, *How Does Artistic Research Decolonise*, 25.

47. Berhanu Ashagrie Deribew, "Closing Address," in Arts Research Africa, *How Does Artistic Research Decolonise*, 337.

48. Samuel Ravengai, "Artistic Research in Africa with Specific Reference to South Africa and Zimbabwe: Formulating the Theory of Afroscenology," in Arts Research Africa, *How Does Artistic Research Decolonise*, 56.

49. See Walter Mignolo, *The Darker Side of Western Modernity: Global Futures, Decolonial Options* (Durham, NC: Duke University Press, 2011); and Walter D. Mignolo and Catherine E. Walsh, *On Decoloniality: Concepts, Analytics, Praxis* (Durham, NC: Duke University Press, 2018).

50. Foluke Ifejola Adebisi, "Why I Say 'Decolonisation is Impossible'," *African Skies* blog, https://folukeafrica.com/why-i-say-decolonisation-is-impossible/ (December 17, 2019).

51. On the problem of metaphor, see Eve Tuck and K. Wayne Yang, "Decolonization Is Not a Metaphor," *Decolonization: Indigeneity, Education & Society* 1,

no. 1 (2012): 1–40. For a helpful reflection on the context and trajectory of this much-cited article, see the opening discussion in "A Third University Is Always Happening: A Conversation with K. Wayne Yang," *Nothing Never Happens* podcast, June 17, 2020, https://nothingneverhappens.org/uncategorized/decolonizing -universities-part-one-of-a-conversation-with-k-wayne-yang/.

52. Both Borgdorff and Ferguson, in the works cited above, take Kant's 1798 *Conflict of the Faculties* as a reference point for their respective treatments of artistic research and identity-based interdisciplines as epistemic incursions into the university.

53. *Another Europe Is Possible*, "Episode 37: Priyamvada Gopal on a Decolonised Europe: Saving Europe from Itself," podcast, October 7, 2019, https:// www.anothereurope.org/episode-37-priyamvada-gopal-on-a-decolonial-europe -saving-europe-from-itself/. See also Priyamvada Gopal, *Insurgent Empire: Anticolonial Resistance and British Dissent* (London: Verso, 2019). For another perspective on decolonization within europe, see Social Science Research / University of Amsterdam, "Decolonising Europe #13: Decolonising Queerness," podcast, March 18, 2021, https://www.youtube.com/watch?v=-ik0QM5QF5Q. In this podcast Sandeep Bakshi discusses "decolonial aesthesis": "What has been conventionally regarded has cultural practice has often ended up in the terrain of non-knowledge. [This is] something that obviously, as we understand today, enacts epistemic violence against knowledge-producing formations from outside Europe that have somehow sneaked their way into Europe" (20:00). See also, in the same episode, Sarah Bracke's comment about the ongoing challenge of recognizing art as knowledge producing while working in the social sciences (25:05).

54. Priyamvada Gopal, "On Decolonisation and the University," *Textual Practice* 35, no. 6 (2021): 876.

55. D'Souza, *Whitewalling*, 37. For an earlier work focusing on dance and performing arts, see Brenda Dixon Gottschild, *Digging the Africanist Presence in American Performance: Dance and Other Contexts* (Westport, CT: Praeger, 1998). As Gottschild observes: "So much of what we see as avant-garde in the postmodern era is informed by recycled Africanist principles" (50).

56. Arts Research Africa, *How Does Artistic Research Decolonise*, 25, italics added.

57. Kelley, "Western Civilization Is Neither," 4.

58. Ferguson, *Reorder of Things*, 214.

59. Ferguson, *Reorder of Things*, 105. The politics of (black) methodology are taken up even more explicitly by McKittrick in *Dear Science and Other Stories*.

60. Saidiya V. Hartman and Frank B. Wilderson, "The Position of the Unthought," *Qui Parle* 13, no. 2 (2003): 198–99, italics original.

61. Hartman and Wilderson, "Position of the Unthought," 199.

62. On the entanglement of antifatness (fatphobia, fatmisia, sizeism) with antiblackness, see Sabrina Strings, *Fearing the Black Body: The Racial Origins of Fat Phobia* (New York: New York University Press, 2019); and Da'Shaun Harrison, *Belly of the Beast: The Politics of Anti-Fatness as Anti-Blackness* (Berkeley, CA: North Atlantic Books, 2021). On class as a particularly "unwieldy object of intersectional study," see Matt Brim, *Poor Queer Studies: Confronting Elitism in the University* (Durham, NC: Duke University Press, 2020), 101.

63. McKittrick, *Dear Science and Other Stories*, 72. The one doing the urging here seems to be Sylvia Wynter, although McKittrick invokes her here without naming her, almost as a figure or incarnation of radical black thought. Sources linking similar arguments to indigenous thought are cited below and in later chapters.

64. Caroline Randall Williams, "You Want a Confederate Monument? My Body Is a Confederate Monument," *New York Times*, June 26, 2020, https://www.nytimes.com/2020/06/26/opinion/confederate-monuments-racism.html.

65. Kesha Fikes, "'Extimacy' as Racial Transparency in the Embodied Relational Field," Embodied Social Justice Summit, February 16–20, 2021, https://www.embodiedsocialjusticesummit.com. On the daily embodiment of identity, see also Alexis Shotwell, *Knowing Otherwise: Race, Gender, and Implicit Understanding* (University Park: Penn State University Press, 2012).

66. Sharpe, *In the Wake*, 21–22.

67. Weheliye, *Habeas Viscus*, 127–32. Weheliye here critiques and extends Giorgio Agamben's work on the nazi concentration camp as a paradigmatic place of death. I consider the relationship between black and jewish histories, politics, and ontologies in chapter 3.

68. King, *Black Shoals*, 200. I return to King's concept of ceremony in the afterword.

69. This book is especially informed by recent critical works that attempt to think through black and indigenous relationality in north america, including King, *Black Shoals*; King, Navarro, and Smith, *Otherwise Worlds*; and Mark Rifkin, *Fictions of Land and Flesh: Blackness, Indigeneity, Speculation* (Durham, NC: Duke University Press, 2019). These vital conversations are the framing context within which I have investigated whiteness, jewishness, and the racialization of knowledge.

70. My undergraduate thesis, written twenty years ago, already attempted to read Deleuze and Guattari against the afrofuturism of Kodwo Eshun and Rammellzee. That project began a theorization of "tech" that has continued throughout all my work, up to and including this book. It also took the form of a written thesis accompanied by a playscript and theatrical production, enacting something like artistic research long before I knew that term. Ben Spatz, "The Electronic Heart" (BA thesis, Wesleyan University, 2001).

71. Dylan Robinson, *Hungry Listening: Resonant Theory for Indigenous Sound Studies* (Minneapolis: University of Minnesota Press, 2020).

72. Martin Buber retells a hasidic tale: "After about an hour he saw how the boy first turned himself restlessly, then how, still steeped in slumber, he seized the page, and finally how, as if held by mighty hands, he buried himself in the writings aided by the gleam of a small oil light. To the onlooker it was as if the room became brighter and larger while the boy read." Martin Buber, *The Legend of the Baal-Shem* (London: Routledge, 2002), 58. The difference between fervent and hungry reading is powerfully evoked in this story, "The Prince of Fire."

73. Institutionally, there are similarities as well as differences between University of Huddersfield and the College of Staten Island, as described by Matt Brim, where I have also taught. See Brim, *Poor Queer Studies*.

Chapter 1

1. Ariane Mnouchkine, Joëlle Gayot, and Nora Armani, "Cultures Are Not Anyone's Property," *PAJ: A Journal of Performance and Art* 41, no. 3 (2019): 65–70.

2. Mnouchkine, Gayot, and Armani, "Cultures Are Not Anyone's Property," 65. For summaries of the controversy around *Kanata*, see Laura Cappelle, "Review: In Robert Lepage's 'Kanata,' the Director, Too, Plays the Victim," *New York Times*, December 17, 2018, https://www.nytimes.com/2018/12/17 /theater/robert-lepage-kanata-review.html; and Lily Climenhaga, "The Power of Presence: Indigenous Representation in Theatre, Reflections on Mnouchkine/ Lepage, Kanata, and Colonial Remains," *Lost Dramaturgin International*, September 9, 2018, https://lostdramaturgininternational.wordpress.com/2018/09 /09/the-power-of-presence-indigenous-representation-in-theatre-reflections-on -mnouchkine-lepage-kanata-and-colonial-remains/.

3. Mnouchkine, Gayot, and Armani, "Cultures Are Not Anyone's Property," 66.

4. Mnouchkine, Gayot, and Armani, "Cultures Are Not Anyone's Property," 67–69. As Cappelle notes: "The French director's stance isn't unusual in her country, where the notion of cultural appropriation isn't widely recognized" ("Review: In Robert Lepage's 'Kanata' "). This is then also a conversation about how the history and legacies of colonialism are understood differently across european and north american geographies. Moreover, the reference by a french artist to the nazis and the jewish holocaust is salient, as the redirection of concerns about racism via references to antisemitism is an increasingly prevalent right-wing political strategy today. For an even more oppressively reductive reading of the issues surrounding the *Kanata* project, see Michel Vaïs, "Lepage and Mnouchkine Collide with Cultural Appropriation," *PAJ: A Journal of Performance and Art*, no. 123 (2019): 71–74.

5. The concept of immunity is developed further below, via Christopher Miller's critique of Deleuze and Guattari's nomadology, which bears striking resemblance to the claims of depoliticized artistic research.

6. Quoted in Marianne Ackerman, "Robert Lepage's Controversial Kanata Opens in Paris as a Rehearsal," *Montreal Gazette*, December 20, 2018, https:// montrealgazette.com/entertainment/local-arts/robert-lepages-controversial -kanata-opens-in-paris-as-a-rehearsal. The original open letter is here: "Encore une fois, l'aventure se passera sans nous, les Autochtones?," *Le Devoir*, July 14, 2018, https://www.ledevoir.com/opinion/libre-opinion/532406/encore-une-fois -l-aventure-se-passera-sans-nous-les-autochtones.

7. While my focus here is on theater and dance, my critique of the "work" concept owes much to Lydia Goehr's history of the invention of musical works, which I extend to a more general critique of white logocentrism in chapter 2. See Goehr, *Imaginary Museum of Musical Works*.

8. I am thinking here of how Matt Damon drew such a line when declaring that diversity in his *Project Greenlight* should apply only to the casting of performers and not to that of directors, saying: "When we're talking about diversity, you do it in the casting of the film, not in the casting of the show." Even more blatantly, the artistic director of a regional performing arts series moved to contain the work of an indigenous artist by declaring: "My idea of social justice is onstage."

Such examples reveal how the structural or methodological division between producers/directors and artists/performers maps onto hegemonies of power. Ellie Harrison, "'I Spoke Up and Got Smacked Down': Producer Effie Brown Recalls Backlash after Her Conflict with Matt Damon over Diversity Went Viral," *Independent*, June 19, 2020, https://www.independent.co.uk/arts-entertainment /tv/news/matt-damon-effie-brown-project-greenlight-diversity-racism-a9574521 .html; Brian Seibert, "A Rift over Art and Activism Ripples through the Performance World," *New York Times*, March 12, 2021, https://www.nytimes.com /2021/03/12/arts/dance/peak-performances-emily-johnson.html.

9. For a concrete example and discussion of how the casting paradigm blocks change, see Lilian Mengesha, "Being and Whiteness: Settler Possession and Performative Wokeness in *The Thanksgiving Play*," *Journal of Dramatic Theory and Criticism* 35, no. 2 (2021): 39–52. While Mengesha's focus is on "the overreliance on representation as equity" (41–42), she concludes by pointing to a future in which "what we call 'theatre' might be entirely unrecognizable" (50). As I have argued elsewhere, moving beyond the casting paradigm invites a radical dismantling of logocentric theatrical forms. See Ben Spatz, "Notes for Decolonizing Embodiment," *Journal of Dramatic Theory and Criticism* 33, no. 2 (2019): 9–22. For a set of related examples in the visual arts, where the politics of representation unfolds through many of the same tropes and tensions despite there being no explicit process of casting, see D'Souza, *Whitewalling*.

10. Wikipedia, s.v. "Casting," last accessed August 12th, 2023, https://en .wikipedia.org/wiki/Casting.

11. Angela C. Pao, *No Safe Spaces: Re-Casting Race, Ethnicity, and Nationality in American Theater* (Ann Arbor: University of Michigan Press, 2010), 23.

12. Amanda Rogers and Ashley Thorpe, "A Controversial Company: Debating the Casting of the RSC's *The Orphan of Zhao*," *Contemporary Theatre Review* 24, no. 4 (2014): 429–30.

13. For the latter, see Youssef Kerkour, "Letter to Malcolm Sinclair, Equity, from *The Orphan of Zhao* Company," *Contemporary Theatre Review* 24, no. 4 (2014): 494–95. Another relevant perspective is Jennifer Kidwell, "Performance and Para-Fiction: Jennifer Kidwell on Playing Donelle Woolford," *Hyperallergic*, December 23, 2014, https://hyperallergic.com/170408/performance-and-para -fiction-jennifer-kidwell-on-playing-donelle-woolford/, originally published in *Movement Research Performance Journal*. For a scholarly study that highlights the complexity of identity formation in long-term actor training processes, see Cláudia Tatinge Nascimento, *Crossing Cultural Borders through the Actor's Work: Foreign Bodies of Knowledge* (New York: Routledge, 2009).

14. Brandi Wilkins Catanese, *The Problem of the Color[blind]: Racial Transgression and the Politics of Black Performance* (Ann Arbor: University of Michigan Press, 2014), 23.

15. Catanese, *Problem of the Color[blind]*, 12.

16. Brian Massumi, *Parables for the Virtual: Movement, Affect, Sensation* (Durham, NC: Duke University Press, 2002), 2–3. Richard Schechner's famous "not not" is an early formulation evoking the conundrum posed to actual identity by the census epistemology. "Olivier is not Hamlet, but also he is not not Hamlet: his performance is between a denial of being another (= I am me) and a denial of not being another (= I am Hamlet). Performer training focuses its techniques not on

making one person into another, but in permitting the performer to act in-between identities." Richard Schechner, "Performers and Spectators Transported and Transformed," *Kenyon Review* 3, no. 4 (1981): 88. This formulation prefigures Kara Keeling's "I = Another: Digital Identity Politics," in *Strange Affinities: The Gender and Sexual Politics of Comparative Racialization*, ed. Grace Kyungwon Hong and Roderick A. Ferguson (Durham, NC: Duke University Press, 2011).

17. Asad Haider, *Mistaken Identity: Race and Class in the Age of Trump* (London: Verso, 2018), 11, 23. Haider writes against identity from a racialized position, as do Kwame Anthony Appiah, in *The Lies that Bind: Rethinking Identity, Creed, Country, Color, Class, Culture* (New York: Liveright, 2018); and Paul Gilroy, in *Against Race: Imagining Political Culture beyond the Color Line* (Cambridge, MA: Belknap Press of Harvard University Press, 2001). For responses to Gilroy, see Sara Ahmed, *On Being Included: Racism and Diversity in Institutional Life* (Durham, NC: Duke University Press, 2012), 219n16; and McKittrick, *Dear Science and Other Stories*, 39–40n15.

18. Bey, *Problem of the Negro*, 22. "Black is . . . an' black ain't" is a quotation from Ralph Ellison's novel, *Invisible Man.* Elsewhere, Alessandra Raengo describes black liquidity as both "the ability for blackness to travel on its own, separate from black people" and "blackness as lived in the body." And R. A. Judy writes: "While indissolubly associated with Negro embodiment, *poiēsis in black* as semiosis is not identical with black people, even though it indisputably belongs with them." There are parallels with Sarah Hammerschlag's analysis of the "figural jew," which I address in chapter 3. See Alessandra Raengo, "Blackness, Aesthetics, Liquidity" (Atlanta: Georgia State University, 2014), 6; R. A. Judy, *Sentient Flesh: Thinking in Disorder, Poiēsis in Black* (Durham, NC: Duke University Press, 2020), xix; and Hammerschlag, *Figural Jew.*

19. Jared Sexton, *Amalgamation Schemes: Antiblackness and the Critique of Multiracialism* (Minneapolis: University of Minnesota Press, 2008), 43–55.

20. Sexton, *Amalgamation Schemes*, 12.

21. Note also that "colorblind" is an ableist appropriation of a physiological impairment.

22. Denise Ferreira da Silva, *Toward a Global Idea of Race* (Minneapolis: University of Minnesota Press, 2007), 250.

23. Sexton, *Amalgamation Schemes*, 11.

24. Ferguson, *The Reorder of Things*, 105–6.

25. Dorinne K. Kondo, *Worldmaking: Race, Performance, and the Work of Creativity* (Durham, NC: Duke University Press, 2018), 25.

26. Kondo, *Worldmaking*, 140. Throughout this book, I use the terms "technique" and "knowledge" almost as synonyms, but with differing connotations. Knowledge is a broader concept in philosophy, but is unfortunately narrowed when it is equated with writing. I use technique to underscore how knowledge, as *ways* of doing and being, extends far beyond the technology of writing.

27. Kondo, *Worldmaking*, 45, italics original.

28. Kondo, *Worldmaking*, 12, 54. This argument, for Kondo, works to "pull aesthetic transcendence back to earth" (55). I take up the concept of grounding or *earthing* at the end of this book.

29. Kondo, *Worldmaking*, 40, 42. A comparison to indigenous "tribally driven participatory research" as a method of decolonizing research is not unwarranted.

If "tribal government agencies and institutions increasingly perform their own research and maintain the power to invite university or industry collaborators to participate" (TallBear, *Native American DNA*, 21), the position of the dramaturg within an artist-led process likewise reverses the conventional power dynamic between scholar and artist. I do not mean to equate these very different situations, but to observe parallel methodological transformations unfolding in different fields.

30. Kondo, *Worldmaking*, 132, italics original. Agonistic relations are contrasted here with antagonistic ones, following the work of Chantal Mouffe (138). On antagonistic relations, see also my discussion of Frank Wilderson's work, below.

31. Kondo, *Worldmaking*, 138.

32. As quoted in the introduction, Kesha Fikes defines extimacy as "racial transparency." I am shifting from transparency to *transparencing* here to acknowledge the processual and provisional nature of such processes, which might aim to work through the racial dynamics of a given moment or encounter but which can never bring race to a final state of transparency.

33. Kondo, *Worldmaking*, 148, 153. I focus on critical whiteness studies in chapter 2.

34. Kondo, *Worldmaking*, 84.

35. Kondo, *Worldmaking*, 97–129. The work in development is *Twilight: Los Angeles* (1994).

36. Kondo, *Worldmaking*, 108.

37. Kondo, *Worldmaking*, 233.

38. Kondo, *Worldmaking*, 236.

39. Katherine Profeta, *Dramaturgy in Motion: At Work on Dance and Movement Performance* (Madison: University of Wisconsin Press, 2015), 168.

40. Profeta, *Dramaturgy in Motion*, 63, xi.

41. A chronology of Lemon's works is provided by the Wikipedia page. Notably, all the works are listed there as having start dates but no dates of completion: *Geography* 1997–; *Tree* 2000–; *Come Home Charley Patton* 2004–; and *How Can you Stay in the House all Day and Not Go Anywhere* 2010–.

42. Profeta, *Dramaturgy in Motion*, 204–5.

43. Profeta, *Dramaturgy in Motion*, 205.

44. Profeta, *Dramaturgy in Motion*, 74.

45. Profeta, *Dramaturgy in Motion*, 205.

46. Kondo, *Worldmaking*, 4.

47. My discussion here resonates with ongoing work on concepts of performativity and the performative in performance studies, as demonstrated in a recent panel discussion called "re: PERFORMATIVE" that took place at the annual conference of the Association for Theatre in Higher Education (August 8, 2021) with Enzo Vasquez Toral, Taylor Black, Michelle Liu Carriger, and James McMaster. But performativity, following the work of Judith Butler and J. L. Austin, remains grounded in a notion of *speech acts* that must be radicalized through a more materialist understanding of embodiment and identity. See also the special section "#PerformativeX," edited by Carriger, in *Journal of Dramatic Theory* 35, no. 2 (2021).

48. Jasbir K. Puar, *Terrorist Assemblages: Homonationalism in Queer Times* (Durham, NC: Duke University Press, 2017), 212. Massumi and Puar rely heavily

on the work of Deleuze and Guattari to rethink the politics of identity, which they formulate in terms of affect and assemblage. Because my aim here is not primarily to compare their approaches with that of intersectionality, but rather to lay groundwork for my own thinking about molecular identity, I hold off on a direct engagement with Deleuze and Guattari until the next section.

49. Tiffany Lethabo King, "Post-Identitarian and Post-Intersectional Anxiety in the Neoliberal Corporate University," *Feminist Formations* 27, no. 3 (2015): 127.

50. King, "Post-Identitarian," 130.

51. For an attempt to work through theories of racialization within the discipline of anthropology, which at the same time reveals the great distance between anthropology and cultural studies (to say nothing of sociology and black studies), see Didier Fassin, "Racialization: How to Do Races with Bodies," in *A Companion to the Anthropology of the Body and Embodiment*, ed. Frances E. Mascia-Lees (Malden, MA: Blackwell Publishing, 2011), 419–34.

52. I first connected intersectionality with radical interdisciplinarity in the essay "Thresholds" in Spatz, *Blue Sky Body*, 1–56. For introductions to intersectionality, see Anna Carastathis, *Intersectionality: Origins, Contestations, Horizons* (Lincoln: University of Nebraska Press, 2016); Ange-Marie Hancock, *Intersectionality: An Intellectual History* (New York: Oxford University Press, 2016); and Jennifer C. Nash, *Black Feminism Reimagined: After Intersectionality* (Durham, NC: Duke University Press, 2019). Nash underscores the point, central to my argument, that "'who people are' can never be understood apart from 'the way things work,' despite the insistance of [some] scholarship that these two categories are distinct" (75).

53. Rosamond S. King, "Radical Interdisciplinarity: A New Iteration of a Woman of Color Methodology," *Meridians: Feminism, Race, Transnationalism* 18, no. 2 (2019): 447. Thanks to Brandi Catanese for sharing this article with me.

54. King, "Radical Interdisciplinarity," 446, 448, 449. Gloria Anzaldúa's *autohistorias* and Audre Lorde's biomythography are two well-known precedents that King names.

55. King, "Radical Interdisciplinarity," 450.

56. Something like this imbrication of knowledge and power was influentially formulated by Michel Foucault, whose work has informed my own prior writing. But in the present context Foucault's *power-knowledge* is not as capable a tool as the intersectional interdisciplinarity of black studies. Perhaps because of his eurocentrism, Foucault's work never moves beyond subsuming one or the other term within the other. Broadly speaking, Foucault's early and better-known work shows how knowledges, as in the discursive formulations of law and medicine and the academic disciplines that underpin them, are operations of power. His later work on "technologies of the self" moves toward a different articulation of knowledge and power, but this is never effectively reconciled with his earlier work on how the body is inscribed by power. From Foucault we can understand that the "docile" body is always also a body that creates itself through techniques of the self, as demonstrated by the double-edged meaning of terms like "power," "knowledge," and "discipline." But we are left with few tools by which to undertake experimental practice in the disarticulation of such terms. For a discussion of Foucault's limitations, see Denise Ferreira da Silva, "Before *Man*: Sylvia Wynter's

Rewriting of the Modern Episteme," in Katherine McKittrick, ed., *Sylvia Wynter: On Being Human as Praxis* (Durham, NC: Duke University Press, 2015).

57. On land as knowledge, see Leanne Betasamosake Simpson, "Land as Pedagogy: Nishnaabeg Intelligence and Rebellious Transformation," *Decolonization: Indigeneity, Education & Society* 3, no. 3 (2014): 1–25.

58. These passages are quoted and discussed in Spatz, *What a Body Can Do*, 51–52. The same distinction is repeated frequently in contemporary debates about identity and solidarity. As R. L. Stephens writes in *Jacobin*: "Solidarity is about what you do, not who you are" (https://www.jacobinmag.com/2016/07 /left-class-racism-identity-struggle-oppression). But this division does not hold up: Who you are structures what you can do; what you do gradually becomes who you are. For a discussion of how Bourdieu's sharp distinction between conscious and tacit knowledge reflects colonial divisions between types of knowers, see Mahmut Mutman, *The Politics of Writing Islam: Voicing Difference* (London: Bloomsbury, 2015), 59–72.

59. Spatz, *What a Body Can Do*, 1, 44.

60. Spatz, *What a Body Can Do*, 51.

61. Spatz, *What a Body Can Do*, chap. 4.

62. For a careful examination of the transrace identification of Nkechi Amare Diallo, formerly known as Rachel Dolezal, see Aniruddha Dutta, "Allegories of Gender: Transgender Autology versus Transracialism," *Atlantis Journal* 39, no. 2 (2018): 86–98. Dutta uses "'transrace' instead of the more usual adjective 'transracial' in order to disambiguate [this] usage from the sense of 'transracial' as pertaining to cross-racial adoptees" (95n1). The generative risk taken by Marquis Bey's formulation of blackness and trans in the same terms is precisely to render race, and specifically blackness, in the more fluid and unknowable terms that have previously been attached to gender. These interventions are deeply informed by critical race studies and black feminist theory and deserve to be taken seriously even by those who might dismiss the comparable arguments of an analytical philosopher like Rebecca Tuvel or a sociologist like Rogers Brubaker. See Marquis Bey, "Incorporeal Blackness: A Theorization in Two Parts—Rachel Dolezal and Your Face in Mine," *CR: The New Centennial Review* 20, no. 2 (2020): 205–41; Marquis Bey and Theodora Sakellarides, "When We Enter: The Blackness of Rachel Dolezal," *Black Scholar* 46, no. 4 (2016): 33–48; as well as Kai M. Green, "'Race and Gender Are Not the Same!' Is Not a Good Response to the 'Transracial'/Transgender Question OR We Can and Must Do Better," *Feminist Wire*, June 14, 2015, https://www.thefeministwire.com/2015/06/race-and-gender-are -not-the-same-is-not-a-good-response-to-the-transracial-transgender-question-or -we-can-and-must-do-better/.

63. In *What a Body Can Do* I touch briefly on race through Harvey Young's concept of a "black habitus" (175). I also take jewishness as my initial point of departure for thinking identity as technique (171), planting a seed that I develop further in chap. 3 of this volume. I do refer to unequal power relations throughout that book. Nevertheless, *What a Body Can Do* offers a theory of radical interdisciplinarity without intersectionality.

64. Here my project chimes with that of Soyica Diggs Colbert, Douglas A. Jones Jr., and Shane Vogel in the edited volume *Race and Performance after Repetition* (Durham, NC: Duke University Press, 2020). My concept of technique

has always linked repetition to knowledge, or deleuzian "generality," rather than reducing it to a matter of ideology and resistance ("Introduction: Tidying Up after Repetition," 12). Joining technique to identity (and eventually to place) is another way of moving beyond repetition: "rather than understanding race and performance as constituted by repetition, [to] deem repetition to be constituted by race and performance" (13). Many of the examples discussed in that volume's introductory essay also foreground the power of *place* as that which grounds and enables repetition in this broader sense.

65. Nina Sun Eidsheim, *The Race of Sound: Listening, Timbre, and Vocality in African American Music* (Durham, NC: Duke University Press, 2019), 55, italics added.

66. Eidsheim, *The Race of Sound*, 197.

67. Eidsheim, *The Race of Sound*, 40, 49.

68. Eidsheim, *The Race of Sound*, 172, 174–57. The latter is a quotation from Emily J. Lordi.

69. Through the seventeenth-century poet Tukaram, Eidsheim likens the experience of open-ended embodied research to being "mingled with the sky" (189). I have explored similar imagery in relation to "blue skies research" (*What a Body Can Do*, 219) and the "blue sky body" (*Blue Sky Body*, xiii–xxi).

70. Eidsheim, *Race of Sound*, 63.

71. Eidsheim, *Race of Sound*, 154. A footnote here cites Eric Lott and Daphne Brooks as scholars who have worked on the cultural appropriation of blackness, but leaves these issues to be addressed in future writing.

72. Eidsheim, *Race of Sound*, 168–69.

73. Eidsheim, *Race of Sound*, 185.

74. "Look, a negro!" Frantz Fanon, *Black Skin, White Masks* (London: Pluto Press, 2008), 82.

75. Eidsheim, *Race of Sound*, 187–88.

76. Keeanga-Yamahtta Taylor, *From #BlackLivesMatter to Black Liberation* (Chicago: Haymarket Books, 2016), 147.

77. Eidsheim, *Race of Sound*, 191. The importance of motherhood here, and the question of how motherhood does or does not resonate across racial divisions, links this example to the controversy around Diana Schutz's painting of Emmett Till, discussed by D'Souza in the first act/chapter of *Whitewalling*.

78. I am thinking here again of Asad Haider, Anthony Appiah, and Paul Gilroy, cited above; see also Bey, *Problem of the Negro*; and Michelle M. Wright, *Physics of Blackness: Beyond the Middle Passage Epistemology* (Minneapolis: University of Minnesota Press, 2015).

79. For an important discussion of how notions of pure sound are deployed in whiteness and support white ontologies, see Marie Thompson, "Whiteness and the Ontological Turn in Sound Studies," *Parallax* 23, no. 3 (2017): 266–82, https://doi.org/10.1080/13534645.2017.1339967. Thompson's critique of "white aurality" necessarily complicates any attempts to escape from racialization into pure sound or vibration.

80. Wilderson, *Red, White & Black*, ix.

81. Linette Park, "Afropessimism and Futures of . . . : A Conversation with Frank Wilderson," *Black Scholar* 50, no. 3 (2020): 29.

82. Wilderson: "I began to understand that inaugural division is not between genders, not between classes, but between humans and blacks." In Park, "Afropessimism and Futures," 31.

83. Wilderson, *Red, White & Black*, 27, 52. Wilderson draws heavily on Hartman's *Scenes of Subjection: Terror, Slavery, and Self-Making in Nineteenth-Century America* (New York: Oxford University Press, 1997) to emphasize the questionable status of performance under conditions of slavery. But Hartman's account is much more ambiguous than Wilderson's. Whereas Wilderson reads Hartman's critique of easy celebration as demonstrating the absolute impossibility of joy and empathy under conditions of subjection, for Hartman, in contrast, song, dance, joy, and empathy are distinctly double edged (17–78). This double-edged quality is further emphasized in a new preface to the twenty-fifth anniversary edition of *Scenes*, where Hartman underscores her original intent "to account for extreme domination *and* the possibilities seized in practice." There she criticizes the extent to which a focus on her book's "arguments about empathy, terror and violence, subjection, and social death has overshadowed the discussion of practice." Saidiya Hartman, "The Hold of Slavery" (2022), https://illwill.com/print/the-hold-of-slavery, italics original.

84. Wilderson, *Red, White & Black*, 31. Wilderson explains his orthographic choices: "I capitalize the words *Red, White, Black, Slave, Savage,* and *Human* in order to assert their importance as ontological positions and to stress the value of theorizing power politically rather than culturally. . . . Capitalizing these words is consistent with my argument that the array of identities that they contain is important but inessential to an analysis of the paradigm of power in which they are positioned" (23–24). As indicated in my prefatory note on lowercasing, I take the opposite approach here. I do this precisely in order to avoid such a bifurcation between two different levels of identification, what Wilderson calls the "political" or "ontological" and the "cultural" or "inessential."

85. Wilderson, *Red, White & Black*, 29.

86. Wilderson, *Red, White & Black*, 58–59. For a discussion that situates afropessimism in the broader context of black studies, see "Afropessimism and Its Others: A Discussion between Hortense J. Spillers and Lewis R. Gordon," Soka University of America, Alisa Viejo, CA, May 24, 2021, https://www.youtube.com/watch?v=Z-s-Ltu06NI. I would add that, while there is much to be learned from the thought experiment of equating blackness with pure abjection, the evident parallels with certain earlier turns in feminist and jewish politics strengthen my courage to critique Wilderson's work. Both as an antizionist jew (see chap. 3) and as someone of non-binary gender who has always had a complex relationship with trans-exclusionary "radical feminist" (TERF) polemics, I am keenly aware of the dangers that attend the reduction/elevation of any identity position to the status of paradigmatic abjection. Wilderson compares his argument to the marxist feminism of Leopoldina Fortunati, dismissing the "lame libidinal economy" of Betty Friedan and Gloria Steinem (135). But the "unflinching" feminism to which Wilderson's work should be compared is that of Andrea Dworkin, whose writing is similarly compelling and problematic. Indeed, Wilderson's racial-structuralist analysis of cinema as merely expressive and never transformative of racial ontologies is closely analogous to Dworkin and Catharine MacKinnon's well-known gender-structuralist account of pornography as merely expressive and never transformative of gender.

87. Wilderson, *Red, White & Black*, 194.

88. Wilderson, *Red, White & Black*, 357n1.

89. Wilderson, *Red, White & Black*, 45.

90. *Always Already Podcast*, "Interview: Frank B. Wilderson III on Afropessimism: Epistemic Unruliness 28," May 11, 2020, https://alwaysalreadypodcast .wordpress.com/2020/05/11/wilderson-interview/ (1:04:35). See also Wilderson, *Red, White & Black* (48), where Wilderson rejects methodological approaches that "might clarify the historical record at the expense of mystifying paradigmatic relations of power."

91. Wilderson, *Red, White & Black*, 59. Tyrone S. Palmer extends Wilderson's argument and similarly takes particular issue with the claim that artmaking practices have the capacity to intervene meaningfully or materially in the world. In an article framed as a critique of affect theory, Palmer's most focused criticism lands on black performance theorists who "hold that the transformative power of performance ceaselessly creates 'new worlds' that resist and escape the enclosure of anti-Black violence." For Palmer, as for Wilderson, no such power can touch the "brutal facticity" of antiblackness as absolute structure. These are effectively arguments against the possibility of artistic research. See Palmer, "Otherwise than Blackness," 278n63, 264.

92. *Always Already Podcast*, "Interview: Frank B. Wilderson III on Afropessimism" (1:37:50).

93. Wilderson, *Red, White & Black*, 340.

94. Wilderson, *Red, White & Black*, 124.

95. For a pragmatic discussion about whether Wilderson's paradigm is ultimately defeatist or instead demands a return to black revolutionary politics, see *Always Already Podcast*, "Ep. 29: Frank B. Wilderson III on Cinema and the Structure of US Racial Antagonisms," podcast, September 22, 2015, https:// alwaysalreadypodcast.wordpress.com/2015/09/22/wilderson/.

96. Wilderson, *Red, White & Black*, 337.

97. Wilderson, *Red, White & Black*, 50.

98. I am not suggesting that audio ontologies are necessarily "colorblind" because they are nonvisual. On the contrary, as I point out in chapter 3, the very substantial literature on black music and black sound studies shows that audio ontologies can be positively racialized. But it does seem that Eidsheim relies upon the particularly nonvisual qualities of the audio and the auditory in proposing her largely colorblind analytics.

99. Wilderson, *Red, White & Black*, 249, 316.

100. Keeling, "I = Another: Digital Identity Politics," 56. Keeling borrows the phrase "house of difference" from Audre Lorde and elaborates it in a digital audiovisual context.

101. Natasha Myers, *Rendering Life Molecular: Models, Modelers, and Excitable Matter* (Durham, NC: Duke University Press, 2015), ix.

102. Myers, *Rendering Life Molecular*, x.

103. My previous work has relied especially on Karin Knorr Cetina's discussion of the unfolding nature of scientific objects and the "libidinal" quality of the relationships scientists develop with them; see Theodore R. Schatzki, K. Knorr Cetina, and Eike von Savigny, eds., *The Practice Turn in Contemporary Theory* (New York: Routledge, 2001); as well as Hans-Jörg Rheinberger's

detailed treatment of the constantly shifting boundary between the known and the unknown through the iteration of experimental systems, in *Toward a History of Epistemic Things: Synthesizing Proteins in the Test Tube* (Stanford, CA: Stanford University Press, 1997); see also Andrew Pickering, *The Mangle of Practice: Time, Agency, and Science* (Chicago: University of Chicago Press, 1995). I find these works more compelling, in their integration of cultural and material histories, than Karen Barad's better-known but limitingly physicalist concept of "intra-action": see Karen Barad, *Meeting the Universe Halfway: Quantum Physics and the Entanglement of Matter and Meaning* (Durham, NC: Duke University Press, 2007).

104. TallBear continues: "The population and population-specified markers that are identified and studies mirror the cultural, racial, ethnic, national, and tribal understandings of the humans who study them. Native American, sub-Saharan African, European, and East Asian DNAs are constituted as scientific objects by laboratory methods and devices, and also by discourses or particular ideas and vocabularies of race, ethnicity, nation, family, and tribe." TallBear, *Native American DNA*, 5–6. See also Noah Tamarkin: "As used by geneticists, population has no inherent content: it can be any group that researchers find meaningful to compare to another. Populations, then, are never neutral: they are made rather than found. And the populations that geneticists make are inexorably entangled with race." Noah Tamarkin, *Genetic Afterlives: Black Jewish Indigeneity in South Africa* (Durham, NC: Duke University Press, 2020), 12.

105. Paul B. Preciado, *Testo Junkie: Sex, Drugs, and Biopolitics in the Pharmacopornographic Era* (New York: Feminist Press at CUNY, 2013), 60.

106. Preciado, *Testo Junkie*, 55, 351. On Preciado's work as a model for embodied artistic research, see "Towards a Queer Laboratory," in Ben Spatz, *Making a Laboratory: Dynamic Configurations with Transversal Video* (New York: Punctum Books, 2020), 147–83. On gender as technique more generally, see Spatz, "Gender as Technique," in *What a Body Can Do*, 171–214. For additional connections between gender and race as techniques or technics of the body, see Julian Gill-Peterson, "The Technical Capacities of the Body: Assembling Race, Technology, and Transgender," *TSQ: Transgender Studies Quarterly* 1, no. 3 (2014): 402–18, https://doi.org/10.1215/23289252-2685660.

107. Preciado, *Testo Junkie*, 353.

108. Mel Y. Chen, *Animacies: Biopolitics, Racial Mattering, and Queer Affect* (Durham, NC: Duke University Press, 2012), 159.

109. Chen, *Animacies*, 166. Chen's discussion of viruses as "nonliving" yet "closer to life" has become even more relevant in the era of Covid, especially given the racialization of its chinese origins.

110. King, *Black Shoals*, 119.

111. King, *Black Shoals*, 130.

112. This is not to suggest that anything and everything exists in molecular form. As I have argued elsewhere, the problem with the "flat ontology" proposed by someone like Graham Harman is that, in its attempt to embrace anything and everything as an equally valid object of study, it jettisons any concern for disciplinarity or depth of knowledge. In my view, such an approach is not even interdisciplinary, since it attempts to flatten or dismiss the epistemic depth cultivated by disciplinarity, let alone intersectional. See Graham Harman, *Object-Oriented*

Ontology: A New Theory of Everything (London: Pelican Books, 2018). My critique of Harman is in "Thresholds," in Spatz, *Blue Sky Body*.

113. Karin Knorr Cetina, "The Couch, the Cathedral, and the Laboratory: On the Relationship between Experiment and Laboratory in Science," in *Science as Practice and Culture*, ed. Andrew Pickering (Chicago: University of Chicago Press, 1992), 116. See also Liboiron, *Pollution Is Colonialism*, 81–83, on the complex ontological status of even the most quantifiable molecules. Liboiron asks: "What is a chemical?" and, even more pointedly, "What is a chemical where you are?" (82, 111). I return to the ontology of song in chapter 3, with the question: "What is a song?"

114. For a detailed explanation of how the elegant equations of mechanical physics gave rise to an impossible dream of perfect coherence in modern science, see Isabelle Stengers, *Cosmopolitics* (Minneapolis: University of Minnesota Press, 2010). On the way in which molecular science "gently releases the ballast of the Periodic Table," with its compelling mathematical symmetries, and "leaves the chemist free to ascend into a world of synthesis, a non-Platonic realm where molecules are designed and made to *do* things," see Philip Ball, *Stories of the Invisible: A Guided Tour of Molecules* (Oxford: Oxford University Press, 2002), 9, italics original. Materiality in this sense might be contrasted to its use in some marxian theory, where it is strictly distinguished from relations that are "immaterial but objective." That distinction allows David Harvey to ask, rhetorically: "Can you see relations? Can you actually have iotas or atoms or *molecules of social relationships*? You can't trace them that way." I argue here that it is indeed possible to trace molecules of social relationships and that this requires a radical shift in onto-epistemology and the forms of knowledge, such as that proposed by artistic research. See David Harvey, "Reading Marx's *Capital* with David Harvey: Class 02 Reading Marx's *Capital Vol I* with David Harvey," January 16, 2011, https://www.youtube.com/watch?v=zwuMrd_Hgww (24:05–24:30).

115. Okpokwasili and Rossi, *Bronx Gothic*, 01:07, cited in the introduction.

116. Sara Ahmed, "Declarations of Whiteness: The Non-Performativity of Anti-Racism," *Borderlands* 3, no. 2 (2004): §49.

117. r. erica doyle in Claudia Rankine, Beth Loffreda, and Max King Cap, eds., *The Racial Imaginary: Writers on Race in the Life of the Mind* (Albany, NY: Fence Books, 2015), 253.

118. Billy-Ray Belcourt, *A History of My Brief Body* (Columbus, OH: Two Dollar Radio, 2020), 56.

119. Bey, *Problem*, 3.

120. Marquis Bey, *Black Trans Feminism* (Durham, NC: Duke University Press, 2022), 26.

121. A chapter by Katve-Kaisa Kontturi in Barrett and Bolt, *Carnal Knowledge*, applies Deleuze and Guattari's concept of the particle-sign to theorize "the molecular action of art" (27).

122. Arun Saldanha, "Reontologising Race: The Machinic Geography of Phenotype," *Environment and Planning D: Society and Space* 24 (2006): 18, italics original.

123. Saldanha, "Reontologising Race," 21, italics original.

124. Arun Saldanha, "So What *Is* Race?," Institute of Advanced Study, *Insights* 2, no. 12 (2009): 9.

125. Philip Ball, *Stories of the Invisible: A Guided Tour of Molecules* (Oxford: Oxford University Press, 2002), 6, 9, 10.

126. Patrick Wolfe, *Traces of History: Elementary Structures of Race* (London: Verso, 2016), 10.

127. Puar, *Terrorist Assemblages*, 161, 162, 202.

128. Amit S. Rai, "Race Racing: Four Theses on Race and Intensity," *WSQ: Women's Studies Quarterly* 40, no. 1–2 (2012): 64–65.

129. Gilles Deleuze and Félix Guattari, *A Thousand Plateaus: Capitalism and Schizophrenia* (Minneapolis: University of Minnesota Press, 1987), 275.

130. Deleuze and Guattari, *Thousand Plateaus*, 379; and see the introduction to Arun Saldanha and Jason Michael Adams, eds., *Deleuze and Race* (Edinburgh: Edinburgh University Press, 2013), 6–34.

131. Félix Guattari, *Molecular Revolution: Psychiatry and Politics* (Harmondsworth, UK: Penguin, 1984), 235.

132. *Online Etymology Dictionary*, s.v. "molecule," https://www.etymonline .com/word/molecule.

133. Christopher L. Miller, "The Postidentitarian Predicament in the Footnotes of *A Thousand Plateaus*: Nomadology, Anthropology, and Authority," *Diacritics* 23, no. 3 (1993): 16; see also Christopher L. Miller, "'We Shouldn't Judge Deleuze and Guattari': A Response to Eugene Holland," *Research in African Literatures* 34, no. 3 (2003): 129–41. These arguments continue into current anthropological debates; for example, see Lucas Bessire and David Bond, "Ontological Anthropology and the Deferral of Critique," *American Ethnologist* 41, no. 3 (2014): 440–56.

134. Miller, "Postidentitarian Predicament," 21.

135. Jodi A. Byrd, *The Transit of Empire: Indigenous Critiques of Colonialism* (Minneapolis: University of Minnesota Press, 2011), 18, 19.

136. Jordana Rosenberg, "The Molecularization of Sexuality: On Some Primitivisms of the Present," *Theory and Event* 17, no. 2 (2014), https://muse.jhu.edu /article/546470.

137. Neel Ahuja, "Post-Mortem on Race and Control," in Frida Beckman, ed., *Control Culture: Foucault and Deleuze after Discipline* (Edinburgh: Edinburgh University Press, 2018), 40.

138. Thomas F. DeFrantz, "I Am Black (You Have to Be Willing to Not Know)," *Theater* 47, no. 2 (2007): 10, italics added.

139. "Asymmetry" is one of the proposals made by Andrew Culp in seeking to exchange a positive, joyful Deleuze with a negative or "dark" Deleuze. I agree with Culp's critique of positivity—which I see as following the work of Miller, Byrd, Rosenberg, and Ahuja to disarm the potentially violent joy of a prematurely celebratory molecular theory—without endorsing his proposal for negativity. In my understanding, an experimental approach to action can never take on a merely positive or negative orientation. Culp acknowledges this when he speaks of each of us needing to live a "double life": one fraught with compromises (in "this world") and another mired in secrecy, conspiracy, and negativity (69). I would instead suggest that every moment is both moments, compromise mixed with revolution, negativity mixed with positivity. A three-part model of positive, negative, and strategic compromise is proposed in my discussion of three modes

of academic artistic research in chapter 2. Andrew Culp, *Dark Deleuze* (Minneapolis: University of Minnesota Press, 2016), 33–34.

140. See Glen Sean Coulthard, *Red Skin, White Masks: Rejecting the Colonial Politics of Recognition* (Minneapolis: University of Minnesota Press, 2014); Joanne Barker, ed., *Critically Sovereign: Indigenous Gender, Sexuality, and Feminist Studies* (Durham, NC: Duke University Press, 2017); and TallBear, *Native American DNA*. I return to this crucial point below and in chapter 3.

141. Denise Ferreira da Silva, "On Difference without Separability," in *Incerteza viva (Living Uncertainty)* (São Paulo: 32a Art Biennial, 2016), https://issuu.com/amilcarpacker/docs/denise_ferreira_da_silva/5.

142. Muñoz, *Sense of Brown*, 3.

143. Anne Anlin Cheng, *Ornamentalism* (New York: Oxford University Press, 2019), 1. The terms "custom," "style," and "way" often gloss what I call, to emphasize their epistemic depth, technique.

144. Hammerschlag, *Figural Jew*, 10. On muslim figurality, see Mutman, *Politics of Writing Islam*, 175–86.

145. Robert Stam and Ella Shohat have also explored these "tropes of color," focusing on black, red, and white "Atlantics" while taking care to avoid a "rainbow metaphor" that "risks implying the facile 'postracial' harmony and transcendence of race." Their premise is that such "colors" are "situated, overlapping, and relational utterances that slip and slide in their reference; they take on meaning only as part of larger sustems striated by power and inequality." Robert Stam and Ella Shohat, *Race in Translation: Culture Wars around the Postcolonial Atlantic* (New York: New York University Press, 2012), 4–5.

146. Bey, *Black Trans Feminism*, 14.

147. See Hari Ziyad, "My Gender Is Black," *Afropunk*, July 12, 2017, https://afropunk.com/2017/07/my-gender-is-black/. This piece is discussed by Tavia Nyong'o in Tavia Nyong'o, "My Gender Is Black?: The Speculative Refusals of Black Queer/Trans/Feminism," Oakland, CA, March 18, 2021, https://performingarts.mills.edu/broadcasts/2021/tavia-nyongo.php. On the inextricability of race and gender, especially black and trans, see also C. Riley Snorton, *Black on Both Sides: A Racial History of Trans Identity* (Minneapolis: University of Minnesota Press, 2017); Jules Gill-Peterson, *Histories of the Transgender Child* (Minneapolis: University of Minnesota Press, 2018); and Bey, *Black Trans Feminism*. Jewishness can also be a gender; see Daniel Boyarin, *Unheroic Conduct: The Rise of Heterosexuality and the Invention of the Jewish Man* (Berkeley: University of California Press, 1997); Ann Pellegrini, "Jewishness as Gender," *Shofar* 14, no. 1 (1995): 138–41.

148. J. Kameron Carter, "Jews and the Religion of Whiteness," Katz Center for Advanced Judaic Studies, University of Pennsylvania, Philadelphia, February 11, 2021, https://www.reconstructingjudaism.org/center-jewish-ethics/jews-race-and-religion/3.

149. On the racialization of islam, see Ghassan Hage, *Is Racism an Environmental Threat?* (Malden, MA: Polity, 2017); Iskander Abbasi, "Islam, Muslims, and the Coloniality of Being: Reframing the Debate on Race and Religion in Modernity," *Journal for the Study of Religion* 33, no. 2 (2021), https://doi.org/10.17159/2413-3027/2020/v33n2a4. On the origins of whiteness in christianity,

see Jonathan Boyarin, *The Unconverted Self: Jews, Indians, and the Identity of Christian Europe* (Chicago: University of Chicago Press, 2009). For more on jewishness and the racial, see chapter 3.

150. On disability as a country, see Neil Marcus, "Disabled Country"; and Petra Kuppers and Neil Marcus, *Cripple Poetics: A Love Story* (Ypsilanti, MI: Homofactus Press, 2008), 155. On Africa as a country, see Sean Jacobs, *Africa Is a Country*, https://africasacountry.com/about.

151. Belcourt, *History of My Brief Body*, 49; see also Scott Lauria Morgensen, *Spaces between Us: Queer Settler Colonialism and Indigenous Decolonization* (Minneapolis: University of Minnesota Press, 2011).

152. Kelley, "Western Civilization Is Neither," 7–8.

153. Profeta, *Dramaturgy in Motion*, 205.

154. Borelli and Monroe, "Screening the Skin, 1.

155. See Myers, *Rendering Life Molecular*, 23–27.

156. Hans-Jörg Rheinberger, *An Epistemology of the Concrete: Twentieth-Century Histories of Life* (Durham, NC: Duke University Press, 2010).

157. John Durham Peters, *The Marvelous Clouds: Toward a Philosophy of Elemental Media* (Chicago: University of Chicago Press, 2015), offers a useful introduction to the materiality of media, but without any decolonial or even seriously critical perspective that would allow one to attend to its racialization or to separate the general problems of human existence from the specific contours of colonial modernity.

158. Beth Coleman, "Race as Technology," *Camera Obscura* 24, no. 1 (70) (2009): 180, https://doi.org/10.1215/02705346-2008-018.

159. Coleman, "Race as Technology," 182, 184.

160. Coleman, "Race as Technology," 188, 189.

161. Wendy Hui Kyong Chun, "Race and/as Technology, or How to Do Things to Race," in *Race After the Internet*, ed. Lisa Nakamura and Peter A. Chow-White (New York: Routledge, 2012), 38.

162. Chun, "Race and/as Technology," 38, italics original.

163. Chun, "Race and/as Technology," 43. On racialized surveillance, see Simone Browne, *Dark Matters: On the Surveillance of Blackness* (Durham, NC: Duke University Press, 2015).

164. Keeling, "I = Another: Digital Identity Politics," 56.

165. The original source of this phrase is Audre Lorde, Zami: A New Spelling of My Name (Berkeley and Toronto: Crossing Press, 1982), 226.

166. Keeling, "I = Another: Digital Identity Politics," 59–67. Third Cinema refers to a wave of decolonial filmmaking practices in twentieth-century latin america and elsewhere. For a discussion of Third Cinema in relation to the university, with relevance to artistic research, see la paperson, *A Third University Is Possible* (Minneapolis: University of Minnesota Press, 2017).

167. Keeling, "I = Another: Digital Identity Politics," 68.

168. For a series of compelling examples of audiovisuality used in this way, see Gil Z. Hochberg, *Becoming Palestine: Toward an Archival Imagination of the Future* (Durham, NC: Duke University Press, 2021).

169. Keeling, "I = Another: Digital Identity Politics," 71–72.

170. Armond R. Towns, "Toward a Black Media Philosophy," *Cultural Studies* 34, no. 6 (2020): 856, https://doi.org/10.1080/09502386.2020.1792524.

Jonathan Sterne offers a related critique of the colonial narrative in media studies, emphasizing the parallel in Ong's work between orality/literacy developmentalism and christian supercessionism. Jonathan Sterne, "The Theology of Sound: A Critique of Orality," *Canadian Journal of Communication* 36 (2011): 207–25. Thanks to Scott Kushner and Duška Radosavljević for these references.

171. Towns, "Toward a Black Media Philosophy," 855, 864.

172. Towns, "Toward a Black Media Philosophy," 858.

173. Towns, "Toward a Black Media Philosophy," 859–60.

174. Towns, "Toward a Black Media Philosophy," 859.

175. Towns explains how the technology of radio, in french colonies, "produced a *white, French communality,* designed to link the settler with empire from afar." See "Toward a Black Media Philosophy," 867, italics original.

176. Towns, "Toward a Black Media Philosophy," 862; see Jussi Parikka, *A Geology of Media* (Minneapolis: University of Minnesota Press, 2015), 46.

Chapter 2

1. "Antifabulation" after Tavia Nyong'o, *Afro-Fabulations: The Queer Drama of Black Life* (New York: New York University Press, 2019); "unwhitely" after Neff, "Performing Unwhitely / Becoming Imaginary I.

2. George Yancy, *Look, a White! Philosophical Essays on Whiteness* (Philadelphia: Temple University Press, 2012), 6, 16. I came across Faedra Carpenter's work on black performances of whiteface too late to incorporate it here. But it is worth noting that Carpenter's openness toward transrace performance (11) is grounded in a "dramaturgical sensibility" (14) and even a concept of "institutional dramaturgy" (31) that resonates with the "white experiments" that conclude this chapter. Faedra Chatard Carpenter, *Coloring Whiteness: Acts of Critique in Black Performance* (Ann Arbor: University of Michigan Press, 2014).

3. Sometimes the invitation is explicit: "There is so much work that could be done on whiteness and how its coherence requires parasitism in order to survive. I think white folks have so much to do in that respect." King, "Staying Ready for Black Study," in King, Navarro, and Smith, *Otherwise Worlds,* 57.

4. It is often pointed out that being trans or nonbinary does not change one's whiteness. This is a necessary corrective to the impulse, expressed by some white trans and nonbinary people, to bypass or too easily disidentify with whiteness through gender noncomformity. But relations of gender, class, nation, language, citizenship, religion, and more do affect and inflect whiteness: not in a simple way, like checking or unchecking a box, but in complex ways that require intersectional and interdisciplinary analysis.

5. Tema Okun, "White Supremacy Culture," 1999, http://www .whitesupremacyculture.info/. Or, as Leanne Betasamosake Simpson writes sarcastically: "everyone knows white people hate typos." Leanne Betasamosake Simpson, Amanda Strong, and Spotted Fawn Productions, "Biidaaban (The Dawn Comes)," *Public: Art, Culture, Ideas,* no. 63 (2021): 106. For a more historicized enumeration of the characteristics of eurocentrism, see Stam and Shohat, *Race in Translation,* 65–68.

6. Dwight Conquergood, *Cultural Struggles: Performance, Ethnography, Praxis,* ed. E. Patrick Johnson (Ann Arbor: University of Michigan Press, 2013), 151.

7. Dwight Conquergood, "Performance Studies: Interventions and Radical Research," *TDR: The Drama Review* 46, no. 2 (2002): 147.

8. Brigitte Fielder and Jonathan Senchyne, eds., *Against a Sharp White Background: Infrastructures of African American Print* (Madison: University of Wisconsin Press, 2019), 6.

9. Fielder and Senchyne, *Against a Sharp White Background*, 10, 14.

10. Russell Means, "The Same Old Song," in *Marxism and Native Americans*, ed. Ward Churchill (Boston: South End Press, 1982), 19, italics added. For a recent discussion of this speech, see Red Media, "YOTED: Are Indian Reservations Socialism?" November 30, 2020, https://www.patreon.com/posts/yoted-are-indian-44389360.

11. Maria Lugones, "The Coloniality of Gender," *Worlds and Knowledges Otherwise* 2 (2008): 4. I place "cognitive" in quotations because I question whether this term has meaning except by implicit reference to writing.

12. Zuberi and Bonilla-Silva, *White Logic, White Methods*, 18–19. For another critique of demographic and sociological methods as racist and antiblack, see McKittrick, *Dear Science and Other Stories*, 103–21.

13. Lisa Lowe, *The Intimacies of Four Continents* (Durham, NC: Duke University Press, 2015), 4.

14. Sexton, *Amalgamation Schemes*, 29; Wilderson, *Red, White & Black*, 106.

15. da Silva, *Toward a Global Idea of Race*, 28.

16. I use the phrase "technology of writing" in deference to Derrida's expanded concept of "writing in general" or "*arche-writing*," discussed below. In this context, I am more interested in what Derrida has to say about the "narrow" or "vulgar" idea of writing as a specific technology. I am not bothered here by a certain slippage between technique and technology. Technique in my usage refers to the relatively reliable pathways of embodied practice; technology to the material objects produced through those pathways and practices. Both together constitute writing as technique in relation to whiteness as an identity formation.

17. This much is acknowledged even by contemporary thinkers who retain, in large part, Ong and McLuhan's colonial teleological narrative of phonetic writing as a grand achievement of human civilization: "The very ideas of an isolated word and of spelling are derivative of writing practices" (Peters, *Marvelous Clouds*, 301; and see 261–313 on writing in general). As the editor of a videographic journal, I can confirm that the labor required to produce a transcript of all text appearing in a video reveals the extent to which it is transcription itself—the act of writing—that severs words from the rest of life and practice. This point is discussed further in chapter 3.

18. Tony Ballantyne, Lachy Paterson, and Angela Wanhalla, eds., *Indigenous Textual Cultures: Reading and Writing in the Age of Global Empire* (Durham, NC: Duke University Press, 2020), 21. The binary opposition of orality and literacy was influentially developed by Walter J. Ong in *Orality and Literacy: The Technologizing of the Word* (London: Routledge, 2009). See Jonathan Sterne, cited below, for a critique relevant to my argument.

19. In classifying chinese writing, Yuk Hui rejects the term "ideogram" (a symbol that represents an idea) and prefers "pictogram" (a symbol that visually resembles a physical object), acknowledging that "Chinese writing as a practice of traces embeds already rich relations and patterns that could not be identified

in phonetic writing." On the other hand, Jin Suh Jirn suggests that the opposition between european and chinese writing systems is overblown, since "Chinese script is and has always been a phonetic/phonological system." Yuk Hui, "Writing and Cosmotechnics," *Derrida Today* 13, no. 1 (2020): 24, 28, https://doi.org/10.3366/drt.2020.0217; Jin Suh Jirn, "A Sort of European Hallucination: On Derrida's 'Chinese Prejudice,'" *Situations* 8, no. 2 (2015): 70. I am equally unequipped to investigate the colonial, postcolonial, and anticolonial dynamics of other profoundly scripted languages such as arabic and persian. Such an investigation would have to carefully examine muslim techniques of reading and writing in relation to jewish and christian ones. As a starting point see Mutman, *Politics of Writing Islam*, 159–73.

20. Walter D. Mignolo, "Afterword: Writing and Recorded Knowledge in Colonial and Postcolonial Situations," in *Writing without Words: Alternative Literacies in Mesoamerica and the Andes*, ed. Elizabeth Hill Boone and Walter Mignolo (Durham, NC: Duke University Press, 1994), 293.

21. Mignolo, "Afterword," 296.

22. Mignolo, "Afterword," 301.

23. Birgit Brander Rasmussen, *Queequeg's Coffin: Indigenous Literacies and Early American Literature* (Durham, NC: Duke University Press, 2012), 29. The forms of indigenous writing studied by Rasmussen include andean quipu, made of knotted ropes, and the haudenosaunee wampum, made of shell beads. The antiliteracy slave codes to which she refers must be thought alongside the forced residential schooling of indigenous people as two sides of the weaponized enforcement of writing *as* whiteness. The phrase "possessive investment in writing" references the idea of a "possessive investment in whiteness," developed by George Lipsitz in *The Possessive Investment in Whiteness: How White People Profit from Identity Politics* (Philadelphia: Temple University Press, 2018). See also D Vance Smith, "Africa Writes Back," *Aeon*, June 17, 2021, https://aeon.co/essays/africas-ancient-scripts-counter-european-ideas-of-literacy.

24. Raúl Sánchez, "Writing," in *Decolonizing Rhetoric and Composition Studies: New Latinx Keywords for Theory and Pedagogy*, ed. Iris D. Ruiz and Raúl Sánchez (Basingstoke, UK: Palgrave Macmillan, 2016), 84.

25. For another analysis of the development of whiteness in relation to textuality, see Jonathan Boyarin, *Unconverted Self*, 91–108. Situated in jewish studies, Boyarin's account highlights the importance of tracing contemporary whiteness back to the development of christianity and not only that of europe. Responding to Mignolo, Boyarin incisively problematizes the assumptions underpinning the assumed coherency of "religions of the book" by highlighting the centuries of active work that were required to make europe synonymous with christianity through the exclusion of jews and muslims. Separating the history of conflicts between christianity, judaism, and islam from colonialism and the rise of whiteness risks "occluding the importance of any legacy of difference 'inside' a West whose reality is accepted and whose basic contours remain unexamined" (94). As Boyarin demonstrates, "European-style textuality" (101), or what I am calling white writing, draws heavily on specifically christian approaches to scripture in the formation of a modern whiteness that brought together "the notions of literacy, civilization, the city (*civitas*), the political (*polis*), and the human" (106). Hence, religious difference cannot be neatly separated from racial difference, nor

can white writing be attributed in the same way to judaism or islam, which may actually—as I discuss in chapter 3—offer valuable alternative techniques of writing and textuality. On the racialization of islam, see Abbasi, "Islam, Muslims, and the Coloniality of Being."

26. Hélène Cixous, "The Laugh of the Medusa," *Signs: Journal of Women in Culture and Society* 1, no. 4 (1976): 879.

27. J. Kameron Carter, "Other Worlds, Nowhere (or, The Sacred Otherwise)," in King, Navarro, and Smith, *Otherwise Worlds*, 174, 182–83. On this poem, see also Sharpe, *In the Wake*, 125–50.

28. Jacques Derrida, trans. Gayatri Chakravorty Spivak, *Of Grammatology* (Baltimore, MD: Johns Hopkins University Press, 2016), 3. I have read Geoffrey Bennington's critique of this translation in the *Los Angeles Review of Books* ("Embarrassing Ourselves," March 20, 2016) and found its complaints not particularly relevant here.

29. Jacques Derrida, *Margins of Philosophy*, trans. Alan Bass (Chicago: University of Chicago Press, 1982), 213.

30. Sánchez, "Writing," 81.

31. Derrida, *Grammatology*, 366. Just after making this point, Spivak concludes her afterword by mentioning some of the concepts developed in Derrida's later works, many of which resonate with the interventions of artistic research: "the plurality of reason"; "the epistemological performance of multidisciplinarity"; "imaginative training for epistemological performance"; "aesthetic education"; and "pluralized institutional rationalities" (366–67).

32. Gil Z. Hochberg, "Between Orientalisms: Derrida, Cixous, and the Specter of the Arab Jew," *Boundary2*, December 17, 2018, http://www.boundary2.org /2018/12/gil-z-hochberg-between-orientalisms-derrida-cixous-and-the-specter-of -the-arab-jew/, italics original. I return to Derrida's jewishness in chapter 3.

33. da Silva, *Toward a Global Idea of Race*, 14.

34. da Silva, *Toward a Global Idea of Race*, 15.

35. da Silva, *Toward a Global Idea of Race*, xv–xvi.

36. da Silva, *Toward a Global Idea of Race*, 25 and passim.

37. da Silva, *Toward a Global Idea of Race*, 26.

38. Derrida, *Grammatology*, 37.

39. da Silva, *Toward a Global Idea of Race*, 7.

40. Derrida, *Grammatology*, 65, 80.

41. Derrida: "Writing will appear to us more and more as another name for [the] structure of supplementarity," that is, "the play of presence and absence" in general. *Grammatology*, 266–67. For a useful critique of Derrida's insensitivity to differences between media, see Mark Poster's introduction to Vilém Flusser and Mark Poster, *Does Writing Have a Future?* (Minneapolis: University of Minnesota Press, 2011). On the one hand, "history is not possible without writing" (xiii). On the other hand, "The cultural study of media is hampered by a philosophical tradition based on the *episteme* of the transcendental, unconditional, and contextless 'I think,'" and Derrida—along with Lacan, Foucault, and Deleuze—fails to seriously engage with the "technological specificity" (xviii) of writing in relation to photography, audio recording, and other media. In this context, it is interesting to note how Derrida's own logocentrism led him to underestimate the audiovisual as an alternative mode of inscription. He is said to have commented, to a cameraperson

working on the film *Derrida*, directed by Kirby Dick and Amy Ziering Kofman (New York: Zeitgeist Films, 2002), 85 min.: "You will never learn anything about the interior of me by filming." But what is this "interior," if not the logos as defined retroactively by a technology of writing that Derrida here directly opposes to that of film? Kirsten Johnson and Alex Lichtenfels, "Finding a Person and Losing a Person: On *Cameraperson*," *Performance Matters* 6, no. 1 (2020): 125.

42. da Silva, *Toward a Global Idea of Race*, 262.

43. Pickering, *Mangle of Practice*, chapter 4.

44. Isabelle Stengers, *Cosmopolitics* (Minneapolis: University of Minnesota Press, 2010). For a related analysis of how quantifiable variables are reified in environmental science, see Liboiron, *Pollution Is Colonialism*, 39–59. Liboiron quotes Maarten Hajer's observation that quantification is considered particularly valuable by (white) institutions because it is a form of knowledge that "institutions can handle" (51n37). The reasoning is circular but has tremendous impact: White institutions value quantified knowledge because white institutionality is constructed on the basis of quantification and, more generally, writing.

45. Sylvia Wynter offers a deflationary account along these lines when she argues that the crucial move of western thought has been to conflate a particular cultural perspective on being human—the european concept of "Man"—with the whole "horizon of humanity." Sylvia Wynter and Katherine McKittrick, "Unparalleled Catastrophe for Our Species? Or, To Give Humanness a Different Future; Conversations," in McKittrick, *Sylvia Wynter*, 24. Denise Ferreira da Silva's concept of "engulfment" further theorizes the impact of such epistemic eurocentrism on the globe.

46. Rasmussen, *Queequeg's Coffin*, 74, italics added.

47. Sánchez, "Writing," 80.

48. Derrida, *Grammatology*, 85.

49. Rizvana Bradley, "Picturing Catastrophe: The Visual Politics of Racial Reckoning," *Yale Review*, May 25, 2021, https://yalereview.org/article/picturing-catastrophe. See also Nicholas Mirzoeff, *The Appearance of Black Lives Matter* (Miami, FL: Name Publications, 2017), https://namepublications.org/item/2017/the-appearance-of-black-lives-matter/.

50. Arts Research Africa, *How Does Artistic Research Decolonise Knowledge*, 56. I have moved the em-dash for clarity.

51. For an example of quipu in artistic research, see micha cárdenas, *Poetic Operations: Trans of Color Art in Digital Media* (Durham, NC: Duke University Press, 2022), 132–33.

52. For a discussion of how nineteenth-century indigenous writers in north america wrestled with various forms of white/colonial writing and institutionality, see Mark Rifkin, *Speaking for the People: Native Writing and the Question of Political Form* (Durham, NC: Duke University Press, 2021). For a discussion of critical theory as jewish in contradistinction from whiteness, see chapter 3.

53. See Kramer and Misa, "Artistic Research as a Tool of Critique."

54. Patricia Hill Collins, *Fighting Words: Black Women and the Search for Justice* (Minneapolis: University of Minnesota Press, 1998), 156–57.

55. Spivak, "Can the Subaltern Speak?," in Patrick Williams and Laura Chrisman, eds., *Colonial Discourse and Post-Colonial Theory: A Reader* (Harlow, UK: Pearson Education, 2011), 87, italics original.

56. Spivak, Can the Subaltern Speak?," 89, italics original.

57. Derrida, *Margins of Philosophy*. Stam and Shohat describe how, "on innumerable occasions, European and Euro-American thinkers deployed 'the Indian' as an inspiration for social critique and utopian desire." They single out Diderot as someone whose writing "is rich in anticipations of subsequent anticolonial thinking." While it is crucial to recognize Jodi Byrd's point that the european figure of "the Indian" can displace actual indigenous life with its own hallucinations, it is equally important not to underestimate the real transmission of knowledge in this direction. Stam and Shohat, *Race in Translation*, 8, 24; Byrd, *Transit of Empire*.

58. Yancy, *Look, a White!*, 8.

59. Yancy, *Look, a White!*, 11.

60. Wiegman, *Object Lessons*, 138.

61. Wiegman, *Object Lessons*, 139. Although Wiegman's account begins from the simpler term "Whiteness Studies," I use "critical whiteness studies" throughout this section to emphasize that formalizing a critical or even explicitly antiracist intention does not alleviate the basic problem of studying whiteness.

62. Wiegman, *Object Lessons*, 156–57.

63. Michael Rothberg, *The Implicated Subject: Beyond Victims and Perpetrators* (Stanford, CA: Stanford University Press, 2019).

64. Wilderson, *Red, White & Black*, 337.

65. The story of the white person at an antiracist meeting asking something like "What can I do?," is common. For an example, see Resmaa Menakem, *My Grandmother's Hands: Racialized Trauma and the Pathway to Mending Our Hearts and Bodies* (Las Vegas, NV: Central Recovery Press, 2017), 262. This book is discussed further below.

66. This process must in fact go even further, through identity and "down" into place, land, and the earth itself. I return to this point at the end of the book. For my earlier discussion of how a focus on antiracist *technique* can detract from the reframing of racism as *principle*, see "Thresholds" in Spatz, *Blue Sky Body*.

67. Wiegman, *Object Lessons*, 189.

68. I need to make two caveats here regarding this idea of "studies" and the "critical." First: in chapter 3, I will claim critical theory to a certain extent for jewishness as a particular margin of whiteness. Second: I acknowledge the reappropration of "study" undertaken by Stefano Harney and Fred Moten in *Undercommons*. These caveats do not undermine my larger point about critical whiteness studies as an academic field, but I want to acknowledge here that the meanings of the critical and of "studies" are ongoingly contested, including by artistic research.

69. Wiegman, *Object Lessons*, 159–60, italics original.

70. This phrasing is borrowed from Tiffany Lethabo King's critique of the framing of "settler colonial studies" as a new and original field of study, in *Black Shoals*, 70.

71. Wiegman, *Object Lessons*, 159.

72. Linda Alcoff, *The Future of Whiteness* (Cambridge, UK: Polity, 2015), 176–77.

73. Yancy, *Look, a White!*, 3.

74. Shotwell, *Knowing Otherwise*, 80; and see Alexis Shotwell, "Is It White Shame?," *Alexis Shotwell Blog*, August 13, 2017, https://alexisshotwell.com/2017/08/13/white-shame/.

75. Alison Bailey, "On White Shame and Vulnerability," *South African Journal of Philosophy* 30, no. 4 (2011): 477.

76. James Baldwin quoted in Bailey, "On White Shame and Vulnerability," 475. See Baldwin, "The Price of the Ticket," in *Collected Essays* (New York: Library of America, 1998), 841, italics original. This brilliant essay is very clear regarding western and british complicity in the jewish holocaust as well as jewish (and irish) complicity with whiteness in america. The call to "Go back to where you started," which Baldwin attributes to the black church, is "precisely what the generality of white Americans cannot afford to do. They do not know how to do it."

77. Neff, "Performing Unwhitely / Becoming Imaginary I."

78. Kevin Rigby Jr. and Hari Ziyad, "White People Have No Place in Black Liberation," *Racebaitr*, March 31, 2016, https://racebaitr.com/2016/03/31/white-people-no-place-black-liberation/.

79. Sara Ahmed, "Declarations of Whiteness": §59, italics added.

80. As noted by the editors of a recent volume critiquing the whiteness of contemporary mindfulness discourse, "many scholars with interests in mind-body health and contemplative practice lack expertise in the study of racism and social inequalities more broadly. Moreover, the vast majority of mindfulness research focuses on white communities." Veronica Womack, Crystal Marie Fleming, and Jeffrey Proulx, eds., *Beyond White Mindfulness: Critical Perspectives on Racism, Well-Being and Liberation* (New York: Routledge Books, 2022), xvi.

81. Fikes, "'Extimacy' as Racial Transparency."

82. The Embodiment Conference, 2020, https://theembodimentconference.org/. Other channels included "Coaching & Therapy" and "Leadership & Business."

83. Tada Hozumi, "Open Letter to Mark Walsh and the Embodiment Conference," *Medium*, October 18, 2020, https://tadahozumi.medium.com/public-letter-to-mark-walsh-and-the-embodiment-conference-ab9319ee4b69. Punctuation has been adjusted for clarity. This article is no longer available online, nor is Hozumi's own blog, cited below.

84. Arran Gare, "The Grand Narrative of the Age of Re-Embodiments: Beyond Modernism and Postmodernism," *Cosmos and History: The Journal of Natural and Social Philosophy* 9, no. 1 (2013): 327–28. Thanks to Thomas Kampe for this reference.

85. I discuss the tension between cultural appropriation and the transmission of knowledge in the context of modern postural yoga in "The Invention of Modern Postural Yoga," chapter 2 in *What a Body Can Do*.

86. Tada Hozumi, "On Somatics Being an Asian Practice," September 9, 2020, https://tadahozumi.com/on-cultural-somatics-being-an-asian-practice/.

87. Tada Hozumi, "What It Means to Heal White Supremacy: Restoring the Cultural Nervous System, Cultivating Hara," November 17, 2017, https://tadahozumi.com/what-it-means-to-heal-white-supremacy/; and see "A Cultural Somatic Seader on Whiteness, Trauma, and Allyship," June 8, 2020, https://tadahozumi.com/a-cultural-somatic-reader-on-whiteness-free-webinar/. A different post, identifying whiteness as a type of PTSD, was taken down after some strong negative reactions that criticized Hozumi's use of biomedical terminology

and emphasized the risk that attributing whiteness to trauma can erase the differences between oppressor and oppressed. For example, see Lisa Xochitl Vallejos, "The Dangerous Game of Calling Whiteness PTSD: A Response to Tada Hozumi," *Medium*, November 13, 2017, https://drlisavallejos.medium.com/the-dangerous-game-of-calling-whiteness-ptsd-a-response-to-tada-hozumi-d8bddccdc062. For a nuanced consideration of this issue in the context of reclaiming black madness, see Bruce, *How to Go Mad without Losing Your Mind*, 27–29.

88. Tada Hozumi in Building Belonging, "Societal Healing & Belonging," August 11, 2020, https://www.youtube.com/watch?v=7j-LEeNJxnc (0:54).

89. Menakem, *My Grandmother's Hands*, xv. For additional works of contemporary popular nonfiction that invite white people to engage differently with their ancestors, see Emma Dabiri, *What White People Can Do next: From Allyship to Coalition* (London: Penguin, 2021); and Layla F. Saad, *Me and White Supremacy: How to Recognise Your Privilege, Combat Racism and Change the World* (London: Quercus, 2022). For a historical analysis of the violence and conflict internal to christianity that gradually constructed whiteness in contradistinction to jewishness, islam, and indigeneity, see Boyarin, *Unconverted Self*.

90. Menakem, *My Grandmother's Hands*, ix. In this context, "belief," "ideology," "cognition," and the "brain" are better understood as affordances of the technology of writing than of anatomy or biology.

91. Manakem's framework is antiracist but resolutely liberal. He calls for "social activism that is body centered" and acknowledges that we "cannot individualize our way out of white-body supremacy" (*My Grandmother's Hands*, 237). But his approach remains grounded in therapy and social work and notably lacks an anticapitalist analysis or any substantial engagement with intersectionality beyond a black-white binary. Menakem's most obvious break with contemporary black activism is his embrace not only of white antiracism and white healing, but also of the capacity of the police to become a force for justice. Menakem, whose brother is a police officer, acknowledges the roots of north american policing in slave patrols, but also works closely with police (and military) agencies and believes that police can become leaders of justice (215–33). Most surprisingly, he repeatedly defines american power dynamics as if they were constituted by three racialized "cultures": "white Americans, African Americans, and police" (248). This is at odds with contemporary abolitionism and highlights the need for ongoing historical, social, and infrastructural critique alongside even the most politicized cultural somatics.

92. Online information and application sheet for "Healing White-Body Supremacy: Somatic Healing Group for White Activists and Organizers," 2021. The group's concept of politicized somatics draws on the Generative Somatics lineage, https://generativesomatics.org/.

93. Staci Haines in Building Belonging, "Societal Healing & Belonging" (1:05–1:09). For another useful perspective on (white) ancestral reconnection, see Daniel Foor, "In Defense of Ancestor Reverence: A Letter to the Editor of *The New Yorker*," https://ancestralmedicine.org/in-defense-of-ancestor-reverence/, June 9, 2022. For a thoughtful conversation about the risks and potentials of conceptualizing european indigeneity, see Red Media, "Reading Vine Deloria Jr.'s *God is Red* (1973) (pt. 2)," April 17, 2022, https://www.patreon.com/posts/reading-vine-jr-65266831.

94. Saldanha, "Reontologising Race."

95. Arun Saldanha, *Psychedelic White: Goa Trance and the Viscosity of Race* (Minneapolis: University of Minnesota Press, 2007), 8. For more on white cultures of exit and flight, see Ronald B. Sakolsky and James Koehnline, eds., *Gone to Croatan: Origins of North American Dropout Culture* (Brooklyn, NY: Autonomedia, 1993).

96. Saldanha, *Psychedelic White*, 12.

97. Saldanha, *Psychedelic White*, 15.

98. Saldanha, *Psychedelic White*, 19.

99. Saldanha, *Psychedelic White*, 38.

100. On the racial politics of rhythm, melody, and repetition in black music, see Colbert, Jones, and Shane, *Race and Performance after Repetition*; as well as Kodwo Eshun, *More Brilliant than the Sun: Adventures in Sonic Fiction* (London: Quartet Books, 1998); and Simon Reynolds, *Generation Ecstasy: Into the World of Techno and Rave Culture* (New York: Routledge, 1999). As Saldanha's example suggests, the pedagogy of repetition is not limited to black music. Rather, repetition and in a sense rhythm itself are specifically absent in european classic music. White people, it might be suggested, are in part those who have forgotten how to repeat, turning repetition into a means rather than an end. This profound forgetting is linked, again, to white technologies of writing, in this case that of classical european musical notation.

101. Saldanha, *Psychedelic White*, 198. Saldanha cites the work of Rachel Adams and Leslie Fiedler on "appropriating *freak* as a critical category."

102. Saldanha, *Psychedelic White*, 198.

103. Saldanha, *Psychedelic White*, 211. In my own social media posts criticizing the Embodiment Conference, I acknowledged that embodiment, which has long been a central concept in my scholarship and artistic practice, has an equally dangerous lineage and potentiality, which we could call *somafascism* by way of comparison to ecofascism. Just as attachments to land and place may underpin white nationalism and other violent social movements, so attachments to the body and embodiment can support cultic, fascist body politics and eugenics. See Ben Spatz, "I have been using the word 'embodiment' for probably about a decade to name something that I believe has ethical and political value," Facebook, November 3, 2020, https://www.facebook.com/benspatz/posts /10158403649520862. For an incisive journalistic interrogation of cultic, fascist, and misogynistic impulses in yoga and other embodied practice modalities, see the work of Matthew Remski, http://matthewremski.com/.

104. George Yancy, ed., *White Self-Criticality beyond Anti-Racism: How Does It Feel to Be a White Problem?* (Lanham, MD: Lexington Books, 2015).

105. My first scholarly publication on Grotowski was Ben Spatz, "To Open a Person: Song and Encounter at Gardzienice and the Workcenter," *Theatre Topics* 18, no. 2 (2008): 205–22, https://doi.org/10.1353/tt.0.0044. All three of the books I have published since then also engage significantly with Grotowski and his legacies.

106. On Paxton and contact improvisation, see Royona Mitra's important work on "unmaking contact" via the "undoing" of its "universalizing principles." As Mitra shows, there is no inherent contradiction in contact improvisation's capacity to radically queer and democratize white embodied relations while

at the same time having racist and colonial effects. Royona Mitra, "Unmaking Contact: Choreographic Touch at the Intersections of Race, Caste, and Gender," *Dance Research Journal* 53, no. 3 (2021): 22. On whiteness and writing in relation to dance and the choreographic, see André Lepecki, *Exhausting Dance: Performance and the Politics of Movement* (New York: Routledge, 2006). For a broader critique of the whiteness underpinning contemporary dance, see Arabella Stanger, *Dancing on Violent Ground: Utopia as Dispossession in Euro-American Theater Dance* (Evanston, IL: Northwestern University Press, 2021). What is strangely limiting in both Lepecki and Stanger is the absence of a critique of the dance theorist as being caught up in the same white institutional dynamics as the dancers and choreographers they study. This absence allows Lepecki and Stanger to critique (white) choreographers as if from a disinterested or purely theoretical position, affording themselves as scholars a critical positioning in relation to whiteness that they do not seem to consider to be plausibly part of the choreographies they analyze.

107. Kris Salata, *The Unwritten Grotowski: Theory and Practice of the Encounter* (New York: Routledge, 2012), 14. See also James Slowiak and Jairo Cuesta, *Jerzy Grotowski* (New York: Routledge, 2018); Jennifer Kumiega, *The Theatre of Grotowski* (London: Methuen, 1985); and Schechner and Wolford, *Grotowski Sourcebook*.

108. For the ongoing force of the Grotowski mythos in poland, see Aleksandra Gajowy, "Staying at the Level of Impulses: Queering the Grotowski Archive in Karol Radziszewski's *The Prince*," *Contemporary Theatre Review* 31, no. 1–2 (2021): 113. A similar exceptionalism continues to limit the work of north american scholars as well, especially those who are closely associated with the Workcenter of Jerzy Grotowski and Thomas Richards. For example, compare the tone of Salata's books on the Workcenter, which defend its uniqueness to the detriment of most other kinds of theater, with Profeta's much more contextualized study of Ralph Lemon's work. For incisive comments on the Workcenter from the perspective of a former team member later trained in ethnomusicology, see Julia Ulehla, "Living Song: An Intergenerational Investigation of Moravian Folk Song" (PhD diss., University of British Columbia, 2021), 4–6, https://open.library.ubc.ca/soa/cIRcle/collections/ubctheses/24/items/1.0401497. Ulehla grapples with some of the same questions as I do, offering related but distinct answers (37–51).

109. Kasia Lech, "Krytyczki as Activists: On Theatre Criticism, Affect, Objectivism and #MeToo in Polish Drama Schools: Interview with Monika Kwaśniewska," *Critical Stages / Scènes critiques*, no. 23 (2021), https://www.critical-stages.org/23/interview-with-monika-kwasniewska/. Ilona Krawczyk also addresses this issue in "Embodying Voice in Training and Performance: A Process-Oriented Approach" (PhD diss., University of Huddersfield, 2021), https://eprints.hud.ac.uk/id/eprint/35659/. For an early critique, see "Let Grotowski Sacrifice Masculinity Too," by Charles Ludlam, in Schechner and Wolford, *Grotowski Sourcebook*. On the underrepresentation of women in Grotowski studies, see Virginie Magnat, *Grotowski, Women, and Contemporary Performance: Meetings with Remarkable Women* (London: Routledge, 2015). For my own analysis of gender and sexuality in Grotowski's work, see Spatz, *Blue Sky Body* and *Making a Laboratory*.

110. In developing this book I have been particularly interested in connections between the Workcenter and contemporary black arts. The Workcenter has been led since 1996 by Thomas Richards, son of Lloyd Richards, a north american theater director best known for staging the work of Lorraine Hansberry and August Wilson. Of the racial and intercultural knowledges explored during his apprenticeship with Grotowski, Richards writes: "I happened to find the way to reconnect to my so-called African line of tradition from a Polish man with a white beard, in California and Italy." Katherine Profeta mentions Richards and the Workcenter in her book on Ralph Lemon, noting their similarity in some key respects (*Dramaturgy*, 82). And filmmaker Arthur Jafa describes a fascinating encounter with the Workcenter, which he associates both with black forms of spiritual knowledge and technique ("they were just doing *voudon* basically; it was voodoo") and with a profound depth and rigor of practice ("I really came out of there, more than anything, thinking, I don't work hard enough, I just don't work hard enough"). See Thomas Richards, *Heart of Practice: Within the Workcenter of Jerzy Grotowski and Thomas Richards* (London: Routledge, 2008), 40; Thomas Richards and Daphne Brooks, "Open Channels: Performance, Politics and Racial Identity Formations in Times of Crisis," Performance Studies International #19 (Stanford, CA: Stanford University, 2013); Profeta, *Dramaturgy in Motion*, 82; and Arthur Jafa in "Love Is the Message: An Evening with Arthur Jafa," Hirshhorn Museum and Sculpture Garden, Washington, DC, March 16, 2018, https://www.youtube.com/watch?v=yOYd_IAPIe0 (8:10). Thanks to Johannes Birringer for this last reference.

111. Harry J. Elam Jr., "Fathers and Sons," *TDR: The Drama Review* 52, no. 2 (2008): 3.

112. Paratheater involved a series of loosely connected, open-ended projects, developed and led by a range of individuals in addition to Grotowski himself, including Laboratory Theatre performers and new associates. These events often took place outdoors and marked a definitive shift away from the creation of performances for an audience and toward a focus on the experience of participants. They are famously discussed in the film *My Dinner with Andre* (Louis Malle, 1981). Building on the embodied knowledge of the Laboratory Theatre ensemble, these events did not revolve around the development of precisely repeatable scores but were largely improvised encounters, more structurally similar to other encounter groups of the period.

113. Grotowski, "Holiday [Święto]," in Schechner and Wolford, *Grotowski Sourcebook*, 215. For ease of reference, I cite the versions of these texts published in the *Sourcebook*.

114. Grotowski, "Holiday," 217. The resemblance between Grotowski's conceptual framework and that of Rousseau, at least as described by Derrida, is striking. Compare Derrida's concluding meditations on theater and festival (*Grammatology*, 329–41) with Grotowski's "Holiday." The following passage, in which Derrida summarizes Rousseau's imagining of a transcendent "public festival," could almost have been spoken by Grotowski: "But what is a stage which presents nothing to the sight? It is the place where the spectator, giving himself as spectacle, will no longer be either seer [*voyant*] or voyeur, will efface within himself the difference between the actor and the spectator, the represented and the representer, the object seen and the seeing subject. With that difference, an

entire series of oppositions will deconstitute themselves one by one. Presence will be full, but not in the way of an object *present* to be seen, to give itself to intuition as an empirical individual or as an *eidos* holding itself *in front of* or *up against*; but as the intimacy of a self-presence, as the consciousness or the sentiment of self-proximity, self-sameness [*propriété*]. That public festival will therefore have a form analogous to the political meetings of a free and legiferant assembled people: the representative difference will be effaced in the self-presence of sovereignty" (*Grammatology*, 333, italics original).

115. Grotowski, "Holiday," 217, italics original.

116. Grotowski, "Holiday," 221.

117. Grotowski, "Theatre of Sources," in Schechner and Wolford, *Grotowski Sourcebook*, 255.

118. Grotowski, "Theatre of Sources," 257.

119. Grotowski also did not distinguish between "traditional" sources (such as chinese, hindu, or jewish) and those that would now be called indigenous. All, for him, could equally be sources of essential human knowledge that has been forgotten by "modern" society. On indigenous conceptions of sovereignty and their complex relations to european political history, see Joanne Barker, ed., *Sovereignty Matters: Locations of Contestation and Possibility in Indigenous Struggles for Self-Determination* (Lincoln: University of Nebraska Press, 2005).

120. Grotowski, "Theatre of Sources," 252. This passage might be compared to the personal need that Tada Hozumi invokes when discussing his relationship to black dance and culture, which he describes as holding knowledge that is essential first for his own personal healing and only then perhaps more broadly. Tada Hozumi in Building Belonging, "Societal Healing & Belonging" (1:02).

121. Grotowski, "Theatre of Sources," 265. This work took place in many different places: "in Poland, in Haiti, in the reservation of the Huichols in Mexico, in Ife and Oshogbo in the Yoruba territory in Nigeria, in Bengal, India" (267). The work of Maud Robart and the haitian group Saint Soleil was of increasingly central importance during this period, although this remains underacknowledged. See Marco De Marinis, "Maud Robart, Student/Teacher: Collaborating with Grotowski," trans. Giulia Vittori, *TDR: The Drama Review* 61, no. 1 (2017): 114–23; and Dominika Laster, *Grotowski's Bridge Made of Memory: Embodied Memory, Witnessing and Transmission in the Grotowski Work* (Calcutta: Seagull Books, 2016). On Grotowski in mexico, see Nicolás Núñez, *Anthropocosmic Theatre: Theatre, Ritual, Consciousness*, ed. Franc Chamberlain and Deborah Middleton (Huddersfield, UK: University of Huddersfield Press, 2019), 72–88. For documents of Grotowski's travels in central asia, iran, india, china, and japan, see Zbigniew Osiński, *Jerzy Grotowski's Journeys to the East*, ed. Iga Rutkowska, trans. Andrzej Wojtasik and Kris Salata (Holstebro, Denmark: Icarus Publishing Enterprise, 2014).

122. Grotowski, "Theatre of Sources," 268.

123. Rustom Bharucha, *Theatre and the World: Performance and the Politics of Culture* (London: Routledge, 1993), 50. Perhaps this question is answered in part by Abani Biswas's recollection, which echoes Thomas Richards's account: "Grotowski explained to me how important our own Indian tradition was to us. He opened my eyes to the Indian past." Quoted in Osiński, *Grotowski's Journeys*, 87.

124. Bharucha, *Theatre and the World*, 49–50.

125. Marcus Cheng Chye Tan, "Double Take: Review of *Theatre and the World* by Rustom Bharucha," *Theatre Research International* 46, no. 1 (2021): 89–91, https://doi.org/10.1017/S0307883320000607. On "new interculturalism" in dance, see Royona Mitra, *Akram Khan: Dancing New Interculturalism* (Basingstoke, UK: Palgrave Macmillan, 2015). For a critical reading of contrastingly hegemonic intercultural theater, see Daphne P. Lei, "Interruption, Intervention, Interculturalism: Robert Wilson's HIT Productions in Taiwan," *Theatre Journal* 63, no. 4 (2011): 571–86.

126. See Ian Watson, *Towards a Third Theatre: Eugenio Barba and the Odin Teatret* (London: Routledge, 1995); Włodzimierz Staniewski and Alison Hodge, *Hidden Territories: The Theatre of Gardzienice* (London: Routledge, 2004); and James Martin Harding and Cindy Rosenthal, eds., *The Rise of Performance Studies: Rethinking Richard Schechner's Broad Spectrum* (Basingstoke, UK: Palgrave Macmillan, 2011).

127. Maria Kapsali, "'I Don't Attack It, but It's Not for Actors': The Use of Yoga by Jerzy Grotowski," *Theatre, Dance and Performance Training* 1, no. 2 (2010): 185–98, https://doi.org/10.1080/19443927.2010.505002.

128. On Objective Drama, see Lisa Wolford, *Grotowski's Objective Drama Research* (Jackson: University Press of Mississippi, 1996).

129. Spatz, *What a Body Can Do*, 132–47. These emphases are not contradictory, as even blue skies research is oriented by particular desires and intentions. See my discussion of "blue sky" as a concept in *Blue Sky Body*, xiv–xvi.

130. Schechner's preface to Schechner and Wolford, *Grotowski Sourcebook*, xxv.

131. Richards, *Heart of Practice*, 4.

132. From 1772 to 1918, the polish nation had no state or territory and "maintained its identity by resisting the occupiers' efforts to annihilate Polish language and culture." Salata, *Unwritten Grotowski*, 62–63. For a discussion of eastern europe in relation to current decolonial thought, including the historicization of whiteness, see Social Science Research / University of Amsterdam, "Decolonising Europe #12: Decolonising the Non-Colonisers?," February 18, 2021, https://www.youtube.com/watch?v=p5FtT5vnBT4.

133. Laster, *Grotowski's Bridge*, 69, 98.

134. Bailey, "On White Shame and Vulnerability"; Baldwin, "The Price of the Ticket."

135. Grotowski, "Tu es le fils de quelqu'un," 300.

136. Philip Auslander, *From Acting to Performance: Essays in Modernism and Postmodernism* (London: Routledge, 2002), 35.

137. Laster's account of Grotowski's connections in haiti are especially revealing in this regard, showing both his deep personal investments and his unwillingness to instrumentalize (*Grotowski's Bridge*, chap. 4, 121–46).

138. Grotowski, "Tu es le fils de quelqu'un," 303–4.

139. Grotowski, "Tu es le fils de quelqu'un," 303–4.

140. Menakem describes his grandmother in largely positive terms, although he does not flinch from acknowledging her own trauma and its manifestation in both the physical punishment of her grandchildren (Menakem, *My Grandmother's Hands*, 187) and her colorism (81).

141. Menakem, *My Grandmother's Hands*, 53, 138–45.

142. Menakem, *My Grandmother's Hands*, 152.

143. Quoted in Laster, *Grotowski's Bridge*, 25. See also Caroline Gatt, "Breathing beyond Embodiment: Exploring Emergence, Grieving and Song in Laboratory Theatre," *Body and Society* 26, no. 2 (2020): 106–29, https://doi.org/10.1177/1357034X19900538.

144. Grotowski, "Performer," 376.

145. See Bey, *Problem of the Negro*, 71.

146. On the synthesis of "folk" or ritual songs with physical actions in Grotowski's work, see Wolford, *Grotowski's Objective Drama Research*; Thomas Richards, *At Work with Grotowski on Physical Actions* (London: Routledge, 1995); and Spatz, *What a Body Can Do*, 136–47.

147. Philip Joseph Deloria, *Playing Indian* (New Haven, CT: Yale University Press, 2007), 7; see also Shari M. Huhndorf, *Going Native: Indians in the American Cultural Imagination* (Ithaca: Cornell University Press, 2001); and Scott Lauria Morgensen, *Spaces between Us: Queer Settler Colonialism and Indigenous Decolonization* (Minneapolis: University of Minnesota Press, 2011).

148. For a description of this place, see Laster, *Grotowski's Bridge*, xii–xiv. Grotowski was also seriously ill during these years, but I do not believe that fully explains his return to working indoors.

149. Janet Mawhinney, "'Giving up the Ghost': Disrupting the (Re)Production of White Privilege in Anti-Racist Pedagogy and Organizational Change" (MA thesis, University of Toronto, 1998). This phrase has been influentially mobilized by Tuck and Yang in "Decolonization Is Not a Metaphor." Following Grotowski, I am interested in the possibility of an ethical or even radically politicizing innocence that would be very different from, and even directly opposed to, the mobilization of innocence by white supremacy. On the latter, see also Robin Bernstein, *Racial Innocence: Performing American Childhood from Slavery to Civil Rights* (New York: New York University Press, 2011).

150. Grotowski, "Performer," 376.

151. For Grotowski's youthful engagement with politics in poland, which he seems to have abandoned after being violently assaulted by paramilitary police, see Laster, *Grotowski's Bridge*, 6–18.

152. Byrd, *Transit of Empire*, 59.

153. Byrd, *Transit of Empire*, 125–26. On the reduction of indigenous national identities to racial minoritization in north america, see also Morgensen, *Spaces between Us*.

154. On these grounds, we could perhaps develop a distinction between *practice*, which I have previously defined generically as "concrete examples of actions, moments of doing, historical instances of materialized activity" (*What a Body Can Do*, 41) and which are necessarily located in time and space; and *praxis*, in which the very parameters of time and space, the materiality of emplacement as mutually constituted with embodiment, are contested. I begin to address the mutual constitution of technique, identity, and place at the end of this book.

155. See King, Navarro, and Smith, *Otherwise Worlds*; and Marisol de la Cadena and Mario Blaser, eds., *A World of Many Worlds* (Durham, NC: Duke University Press, 2018).

156. Salata, *Unwritten Grotowski*, 173–74.

157. Salata, *Unwritten Grotowski*, 38.

158. Salata, *Unwritten Grotowski*, 39. The last quoted phrase is attributed to Roland Barthes.

159. I am thinking here of the history of theater laboratories since long before Grotowski, including the Reduta Theatre that inspired Grotowski and Charles Dullin's Théâtre de l'Atelier, as well as the more recent ensembles that Eugenio Barba calls "floating islands" and Kathleen Cioffi calls "microcultures." See Zbigniew Osiński, "Returning to the Subject: The Heritage of Reduta in Grotowski's Laboratory Theatre," trans. Kris Salata, *TDR: The Drama Review* 52, no. 2 (2008): 52–74, https://doi.org/10.1162/dram.2008.52.2.52; Eugenio Barba, *Beyond the Floating Islands* (New York: PAJ Publications, 1985); and Kathleen Cioffi, "Zar and Other Microcultures of 'Grotland,'" *Slavic and Eastern European Performance* 28, no. 2 (2008): 20–29. These case studies can be valuably compared with Scott Morgensen's critical ethnographic analysis of the Radical Faeries and other nonindigenous queer conversations with indigeneity in *Spaces between Us*, especially 127–59. There are parallels in the idea that an authentic "nature realized at rural gatherings is endangered by an inauthenticity in urban life" (163–64) and Morgensen explicitly links queer primitivism to performing arts such as contact improvisation (171) and the ecosexuality of Annie Sprinkle (172). But the zone between cultural appropriation and epistemic transmission, indexed in Morgensen by an unresolved slippage between "primitivism" and "primitivity" (e.g., 167–77), needs to be carefully examined in each of these specific cases.

160. Derrida, *Grammatology*, 148.

161. Grotowski, "Theatre of Sources," 299. Here Grotowski contrasts his own embodied ("oral") ontology of song with a written ontology (musical notation) and an audio ontology (tape recordings). See my discussion of multiple ontologies of song in chapter 3, where I also consider a fourth ontology, the audiovisual.

162. Byrd, *Transit of Empire*, 17.

163. A relevant perspective on blood, authenticity, narrative, and embodiment in contemporary indigenous identity is found in Joseph M. Pierce, "Adopted: Trace, Blood, and Native Authenticity," *Critical Ethnic Studies* 3, no. 2 (2017): 57–76. Pierce offers a complex understanding of north american native identity, recognizing both the importance of formal tribal citizenship and the reality of other ways of being and becoming indigenous, including those more related to the "spectral" body and the "ambiguity of racial subjects" (64, 71). I refer to such ambiguities with my reluctant lowercasing of indigenous identities.

164. With Odin, I am thinking of how the organization has supported the increasingly independent work of its original ensemble members across many decades. With Double Edge, I am thinking of how it has developed local community relations, again over decades, as well as its recent engagements with indigenous leaders. See Richard Schechner, "Double Edge Theatre in Its Ashfield Community: An Interview with Stacy Klein," *TDR: The Drama Review* 64, no. 4 (2020). On indigenous practices of kinship that do not begin from a strict division between the personal or domestic sphere and that of community and governance, see Mark Rifkin, "Queering Temporality and Moving beyond Settler Time (Episode 314)," *Green Dreamer* podcast, 2021, https://greendreamer.com /podcast/dr-mark-rifkin-beyond-settler-time. For the limitations of even queer

white "back-to-the-land" projects, especially in their complex relations to indigeneity and settler colonialism, see Morgensen, *Spaces between Us*.

165. See Salata, *Unwritten Grotowski*, 170–71. For a description of recent Workcenter practice, see Richard Schechner, "Oh, I Know I've Been Changed," *Theatre Research International* 46, no. 3 (2021): 346–70, https://doi.org/10.1017/S0307883321000304.

166. These announcements were distributed to the Workcenter's email list on January 18 and 31, 2022. They are reprinted in *TDR: The Drama Review* 66, no. 3 (2022), along with a remarkable piece of writing by Mario Biagini that begins to engage directly with feminist and antiracist critiques of patriarchy and privilege in postgrotowskian practices. Biagini here explicitly raises the question of the return to a public sphere, asking "what turns a room, a square, or a parking lot into a public space" (189). He also reads Grotowski's statement "you are someone's son" as I have been suggesting, so that it refers not to a transcendent or universal genesis but to each person's specific cultural formation, which for Biagini includes acknowledgments of both patriarchy and whiteness (190). Finally, he states that he will no longer be singing songs from the african diaspora, at least not publicly (191). Mario Biagini, "Changes: From the Workcenter to the Academy of the Unfulfilled," *TDR: The Drama Review* 66, no. 3 (2022): 184–93, https://doi.org/10.1017/S1054204322000466.

167. See Truman, "Intimacies of Doing Research-Creation."

168. On the crisis of the contemporary university, see Facer and Newfield, "Special Section: Global Higher Education in 2050." The dismantling of university-based arts and humanities has rapidly intensified during the production process for this book.

169. While my own proclivity is to formulate grand questions of historical judgment as matters of concrete action through particular positions and institutions, I readily acknowledge that it is impossible to ask "what can be done" without implying an affirmative or critical attitude to what is. For a comparable mapping of diverse strategies for structural reform and decolonization, see Sharon Stein et al., "Gesturing Towards Decolonial Futures: Reflections on Our Learnings Thus Far," *Nordic Journal of Comparative and International Education (NJCIE)* 4, no. 1 (2020): 43–65, https://doi.org/10.7577/njcie.3518.

170. Alliance for the Arts in Research Universities (a2ru), https://www.a2ru.org/. a2ru launched a redesigned website in August 2021. All quotations here are taken from the previous version.

171. On the epistemic and political implications of the category of the research university, see Brim, *Poor Queer Studies*.

172. The statement highlights the previous diversity and equity work of a2ru and makes several commitments, such as to "further examining ways as an organization and as an alliance that we can deliberately, systemically work to root-out the layers of anti-black practices, language, and structures." It also commits to making a2ru "more inclusive by widening our membership base beyond Research 1 and Research 2 institutions to include liberal arts institutions, community colleges, art and design schools, and individual artists, scholars, teachers, and practitioners."

173. Mirzoeff, "Whiteness." Mirzoeff is a white jewish writer whose recent work engages deeply with antiracist themes. In his keynote he discussed the

contemporary relations of whiteness and jewishness, a central issue in chapter 3 of this book.

174. Adrienne Keene, "Conference Keynote: Native Appropriations, Indigenous Social Media, and Responding to Racism," 2020 a2ru National Conference, University of Wisconsin–Madison, October 15–30, 2020, https://vimeo.com/472289555.

175. This also may be changing. In his opening remarks preceding Mirzoeff's talk, Spencer Museum of Art curator Joey Orr introduced a series of claims that are closer to the european model of artistic research than to a2ru's "arts-integrated" research. The 2019 National Conference was titled "knowledges: artistic practice as method," while the 2022 National Conference theme was "Exploring Artistic Research," phrases that suggest an increasing engagement with methodological issues. See also Joey Orr, ed., *Inquiries* (Lawrence, KA: Spencer Museum of Art, 2019), https://spencerart.ku.edu/athome/teaser/inquiries, 140–41.

176. The item that comes closest to engaging this prior work is the report "What is Research?," one of a "series of research briefs" offered to a2ru alliance partner institutions. See Alliance for the Arts in Research Universities, *What Is Research? Practices in the Arts, Research, and Curricula* (Ann Arbor, MI: University of Michigan, 2018). This is a summary of interviews rather than a scholarly study. Also notable is the launch of a2ru's own online "platform for exemplary arts-inclusive research projects" called *Ground Works* (https://groundworks.io/). I am grateful that, following a lengthy submission and peer-review process, my Judaica project, which I discuss in chapter 3, has been included in its "compendium of arts integrative exemplars." But I also note that, while a2ru describes *Ground Works* as offering a "ground-breaking, streamlined submission process" (*Annual Report 2018/2019*, 2), there was no evidence in the actual publication process that the organizers are aware of or engaged with major european, canadian, australian, or south african initiatives related to artistic research, or the sustained conversations around them.

177. Bruce M. Mackh, "Surveying the Landscape: Arts Integration at Research Universities. A Review of Best Practices and Challenges for Arts Integration in Higher Education" (Ann Arbor, MI: ArtsEngine, 2015), 113, 111–12.

178. Mackh, "Surveying the Landscape," 17, 18.

179. Ahmed, *On Being Included*, 1, italics added. Ahmed's focus in this book is the united kingdom and australia (7), but her arguments are just as relevant to predominantly white institutions in north america.

180. Ahmed, *On Being Included*, 175.

181. Ahmed, *On Being Included*, 42.

182. Ahmed, *On Being Included*, 41, italics original.

183. Ahmed, *On Being Included*, 19.

184. Ahmed, *On Being Included*, 24, 6.

185. Ahmed, *On Being Included*, 85. The latter phrase is quoted from Annelise Riles, ed., *Documents: Artifacts of Modern Knowledge* (Ann Arbor: University of Michigan Press, 2006), 2.

186. Ahmed, *On Being Included*, 90.

187. Ahmed, *On Being Included*, 33.

188. Ahmed, *On Being Included*, 34, italics original.

189. Ahmed, *On Being Included*, 151.

190. Ahmed, *On Being Included*, 43.

191. Ahmed, *On Being Included*, 72.

192. Ahmed, *On Being Included*, 10. On the politics of happiness, see also Sara Ahmed, *The Promise of Happiness* (Durham, NC: Duke University Press, 2010).

193. "The empire has even been imagined as a history of happiness," such that "the violence of colonial occupation is reimagined as a history of happiness." Ahmed, *On Being Included*, 164.

194. Ahmed, *On Being Included*, 110.

195. Ahmed, *On Being Included*, 113.

196. Peggy Phelan, *Unmarked: The Politics of Performance* (London: Routledge, 1993); Jon McKenzie, "The liminal-norm," in Henry Bial, ed., *The Performance Studies Reader*, 2d ed. (London: Routledge, 2007), 26–31.

197. Simon Jones, "The Courage of Complementarity: Practice-as-Research as a Paradigm Shift in Performance Studies," in Ludivine Allegue et al., *Practice-as-Research*, 30.

198. I made a related point above regarding Grotowski's work with songs. Here again the point is to situate uncapturability, in contrast to textuality or more broadly mediation, within a decolonial analysis of the racialization of knowledge, rather than reifying it as transcendent or universal presence.

199. In addition to the volume cited above, see, e.g., Riley and Hunter, *Mapping Landscapes*; Arlander et al., *Performance as Research*; Borgdorff, Peters, and Pinch, *Dialogues between Artistic Research and Science and Technology Studies*; and Arts Research Africa, *How Does Artistic Research Decolonise*. I define the "trope of excess" in *What a Body Can Do*, 56–60, 234–42.

200. Erin Manning, *The Minor Gesture* (Durham, NC: Duke University Press, 2016), 237n20. See also SenseLab, http://senselab.ca/.

201. Erin Manning, *For a Pragmatics of the Useless* (Durham, NC: Duke University Press, 2020), 15.

202. On membership in SenseLab, see Manning, *Pragmatics*, 119.

203. For descriptions of both International Federation for Theatre Research working groups, see https://iftr.org/working-groups. I was a member of the Performance as Research Working Group (PaR WG) in 2013–16; from 2017–2023, I coconvened the Embodied Research Working Group (ERWG). Manning's descriptions of specific SenseLab activities, such as a 2014 gathering in Australia (*Pragmatics*, 124–39) and the 2016 "bench talks" (163–64), seem similar to the experiences I have had in the PaR WG and ERWG at IFTR conferences in various locations.

204. Manning, *Minor Gesture*, 44.

205. Manning, *Minor Gesture*, 31.

206. Manning, *Minor Gesture*, 32.

207. Manning, *Minor Gesture*, 40. On technique and method, see also Manning, *Pragmatics*, 78–79.

208. Manning here attributes this unparsed perception to "the autistic" (Manning, *Minor Gesture*, 10, 14); the parallels with Grotowski are significant. What Grotowski claims for traditional and indigenous knowledge, Manning locates in autism and more recently in blackness. My project here also attempts to valorize and validate such subjugated knowledges, but through fragmentation and formal complexity (via the variously mediated forms of knowledge, for example) rather than dichotomization.

209. Manning, *Minor Gesture*, 27, and *Pragmatics*, 221.

210. Harney and Moten, *Undercommons*, 29.

211. King, *Black Shoals*, 26.

212. Manning, *Pragmatics*, 1.

213. Manning, *Pragmatics*, 287.

214. Even in Wilderson's afropessimism, while he might wish to position blackness and whiteness as universal structuralist positions, the contextualization of his work as part of radical black thought means that his concept of enslavement, while highly abstracted, can never be completely severed from history.

215. Manning quotes Duchamp: "Infrathin: one must never make it a noun" (*Pragmatics*, 15). But she goes on precisely to use infrathin as a noun, as well as turning relative phrases like "more than" into nouns. This is a grammatical illustration of the tension that arises from the attempt to valorize not specific emergent technique, which may not yet have been named, but an abstract concept of that which *cannot* be named.

216. Each pocket practice has a composite name: "nestingpatching," "backgroundingforegrounding," "livingloving," "ticcingflapping," "schizzinganarchiving."

217. Manning, *Pragmatics*, 13–14. The 3Ecologies Institute is named for Félix Guattari, *The Three Ecologies* (London: Bloomsbury Academic, 2014); see http://senselab.ca/wp2/3-ecologies/3-ecologies-institute/.

218. "The crafting of the digital platform for the 3E Process Seed Bank is deeply committed to a sensitivity toward the outside of nonhuman expression that courses through us, computational and extracomputational. In the context of the 3E Process Seed Bank, what this requires in practice is that we design techniques that foster compelling ways of encountering how the coded world might collaborate with the more-than that courses through the analog." Manning, *Pragmatics*, 304. Brian Massumi, whose recent work is closely associated with that of Manning and SenseLab, reexamines value, money, and finance in *99 Theses on the Revaluation of Value: A Postcapitalist Manifesto* (Minneapolis: University of Minnesota Press, 2018).

219. Manning, *Pragmatics*, 14.

220. For another perspective on money as form, see *Money on the Left*, "Abstractions also Liberate with Anna Kornbluh," podcast, October 1, 2021, https://moneyontheleft.org/2021/10/01/abstractions-also-liberate-with-anna-kornbluh/.

221. Manning refers to her own practices as "pragmatic" in the philosophical sense, but practical details of form and content are largely absent from her accounts. Manning's theory of the pragmatic attempts to name it without describing it, to theorize it in the abstract, rather than getting down into the nitty-gritty, talking shop. I would argue that an actual pragmatics, without denying the importance of "the" more-than, should consistently lower its gaze to focus on a specific more-than as it appears in a given context or moment. This means acknowledging rather than disavowing *that which the "more-than" is more than*: the known that subtends a specific unknown, or the local and emplaced context in which experimental practice is undertaken.

222. Deleuze and Guattari, *Thousand Plateaus*, 161; see also Spatz, *What a Body Can Do*, 70n19.

223. I have proposed a somewhat abstract mapping of this process in "Thresholds," in *Blue Sky Body*, where I attempt to ground the abstraction of the spatial metaphor for knowledge in specific examples. Yet I remain unsatisfied with the tension in that essay between schematizing knowledge and contextualizing its politics.

224. See the important critique of Harney and Moten in Brim, *Poor Queer Studies*, 181–93. As Brim suggests, "the undercommons disorganizes itself *in relation to rather than beyond* the organization that bids it to speak: the university" (191, italics added).

225. McKittrick, *Dear Science and Other Stories*, 41.

226. Arts Research Africa, *How Does Artistic Research*, 222–23, italics added. In a recent conversation Fred Moten approaches the question of academic form by suggesting that academia's contribution to broader social movement might be through the work of "experimentalists" rather than "theorists" (1:08:05–1:08:53). He says: "If black study, or for that matter black studies, has some task, has some role to play in the preservation and the mobilization of the radical resources that are given in black social life, that role will have been played out *in its practice, in its experimental practices*. So there's no overarching theoretical or conceptual formulation that we have to arrive at in order to unlock those practices and that potential. We just have to start working different." And then, more concretely: "I really don't know why any black studies program would ever have exams. I kind of don't quite understand why any black studies program would have classes. There might be a reason for it. It might be possible to justify. But to simply assume? And then to simply accept an already given structure of how a certain kind of advanced intellectual life is supposed to be lived in the university? How could we possibly assume that shit? *These are questions that are about experimental practice*." Fred Moten in "The Multiplicity Turn: Theories of Identity from Poetry to Mathematics Seminar: November 24, 2021," Stanford DLCL, December 17, 2021, https://www.youtube.com/watch?v=hRfsGzvK144 (1:08:05–1:08:53).

227. Esa Kirkkopelto, "Artistic Research as Institutional Practice," in *Yearbook on Artistic Research* (Stockholm: Swedish Research Council, 2015), 52–53, italics original.

228. Kirkkopelto, "Artistic Research as Institutional Practice," 53–54, final italics added.

229. "Another benefit of this kind of reasoning is that it liberates the evaluation of artistic research from superfluous epistemic speculations concerning the nature of artistic knowledge." Kirkkopelto, "Artistic Research as Institutional Practice," 53. Compare this with Ahmed: "I offer a way of thinking about diversity work as a phenomenological practice. Diversity work does not simply generate knowledge *about* institutions (in which the institution becomes a thematic); it generates knowledge of institutions in the process of attempting to transform them." Ahmed, *On Being Included*: 173.

230. Ahmed, *On Being Included*, 93. On the image of the lever and its leverage, see Bruno Latour, "Give Me a Laboratory and I Will Raise the World," in *Science Observed: Perspectives on the Social Study of Science*, ed. Karin Knorr-Cetina and Michael Mulkay (London: Sage Publications, 1983), 141–70; and Jacques Derrida, "Mochlos; or, The Conflict of the Faculties," in Richard Rand,

ed., *Logomachia: The Conflict of the Faculties* (Lincoln: University of Nebraska Press, 1992), 2–34.

231. Carson, "Owning My Masters: The Rhetorics of Rhymes & Revolutions" and *I Used to Love to Dream*.

232. See James Bulley and Özden Şahin, "Practice Research—Report 1: What Is Practice Research? and Report 2: How Can Practice Research Be Shared?" (London: PRAG-UK, 2021), https://doi.org/10.23636/1347, §1.3.2.4; Artistic Doctorates in Europe, "Experiences and Perceptions of the Artistic Doctorate in Dance and Performance," 2017, https://www.artisticdoctorates.com/; and Ben Spatz, "Earthing the Laboratory: Speculations for Doctoral Training," *Performance Research* 25, no. 8 (2020): 33–41, https://doi.org/10.1080/13528165 .2020.1909896.

233. Another such "pressure point" might be the form of the academic conference or conference session, as explored for example by the Performance as Research and Embodied Research Working Groups of the International Federation for Theatre Research; see note 203 above.

Chapter 3

1. The Judaica project, *steampunk version* ("Tales of the Hasidim" with Margot Bassett, 2012) at Triskelion Arts, Earthdance, and the Center for Performance Research in brooklyn. Later phases of the Judaica project include the *aleph version* ("Tales" with projections by Bruce Steinberg, 2013) at Performance Mix Festival, new york city; *dybbuk version* ("Judaica 1" with Sióbhán Harrison, Nicola Fisher, Jennifer Parkin, and Karoliina Sandström, 2014) at the British Library and ("Judaica 2" with Sióbhán Harrison and Jennifer Parkin, 2015) at the Centre for Psychophysical Performance Research, huddersfield; *performance art intervention* ("Behold How Good" directed by Maiada Aboud, 2017) at Byram Arcade, huddersfield, and the Midlands Arts Centre, birmingham; *chorus* (Holocaust Memorial Procession, huddersfield, 2017 and 2018); and *laboratory phase* ("Judaica: An Embodied Laboratory for Songwork" with Nazlıhan Eda Erçin, Agnieszka Mendel, and additional guests, 2017), with funding (2016–18) from the UK Arts and Humanities Research Council, at the University of Huddersfield and other venues including the White Stork Synagogue (wroclaw), POLIN Museum (warsaw), Galicia Jewish Museum (kraków), NN Theatre (lublin), JW3 Jewish Community Centre (london), Royal Central School of Speech and Drama, Goldsmiths University of London, University of Kent, University of Manchester, Leimay/Cave NYC, New York University, Martin E. Segal Theatre Center, FringeArts (philadephia), and Wesleyan University (middletown).

2. Bey, *Problem of the Negro.*

3. In an extraordinary talk, Daniel Boyarin argues that "religion" is an anachronistic and misleading term when associated with historical judaism, which was understood very differently before the modern period. Although Boyarin does not directly suggest this, what I take from his argument is the possibility that juda*ism* and not only jewish*ness* can be approached as a molecular identity in the sense developed here. We can start by returning to the suffix "-ism" its sense of transmissible culture and knowledge, as in the comparable term "hellenism," rather than treating "Judaism" as a monolithic or institutionally structured whole by analogy with the christian church. Daniel Boyarin, "20th Anniversary

Lecture, Judaic Studies: Daniel Boyarin: No 'Judaism' In Josephus," McClung Museum of Natural History and Culture, October 24, 2013, posted January 16, 2014, https://www.youtube.com/watch?v=9iL3NZrxp28 (15:30). According to the editors of *Queer Theory and the Jewish Question,* the secularization and racialization of jewishness in modernity meant that "modern Jewishness became as much a category of gender as of race." Daniel Boyarin, Daniel Itzkovitz, and Ann Pellegrini, eds., *Queer Theory and the Jewish Question* (New York: Columbia University Press, 2003), 4.

4. See Jonathan Boyarin, *Unconverted Self.* As Boyarin explains, the development of europe as a colonizing entity is inextricable from the ways in which christianity worked to distinguish itself from its others. I use modern racial terms here because I am in dialogue with an emergent decolonial grammar of colors and with critical black and native studies. My focus is on how judaism and jewishness can be reexamined in that context. While I am not able to delve into the religious prehistory of race described by Boyarin, any attempt to reposition jewishness today must keep in mind the extent to which the invention of whiteness through colonialism was built on centuries of christian policy and theology. The historically recent formulation "Judeo-Christian" is itself one of the ways in which jewish difference "is cancelled out, further obscuring what is specifically Christian (and *not,* or surely not in any simple way, Judeo-Christian) about the work of global colonization from a European base" (18). See also Ariella Aïsha Azoulay, "Open Letter to Sylvia Wynter: Unlearning the Disappearance of Jews from Africa," *The Funambulist,* no. 30 (2020), https://thefunambulist .net/magazine/reparations; and Anya Topolski, "The Dangerous Discourse of the 'Judaeo-Christian' Myth: Masking the Race–Religion Constellation in Europe," *Patterns of Prejudice* 54, no. 1–2 (2020): 71–90, https://doi.org/10.1080 /0031322X.2019.1696049.

5. Jonathan Boyarin, *Thinking in Jewish* (Chicago: University of Chicago Press, 1996), 6. The exemplary status of jewishness is not merely of theoretical interest. It is politically urgent, as demonstrated by the increasing right-wing weaponization of accusations of antisemitism in the past decade. For a detailed report on the "antisemitism crisis" that contributed to the removal of Jeremy Corbyn as the leader of the Labour Party in the united kingdom, see David Renton, *Labour's Antisemitism Crisis: What the Left Got Wrong and How to Learn from It* (Abingdon, UK: Routledge, 2022).

6. At the start of the Judaica project, in 2012, I had not yet realized that it would be impossible to develop a molecular—let alone decolonial—approach to jewishness without confronting whiteness. Yet I did already sense that I needed to avoid some of the conventional ways in which jewish identity has been analyzed, particularly in relation to performing arts. Scholarly production on (white) jewishness in the united states has been massive. Approaching my own artistic practice through that lens would have drowned me in a vast narrative that did not reflect how I wanted to situate either my artistic practice or my identity. For this reason, I did not read certain books on jewish performing arts until the last phase of the research described here. Three works that seem obviously related to my project, but which I did not consult until beginning to write this chapter, are Henry Bial, *Acting Jewish: Negotiating Ethnicity on the American Stage and Screen* (Ann Arbor: University of Michigan Press, 2005); Roberta Mock, *Jewish*

Women on Stage, Film, and Television (Basingstoke, UK: Palgrave Macmillan, 2007); and Abigail Wood, *And We're All Brothers: Singing in Yiddish in Contemporary North America* (Farnham, UK: Ashgate, 2013). These books felt at once too close to home and too distant from my critical and political intentions, particularly regarding how I want to name and examine whiteness. As one example, Bial's *Acting Jewish* aims to develop a "fluid, affective understanding of identity" (154). But references to whiteness and blackness appear only a handful of times, while the book's overarching framework positions judaism and jewishness in relation to what Bial calls "mainstream," "universal," "generic," "nonspecific," or (even more problematically) "gentile" visions of "American" culture (3, 4, 16). These terms are not strictly incorrect, but they can all be read as euphemisms for whiteness that, in failing to name that whiteness, unintentionally reinscribe a white narrative. I cite Bial only as an example of a larger trend, a wealth of scholarly production on "the landscape of American Jewishness" that Wood calls "almost obsessive" in its extent (*And We're All Brothers*, 13). The dominance of this particular narrative of jewishness, which uncritically centers "American Jewishness" rather than interrogating jewishness in relation to whiteness, explains why I had to avoid these works throughout most of the Judaica project and also why I have found it necessary to devote an entire chapter to analyzing whiteness before turning to focus on jewishness.

7. Efraim Sicher, ed., *Race, Color, Identity: Rethinking Discourses about "Jews" in the Twenty-First Century* (New York: Berghahn Books, 2013), 13. See also Melanie Kaye/Kantrowitz, *The Colors of Jews: Racial Politics and Radical Diasporism* (Bloomington, IN: Indiana University Press, 2007); and Lisa Tessman and Bat-Ami Bar On, eds., *Jewish Locations: Traversing Racialized Landscapes* (Lanham, MD: Rowman and Littlefield, 2001).

8. Walter Isaac, "Locating Afro-American Judaism: A Critique of White Normativity," in *A Companion to African-American Studies*, ed. Lewis R. Gordon and Jane Anna Gordon (Malden, MA: Blackwell Publishing, 2006), 538.

9. See Noah Tamarkin, *Genetic Afterlives: Black Jewish Indigeneity in South Africa* (Durham, NC: Duke University Press, 2020), on black jewish lemba people in south africa. The lemba people are simultaneously black, indigenous, and jewish—a subject position that is nearly unthinkable from within dominant white imaginaries today. Other jewish african communities include the abayudaya community in uganda, whose songs I discuss below.

10. Carter, "Jews and the Religion of Whiteness" (20:22).

11. Shaul Magid, "Jews, Whiteness, and becoming 'Judeo-Christian': A Response to J. Kameron Carter," *Reconstructing Judaism*, n.d., https://www.reconstructingjudaism.org/jews-whiteness-and-becoming-judeo-christian-response-j-kameron-carter. On the whiteness of white jews in the united states, see Eric L. Goldstein, *The Price of Whiteness: Jews, Race, and American Identity* (Princeton, NJ: Princeton University Press, 2008). Additional sources can be found in Goldstein, *Price of Whiteness*, 242n7; and see also Ben Ratskoff, "'Improbable Spectacles': White Supremacy, Christian Hegemony, and the Dark Side of the Judenfrage," *Studies in American Jewish Literature* 39, no. 1 (2020): 17–43. For a historical overview of how european jewishness changed its political meaning during the twentieth century, see Enzo Traverso, *The End of Jewish Modernity* (London: Pluto Press, 2016).

12. Tamara Deutscher, "Introduction," in Isaac Deutscher, *The Non-Jewish Jew and Other Essays* (London: Verso, 2017), 22; cf. Boyarin, *Thinking in Jewish*, 175.

13. Judith Butler, *Parting Ways: Jewishness and the Critique of Zionism* (New York: Columbia University Press, 2012); Michael Rothberg, *Multidirectional Memory: Remembering the Holocaust in the Age of Decolonization* (Stanford, CA: Stanford University Press, 2009), and *The Implicated Subject*.

14. Mirzoeff, "Whiteness."

15. Rifkin, *Fictions of Land and Flesh*. Rifkin writes that this book "came from a sense that I could and wanted to contribute something to the conversations that were happening about relations between blackness and indigeneity" (vii). It seems to me that such a project has a different meaning when it is understood as a particularly jewish contribution rather than an unmarked and implicitly white one. Rifkin applies his understanding of indigeneity to a critique of israel in "Indigeneity, Apartheid, Palestine: On the Transit of Political Metaphors," *Cultural Critique*, no. 95 (2017): 25–70, but even there he does not offer any pointers toward approaching or imagining jewishness as distinct from whiteness.

16. Hélène Cixous, *Portrait of Jacques Derrida as a Young Jewish Saint* (New York: Columbia University Press, 2005); Bettina Bergo, Joseph D. Cohen, and Raphael Zagury-Orly, eds., *Judeities: Questions for Jacques Derrida* (New York: Fordham University Press, 2007); Hammerschlag, *Figural Jew*.

17. Jack Lester Jacobs, *The Frankfurt School, Jewish Lives, and Antisemitism* (New York: Cambridge University Press, 2015). "All of the full members of the Institute in residence in Frankfurt and actively involved in its affairs in the period immediately preceding the Institute's relocation out of Germany . . . were Jews" (3).

18. Fred Moten, *The Universal Machine* (Durham, NC: Duke University Press, 2018), xi.

19. Sergey Dolgopolski, *What Is Talmud? The Art of Disagreement* (New York: Fordham University Press, 2009), 25. For a crucial treatment of Freud's jewishness that underscores its racial and colonial context, see Daniel Boyarin, "Freud's Baby, Fliess's Maybe," in *Unheroic Conduct: The Rise of Heterosexuality and the Invention of the Jewish Man* (Berkeley: University of California Press, 1997), 189–220. But it is disappointing that the work of Hortense Spillers, which contributes directly to the naming and content of this chapter, is referenced without being fully cited (193) and does not appear in that book's bibliography.

20. Dolgopolski, *What Is Talmud*, 12. Dolgopolski removes the definite article "the," which objectifies "The Talmud" as a closed text or set of books. I further lowercase the term to render it as a porous zone of technique. For a set of articles that add depth to associations between talmud and the critical as a mode of thought, see Avraham Rosen and Jillian Davidson, eds., "There's a Jewish Way of Saying Things: Essays In Honor of David Roskies," special issue, *In geveb: A Journal of Yiddish Studies* (June 2020), https://ingeveb.org/issues/theres-a-jewish-way-of-saying-things, especially the contributions by David Kraemer and Edward Greenstein.

21. Dolgopolski, *What Is Talmud*, 237.

22. Dolgopolski, *What Is Talmud*, 238.

23. Jonathan Boyarin, *Thinking in Jewish* (Chicago: University of Chicago Press, 1996), 84. See also Boyarin's discussion of talmudic citation—the act and practice

of citation itself rather than the content or truth value of any given quotation—as redemptive. "As the Talmud avers: 'One who cites an utterance in the name of its original speaker brings redemption to the world' " (50). Another name for talmudic thought might be "Yiddish science": a "conversation that goes on around and against and under the Western conversation" of proper historical and philosophical thought (193). Daniel Boyarin calls this mode of thought "jumbled, carnivalesque, raucous, bawdy, vital, exciting," its sensibility evoked by Eve Kosofsky Sedgwick's description of "Talmudic desires, to reproduce or unfold the text and to giggle." Daniel Boyarin, *Unheroic Conduct: The Rise of Heterosexuality and the Invention of the Jewish Man* (Berkeley: University of California Press, 1997), xvi.

24. Historically, cryptojudaism most often refers to spanish and portuguese jews who were compelled to formally renounce their religion and become christian, while they continued to practice jewish rituals in secret. The lineages of those cryptojews continue to exist, both in europe and elsewhere, including in the american southwest where they may be blended with indigenous and/or latinx identities including christianity. On the other hand, the concept of cryptojudaism might refer more broadly to that which remains distinct from hegemonic christianity (or in some contexts perhaps islam) and whiteness but is hidden and practiced in secret. This is the sense in which the "critical" in critical theory and critical race theory can be recognized as a cryptojudaic trace. See Michael Alpert, *Crypto-Judaism and the Spanish Inquisition* (Basingstoke, UK: Palgrave, 2001); Agata Bielik-Robson, *Jewish Cryptotheologies of Late Modernity: Philosophical Marranos* (London: Routledge, 2014); Seth Daniel Kunin, *Juggling Identities: Identity and Authenticity among the Crypto-Jews* (New York: Columbia University Press, 2009); Hilda Nissimi, *The Crypto-Jewish Mashhadis: The Shaping of Religious and Communal Identity in Their Journey from Iran to New York* (Eastbourne, UK: Sussex Academic Press, 2021); and Stanley M. Hordes, *To the End of the Earth: A History of the Crypto-Jews of New Mexico* (New York: Columbia University Press, 2005).

25. On the slowness of jewish studies to engage with cultural and corporeal turns across the critical humanities, see Barbara Kirshenblatt-Gimblett, "The Corporeal Turn," *Jewish Studies Quarterly* 95, no. 3 (2005): 447–61; and Adam Zachary Newton, *Jewish Studies as Counterlife: A Report to the Academy* (New York: Fordham University Press, 2019). This may gradually be changing now, due in part to the rise of a stronger critique of zionism in solidarity with initiatives like the palestinian-led Boycott, Divestment, Sanctions movement and a concomitant potential to rearticulate an oppositional jewish positionality that would once again be part of critical theory and could align with decolonial thought and politics. See Neil Levi and Michael Rothberg, eds., "Trump and the 'Jewish Question,' " special issue, *Studies in American Jewish Literature* 39, no. 1 (2020). In that issue Dean Franco, "The Jews are 'The New Jews,' " argues that in "recent work in Black and Latinx Studies, which historicizes the discursive formation of their respective fields, we find models for how to analyze the cultural production of Jewishness without naturalizing a racial, cultural, or ethno-national Jewish subject as the desired outcome or object of Jewish Studies" (156). Elsewhere Lila Corwin Berman invokes queer studies and critical race theory to propose a radically constructivist approach to jewish studies. Berman, "Jewish History beyond the Jewish People," *AJS Review* 42, no. 2 (2018): 269–92.

26. Jacobs, while highlighting the foundational role of jewish culture and tradition in the development of the Frankfurt School of critical theory, at the same time clarifies: "I do not believe that Critical Theory is a Jewish theory, any more than psychoanalysis is a 'Jewish science.' The latter assertion was a Nazi calumny. The former is deeply suspect" (*Frankfurt School*, 6). Jacobs is rightly concerned about antisemitic tropes that remain alive and well today, as in the wide circulation of the idea of "cultural marxism" and the implicit or explicit antisemitism of recent attacks on critical race theory. Nevertheless, I am willing to reclaim the jewishness of psychoanalysis, marxism, and critical theory, as long as this is understood not as a demographic constraint but as a decolonial reontologization of racial matter. See also the recently launched radical jewish journal *Protocols*, which takes as its title the name of one of the most infamous antisemitic conspiracy theories: https://prtcls.com/.

27. The whitening of european jewishness, which Goldstein and others describe in sociological and political terms, is also philosophical. Thus, it is unremarkable today for a philosopher to compare the "shared materialism" of Marx and Spinoza without even mentioning their common jewish backgrounds. This is no doubt because, in accordance with the principles of white writing and the strict separation of technique and identity, to call their shared materialism *jewish* would seem to many readers to be a reduction or denigration of the philosophical—rendering it merely religious or racial—rather than a necessary grounding of philosophical technique in much older lineages of thought and practice. See Jason Read, "Preemptive Strike (of a Philosophical Variety): Marx and Spinoza," *Crisis and Critique* 8, no. 1 (2021): 289.

28. Adin Steinsaltz, *The Essential Talmud* (New York: Basic Books, 2006), 262, 301–3.

29. For a relevant examination of logos in contemporary media theory, see Jonathan Sterne's critique of Walter Ong's derivation of his orality-literacy binary from suspect etymologies of jewish and greek modes of thought. Sterne, in "Theology of Sound," sharply critiques an "audiovisual litany" according to which the history of communication is dichotomized as stemming from biological differences between hearing and vision, this account being "rhetorically powerful, but not very accurate" (212). I am grateful to Duška Radosavljević for pointing me to this article and to this passage in particular: "What if the invention of writing and its stabilization in print were not the single most important turning point in communication history, but only one of many technological turning points? What if scholars—whose lives' work is dedicated to the written word—have overestimated its world-historical importance? We want to believe Plato that everything changed with writing. We are inclined to imagine writing as the moment that consciousness first allowed itself to be *externalized in physical form*. But what would happen if we instead submitted the history of communication technology to the rigours of the broader history of technology?" (221, italics added). My aim here is to contribute to such a project, building on the work of decolonial historians to rethink whiteness and jewishness not as a binary schematic opposition for all of history but as historically interwoven technologies of identity. Hence I theorize artistic research as a contestation of consciousness, thought, and knowledge via their externalization in multiple forms.

30. Daniel Boyarin writes in *Unheroic Conduct: The Rise of Heterosexuality and the Invention of the Jewish Man* (Berkeley: University of California Press, 1997): "This is not to say that all male Ashkenazi Jews actually studied Torah, any more than all medieval German men were knights, but this social marker was what defined the ideal male, indeed defined maleness itself. . . . If study defined the rabbinic male, then the exclusion of women was the practice that constructed gender differentiation and hierarchy within that society" (151–52). For a contemporary project to read and write talmud as queer embodied practice, see Benay Lappe's reclamation of the term *svara*: "Hot Off the Shtender: The Word that Changed the World" (February 12, 2021), *svara.org*, https://svara.org/hot-off-the-shtender-the-word-that-changed-the-world/.

31. See Isaac, "Locating Afro-American Judaism." Fred Moten conducts an extensive examination of antiblackness in Emmanuel Levinas and Hannah Arendt in Moten, *Universal Machine*.

32. "It is the result of the expulsion of Muslims and Jews from the continent, the subjugation of the Native populations in the Americas, and the enslavement of Africans that Europe was able to find the resources that later would become critical to launching the Industrial Revolution and the second modernity. In other words, what became a colonial racialization of people funded the possibility of an economic revolution that gave a new bourgeois class the chance to demand individual freedoms. It is thus at the expense of exploitation, expropriation, and enslavement of, among others, barbarians, that Western liberties were achieved." Santiago Slabodsky, *Decolonial Judaism: Triumphal Failures of Barbaric Thinking* (New York: Palgrave Macmillan, 2014), 33.

33. Butler, *Parting Ways*; Atalia Omer, *Days of Awe: Reimagining Jewishness in Solidarity with Palestinians* (Chicago: University of Chicago Press, 2019); Jonathan Boyarin and Daniel Boyarin, *Powers of Diaspora: Two Essays on the Relevance of Jewish Culture* (Minneapolis: University of Minnesota Press, 2002). Kaye/Kantrowitz also names "Diasporism" as an "identity and practice of Jewish anti-racism" (*Colors of Jews*, xi). In fact, Daniel Boyarin's reading of jewishness in *Unheroic Conduct* goes much further to address issues of racialization, nationalism, and colonialism (including zionism) than the book's title or cover material—all of which emphasize gender over race—suggest. As Boyarin shows, zionism is a form of racial whitening not only in its eventual effects but also in its origins (302–3). He does not hesitate to paraphrase the racial and masculinist impulse behind Theodor Herzl's nationist project of "white-settler-state-making" (310): "Make the Jews into colonists, and then they will turn white!" (305).

34. Slabodsky, *Decolonial Judaism*, 196.

35. Slabodsky, *Decolonial Judaism*, 211.

36. Slabodsky, *Decolonial Judaism*, 204. For Slabodsky, the repositioning of jewishness in relation to whiteness is global, not limited to the americas. Yet if Slabodky's jewishness whitens him, in other cases racialization and especially blackness render jewishness invisible. Hence, black jewish performers are often seen "only as black women, not as Jews," with their blackness perceived to supersede their jewishness. On the power of jewishness to produce whiteness in post-1948 north america, see Isaac, "Locating Afro-American Judaism"; Lewis Gorden in Kaye/Kantrowitz, *Colors of Jews*, 173–81; Kunin, *Juggling Identities*, 62–63, 81, 93–94; and MaNishtana, "The 'Jewface' Debate

about Casting Non-Jews as Jews Betrays an Ashkenazi Bias," *Jewish Telegraphic Agency*, October 13, 202, https://www.jta.org/2021/10/13/opinion/the-jewface-debate-about-casting-non-jews-as-jews-betrays-an-ashkenazi-bias.

37. Slabodsky, *Decolonial Judaism*, 30.

38. Slabodsky, *Decolonial Judaism*, 210.

39. Slabodsky has confirmed that he is open to this interpretation of his work.

40. Gil Hochberg, "Forget Pinkwashing, It's Brownwashing Time: Self-Orientalizing on the US Campus," *Mondoweiss*, November 28, 2017, https://mondoweiss.net/2017/11/pinkwashing-brownwashing-orientalizing/;   Michael Zalta, "Hallucinatory Ethnicization," *Protocols*, no. 8 (2021), https://prtcls.com/article/hallucinatory-ethnicization/. Hochberg describes her encounter with a poster image that jarringly positions an image of (male) orthodox judaism alongside four ostensibly indigenous figures. She observes: "There is, of course, nothing wrong in suggesting an alliance between Jews and Indigenous people . . . However, placing such images underneath the Israeli flag makes them, at best, tasteless depictions of a pseudo alliance. Suggesting, as the posters do, that Jews have been driven out of their land (like indigenous people) and have finally returned to Israel—a trajectory that all indigenous people should unite behind—is a crude and cynical manipulation of (Jewish) history and a vulgar fabrication that not only makes no sense, but is also offensive in its use and abuse of indigenous peoples' histories of oppression."

41. An instructive point of contention in this regard is Frantz Fanon's discussion of the jewish holocaust in *Black Skin, White Masks*. Frank Wilderson reads this passage approvingly, as a diminution of the holocaust to a matter of "little family quarrels," hence "a conflict rather than an antagonism." Michael Rothberg, following the same interpretation, critiques Fanon for his "deliberate minimization of Nazi genocide." But Benjamin Steinhardt Case suggests that this reading of Fanon is in fact based on a mistranslation: "The 'family stories' Fanon refers to are the Jewish family's stories of oppression, not intra-white family quarrels between white non-Jews and white Jews." See Wilderson, *Red, White & Black*, 36; Rothberg, *Multidirectional Memory*, 93–94; and Benjamin Steinhardt Case, "Decolonizing Jewishness: On Jewish Liberation in the 21st Century," *Tikkun Magazine*, April 18, 2018, https://www.tikkun.org/nextgen/2018/04/18/decolonizing-jewishness-on-jewish-liberation-in-the-21st-century/. See Case for page references in Fanon.

42. Tamarkin, *Genetic Afterlives*, 23.

43. The prefix "ethno" here means more than the contemporary ethnic. It refers to groupings of human beings via imaginaries that range from blood kinship to formal politics, embracing commonalities as apparently distinct as those variously called communities, religions, ethnic groups, nations, and races. See Cynthia M. Baker, *Jew* (New Brunswick, NJ: Rutgers University Press, 2017), 33–46. Ethnotechnics can also be situated alongside the cognate terms *phenomenotechnics*, *anthropotechnics*, and *somatechnics*. See Ben Spatz, "Colors Like Knives: Embodied Research and Phenomenotechnique in Rite of the Butcher," *Contemporary Theatre Review* 27, no. 2 (2017): 195–215, https://doi.org/10.1080/10486801.2017.1300152, reprinted in *Blue Sky Body*; Peter Sloterdijk, *You Must Change Your Life: On Anthropotechnics*, trans. Wieland Hoban (Cambridge, UK: Polity, 2013); and the Edinburgh University Press journal *Somatechnics*.

44. Some of the other performing artists I know who are also currently exploring the borders of (critical) whiteness and jewishness through artistic research include Hadar Ahuvia, Tatyana Tenenbaum, Tobaron Waxman, and Michael Dudeck. See also Cindy Milstein, ed., *There Is Nothing So Whole as a Broken Heart: Mending the World as Jewish Anarchists* (Chico, CA: AK Press, 2021); Gabriel Levine's description of a queer purim party in new york city, in *Art and Tradition in a Time of Uprisings* (Cambridge, MA: MIT Press, 2020); and Celia Weiss Bambara, "On locating interculturalism and somatics: Looseness, holding on and swimming," Journal of Dance & Somatic Practices 14, no. 2 (2022): 217–30. For a historical example of jewishly racialized artistic technique, see Nicholas Mirzoeff's chapter on Camille Pissarro in Mirzoeff, ed., *Diaspora and Visual Culture: Representing Africans and Jews* (London: Routledge, 2000), 57–75.

45. This was during a sweat lodge ceremony led by Charles Red Hawk Thom, a karuk elder from california, on long island (see "Sweat" in *Blue Sky Body*, 87–88). I would also like to acknowledge a much older and for many years unrecognized impact of indigenous songwork on me, which took place when I was a teenager. When I was in high school in the late 1990s, the pop song "Return to Innocence" by Michael Cretu's Enigma project became a kind of anthem for me, with deep personal significance. Two decades later, while researching the politics of digital copyright as part of the Judaica project, I learned that this track's core vocal performance was appropriated from an ethnographic archive, a process that I would now interpret very differently. See Nancy Guy, "Trafficking in Taiwan Aboriginal Voices," in *Handle with Care: Ownership and Control of Ethnographic Materials*, ed. Sjoerd R. Jaarsma (Pittsburgh, PA: University of Pittsburgh Press, 2002), 195–209.

46. Some of the practitioners I worked with or have been influenced by include the Gardzienice Theatre, Song of the Goat Theatre, Theatre Zar, Theatre Wegajty, Studium Teatralne, Odin Teatret, the Workcenter of Jerzy Grotowski and Thomas Richards, New World Performance Laboratory, North American Cultural Laboratory, Farm in the Cave, Milon Mela, U Theatre, Double Edge Theatre, Dzieci Theater, and Massimiliano Balduzzi, as well as Zygmunt Molik, Rena Mirecka, Gey Pin Ang, and Maud Robart. The lineages of song I have mentioned arrived to me through these practitioners. Because of their approach to embodied transmission, in many cases I cannot be any more specific about the songs' origins or histories. Those who are familiar with postgrotowskian communities of practice will know which practitioners have worked in sustained ways with which lineages of song. I have written about postgrotowskian songwork practices in various contexts, beginning with "To Open a Person" and most recently with Ilona Krawczyk in "Dreaming Voice: A Dialogue," in *Somatic Voices in Performance Research and Beyond*, ed. Christina Kapadocha (Abingdon, UK: Routledge, 2021), 140–54.

47. I conducted a series of brief interviews with artists around this question, published as Gey Pin Ang et al., "What Is a Song?," *Performance Research* 24, no. 1 (2019): 80–93, https://doi.org/10.1080/13528165.2019.1601945.

48. The term "songwork" comes from Gary Tomlinson's historical study of indigenous nahuatl song in the colonial era. (Before encountering this term I used the phrase "song-action," referring to the concept of "action" developed by Jerzy Grotowski and Konstantin Stanislavski.) Tomlinson coins the word "songwork"

to name a "supraperformative level" or "nexus" at which the technical or sonic elements of song interact with, and perhaps mutually construct, "the non-songish things around them." This evocation of how songs can interweave and interpenetrate with "non-songish" things resonates with my discussion of indigenous ontologies of song below and particularly with Dylan Robinson's descriptions of indigenous song as knowledge, law, and history rather than aesthetic objects that float apart from the social world. Gary Tomlinson, *The Singing of the New World: Indigenous Voice in the Era of European Contact* (Cambridge: Cambridge University Press, 2007), 51.

49. Since 2004, I have developed my artistic research under the name Urban Research Theater (originally "Badawczy Teatr Miejski"). The first Urban Research Theater ensemble, in wrocław (2004–5), practiced songs that I adapted from the following audio tracks: the opening to *St John Passion* (Bach), "Victory" (Puff Daddy), "3:7:8" (Emergency Broadcast Network), and "A'oun Douash-maya Notre père chaldéen" (Esther Lamandier).

50. *First Song Cycle* (2005–9) and *Second Song Cycle* (created with Michele Farbman, 2007–9) followed an intuitive approach to melody and resonance, inspired by my brief but impactful encounters with the Workcenter of Jerzy Grotowski and Thomas Richards. The *PLAYWAR* song cycle, created with Massimiliano Balduzzi (2008–12), took a different approach: I transformed existing songs onto new ones by changing the lyrics and melodies, while attempting to keep everything else the same. The song cycle for *Rite of the Butcher* (2010–13) used a third strategy: A single session of extended vocal improvisation was recorded and then broken into sections and learned as songs. These three approaches have distinct relationships with technology: the first eschewed any form of recording or notation, developing songs entirely through embodied repetition; the second used writing to record nonlexical syllables; and the third relied on audio recording to transform improvised material into learnable songs. I discuss these technologies and ontologies of song further below.

51. Thompson, "Whiteness and the Ontological Turn," 273; and see my critique of Eidsheim in chapter 1.

52. This shift also coincided with my return to academia. Between 2001 and 2007, I intentionally separated myself from academic and scholarly modes of thought in order to (re)discover embodiment through artistic practice. The Judaica project can be seen as an attempt to reintegrate what I had learned on that journey with a return to critical theory, alongside the PhD that I began in 2007.

53. Memmi, "Negritude and Judeity," 4–12; see also Bergo, Cohen, and Zagury-Orly, *Judeities*. Jonathan Boyarin writes of contemporary yiddish language practices: "We must begin with the fragmentation of our language and encourage the possibilities of the various fragments," gathering "fragmented Torah-sparks of Yiddish" while guarding "against an artificial wholeness" (*Thinking in Jewish*, 198–99). The Judaica project's songwork extends well beyond the linguistic territory of yiddish, but its approach resonates with Boyarin's account of fragmentary creative practice. See also Boyarin's comparison of Alain Finkelkraut's retrospective rejection of his own jewish ancestral imaginary as mere pretense with Walter Benjamin's more nuanced approach to history. While Finkelkraut "evinces no critical reintegration of recuperated fragments of his annihilated ancestral culture," perhaps because he "still imagines identity as an all-or-nothing affair,"

Benjamin on the other hand shows us "how to work with fragments of culture without the need to reinvent a fantasized whole" (165, 166, 164).

54. By enumerating these five, I do not mean to foreclose the existence of other song ontologies or to suggest a general symmetry between them. On the contrary, I see the Judaica project as mapping a specific relationship between diverse ontologies of song through its emergent methodological form. The five ontologies enumerated here are those I have most directly investigated. As with the identity categories to which they are linked, my interest is in exploring their asymmetries rather than trying to fit them into a single overarching scheme.

55. See chap. 2; also Spatz, "Molecular Identities," 66; Spatz, "Colors Like Knives," 122n48.

56. Caroline Bithell, *A Different Voice, A Different Song: Reclaiming Community through the Natural Voice and World Song* (Oxford: Oxford University Press, 2014). Bithell touches briefly on postgrotowskian songwork, as well as the theater-oriented song and voice work of Kristin Linklater and Roy Hart (55–63).

57. Dylan Robinson, *Hungry Listening: Resonant Theory for Indigenous Sound Studies* (Minneapolis: University of Minnesota Press, 2020), 15.

58. Robinson, *Hungry Listening*, 141.

59. Robinson, *Hungry Listening*, 37–47. The phrase "tin ear" could just as easily refer to Grotowski's assessment of "Occidental" listeners, quoted in the previous chapter: "Anything belonging to the quality of the vibration, the resonance of the space, the resonating chambers in the body, the way in which exhalation carries the voice, all this they are not even able to grasp in the beginning."

60. Jeanette Bicknell and John Andrew Fisher, "Introduction: Making a Space for Song," *Journal of Aesthetics and Art Criticism* 71, no. 1 (2013): 4; and see Jeanette Bicknell, *A Philosophy of Song and Singing: An Introduction* (New York: Routledge, 2015). These works acknowledge that the inclusion of song in philosophy—*even when song is defined logocentrically, as music plus words*—is a risky and radical move.

61. For a set of anthropological interventions that aim to move beyond this logocentric dualism, see the special section "Knowing by Singing," in *American Anthropologist* 124, no. 4 (2022): 830–40, edited by Caroline Gatt and Valeria Lembo, https://anthrosource.onlinelibrary.wiley.com/toc/15481433/2022/124/4.

62. On this topic, I have learned much from Sophie Fetokaki's rigorous critique of ongoingly colonial modes of white and western music education, as developed in her PhD dissertation, which I had the privilege to supervise: "A Handbook of Situated Making" (PhD diss., University of Huddersfield, 2022), https://eprints .hud.ac.uk/id/eprint/35684/.

63. On the logocentric ontology of european music, see Goehr, *Imaginary Museum of Musical Works*.

64. Writing in a different geographical and cultural context, Brett Pyper analyzes the colonial hierarchy of knowledges in similar terms, arguing that they map "all too easily onto the binary between musical literacy and orality, privileging the notion that *the music worth knowing through systematic study must be a form of writing*. For all its own colonial baggage, ethnomusicology has, since its consolidation as a discipline in the mid-twentieth century, critiqued this narrow conception of music." Arts Research Africa, *How Does Artistic Research Decolonise*, 27, italics added.

65. Robinson, *Hungry Listening*, 46, italics added.

66. Robinson, *Hungry Listening*, 149.

67. Robinson, *Hungry Listening*, 151–52.

68. Robinson, *Hungry Listening*, 152.

69. Robinson, *Hungry Listening*, 167–68.

70. While jewish and black diasporic positionalities are different, my understanding of diaspora as distinct from both settler colonialism and indigeneity is informed by recent work on black-indigenous relations. See King, Navarro, and Smith, *Otherwise Worlds*; and Rifkin, *Fictions of Land and Flesh*. I return to this point at the end of the chapter.

71. Robinson, *Hungry Listening*, 154.

72. Bithell, *A Different Voice, A Different Song*, 18; and see 200–203. I put "oral" in quotations as a reminder that direct, interpersonal transmission is much more than just oral, or even aural. See Sterne, "Theology of Sound," for a critique of the concept of the oral in Walter Ong.

73. Rebecca Joy Fletcher (https://www.rebeccajoyfletcher.com/) taught me "Avinu Malkeinu," an important jewish prayer that I had never learned in the context of my secular childhood.

74. Joey Weisenberg has released numerous albums, as well as a book: *Building Singing Communities: A Practical Guide to Unlocking the Power of Music in Jewish Prayer* (New York: Mechon Hadar, 2011).

75. The assumed difference between the citation of written knowledge and the performance of song, specifically regarding the question of appropriation, is a central concern of this book. If we simply assume that citing the work of marginalized scholars is a positive intervention, while performing the songs of marginalized practitioners is an act of appropriation, then we have already taken for granted that songs are not knowledge—with the potential to transform—but instead merely objects, which can only be possessed. For an excellent consideration of the difference between citation and performance in theatre pedagogy, see Brandi Wilkins Catanese, "Teaching *A Day of Absence* 'at [Your] Own Risk,'" *Theatre Topics* 19, no. 1 (2009): 29–38, https://doi.org/10.1353/tt.0.0049. Catanese writes: "Put simply, a white instructor could teach a classroom full of white students a very productive course on African American theatre history, but a white instructor leading a classroom full of white students through an acting class focused on black performance styles would be subject to scrutiny that belies our supposed dismissive turn away from race as just a social construct" (35). The question raised here is how to rework the apparent assumption that, unlike history, performance styles are not fields of knowledge.

76. This literature is far too deep and wide to explore here. One could begin with Eshun, *More Brilliant than the Sun*; Anthony Reed, *Soundworks: Race, Sound, and Poetry in Production* (Durham, NC: Duke University Press, 2021); and Alexander G. Weheliye, *Phonographies: Grooves in Sonic Afro-Modernity* (Durham, NC: Duke University Press, 2005). The slave songs, sorrow songs, or spirituals are canonically described in Frederick Douglass, *Narrative of the Life of Frederick Douglass, an American Slave* (1845); and W. E. B. Du Bois, *The Souls of Black Folk* (1903).

77. McKittrick, *Dear Science and Other Stories*, 151, italics added.

78. McKittrick, *Dear Science and Other Stories*, 154, and see 160–67.

79. Eidsheim, *Race of Sound*; see my critique of this book in chapter 1.

80. The eighteen albums, in chronological order, were *Religious Music of the Falashas* (1951); *Jewish Life: The Old Country* (1958); Gloria Levy, *Sephardic Folk Songs* (1958); Ruth Rubin, *Jewish Folk Songs* (1959); *Music of the Spanish and Portuguese Synagogue* (1960); Abraham Brun, *Songs of the Ghetto* (1965); *Ethiopia: The Falasha and the Adjuran Tribe* (1975); *The Yemenite Jews* (1978); *Greek-Jewish Musical Traditions* (1978); *Hassidic Tunes of Dancing and Rejoicing* (1978); *Morasha: Traditional Jewish Musical Heritage* (1978); The Golden Gate Gypsy Orchestra, *The Travelling Jewish Wedding* (1981); *Chad Gadya: Passover Chant* (1982); *Ballads, Wedding Songs, and Piyyutim of the Sephardic Jews of Tetuan and Tangier, Morocco* (1983); *Bukhara: Musical Crossroads of Asia* (1991); *Abayudaya: Music from the Jewish People of Uganda* (2003); Feenjon Group and the El Avram Group, *Salute to Israel* (no date); and Feenjon Group, *An Evening at Cafe Feenjon* (n.d.). All these can be explored and downloaded from the online Smithsonian Folkways Recordings website, https://folkways.si .edu/. Before settling on the Folkways archive, I learned songs from the israeli database Invitation to Piyut, http://www.piyut.org.il/english/; the Judaic Collection in Recorded Sound Archives, Florida Atlantic University, https://rsa.fau.edu/; and the online music archive of Chabad, https://www.chabad.org/.

81. The Folkways archive also provides a starting point for grappling with questions of intellectual property (IP). While IP is in some ways a very limited and crudely commercial way of thinking about the ownership of songs, it is by no means static and the ongoing debates arising from the prevalence of new media technologies are crucial for the future of embodied and artistic research. Recordings in the Folkways archive are available for use through a standard licensing agreement. The income from this licensing goes to support Smithsonian Folkways as a nonprofit organization and in some cases is also returned directly to the artists and practitioners recorded. But these agreements apply only to the recordings, for example when used in the soundtrack of a film. As the Folkways licensing page makes clear, the "song" itself is understood as a separate entity, which may require separate permission from another copyright holder. While much commercial music negotiates these two distinct ontologies of song with relative ease, the emphasis of Folkways on "folk" music means that many of their recordings document performances of songs for which no separate rights holder can be found. On folk music and contemporary copyright law, see Richard Jones and Euan Cameron, "Full Fat, Semi-Skimmed or No Milk Today—Creative Commons Licences and English Folk Music," *Review of Law, Computers & Technology* 19, no. 3 (2005): 259–75.

82. Robinson's comments on the diverse media of songwork are relevant here. On the one hand, he carefully considers the capacity of alternative styles and forms of "performative writing" to write with and alongside music, rather than *about* it an an objectifying way (77–105). At the same time, he acknowledges that "perhaps writing is *not* always the best medium for understanding the presence and time of certain musical experiences" (86, italics original) and suggests that music scholars consider "transposing our analyses from the page to the concert hall, the gallery, the cinema, and site-specific contexts" (101). With reference to artistic research, Robinson suggests that, in some cases, "research-creation forms for conveying knowledge about music extend music subdisciplines into . . .

Indigenous forms of conveying knowledge," such as "song, oration, story, and dance." Moreover, "integrations of these are not simply primary forms for conveying knowledge; their forms allow us to uphold Indigenous values (and refuse epistemic violence of other forms)" (101). Robinson's examples of how audiovisual forms can extend and recontextualize songwork include a documentary film that relocates throat singing in the context of "wider expressions of Inuit spirituality" (138), as well as one of his own scores, which adds textual and audiovisual projections to the performance of a musical work (191–99).

83. Numerous audio and audiovisual versions of the songs described here can be found on the website of Urban Research Theater (2023), https:// urbanresearchtheater.com/. I do not link to specific pages as the site structure could change, but they can be found through a keyword search. The most summative and authoritive audiovisual outcomes from the Judaica project are those published on other platforms, several of which are cited below.

84. For a stirring performance and discussion of this song, see Rabbi Mónica Gomery's Yom Kippur Sermon 5782, https://www.youtube.com/watch?v= QMxMKEvhP-A (26:05–27:55), September 16, 2021. Thanks to Cara Herbitter for this reference.

85. Avraham Fried, *The Baal Shem Tov's Song* (2010), https://www.chabad .org/multimedia/music_cdo/aid/254270/jewish/Nigun-Simcha-1.htm.

86. Wood, *And We're All Brothers*, 146.

87. Wood, *And We're All Brothers*, 135.

88. The cultural division Wood describes is as much about gender as any other cultural dimension. It was never on the table for me, as a nonbinary person, to approach the strictly male spaces of hasidic religious song. I find even the small but powerful ways in which maleness is projected onto me in orthodox spaces to be deeply unsettling. For a contrasting experience, see the work of Tobaron Waxman as discussed in Dominic Johnson, "Voice, Performance, and Border Crossings: An Interview with Tobaron Waxman," *TSQ: Transgender Studies Quarterly* 1, no. 4 (2014): 614–19, http://www.tobaron.com/.

89. Wood, *And We're All Brothers*, 139. As noted above, Woods juxtaposition of "East European Jewish" and "modern American culture"—without reference to whiteness, blackness, or indigeneity—is part of why I could not engage with this monograph until late in the process of writing this book, after I had established my own ways of locating jewishness in relation to those crucial contemporary categories of identity.

90. Wood, *And We're All Brothers*, 1, 14.

91. "Queen Anne's Lace / Ale Brider," *Potluck* (1998), Wintergreen (Alice Spatz, Larry Spatz, Jared Polens), https://wintergreentrio.com/.

92. "Day by day Israel led a singing procession of children through the streets to school, and later led them home again by a wide detour through meadow and forest." Buber, *Legend of the Baal-Shem*, 40. This is the story about a werewolf and a magical child that I mentioned above. See also Martin Buber, *Tales of the Hasidim* (New York: Schocken Books, 1991).

93. This and other songs in the Judaica project were developed with Sióbhán Harrison, Jennifer Parkin, and later Ilona Krawczyk at the University of Huddersfield.

94. Liner notes to "Yafim Halelot," from Ruth Rubin, *Jewish Folk Songs* (Folkways Recordings, 1959).

95. See Jeffrey A. Summit, "The Participating Observer: Fieldwork in Jewish Settings," *Musica Judaica* 20 (2014): 117–42.

96. Summit's relationship with the abayudaya did not end with the production of that album, which was itself nominated for a Grammy award. Folkways has also released an album created and performed "by the coffee farmers of the Peace Kawomera (Delicious Peace) Fair Trade cooperative in Mbale, Uganda," in which "Jewish, Christian, and Muslim farmers work together to overcome generations of conflict and poverty" (*Delicious Peace: Coffee, Music & Interfaith Harmony in Uganda*, Folkways Recordings, 2012). For more on the abayudaya, see Richard Sobol and Jeffrey A. Summit, *Abayudaya: The Jews of Uganda* (New York: Abbeville Press, 2002). On their rejection from israel, see Judy Maltz, "Israel Rules Not to Recognize Ugandan Jewish Community," *Haaretz*, May 31, 2018, https://www.haaretz.com/israel-news/.premium-exclusive-israel-rules-not -to-recognize-ugandan-jewish-community-1.6137079. Some of these complexities are analogous to those involving the lemba (Tamarkin, *Genetic Afterlives*), including the ongoing antiblack racism that excludes them from dominant white and white supremacist jewish communities. But the situation of the abayudaya is particularly interesting to me because they do not claim a genetic or blood lineage to ancestral judaism.

97. "Hinei Ma Tov," Various Artists, *Abayudaya: Music from the Jewish People of Uganda* (Folkways Recordings, 2003); cf. "Hineh Ma Tov," *Old Songs and New* (2005), Wintergreen (Alice Spatz, Larry Spatz, and Jared Polens), https:// wintergreentrio.com/.

98. The lullaby is "Tulo, Tulo (Sleep, Sleep)," from *Abayudaya*. I sing it alongside "Hinei Ma Tov" in a video article that is discussed further below: Ben Spatz, N. Eda Erçin, Caroline Gatt, and Agnieszka Mendel, "He Almost Forgets That There Is a Maker of the World," *Journal of Embodied Research* 4, no. 2 (2021): 32:06, https://doi.org/10.16995/jer.71.

99. Nazlıhan Eda Erçin, "From-Ness: The Identity of the Practitioner in the Laboratory," *Journal of Interdisciplinary Voice Studies* 3, no. 2 (2018): 195–202, https://doi.org/10.1386/jivs.3.2.195_1. This article discusses her work with the song "Shishelai" (Şişeler), from the Feenjon Group, *An Evening at Cafe Feenjon* (Folkways Recordings, n.d.), during the Judaica project.

100. "Fel Sharah Canet Betet Masha—Walking Down the Street," from Gloria Levy, *Sephardic Folk Songs* (Folkways Recordings, 1958). Here is a taste, as transcribed by M. J. Benardete: "Velevo parlar shata metni / Because her father was a la gare / E con su umbrella darabetni / En rosponse a mon bonsoir."

101. *Chia e Tazi Pesen? [Whose Is This Song?]* (Sofia, Bulgaria: Adela Media Film and TV Productions, 2003), http://www.adelamedia.net/movies/whose-is -this-song.php.

102. Wood, *And We're All Brothers*, 105.

103. Posted March 23, 2017, on the Urban Research Theater website, https:// urbanresearchtheater.com/2017/03/23/expedition-swietokrzyskie/. The resonances with the genocide of indigenous nations in north american history are particularly striking to me, as in this context I stand on the other side of the erasure.

104. Yaron Trio, *Carmina Judaica* (Poland: AAUU Records, 2020), https://voicewild.wixsite.com/aauu.

105. This question was contributed to the Judaica project by Eda Erçin.

106. José Esteban Muñoz, *Disidentifications: Queers of Color and the Performance of Politics* (Minneapolis: University of Minnesota Press, 1999), 20.

107. Omise'eke Natasha Tinsley, *Ezili's Mirrors: Imagining Black Queer Genders* (Durham, NC: Duke University Press, 2018), 1.

108. A lovely example of the power of transmissible melody is provided by Wood. "One informant laughed," she tells us, "that her brother and his friends, studying at a yeshiva (religious school) in Jerusalem, had fooled an old rabbi into singing the theme tune from the computer game 'Tetris' as a nigun, in which guise the melody then spread around the yeshiva world." Yet, Wood goes on, "the Tetris theme tune she refers to is likely 'Korobeiniki', originally a Russian folk song, thus not wholly distant from the aesthetic world of East European Jewish music." Wood, *And We're All Brothers*, 149 and 149n17. This anecdote could be compared with that related in Thomas Richards, *Heart of Practice: Within the Workcenter of Jerzy Grotowski and Thomas Richards* (London: Routledge, 2008), 44. We do not know what a song can do.

109. Ben Spatz, Nazlıhan Eda Erçin, and Agnieszka Mendel, "Ancestors: An Illuminated Video," *International Journal of Performance Arts and Digital Media* 17, no. 1 (2021): 46–55, https://doi.org/10.1080/14794713.2021.1880140.

110. Ben Spatz, Nazlıhan Eda Erçin, Agnieszka Mendel, and Elaine Spatz-Rabinowitz, "Diaspora (An Illuminated Video Essay)," *Global Performance Studies* 2, no. 1 (2018), 30 min.

111. Nazlıhan Eda Erçin, Agnieszka Mendel, and Ben Spatz, "Działoszyce: Body, Song, Border," 1st International Ecoperformance Festival, March 16–19, 2021, 18 min., https://taanteatro.wixsite.com/ecoperformance/ecopoethics-in-progress. The book carried and sung in this session is Ghassan Hage, *Is Racism an Environmental Threat?* (Malden, MA: Polity, 2017).

112. On performance documentation, see Matthew Reason, *Documentation, Disappearance and the Representation of Live Performance* (Basingstoke, UK: Palgrave Macmillan, 2006); and Toni Sant, ed., *Documenting Performance: The Context and Processes of Digital Curation and Archiving* (London: Bloomsbury Methuen Drama, 2017).

113. Truman, "Intimacies of Doing Research-Creation, 230.

114. Loveless, *How to Make Art*, 102, italics original.

115. Annette Michelson, introduction to Dziga Vertov, *Kino-Eye: The Writings of Dziga Vertov* (Berkeley: University of California Press, 1984), xix. It is beyond the scope of this book to examine how videographic ways of thinking have developed in other approaches to cinema, from improvised narrative to video essays to visual ethnography. As starting points, see Gilles Mouëllic, *Improvising Cinema*, trans. Caroline Taylor Bouché (Amsterdam: Amsterdam University Press, 2013); Jean Rouch, *Ciné-Ethnography*, ed. Steven Feld (Minneapolis: University of Minnesota Press, 2003); Lucien Taylor, *Visualizing Theory: Selected Essays from V.A.R., 1990–1994* (New York: Routledge, 2014); Elizabeth Papazian and Caroline Eades, *The Essay Film: Dialogue, Politics, Utopia* (New York: Columbia University Press, 2016). Thanks to Caroline Gatt for ongoing conversations at the borders of theater and anthropology.

116. Katariina Kyrölä, "Music Videos as Black Feminist Thought: From Nicki Minaj's *Anaconda* to Beyoncé's *Formation*," *Feminist Encounters: A Journal of Critical Studies in Culture and Politics* 1, no. 1 (2017): article 8, https://doi.org /10.20897/femenc.201708.

117. Tomlinson, *Singing of the New World*, 51.

118. During the finalizing of this book, artificial intelligence (AI) capabilities improved very significantly, as seen in image generation platforms like Dall-E and writing platforms like ChatGPT. While it is still not possible to easily create a photorealistic video of me without recording my actual body, that possibility seems close at hand. This means that the same attitudes of skepticism and verification that now attend textual material (always asking where such material comes from and whether it can be verified) must ever more acutely attend audiovisual material. Moreover, as micha cárdenas writes, "today algorithms have much of the power of law, if not more." cárdenas, *Poetic Operations*, 173.

119. Alexander R. Galloway and Bernard Dionysius Geoghegan, "Shaky Distinctions: A Dialogue on the Digital and the Analog," *e-flux journal*, no. 121 (October 2021), https://www.e-flux.com/journal/121/423015/shaky-distinctions -a-dialogue-on-the-digital-and-the-analog/.

120. *Journal for Artistic Research*, https://jar-online.net/en.

121. Artistic research projects in music increasingly rely centrally on coding as a way to shift and expand the ontology of sound; for example, see the FluCoMa (https://www.flucoma.org/) and IRiMaS (https://research.hud.ac.uk/institutes -centres/irimas/) projects at University of Huddersfield. On the enticing but challenging possibility of research-creation in finance, see my discussion of SenseLab and the 3Ecologies Institute in chapter 2.

122. For some perspectives on indigenous video, see Pamela Wilson and Michelle Stewart, *Global Indigenous Media: Cultures, Poetics, and Politics* (Durham, NC: Duke University Press, 2008); and Macarena Gómez-Barris, *The Extractive Zone: Social Ecologies and Decolonial Perspectives* (Durham, NC: Duke University Press, 2017).

123. Cixous, "Laugh of the Medusa," 75.

124. Nancy K. Miller, *Getting Personal: Feminist Occasions and Other Autobiographical Acts* (New York: Routledge, 1991).

125. Miller, *Getting Personal*, back cover.

126. Kwame Anthony Appiah, "Go Ahead, Speak for Yourself," *New York Times*, August 10, 2018, https://www.nytimes.com/2018/08/10/opinion/sunday /speak-for-yourself.html.

127. Sara Ahmed, *Living a Feminist Life* (Durham, NC: Duke University Press, 2017), 214.

128. G Patterson, "Entertaining a Healthy Cispicion of the Ally Industrial Complex in Transgender Studies," *Women and Language* 41, no. 1 (2018): 146. For a contrasting meditation on the limits of these kinds of declaration, see Bey, *Black Trans Feminism*, 230–34n8.

129. Madison Moore, *Fabulous: The Rise of the Beautiful Eccentric* (New Haven, CT: Yale University Press, 2018), 42, 44.

130. Mirzoeff, *Appearance of Black Lives Matter*, 17–18, italics added.

131. Laura Horak, "Trans on YouTube: Intimacy, Visibility, Temporality," *TSQ: Transgender Studies Quarterly* 1, no. 4 (2014): 582, https://doi.org/10.1215/23289252-2815255.

132. Horak, "Trans on YouTube," 579, 574–75. This might be compared with Robinson's proposal to augment a performance of western classical music with projected critical and contextual annotations (191–99). In both cases the rearticulation of power comes from a strategic juxtaposition of textuality and audiovisuality.

133. See Steven Shaviro, *The Cinematic Body* (Minneapolis: University of Minnesota Press, 1993); Laura U. Marks, *Touch: Sensuous Theory and Multisensory Media* (Minneapolis: University of Minnesota Press, 2002); Eliza Steinbock, *Shimmering Images: Trans Cinema, Embodiment, and the Aesthetics of Change* (Durham, NC: Duke University Press, 2019); Catherine Grant, "The Shudder of a Cinephiliac Idea? Videographic Film Studies Practice as Material Thinking," *ANIKI: Portuguese Journal of the Moving Image* 1, no. 1 (2014): 49–62; and Christian Keathley, Jason Mittell, and Catherine Grant, *The Videographic Essay: Criticism in Sound and Image* (Montreal: caboose books, 2019).

134. *Liminalities: A Journal of Performance Studies*, http://www.liminalities.net/; *Journal for Artistic Research*, https://jar-online.net/; Research Catalogue: An International Database for Artistic Research, https://www.researchcatalogue.net/.

135. *Journal of Embodied Research*, Open Library of Humanities, https://jer.openlibhums.org/. As a practical way of working through issues of videographic form, *JER* published its first style guide, with a glossary and bibliography, in November 2022: https://jer.openlibhums.org/site/styleguide/.

136. For a fuller discussion of the difference between these earlier, more rigidly structured videos and the more recent ones examined here, see Ben Spatz, "Artistic Research and the Queer Prophetic," *Text and Performance Quarterly* 41, no. 1–2 (2021): 81–105, https://doi.org/10.1080/10462937.2021.1908585.

137. For a detailed description of the audiovisual embodied research method, including the configuration of practice-based lab sessions ("Dynamic Configurations") and the analysis and editing of the resulting video materials ("Transversal Video"), see Spatz, *Making a Laboratory*.

138. Nazlıhan Eda Erçin, Agnieszka Mendel, and Ben Spatz, The Songwork Catalogue (2020), https://urbanresearchtheater.com/songwork/.

139. Video methods in the social sciences are discussed in Edgar Gómez Cruz, Shanti Sumartojo, and Sarah Pink, eds., *Refiguring Techniques in Digital Visual Research* (Basingstoke, UK: Palgrave Macmillan, 2017); Sarah Pink, *Doing Visual Ethnography* (Los Angeles: SAGE, 2013); and Phillip Vannini, ed., *Non-Representational Methodologies: Re-Envisioning Research* (London: Routledge, 2015).

140. On the distinct forms of catalogue, lexicon, and index, see "A Thousand Tiny Viewpoints" in Spatz, *Blue Sky Body*, 161–73.

141. Erçin, Mendel, and Spatz, "Działoszyce," 12:43.

142. Robinson, *Hungry Listening*, 168–69.

143. Ingold's books, highly relevant to this project, include *Being Alive: Essays on Movement, Knowledge and Description* (London: Routledge, 2011), and

Making: Anthropology, Archaeology, Art and Architecture (London: Routledge, 2013). Ang's website is https://sourcingwithin.org/.

144. See Caroline Gatt, ed., *The Voices of the Pages* (Aberdeen, Scotland: University of Aberdeen, 2017).

145. Karin Knorr Cetina, "The Couch, the Cathedral, and the Laboratory: On the Relationship between Experiment and Laboratory in Science," in *Science as Practice and Culture*, ed. Andrew Pickering (Chicago: University of Chicago Press, 1992), 116–17, italics original. For more recent work on the emplacement of scientific laboratories, see Charlotte Klonk, ed., *New Laboratories: Historical and Critical Perspectives on Contemporary Developments* (Berlin: De Gruyter, 2016).

146. In Sarah E. Truman's interview with four leading figures in canadian artistic research, every one of them refers to a "lab" that they lead or are involved with. See Truman, "Intimacies of Doing Research-Creation." Compare also the sites and practices discussed in "Laboratories in Flux," special issue, *Brazilian Journal on Presence Studies* 11, no. 4 (2021), https://seer.ufrgs.br/presenca/issue/view/4230/showToc.

147. Eve Tuck and Marcia McKenzie, *Place in Research: Theory, Methodology, and Methods* (London: Routledge, 2014), xvii.

148. Tuck and McKenzie, *Place in Research*, 2, 5, 9.

149. Tuck and McKenzie, *Place in Research*, 100.

150. Frank Camilleri, *Performer Training Reconfigured: Post-Psychophysical Perspectives for the Twenty-First Century* (London: Methuen Drama, 2020), 8. This point is made explicitly in response to my theorization of embodied technique in *What a Body Can Do*. Throughout the book Camilleri extends the concept of embodied knowledge to embrace that which might otherwise be backgrounded as environment.

151. Barba, *Beyond the Floating Islands*. I am thinking of the complex relationships to place that have been developed in small towns and villages like Holstebro (Odin Teatret), Gardzienice, Pontedera (Workcenter of Jerzy Grotowski and Thomas Richards), and Ashfield (Double Edge Theatre). This issue is explored in Schechner, "Double Edge Theatre in Its Ashfield Community." As noted in chapter 2, it may be valuable to rethink these relations to place in light of the discussion and critique of white queer "back-to-the-land" movements found in Morgensen, *Spaces between Us*.

152. Tuck and McKenzie, *Place in Research*, 105. Part of this passage is a quotation from David Howes. See also the relationship between biopolitics and geopolitics in Mark Rifkin, "Indigenizing Agamben: Rethinking Sovereignty in Light of the 'Peculiar' Status of Native Peoples," *Cultural Critique* 73 (2009): 88–124.

153. Tuck and Yang, "Decolonization Is Not a Metaphor."

154. For a recent reflection on Tuck and Yang's influential article, see *Nothing Never Happens*, "A Third University Is Always Happening." For a careful and incisive critique, see Gopal, "On Decolonisation and the University." For an overview of the difference between political decolonization and epistemic decoloniality, see Mignolo and Walsh, *On Decoloniality*. I am looking here especially for how a european jewish diasporic perspective might contribute to conversations

between black diasporic, asian diasporic, and south and north american indigenous perspectives, as well as those of critical whiteness studies.

155. Tapji Garba and Sara-Maria Sorentino, "Slavery Is a Metaphor: A Critical Commentary on Eve Tuck and K. Wayne Yang's 'Decolonization Is Not a Metaphor,'" *Antipode* 52, no. 3 (2020): 772.

156. Garba and Sorentino, "Slavery Is a Metaphor," 770, italics original.

157. See Barker, *Sovereignty Matters*; Coulthard, *Red Skin, White Masks*, 2014; Leanne Betasamosake Simpson, *As We Have Always Done: Indigenous Freedom through Radical Resistance* (Minneapolis: University of Minnesota Press, 2017); Darryl Leroux, *Distorted Descent: White Claims to Indigenous Identity* (Winnipeg: University of Manitoba Press, 2019). For a synthesizing anthropological treatment of indigenous relations to place, see Soren C. Larsen and Jay T. Johnson, *Being Together in Place: Indigenous Coexistence in a More than Human World* (Minneapolis: University of Minnesota Press, 2017). For a white european approach to earthing that does not cite indigenous sources, see Bruno Latour, *Down to Earth: Politics in the New Climatic Regime*, trans. Catherine Porter (Cambridge, UK: Polity, 2018).

158. King, Navarro, and Smith, *Otherwise Worlds*, 12, italics added. Nandita Sharma also criticizes the tendency in some indigenous scholarship and activism to implement a native-nonnative binary that ignores important differences between the enslaved, the migrant, and the colonizer, reducing all to the category of settler. But in my view Sharma's approach is too hasty and simplistic in its dismissal of indigenous politics and of the politics of identity. Sharma, "Strategic Anti-Essentialism: Decolonizing Decolonization," in McKittrick, *Sylvia Wynter*, 164–82.

159. King, *Black Shoals*, 191.

160. Coulthard, *Red Skin, White Masks*, makes this argument most explicitly.

161. Rifkin, *Fictions of Land and Flesh*.

162. See King, *Black Shoals*; Weheliye, *Habeas Viscus*; Bey, *Problem of the Negro*; Wilderson, *Red, White & Black*; and Hartman, *Scenes of Subjection*.

163. Bey, *Problem of the Negro*, 47.

164. There is no contradiction between positing the Ten Commandments as an origin point for white writing and seeking alternatives to white writing in the development of talmudic jewish thought. On the intensely gendered relations between rabbinic (talmudic) judaism and logocentrism, see Boyarin, *Unheroic Conduct*. Boyarin links the commandment against graven images directly to patriarchal, colonial, white supremacist logocentrism (254–70). The much-vaunted spirituality, abstraction, and "intellectuality" of this masculinist "rule of law" (255) is precisely the replacement of the analogue image with alphabetic texuality as a technique of control. White writing in this sense follows a "Christian tradition dating back to the thirteenth century which admired 'the Mosaic law but despised the legalistic accretions of the Talmudists'" (262n158). These very different ways in which textuality evolved over centuries suggest important, more media-critical layers of meaning for ongoing jewish racial ambivalence as "off-white" (262).

165. McKittrick, *Dear Science and Other Stories*, ix.

166. McKittrick, *Demonic Grounds: Black Women and the Cartographies of Struggle* (Minneapolis: University of Minnesota Press, 2006), xxii. I have been

using the phrase "technique, identity, and place" since 2017 and only in 2021 discovered McKittrick's much earlier discussion of "identity and place." Earlier thinkers of black geography on whom McKittrick draws include Édouard Glissant, Sylvia Wynter, and Paul Gilroy. See also the Black/Land Project, http://www.blacklandproject.org/.

167. McKittrick, *Demonic Grounds*, xxiii, xxxi.

168. Paul Gilroy, *The Black Atlantic: Modernity and Double Consciousness* (Cambridge, MA: Harvard University Press, 2003); McKittrick, *Demonic Grounds*, xiv, 149n8.

169. Liboiron, *Pollution Is Colonialism*, 28–29.

170. Ian Baucom, *History 4° Celsius: Search for a Method in the Age of the Anthropocene* (Durham, NC: Duke University Press, 2020), 56.

171. See Spatz, "Thresholds," in *Blue Sky Body*. I use these conceptual categories to analyze a different video from the Judaica project in a recent talk: "Thresholds: Race, Artistic Research, and the Forms of Knowledge," University of Leeds, July 21, 2021, https://cepra.leeds.ac.uk/2021/07/04/538/.

172. Illuminated video can be seen as a synthesizing response to what has often been posed as a dichotomy between textual and audiovisual forms of mediation. For a fascinating account of this polarization in the early twentieth century, and more specifically in the life and work of Franz Kafka, see Roger F. Cook, *Postcinematic Vision: The Coevolution of Moving-Image Media and the Spectator* (Minneapolis: University of Minnesota Press, 2020), 113–53. Cook's analysis of media relations is explicitly universalist (14) and does not mention Kafka's jewishness. But the tensions between audiovisuality and textuality that Cook traces only become more significant when the racial dimensions of media are acknowledged.

173. Spatz et al., "He Almost Forgets."

174. As previously noted, the academic field of jewish studies has been slow to engage with the radical shifts in critical theory and audiovisuality that I am tracking here. As a counterexample, see Adam Zachary Newton's stimulating discussion of the *Lehrhaus* as a possible site for the "temporality of the living moment, outside the university walls," a site and practice that could be at once "bookless" and at the same time "thoroughly and immersively textual" (Newton, *Jewish Studies as Counterlife*, 146). I would propose to think Newton's *Lehrhaus* alongside Moten and Harney's concept of "study" in *Undercommons*.

175. Houria Bouteldja, *Whites, Jews, and Us: Toward a Politics of Revolutionary Love*, trans. Rachel Valinsky (Los Angeles: Semiotext(e), 2017), 140, 67.

176. Moten, *Universal Machine*, 25.

177. Moten, *Universal Machine*, 25. Levinas's failure to fully grasp the decolonial potential of jewishness is also discussed in Slabodsky, *Decolonial Judaism*, chapter 4.

178. Robinson, *Hungry Listening*, 8.

Afterword

1. Ben Spatz, Nazlıhan Eda Erçin, Ilona Krawczyk, and Agnieszka Mendel, "whiteness," *Performance Philosophy* 7, no. 2 (2022): 169–72, https://doi.org/10.21476/PP.2022.72349. The coauthors of this publication cocreated its audiovisual content but I accept responsibility for its textual content, including the title,

which radically reframes its meaning. The book is Giorgio Agamben, *The Open: Man and Animal* (Stanford, CA: Stanford University Press, 2004).

2. Spatz, *Blue Sky Body*, 255–56.

3. Hagar Kotef, *The Colonizing Self: Or, Home and Homelessness in Israel/ Palestine* (Durham, NC: Duke University Press, 2020), 127–35.

4. Lorenzo Veracini, "Decolonizing Settler Colonialism: Kill the Settler in Him and Save the Man," *American Indian Culture and Research Journal* 41, no. 1 (2017): 1–18, https://doi.org/10.17953/aicrj.41.1.veracini.

5. Veracini, "Decolonizing Settler Colonialism," 12, 10.

6. Kotef, *Colonizing Self*, 131.

7. Kotef, *Colonizing Self*, 133.

8. Kotef, *Colonizing Self*, 132, italics added.

9. Kotef, *Colonizing Self*, 134.

10. Thanks to Einav Katan-Schmid for this translation.

11. Elaine Spatz Rabinowitz, http://www.espatzrabinowitz.com/.

12. *Postmemory: Fragments* and *Postmemory: Crypt* ran for eight weeks (June–August 2022) at Holocaust Centre North, University of Huddersfield. Both videos were created by Ben Spatz with Nazlıhan Eda Erçin and Agnieszka Mandel. As of this writing, these are the only Judaica project video works that have been presented publicly but not made available online.

13. Shawn Wilson, *Research Is Ceremony: Indigenous Research Methods* (Winnipeg: Fernwood Publishing, 2008).

14. For a longer discussion of these works, see Ben Spatz with Lxo Cohen, Lindsey Dodd, Nazlıhan Eda Erçin, Paula Kolar, and Agnieszka Mendel, "Postmemory: Fragments / Crypt," *Performance Matters* 9, no. 1–2 (2023): 171–86.

15. King, *Black Shoals*, 189. King's discussion of ceremony responds to a pair of articles by Sylvia Wynter, written thirty years apart, in which the search for ceremony is directly thematized: Sylvia Wynter, "The Ceremony Must Be Found: After Humanism," *Boundary 2* 12, no. 3 (1984): 19, https://doi.org/10.2307 /302808; and "The Ceremony Found: Towards the Autopoetic Turn/Overturn, Its Autonomy of Human Agency and Extraterritoriality of (Self-)Cognition," in *Black Knowledges/Black Struggles: Essays in Critical Epistemology*, ed. Jason R. Ambroise and Sabine Bröck-Sallah (Liverpool: Liverpool University Press, 2015), 184–245.

16. King, *Black Shoals*, 176–78.

17. King, *Black Shoals*, 184, 186.

18. King, *Black Shoals*, 190.

19. Keeling, "I = Another: Digital Identity Politics," discussed in chapter 1.

WORKS CITED

Abbasi, Iskander. "Islam, Muslims, and the Coloniality of Being: Reframing the Debate on Race and Religion in Modernity." *Journal for the Study of Religion* 33, no. 2 (2021). https://doi.org/10.17159/2413-3027/2020/v33n2a4.

Ackerman, Marianne. "Robert Lepage's Controversial Kanata Opens in Paris as a Rehearsal." *Montreal Gazette*, December 20, 2018. https://montrealgazette .com/entertainment/local-arts/robert-lepages-controversial-kanata-opens-in -paris-as-a-rehearsal.

"Afropessimism and Its Others: A Discussion between Hortense J. Spillers and Lewis R. Gordon." Soka University of America, Alisa Viejo, CA, May 24, 2021. https://www.youtube.com/watch?v=Z-s-Ltu06NI.

Ahmed, Sara. "Declarations of Whiteness: The Non-Performativity of Anti-Racism." *Borderlands* 3, no. 2 (2004).

———. *Living a Feminist Life*. Durham, NC: Duke University Press, 2017.

———. *On Being Included: Racism and Diversity in Institutional Life*. Durham, NC: Duke University Press, 2012.

———. *The Promise of Happiness*. Durham, NC: Duke University Press, 2010.

Alcoff, Linda. *The Future of Whiteness*. Cambridge, UK: Polity Press, 2015.

Allegue, Ludivine, Simon Jones, Baz Kershaw, and Angela Piccini, eds. *Practice-as-Research in Performance and Screen*. New York: Palgrave Macmillan, 2009.

Alliance for the Arts in Research Universities. *What Is Research? Practices in the Arts, Research, and Curricula*. Ann Arbor: University of Michigan, 2018.

Alpert, Michael. *Crypto-Judaism and the Spanish Inquisition*. Basingstoke, UK: Palgrave, 2001.

Always Already Podcast. "Ep. 29: Frank B. Wilderson III on Cinema and the Structure of US Racial Antagonisms." Podcast, September 22, 2015. https:// alwaysalreadypodcast.wordpress.com/2015/09/22/wilderson/.

———. "Interview: Frank B. Wilderson III on Afropessimism: Epistemic Unruli-ness 28." Podcast, May 11, 2020. https://alwaysalreadypodcast.wordpress.com /2020/05/11/wilderson-interview/.

Andrews, Kehinde. "The Radical 'Possibilities' of Black Studies." *Black Scholar* 50, no. 3 (2020): 17–28.

Ang, Gey Pin, Massimiliano Balduzzi, Ditte Berkeley, Daniel Alexander Jones, M. Lamar, Samita Sinha, Tatyana Tenenbaum, and Ben Spatz. "What Is a Song?" *Performance Research* 24, no. 1 (2019): 80–93. https://doi.org/10.1080 /13528165.2019.1601945.

Another Europe Is Possible. "Episode 37: Priyamvada Gopal on a Decolonised Europe: Saving Europe from Itself." Podcast, October 7, 2019. https://www .anothereurope.org/episode-37-priyamvada-gopal-on-a-decolonial-europe -saving-europe-from-itself/.

Appiah, Kwame Anthony. "Go Ahead, Speak for Yourself." *New York Times*, August 10, 2018. https://www.nytimes.com/2018/08/10/opinion/sunday/speak -for-yourself.html.

———. *The Lies that Bind: Rethinking Identity, Creed, Country, Color, Class, Culture*. 1st ed. New York: Liveright, 2018.

Arlander, Annette, Bruce Barton, Melanie Dreyer-Lude, and Ben Spatz, eds. *Performance as Research: Knowledge, Methods, Impact*. 1st ed. New York: Routledge, 2017.

Artistic Doctorates in Europe. "Experiences and Perceptions of the Artistic Doctorate in Dance and Performance." 2017. https://www.artisticdoctorates.com/.

Arts Research Africa. *How Does Artistic Research Decolonise Knowledge and Practice in Africa?* Johannesburg: University of the Witwatersrand, 2020. http://wiredspace.wits.ac.za/handle/10539/29181.

Auslander, Philip. *From Acting to Performance Essays in Modernism and Postmodernism*. London: Routledge, 2002.

Azoulay, Ariella Aïsha. "Open Letter to Sylvia Wynter: Unlearning the Disappearance of Jews from Africa." *Funambulist*, no. 30 (2020). https://thefunambulist .net/magazine/reparations.

Bailey, Alison. "On White Shame and Vulnerability." *South African Journal of Philosophy* 30, no. 4 (2011): 472–83.

Baker, Cynthia M. *Jew*. Key Words in Jewish Studies 7. New Brunswick, NJ: Rutgers University Press, 2017.

Baldwin, James. *Collected Essays*. Library of America 98. New York: Library of America, 1998.

Ball, Philip. *Stories of the Invisible: A Guided Tour of Molecules*. Oxford: Oxford University Press, 2002.

Ballantyne, Tony, Lachy Paterson, and Angela Wanhalla, eds. *Indigenous Textual Cultures: Reading and Writing in the Age of Global Empire*. Durham, NC: Duke University Press, 2020.

Bambara, Celia Weiss. "On locating interculturalism and somatics: Looseness, holding on and swimming." *Journal of Dance & Somatic Practices* 14, no. 2 (2022): 217–30.

Barad, Karen. *Meeting the Universe Halfway: Quantum Physics and the Entanglement of Matter and Meaning*. Durham, NC: Duke University Press, 2007.

Barba, Eugenio. *Beyond the Floating Islands*. New York: PAJ Publications, 1985.

Barker, Joanne, ed. *Critically Sovereign: Indigenous Gender, Sexuality, and Feminist Studies*. Durham, NC: Duke University Press, 2017.

———. *Sovereignty Matters: Locations of Contestation and Possibility in Indigenous Struggles for Self-Determination*. Contemporary Indigenous Issues. Lincoln: University of Nebraska Press, 2005.

Barrett, Estelle, and Barbara Bolt, eds. *Carnal Knowledge: Towards a "New Materialism" through the Arts*. New York: I. B. Tauris, 2013.

Baucom, Ian. *History 4° Celsius: Search for a Method in the Age of the Anthropocene*. Theory in Forms. Durham, NC: Duke University Press, 2020.

Beckman, Frida, ed. *Control Culture: Foucault and Deleuze after Discipline*. Edinburgh: Edinburgh University Press, 2018.

Belcourt, Billy-Ray. *A History of My Brief Body*. Columbus, OH: Two Dollar Radio, 2020.

Bergo, Bettina, Joseph D. Cohen, and Raphael Zagury-Orly, eds. *Judeities: Questions for Jacques Derrida*. New York: Fordham University Press, 2007.

Berman, Lila Corwin. "Jewish History beyond the Jewish People." *AJS Review* 42, no. 2 (2018): 269–92.

Bernstein, Robin. *Racial Innocence: Performing American Childhood from Slavery to Civil Rights*. New York: New York University Press, 2011.

Bessire, Lucas, and David Bond. "Ontological Anthropology and the Deferral of Critique." *American Ethnologist* 41, no. 3 (2014): 440–56.

Bey, Marquis. *Black Trans Feminism*. Black Outdoors: Innovations in the Poetics of Study. Durham, NC: Duke University Press, 2022.

———, "Incorporeal Blackness: A Theorization in Two Parts—Rachel Dolezal and Your Face in Mine." *CR: The New Centennial Review* 20, no. 2 (2020): 205–41.

———. *The Problem of the Negro as a Problem for Gender*. Minneapolis: University of Minnesota Press, 2020.

Bey, Marquis, and Theodora Sakellarides. "When We Enter: The Blackness of Rachel Dolezal." *Black Scholar* 46, no. 4 (2016): 33–48.

Bharucha, Rustom. *Theatre and the World: Performance and the Politics of Culture*. London: Routledge, 1993.

Biagini, Mario. "Changes: From the Workcenter to the Academy of the Unfulfilled." *TDR: The Drama Review* 66, no. 3 (2022): 184–93. https://doi.org/10.1017/S1054204322000466.

Bial, Henry. *Acting Jewish: Negotiating Ethnicity on the American Stage and Screen*. Ann Arbor: University of Michigan Press, 2005.

———, ed. *The Performance Studies Reader*. 2d ed. London: Routledge, 2007.

Bicknell, Jeanette. *A Philosophy of Song and Singing: An Introduction*. New York: Routledge, 2015.

Bicknell, Jeanette, and John Andrew Fisher. "Introduction: Making a Space for Song." *Journal of Aesthetics and Art Criticism* 71, no. 1 (2013): 1–11.

Bielik-Robson, Agata. *Jewish Cryptotheologies of Late Modernity: Philosophical Marranos*. Routledge Jewish Studies Series. London: Routledge, 2014.

Bithell, Caroline. *A Different Voice, A Different Song: Reclaiming Community through the Natural Voice and World Song*. Oxford: Oxford University Press, 2014.

Blaser, Mario. "Ontology and Indigeneity: On the Political Ontology of Heterogeneous Assemblages." *Cultural Geographies* 21, no. 1 (January 2014): 49–58. https://doi.org/10.1177/1474474012462534.

Boone, Elizabeth Hill, and Walter Mignolo, eds. *Writing without Words: Alternative Literacies in Mesoamerica and the Andes*. Durham, NC: Duke University Press, 1994.

Borelli, Melissa Blanco, and Raquel Monroe, eds. "Screening the Skin: Issues of Race and Nation in Screendance." *International Journal of Screendance* 9 (2018).

Borgdorff, Henk. *The Conflict of the Faculties: Perspectives on Artistic Research and Academia*. Leiden, Netherlands: Leiden University Press, 2012.

Borgdorff, Henk, Peter Peters, and Trevor Pinch, eds. *Dialogues between Artistic Research and Science and Technology Studies*. Routledge Advances in Art and Visual Studies. New York: Routledge, 2020.

Bouteldja, Houria. *Whites, Jews, and Us: Toward a Politics of Revolutionary Love*. Translated by Rachel Valinsky, 2017.

Boyarin, Daniel. *Unheroic Conduct: The Rise of Heterosexuality and the Invention of the Jewish Man*. Berkeley: University of California Press, 1997.

————. "20th Anniversary Lecture, Judaic Studies: Daniel Boyarin: No 'Judaism' In Josephus." McClung Museum of Natural History and Culture, University of Tennessee, Knoxville, October 24, 2013, posted January 16, 2014. https://www.youtube.com/watch?v=9iL3NZrxp28.

Boyarin, Daniel, Daniel Itzkovitz, and Ann Pellegrini, eds. *Queer Theory and the Jewish Question*. New York: Columbia University Press, 2003.

Boyarin, Jonathan. *Thinking in Jewish*. Chicago: University of Chicago Press, 1996.

————. *The Unconverted Self: Jews, Indians, and the Identity of Christian Europe*. Chicago: University of Chicago Press, 2009.

Boyarin, Jonathan, and Daniel Boyarin. *Powers of Diaspora: Two Essays on the Relevance of Jewish Culture*. Minneapolis: University of Minnesota Press, 2002.

Bradley, Rizvana. "Picturing Catastrophe: The Visual Politics of Racial Reckoning." *Yale Review*, May 25, 2021. https://yalereview.org/article/picturing-catastrophe.

Brander Rasmussen, Birgit. *Queequeg's Coffin: Indigenous Literacies and Early American Literature*. Durham, NC: Duke University Press, 2012.

Brim, Matt. *Poor Queer Studies: Confronting Elitism in the University*. Durham, NC: Duke University Press, 2020.

Browne, Simone. *Dark Matters: On the Surveillance of Blackness*. Durham, NC: Duke University Press, 2015.

Bruce, La Marr Jurelle. *How to Go Mad without Losing Your Mind: Madness and Black Radical Creativity*. Durham, NC: Duke University Press, 2020.

Buber, Martin. *The Legend of the Baal-Shem*. London: Routledge, 2002.

————. *Tales of the Hasidim*. New York: Schocken Books, 1991.

Building Belonging. "Societal Healing and Belonging." August 11, 2020. https://www.youtube.com/watch?v=7j-LEeNJxnc.

Bulley, James, and Özden Şahin. "Practice Research—Report 1: What Is Practice Research? And Report 2: How Can Practice Research Be Shared?" London: PRAG-UK, 2021. https://doi.org/10.23636/1347.

Butler, Judith. *Parting Ways: Jewishness and the Critique of Zionism*. New York: Columbia University Press, 2012.

Byrd, Jodi A. *The Transit of Empire: Indigenous Critiques of Colonialism*. First Peoples: New Directions Indigenous. Minneapolis: University of Minnesota Press, 2011.

Camilleri, Frank. *Performer Training Reconfigured: Post-Psychophysical Perspectives for the Twenty-First Century*. London: Methuen Drama, 2020.

Cappelle, Laura. "Review: In Robert Lepage's 'Kanata,' the Director, Too, Plays the Victim." *New York Times*, December 17, 2018. https://www.nytimes.com/2018/12/17/theater/robert-lepage-kanata-review.html.

Carastathis, Anna. *Intersectionality: Origins, Contestations, Horizons*. Expanding Frontiers, Interdisciplinary Approaches to Studies of Women, Gender, and Sexuality. Lincoln: University of Nebraska Press, 2016.

cárdenas, micha. *Poetic Operations: Trans of Color Art in Digital Media.* Durham, NC: Duke University Press, 2022.

Carpenter, Faedra Chatard. *Coloring Whiteness: Acts of Critique in Black Performance.* Ann Arbor: University of Michigan Press, 2014.

Carriger, Michelle Liu, ed. "#PerformativeX," special section of *Journal of Dramatic Theory* 35, no. 2 (2021): 9–148.

Carson, A. D. *I Used to Love to Dream.* Ann Arbor: University of Michigan Press, 2020. https://doi.org/10.3998/mpub.11738372.

———. "Owning My Masters: The Rhetorics of Rhymes & Revolutions." PhD diss., Clemson University, 2017. https://tigerprints.clemson.edu/all_dissertations/1885/.

Carter, J. Kameron. "Jews and the Religion of Whiteness." Katz Center for Advanced Judaic Studies, University of Pennsylvania, Philadephia, February 11, 2021. https://www.reconstructingjudaism.org/center-jewish-ethics/jews-race-and-religion/3.

Case, Benjamin Steinhardt. "Decolonizing Jewishness: On Jewish Liberation in the 21st Century." *Tikkun Magazine,* April 18, 2018. https://www.tikkun.org/nextgen/2018/04/18/decolonizing-jewishness-on-jewish-liberation-in-the-21st-century/.

Catanese, Brandi Wilkins. *The Problem of the Color[blind]: Racial Transgression and the Politics of Black Performance.* Ann Arbor: University of Michigan Press, 2014.

———. "Teaching *A Day of Absence* 'at [Your] Own Risk.' " *Theatre Topics* 19, no. 1 (2009): 29–38. https://doi.org/10.1353/tt.0.0049.

Cetina, Karin Knorr. "The Couch, the Cathedral, and the Laboratory: On the Relationship between Experiment and Laboratory in Science." In *Science as Practice and Culture,* edited by Andrew Pickering, 113–38. Chicago: University of Chicago Press, 1992.

Chaudhuri, Una, and Shonni Enelow. *Research Theatre, Climate Change, and the Ecocide Project.* Basingstoke, UK: Palgrave Macmillan, 2016.

Chen, Mel Y. *Animacies: Biopolitics, Racial Mattering, and Queer Affect.* Perverse Modernities. Durham, NC: Duke University Press, 2012.

Cheng, Anne Anlin. *Ornamentalism.* New York: Oxford University Press, 2019.

Chia e Tazi Pesen? [Whose Is This Song?]. Sofia, Bulgaria: Adela Media Film and TV Productions, 2003. http://www.adelamedia.net/movies/whose-is-this-song.php.

Chun, Wendy Hui Kyong. "Race and/as Technology, or How to Do Things to Race." In *Race after the Internet,* edited by Lisa Nakamura and Peter A. Chow-White, 38–60. New York: Routledge, 2012.

Cioffi, Kathleen. "Zar and Other Microcultures of 'Grotland.' " *Slavic and Eastern European Performance* 28, no. 2 (2008): 20–29.

Cixous, Hélène. "The Laugh of the Medusa." *Signs: Journal of Women in Culture and Society* 1, no. 4 (1976): 875–93.

———. *Portrait of Jacques Derrida as a Young Jewish Saint.* New York: Columbia University Press, 2005.

Climenhaga, Lily. "The Power of Presence: Indigenous Representation in Theatre, Reflections on Mnouchkine/Lepage, Kanata, and Colonial Remains." *Lost Dramaturgin International,* September 9, 2018. https://lostdramaturgininternational

.wordpress.com/2018/09/09/the-power-of-presence-indigenous-representation
-in-theatre-reflections-on-mnouchkine-lepage-kanata-and-colonial-remains/.

Colbert, Soyica Diggs, Douglas A. Jones Jr., and Shane Vogel, eds. *Race and Performance after Repetition*. Durham, NC: Duke University Press, 2020.

Coleman, Beth. "Race as Technology." *Camera Obscura* 24, no. 1 (70) (2009): 177–207. https://doi.org/10.1215/02705346-2008-018.

Conquergood, Dwight. *Cultural Struggles: Performance, Ethnography, Praxis*. Edited by E. Patrick Johnson. Ann Arbor: University of Michigan Press, 2013.

———. "Performance Studies: Interventions and Radical Research." *TDR: The Drama Review* 46, no. 2 (2002): 145–56.

Cook, Roger F. *Postcinematic Vision: The Coevolution of Moving-Image Media and the Spectator*. Posthumanities. Minneapolis: University of Minnesota Press, 2020.

Coole, Diana H., and Samantha Frost, eds. *New Materialisms: Ontology, Agency, and Politics*. Durham, NC: Duke University Press, 2010.

Coulthard, Glen Sean. *Red Skin, White Masks: Rejecting the Colonial Politics of Recognition*. Indigenous Americas. Minneapolis: University of Minnesota Press, 2014.

Cruz, Edgar Gómez, Shanti Sumartojo, and Sarah Pink, eds. *Refiguring Techniques in Digital Visual Research*. Basingstoke, UK: Palgrave Macmillan, 2017. https://www.palgrave.com/de/book/9783319612218.

Cull Ó Maoilearca, Laura, and Alice Lagaay, eds. *The Routledge Companion to Performance Philosophy*. Routledge Companions 18. Abingdon, UK: Routledge, 2020.

Culp, Andrew. *Dark Deleuze*. Minneapolis: University of Minnesota Press, 2016.

da Silva, Denise Ferreira. "On Difference without Separability." In *Incerteza viva (Living Uncertainty)*. São Paulo: 32a Art Biennial, 2016. https://issuu.com /amilcarpacker/docs/denise_ferreira_da_silva/5.

———. *Toward a Global Idea of Race*. Borderlines 27. Minneapolis: University of Minnesota Press, 2007.

Dabiri, Emma. *What White People Can Do next: From Allyship to Coalition*. London: Penguin, 2021.

de la Cadena, Marisol, and Mario Blaser, eds. *A World of Many Worlds*. Durham, NC: Duke University Press, 2018.

De Marinis, Marco. "Maud Robart, Student/Teacher: Collaborating with Grotowski." Translated by Giulia Vittori. *TDR: The Drama Review* 61, no. 1 (2017): 114–23.

DeFrantz, Thomas F. "I Am Black (You Have to Be Willing to Not Know)." *Theater* 47, no. 2 (2007): 8–21.

Deleuze, Gilles, and Félix Guattari. *A Thousand Plateaus: Capitalism and Schizophrenia*. Minneapolis: University of Minnesota Press, 1987.

Deloria, Philip Joseph. *Playing Indian*. New Haven, CT: Yale University Press, 2007.

Derrida, Jacques. *Margins of Philosophy*. Translated by Alan Bass. Chicago: University of Chicago Press, 1982.

———. *Of Grammatology*. Translated by Gayatri Chakravorty Spivak. 40th anniversary ed. Baltimore, MD: Johns Hopkins University Press, 2016.

Deutscher, Isaac. *The Non-Jewish Jew and Other Essays*. Radical Thinkers. London: Verso, 2017.

Dolgopolski, Sergey. *What Is Talmud? The Art of Disagreement*. New York: Fordham University Press, 2009.

Dolphijn, Rick, and Iris van der Tuin. *New Materialism: Interviews and Cartographies*. 1st ed. New Metaphysics. Ann Arbor, MI: Open Humanities Press, 2012.

D'Souza, Aruna. *Whitewalling: Art, Race & Protest in 3 Acts*. New York: Badlands Unlimited, 2018.

Dutta, Aniruddha. "Allegories of Gender: Transgender Autology versus Transracialism." *Atlantis Journal* 39, no. 2 (2018): 86–98.

Eidsheim, Nina Sun. *The Race of Sound: Listening, Timbre, and Vocality in African American Music*. Refiguring American Music. Durham, NC: Duke University Press, 2019.

Elam, Harry J., Jr. "Fathers and Sons." *TDR: The Drama Review* 52, no. 2 (2008): 2–3.

"Encore une fois, l'aventure se passera sans nous, les Autochtones?" *Le Devoir*, July 14, 2018. https://www.ledevoir.com/opinion/libre-opinion/532406/encore-une-fois-l-aventure-se-passera-sans-nous-les-autochtones.

Erçin, Nazlıhan Eda. "From-Ness: The Identity of the Practitioner in the Laboratory." *Journal of Interdisciplinary Voice Studies* 3, no. 2 (2018): 195–202. https://doi.org/10.1386/jivs.3.2.195_1.

Erçin, Nazlıhan Eda, Agnieszka Mendel, and Ben Spatz. "Działoszyce: Song, Border, Body." 1st International Ecoperformance Festival, March 16–19, 2021. 18 min. https://taanteatro.wixsite.com/ecoperformance/ecopoethics-in-progress.

Eshun, Kodwo. *More Brilliant than the Sun: Adventures in Sonic Fiction*. London: Quartet Books, 1998.

Facer, Keri, and Christopher Newfield, eds. "Special Section: Global Higher Education in 2050: Building Universities for Sustainable Societies." *Critical Times* 5, no. 1 (2022): 77–216.

Fanon, Frantz. *Black Skin, White Masks*. London: Pluto Press, 2008.

Fassin, Didier. "Racialization: How to Do Races with Bodies." In *A Companion to the Anthropology of the Body and Embodiment*, edited by Frances E. Mascia-Lees, 419–34. Malden, MA: Blackwell Publishing, 2011.

Ferguson, Roderick A. *The Reorder of Things: The University and Its Pedagogies of Minority Difference*. Minneapolis: University of Minnesota Press, 2012.

Fetokaki, Sophie. "A Handbook of Situated Making." PhD diss., University of Huddersfield, 2022. https://eprints.hud.ac.uk/id/eprint/35684/.

Fielder, Brigitte, and Jonathan Senchyne, eds. *Against a Sharp White Background: Infrastructures of African American Print*. Madison: University of Wisconsin Press, 2019.

Fikes, Kesha. *"Extimacy" as Racial Transparency in the Embodied Relational Field*. Embodied Social Justice Summit, February 16–20, 2021. https://www.embodiedsocialjusticesummit.com.

Flusser, Vilém, and Mark Poster. *Does Writing Have a Future?* Minneapolis: University of Minnesota Press, 2011.

Franco, Dean. "The Jews are 'The New Jews.'" *Studies in American Jewish Literature* 39, no. 1 (2020): 139–59.

Gajowy, Aleksandra. "Staying at the Level of Impulses: Queering the Grotowski Archive in Karol Radziszewski's *The Prince*." *Contemporary Theatre Review* 31, no. 1–2 (2021): 113–31.

Galloway, Alexander R., and Bernard Dionysius Geoghegan. "Shaky Distinctions: A Dialogue on the Digital and the Analog." *e-flux journal*, no. 121 (October 2021). https://www.e-flux.com/journal/121/423015/shaky-distinctions-a-dialogue-on-the-digital-and-the-analog/.

Garba, Tapji, and Sara-Maria Sorentino. "Slavery Is a Metaphor: A Critical Commentary on Eve Tuck and K. Wayne Yang's 'Decolonization Is Not a Metaphor.'" *Antipode* 52, no. 3 (2020): 764–82.

Gare, Arran. "The Grand Narrative of the Age of Re-Embodiments: Beyond Modernism and Postmodernism." *Cosmos and History: The Journal of Natural and Social Philosophy* 9, no. 1 (2013): 327–57.

Gatt, Caroline. "Breathing beyond Embodiment: Exploring Emergence, Grieving and Song in Laboratory Theatre." *Body & Society* 26, no. 2 (2020): 106–29. https://doi.org/10.1177/1357034X19900538.

———, ed. *The Voices of the Pages*. Knowing from the Inside. Aberdeen, Scotland: University of Aberdeen, 2017.

Gatt, Caroline, and Valeria Lembo. "Knowing by Singing." Special section. *American Anthropologist* 24, no. 4 (2022): 830–40. https://anthrosource.onlinelibrary.wiley.com/toc/15481433/2022/124/4.

Gill-Peterson, Jules. *Histories of the Transgender Child*. Minneapolis: University of Minnesota Press, 2018.

———. "The Technical Capacities of the Body Assembling Race, Technology, and Transgender." *TSQ: Transgender Studies Quarterly* 1, no. 3 (2014): 402–18. https://doi.org/10.1215/23289252-2685660.

Gilman, Sander L. *The Jew's Body*. New York: Routledge, 1991.

Gilroy, Paul. *Against Race: Imagining Political Culture beyond the Color Line*. Cambridge, MA: Belknap Press of Harvard University Press, 2001.

———. *The Black Atlantic: Modernity and Double Consciousness*. Cambridge, MA: Harvard University Press, 2003.

Goehr, Lydia. *The Imaginary Museum of Musical Works: An Essay in the Philosophy of Music*. Oxford: Oxford University Press, 1992.

Goldstein, Eric L. *The Price of Whiteness: Jews, Race, and American Identity*. Princeton, NJ: Princeton University Press, 2008.

Gómez-Barris, Macarena. *The Extractive Zone: Social Ecologies and Decolonial Perspectives*. Durham, NC: Duke University Press, 2017.

Gopal, Priyamvada. *Insurgent Empire: Anticolonial Resistance and British Dissent*. London: Verso, 2019.

———. "On Decolonisation and the University." *Textual Practice* 35, no. 6 (2021): 873–99.

Gottschild, Brenda Dixon. *Digging the Africanist Presence in American Performance: Dance and Other Contexts*. Westport, CT: Praeger, 1998.

Grant, Catherine. "The Shudder of a Cinephiliac Idea? Videographic Film Studies Practice as Material Thinking." *ANIKI: Portuguese Journal of the Moving Image* 1, no. 1 (2014): 49–62.

Green, Kai M. "'Race and Gender Are Not the Same!' Is Not a Good Response to the 'Transracial'/Transgender Question OR We Can and Must Do Better."

Feminist Wire, June 14, 2015. https://www.thefeministwire.com/2015/06
/race-and-gender-are-not-the-same-is-not-a-good-response-to-the-transracial
-transgender-question-or-we-can-and-must-do-better/.

Guattari, Félix. *Molecular Revolution: Psychiatry and Politics*. Harmondsworth, UK Penguin, 1984.

———. *The Three Ecologies*. London: Bloomsbury Academic, 2014.

Guy, Nancy. "Trafficking in Taiwan Aboriginal Voices." In *Handle with Care: Ownership and Control of Ethnographic Materials*, edited by Sjoerd R. Jaarsma, 195–209. Pittsburgh, PA: University of Pittsburgh Press, 2002.

Hage, Ghassan. *Is Racism an Environmental Threat?* Debating Race. Malden, MA: Polity, 2017.

Haider, Asad. *Mistaken Identity: Race and Class in the Age of Trump*. London: Verso, 2018.

Hammerschlag, Sarah. *The Figural Jew: Politics and Identity in Postwar French Thought*. Chicago: University of Chicago Press, 2010.

Hancock, Ange-Marie. *Intersectionality: An Intellectual History*. New York: Oxford University Press, 2016.

Harding, James Martin, and Cindy Rosenthal, eds. *The Rise of Performance Studies: Rethinking Richard Schechner's Broad Spectrum*. Studies in International Performance. Basingstoke, UK: Palgrave Macmillan, 2011.

Harman, Graham. *Object-Oriented Ontology: A New Theory of Everything*. Pelican Book 18. London: Pelican Books, 2018.

Harney, Stefano, and Fred Moten. *The Undercommons: Fugitive Planning and Black Study*. Wivenhoe: Minor Compositions, 2013.

Harrison, Da'Shaun. *Belly of the Beast: The Politics of Anti-Fatness as Anti-Blackness*. Berkeley, CA: North Atlantic Books, 2021.

Harrison, Ellie. "'I Spoke Up and Got Smacked Down': Producer Effie Brown Recalls Backlash after Her Conflict with Matt Damon over Diversity Went Viral." *Independent*, June 19, 2020. https://www.independent.co.uk/arts
-entertainment/tv/news/matt-damon-effie-brown-project-greenlight-diversity
-racism-a9574521.html.

Hartman, Saidiya V. *Scenes of Subjection: Terror, Slavery, and Self-Making in Nineteenth-Century America*. New York: Oxford University Press, 1997.

Hartman, Saidiya V., and Frank B. Wilderson. "The Position of the Unthought." *Qui Parle* 13, no. 2 (2003): 183–201.

Harvey, David. "Reading Marx's *Capital* with David Harvey: Class 02 Reading Marx's *Capital Vol I* with David Harvey." January 16, 2011. https://www
.youtube.com/watch?v=zwuMrd_Hgww&t=4043s.

Hill Collins, Patricia. *Fighting Words: Black Women and the Search for Justice*. Minneapolis: University of Minnesota Press, 1998.

Hochberg, Gil Z. *Becoming Palestine: Toward an Archival Imagination of the Future*. Durham, NC: Duke University Press, 2021.

———. "Between Orientalisms: Derrida, Cixous, and the Specter of the Arab Jew." *Boundary2*, December 17, 2018. http://www.boundary2.org/2018/12/gil
-z-hochberg-between-orientalisms-derrida-cixous-and-the-specter-of-the-arab
-jew/#_ednref2.

———. "Forget Pinkwashing, It's Brownwashing Time: Self-Orientalizing on the US Campus." *Mondoweiss*, November 28, 2017. https://mondoweiss.net/2017/11/pinkwashing-brownwashing-orientalizing/.

Hong, Grace Kyungwon, and Roderick A. Ferguson, eds. *Strange Affinities: The Gender and Sexual Politics of Comparative Racialization*. Perverse Modernities. Durham, NC: Duke University Press, 2011.

Horak, Laura. "Trans on YouTube: Intimacy, Visibility, Temporality." *TSQ: Transgender Studies Quarterly* 1, no. 4 (2014): 572–85. https://doi.org/10.1215/23289252-2815255.

Horbury, Ezra, and Christine "Xine" Yao. "Empire and Eugenics: Trans Studies in the United Kingdom." *TSQ: Transgender Studies Quarterly* 7, no. 3 (202AD): 445–54. https://doi.org/10.1215/23289252–8553104.

Hordes, Stanley M. *To the End of the Earth: A History of the Crypto-Jews of New Mexico*. New York: Columbia University Press, 2005.

Hozumi, Tada. "A Cultural Somatic Seader on Whiteness, Trauma, and Allyship." June 8, 2020. https://tadahozumi.com/a-cultural-somatic-reader-on-whiteness-free-webinar/.

———. "On Somatics Being an Asian Practice." September 9, 2020. https://tadahozumi.com/on-cultural-somatics-being-an-asian-practice/.

———. "Open Letter to Mark Walsh and the Embodiment Conference." *Medium*, October 18, 2020. https://tadahozumi.medium.com/public-letter-to-mark-walsh-and-the-embodiment-conference-ab9319ee4b69.

———. "What It Means to Heal White Supremacy: Restoring the Cultural Nervous System, Cultivating Hara." November 17, 2017. https://tadahozumi.com/what-it-means-to-heal-white-supremacy/.

Huhndorf, Shari M. *Going Native: Indians in the American Cultural Imagination*. Ithaca, NY: Cornell University Press, 2001.

Hui, Yuk. "Writing and Cosmotechnics." *Derrida Today* 13, no. 1 (2020): 17–32. https://doi.org/10.3366/drt.2020.0217.

Ingold, Tim. *Being Alive: Essays on Movement, Knowledge and Description*. London: Routledge, 2011.

———. *Making: Anthropology, Archaeology, Art and Architecture*. London: Routledge, 2013.

———. *The Perception of the Environment: Essays on Livelihood, Dwelling and Skill*. London: Routledge, 2000.

Isaac, Walter. "Locating Afro-American Judaism: A Critique of White Normativity." In *A Companion to African-American Studies*, edited by Lewis R. Gordon and Jane Anna Gordon, 512–42. Malden, MA: Blackwell Publishing, 2006.

Jackson, Zakiyyah Iman. *Becoming Human: Matter and Meaning in an Antiblack World*. New York: New York University Press, 2020.

Jacobs, Jack Lester. *The Frankfurt School, Jewish Lives, and Antisemitism*. New York: Cambridge University Press, 2015.

Jirn, Jin Suh. "A Sort of European Hallucination: On Derrida's 'Chinese Prejudice.'" *Situations* 8, no. 2 (2015): 67–83.

Johnson, Dominic. "Voice, Performance, and Border Crossings: An Interview with Tobaron Waxman." *TSQ: Transgender Studies Quarterly* 1, no. 4 (2014): 614–19.

Johnson, Kirsten, and Alex Lichtenfels. "Finding a Person and Losing a Person: On Cameraperson." *Performance Matters* 6, no. 1 (2020): 122–35.

Jones, Richard, and Euan Cameron. "Full Fat, Semi-Skimmed or No Milk Today—Creative Commons Licences and English Folk Music." *Review of Law, Computers and Technology* 19, no. 3 (2005): 259–75.

Judy, R. A. *Sentient Flesh: Thinking in Disorder, Poiēsis in Black*. Black Outdoors. Durham, NC: Duke University Press, 2020.

Kapsali, Maria. "'I Don't Attack It, but It's Not for Actors': The Use of Yoga by Jerzy Grotowski." *Theatre, Dance and Performance Training* 1, no. 2 (2010): 185–98. https://doi.org/10.1080/19443927.2010.505002.

Kaye/Kantrowitz, Melanie. *The Colors of Jews: Racial Politics and Radical Diasporism*. Bloomington, IN: Indiana University Press, 2007.

Keathley, Christian, Jason Mittell, and Catherine Grant. *The Videographic Essay: Criticism in Sound and Image*. Montreal: caboose books, 2019.

Keeling, Kara. "I = Another: Digital Identity Politics." In *Strange Affinities: The Gender and Sexual Politics of Comparative Racialization*, edited by Grace Kyungwon Hong and Roderick A. Ferguson, 53–75. Perverse Modernities. Durham, NC: Duke University Press, 2011.

Kelley, Robin D. G. "'Western Civilization Is Neither': Black Studies' Epistemic Revolution." *Black Scholar* 50, no. 3 (2020): 4–10.

Kerkour, Youssef. "Letter to Malcolm Sinclair, Equity, from *The Orphan of Zhao* Company." *Contemporary Theatre Review* 24, no. 4 (2014): 494–95.

Kidwell, Jennifer. "Performance and Para-Fiction: Jennifer Kidwell on Playing Donelle Woolford." *Hyperallergic*, December 23, 2014. https://hyperallergic .com/170408/performance-and-para-fiction-jennifer-kidwell-on-playing -donelle-woolford/.

King, Rosamond S. "Radical Interdisciplinarity: A New Iteration of a Woman of Color Methodology." *Meridians: Feminism, Race, Transnationalism* 18, no. 2 (2019): 445–56.

King, Tiffany Lethabo. *The Black Shoals: Offshore Formations of Black and Native Studies*. Durham, NC: Duke University Press, 2019.

———. "Post-Identitarian and Post-Intersectional Anxiety in the Neoliberal Corporate University." *Feminist Formations* 27, no. 3 (2015): 114–38.

King, Tiffany Lethabo, Jenell Navarro, and Andrea Smith, eds. *Otherwise Worlds: Against Settler Colonialism and Anti-Blackness*. Durham, NC: Duke University Press, 2020.

Kirkkopelto, Esa. "Artistic Research as Institutional Practice." In *Yearbook on Artistic Research*, 48–54. Stockholm: Swedish Research Council, 2015.

Kirshenblatt-Gimblett, Barbara. "The Corporeal Turn." *Jewish Studies Quarterly* 95, no. 3 (2005): 447–61.

Klonk, Charlotte, ed. *New Laboratories: Historical and Critical Perspectives on Contemporary Developments*. Berlin: De Gruyter, 2016.

Kondo, Dorinne K. *Worldmaking: Race, Performance, and the Work of Creativity*. Durham, NC: Duke University Press, 2018.

Kotef, Hagar. *The Colonizing Self: Or, Home and Homelessness in Israel/Palestine*. Theory in Forms. Durham, NC: Duke University Press, 2020.

Kramer, Paula, and Stephanie Misa. "Artistic Research as a Tool of Critique." *Nivel–Artistic Research in the Performing Arts* 10 (2019). https://nivel.teak.fi /adie/artistic-research-as-a-tool-of-critique/.

Krawczyk, Ilona. "Embodying Voice in Training and Performance: A Process-Oriented Approach." PhD diss., University of Huddersfield, 2021. https:// eprints.hud.ac.uk/id/eprint/35659/.

Krawczyk, Ilona, and Ben Spatz. "Dreaming Voice: A Dialogue." In *Somatic Voices in Performance Research and Beyond*, edited by Christina Kapadocha, 140–54. Abingdon, UK: Routledge, 2021.

Kumiega, Jennifer. *The Theatre of Grotowski*. London: Methuen, 1985.

Kunin, Seth Daniel. *Juggling Identities: Identity and Authenticity among the Crypto-Jews*. New York: Columbia University Press, 2009.

Kuppers, Petra, and Neil Marcus. *Cripple Poetics: A Love Story*. Ypsilanti, MI: Homofactus Press, 2008.

Kyrölä, Katariina. "Music Videos as Black Feminist Thought: From Nicki Minaj's *Anaconda* to Beyoncé's *Formation*." *Feminist Encounters: A Journal of Critical Studies in Culture and Politics* 1, no. 1 (2017): article 8. https://doi.org/10 .20897/femenc.201708.

la paperson. *A Third University Is Possible*. Minneapolis: University of Minnesota Press, 2017.

Lappe, Benay. "Hot Off the Shtender: The Word that Changed the World." February 12, 2021. https://svara.org/hot-off-the-shtender-the-word-that-changed -the-world/.

Larsen, Soren C., and Jay T. Johnson. *Being Together in Place: Indigenous Coexistence in a More than Human World*. Minneapolis: University of Minnesota Press, 2017.

Laster, Dominika. *Grotowski's Bridge Made of Memory: Embodied Memory, Witnessing and Transmission in the Grotowski Work*. Enactments. Calcutta: Seagull Books, 2016.

Latour, Bruno. *Down to Earth: Politics in the New Climatic Regime*. Trans. Catherine Porter. Cambridge, UK: Polity, 2018.

———. "Give Me a Laboratory and I Will Raise the World." In *Science Observed: Perspectives on the Social Study of Science*, edited by Karin Knorr-Cetina and Michael Mulkay, 141–70. London: Sage Publications, 1983.

Lech, Kasia. "Krytyczki as Activists: On Theatre Criticism, Affect, Objectivism and #MeToo in Polish Drama Schools: Interview with Monika Kwaśniewska." *Critical Stages / Scènes critiques*, no. 23 (2021). https://www.critical-stages.org /23/interview-with-monika-kwasniewska/.

Lei, Daphne P. "Interruption, Intervention, Interculturalism: Robert Wilson's HIT Productions in Taiwan." *Theatre Journal* 63, no. 4 (2011): 571–86.

Lepecki, André. *Exhausting Dance: Performance and the Politics of Movement*. New York: Routledge, 2006.

Leroux, Darryl. *Distorted Descent: White Claims to Indigenous Identity*. Winnipeg: University of Manitoba Press, 2019.

Levine, Gabriel. *Art and Tradition in a Time of Uprisings*. Cambridge, MA: MIT Press, 2020.

Liboiron, Max. *Pollution Is Colonialism*. Durham, NC: Duke University Press, 2021.

Lipsitz, George. *The Possessive Investment in Whiteness: How White People Profit from Identity Politics*. 20th anniversary ed. Philadelphia: Temple University Press, 2018.

Lorde, Audre. *Zami: A New Spelling of My Name*. Berkeley and Toronto: Crossing Press, 1982.

"Love Is the Message: An Evening with Arthur Jafa." Hirshhorn Museum and Sculpture Garden, Washington, DC, March 16, 2018. 42:47 min. https://www.youtube.com/watch?v=yOYd_IAPIe0.

Loveless, Natalie. *How to Make Art at the End of the World: A Manifesto for Research-Creation*. Durham, NC: Duke University Press, 2019.

Lowe, Lisa. *The Intimacies of Four Continents*. Durham, NC: Duke University Press, 2015.

Lugones, Maria. "The Coloniality of Gender." *Worlds and Knowledges Otherwise* 2 (2008): 1–17.

Lyotard, Jean François. *Heidegger and "the jews."* Minneapolis: University of Minnesota Press, 1990.

Mackh, Bruce M. *Surveying the Landscape: Arts Integration at Research Universities. A Review of Best Practices and Challenges for Arts Integration in Higher Education*. Ann Arbor, MI: ArtsEngine, 2015.

Magnat, Virginie. *Grotowski, Women, and Contemporary Performance: Meetings with Remarkable Women*. London: Routledge, 2015.

MaNishtana. "The 'Jewface' Debate about Casting Non-Jews as Jews Betrays an Ashkenazi Bias." *Jewish Telegraphic Agency*, October 13, 2021. https://www.jta.org/2021/10/13/opinion/the-jewface-debate-about-casting-non-jews-as-jews-betrays-an-ashkenazi-bias.

Manning, Erin. *For a Pragmatics of the Useless*. Thought in the Act. Durham, NC: Duke University Press, 2020.

———. *The Minor Gesture*. Thought in the Act. Durham, NC: Duke University Press, 2016.

Manning, Erin, and Brian Massumi. *Thought in the Act: Passages in the Ecology of Experience*. Minneapolis: University of Minnesota Press, 2014.

Marable, Manning. *Beyond Black and White: From Civil Rights to Barack Obama*. Radical Thinkers. London: Verso Books, 2016.

Marks, Laura U. *Touch: Sensuous Theory and Multisensory Media*. Minneapolis: University of Minnesota Press, 2002.

Massumi, Brian. *99 Theses on the Revaluation of Value: A Postcapitalist Manifesto*. Minneapolis: University of Minnesota Press, 2018.

———. *Parables for the Virtual: Movement, Affect, Sensation*. Post-Contemporary Interventions. Durham, NC: Duke University Press, 2002.

Mawhinney, Janet. "'Giving up the Ghost': Disrupting the (Re)Production of White Privilege in Anti-Racist Pedagogy and Organizational Change." MA thesis, University of Toronto, 1998.

McKittrick, Katherine. *Dear Science and Other Stories*. Errantries. Durham, NC: Duke University Press, 2021.

———. *Demonic Grounds: Black Women and the Cartographies of Struggle*. Minneapolis: University of Minnesota Press, 2006.

———, ed. *Sylvia Wynter: On Being Human as Praxis*. Durham, NC: Duke University Press, 2015.

Means, Russell. "The Same Old Song." In *Marxism and Native Americans*, edited by Ward Churchill. Boston: South End Press, 1982.

Memmi, Albert. "Negritude and Judeity." *European Judaism: A Journal for the New Europe* 3, no. 2 (1968): 4–12.

Menakem, Resmaa. *My Grandmother's Hands: Racialized Trauma and the Pathway to Mending Our Hearts and Bodies*. Las Vegas, NV: Central Recovery Press, 2017.

Mengesha, Lilian. "Being and Whiteness: Settler Possession and Performative Wokeness in *The Thanksgiving Play*." *Journal of Dramatic Theory and Criticism* 35, no. 2 (2021): 39–52.

Mignolo, Walter. *The Darker Side of Western Modernity: Global Futures, Decolonial Options*. Latin America Otherwise: Languages, Empires, Nations. Durham, NC: Duke University Press, 2011.

Mignolo, Walter D., and Catherine E. Walsh. *On Decoloniality: Concepts, Analytics, Praxis*. Duke University Press, 2018.

Miller, Christopher L. "The Postidentitarian Predicament in the Footnotes of *A Thousand Plateaus*: Nomadology, Anthropology, and Authority." *Diacritics* 23, no. 3 (1993): 6–35.

———. "'We Shouldn't Judge Deleuze and Guattari': A Response to Eugene Holland." *Research in African Literatures* 34, no. 3 (2003): 129–41.

Miller, Nancy K. *Getting Personal: Feminist Occasions and Other Autobiographical Acts*. New York: Routledge, 1991.

Milstein, Cindy, ed. *There Is Nothing So Whole as a Broken Heart: Mending the World as Jewish Anarchists*. Chico, CA: AK Press, 2021.

Mirzoeff, Nicholas. *The Appearance of Black Lives Matter*. Miami, FL: Name Publications, 2017. https://namepublications.org/item/2017/the-appearance-of-black-lives-matter/.

———, ed. *Diaspora and Visual Culture: Representing Africans and Jews*. London: Routledge, 2000.

———. "Whiteness: What Is to Be Done?" Opening keynote at 2019 a2ru National Conference. Lawrence, University of Kansas, November 7–9, 2019. https://vimeo.com/378612639.

Mitra, Royona. *Akram Khan: Dancing New Interculturalism*. New World Choreographies. Basingstoke, UK: Palgrave Macmillan, 2015.

———. "Unmaking Contact: Choreographic Touch at the Intersections of Race, Caste, and Gender." *Dance Research Journal* 53, no. 3 (2021): 6–24.

Mnouchkine, Ariane, Joëlle Gayot, and Nora Armani. "Cultures Are Not Anyone's Property." *PAJ: A Journal of Performance and Art* 41, no. 3 (2019): 65–70.

Mock, Roberta. *Jewish Women on Stage, Film, and Television*. Basingstoke, UK: Palgrave Macmillan, 2007.

Money on the Left. "Abstractions also Liberate with Anna Kornbluh." Podcast, October 1, 2021. https://moneyontheleft.org/2021/10/01/abstractions-also-liberate-with-anna-kornbluh/.

Moore, Madison. *Fabulous: The Rise of the Beautiful Eccentric*. New Haven, CT: Yale University Press, 2018.

Morgensen, Scott Lauria. *Spaces between Us: Queer Settler Colonialism and Indigenous Decolonization*. Minneapolis: University of Minnesota Press, 2011.

Moten, Fred. *The Universal Machine*. Durham, NC: Duke University Press, 2018.

Mouëllic, Gilles. *Improvising Cinema*. Translated by Caroline Taylor Bouché. Film Culture in Transition. Amsterdam: Amsterdam University Press, 2013.

"The Multiplicity Turn: Theories of Identity from Poetry to Mathematics Seminar: November 24, 2021." Stanford DLCL, December 17, 2021. https://www.youtube.com/watch?v=hRfsGzvK144&t=3995s.

Muñoz, José Esteban. *Disidentifications: Queers of Color and the Performance of Politics*. Minneapolis: University of Minnesota Press, 1999.

———. *The Sense of Brown*. Edited by Tavia Amolo Ochieng' Nyongó and Joshua Takano Chambers-Letson. Perverse Modernities. Durham, NC: Duke University Press, 2020.

Mutman, Mahmut. *The Politics of Writing Islam: Voicing Difference*. London: Bloomsbury, 2015.

Myers, Natasha. *Rendering Life Molecular: Models, Modelers, and Excitable Matter*. Durham, NC: Duke University Press, 2015.

Nascimento, Cláudia Tatinge. *Crossing Cultural Borders through the Actor's Work: Foreign Bodies of Knowledge*. Routledge Advances in Theatre and Performance Studies 9. New York: Routledge, 2009.

Nash, Jennifer C. *Black Feminism Reimagined: After Intersectionality*. Next Wave New Directions in Women's Studies. Durham, NC: Duke University Press, 2019.

Neff, Esther. "Performing Unwhitely / Becoming Imaginary I: Theory 07/12/2016." *Medium*, November 9, 2017. https://medium.com/@esthermneff/performing-unwhitely-becoming-imaginary-part-i-theory-07-12-2016-48b04830f77d.

Nelson, Robin. *Practice as Research in the Arts: Principles, Protocols, Pedagogies, Resistances*. Basingstoke, UK: Palgrave Macmillan, 2013. www.palgrave.com/de/book/9781137282897.

Newton, Adam Zachary. *Jewish Studies as Counterlife: A Report to the Academy*. 1st ed. New York: Fordham University Press, 2019.

Nissimi, Hilda. *The Crypto-Jewish Mashhadis: The Shaping of Religious and Communal Identity in Their Journey from Iran to New York*. Eastbourne, UK: Sussex Academic Press, 2021.

Nothing Never Happens. "A Third University Is Always Happening: A Conversation with K. Wayne Yang." Podcast, June 17, 2020. https://nothingneverhappens.org/uncategorized/decolonizing-universities-part-one-of-a-conversation-with-k-wayne-yang/.

Núñez, Nicolás. *Anthropocosmic Theatre: Theatre, Ritual, Consciousness*. Edited by Franc Chamberlain and Deborah Middleton. Huddersfield, UK: University of Huddersfield Press, 2019.

Nyong'o, Tavia. *Afro-Fabulations: The Queer Drama of Black Life*. New York: New York University Press, 2019.

———. "My Gender Is Black?: The Speculative Refusals of Black Queer/Trans/Feminism." Oakland, CA, March 18, 2021. https://performingarts.mills.edu/broadcasts/2021/tavia-nyongo.php.

Okpokwasili, Okwui, and Andrew Rossi. *Bronx Gothic*. New York: Grasshopper Film, 2017. 91 min.

Okun, Tema. "White Supremacy Culture." White Supremacy Culture, 1999. http://www.whitesupremacyculture.info/.

Omer, Atalia. *Days of Awe: Reimagining Jewishness in Solidarity with Palestinians*. Chicago: University of Chicago Press, 2019.

Ong, Walter J. *Orality and Literacy: The Technologizing of the Word*. Reprint. New Accents. London: Routledge, 2009.

Orr, Joey, ed. *Inquiries*. Lawrence, KA: Spencer Museum of Art, 2019. https://spencerart.ku.edu/athome/teaser/inquiries.

Osiński, Zbigniew. *Jerzy Grotowski's Journeys to the East*. Edited by Iga Rutkowska. Translated by Andrzej Wojtasik and Kris Salata. Holstebro, Denmark: Icarus Publishing Enterprise, 2014.

———. "Returning to the Subject: The Heritage of Reduta in Grotowski's Laboratory Theatre." Translated by Kris Salata. *TDR: The Drama Review* 52, no. 2 (2008): 52–74. https://doi.org/10.1162/dram.2008.52.2.52.

Palmer, Tyrone S. "Otherwise than Blackness: Feeling, World, Sublimation." *Qui Parle* 29, no. 2 (2020): 247–83.

Pao, Angela C. *No Safe Spaces: Re-Casting Race, Ethnicity, and Nationality in American Theater*. Ann Arbor: University of Michigan Press, 2010.

Papazian, Elizabeth, and Caroline Eades. *The Essay Film: Dialogue, Politics, Utopia*. New York: Columbia University Press, 2016.

Parikka, Jussi. *A Geology of Media*. Minneapolis: University of Minnesota Press, 2015.

Park, Linette. "Afropessimism and Futures of . . . : A Conversation with Frank Wilderson." *Black Scholar* 50, no. 3 (2020): 29–41.

Patterson, G. "Entertaining a Healthy Cispicion of the Ally Industrial Complex in Transgender Studies." *Women and Language* 41, no. 1 (2018): 146–51.

Pellegrini, Ann. "Jewishness as Gender." *Shofar* 14, no. 1 (1995): 138–41.

Perry, Keisha-Khan Y., and Tasneem Siddiqui. "Contours, Continuities, and Evolutions in Africana Radical Thought: A Conversation with Keeanga-Yamahtta Taylor." *Black Scholar* 50, no. 3 (2020): 64–74. https://doi.org/10.1080/00064246.2020.1780864.

Peters, John Durham. *The Marvelous Clouds: Toward a Philosophy of Elemental Media*. Chicago: University of Chicago Press, 2015.

Phelan, Peggy. *Unmarked: The Politics of Performance*. London: Routledge, 1993. https://www.taylorfrancis.com/books/e/9781134916412.

Pickering, Andrew. *The Mangle of Practice: Time, Agency, and Science*. Chicago: University of Chicago Press, 1995.

Pierce, Joseph M. "Adopted: Trace, Blood, and Native Authenticity." *Critical Ethnic Studies* 3, no. 2 (2017): 57–76.

Pink, Sarah. *Doing Visual Ethnography*. 3d ed. Los Angeles: Sage, 2013.

Preciado, Paul B. *Testo Junkie: Sex, Drugs, and Biopolitics in the Pharmacopornographic Era*. New York: Feminist Press at CUNY, 2013.

Profeta, Katherine. *Dramaturgy in Motion: At Work on Dance and Movement Performance*. Madison: University of Wisconsin Press, 2015.

Puar, Jasbir K. *Terrorist Assemblages: Homonationalism in Queer Times*. 2d ed. Next Wave. Durham, NC: Duke University Press, 2017.

Rabaka, Reiland. "24th Annual W. E. B. Du Bois Lecture." UMass Amherst Libraries, February 21, 2018. https://www.youtube.com/watch?v=6SEJoRCWLCk.

Raengo, Alessandra. "Blackness, Aesthetics, Liquidity." Atlanta: Georgia State University, 2014.

Raengo, Alessandra, and Lauren McLeod Cramer. "Editors' Notes." *Liquid Blackness* 5, no. 1 (2021): 1–3. https://doi.org/10.1215/26923874-8932545.

Rai, Amit S. "Race Racing: Four Theses on Race and Intensity." *WSQ: Women's Studies Quarterly* 40, no. 1–2 (2012): 64–75.

Rand, Richard, ed. *Logomachia: The Conflict of the Faculties*. Lincoln: University of Nebraska Press, 1992.

Rankine, Claudia, Beth Loffreda, and Max King Cap, eds. *The Racial Imaginary: Writers on Race in the Life of the Mind*. Albany, NY: Fence Books, 2015.

Ratskoff, Ben. "'Improbable Spectacles': White Supremacy, Christian Hegemony, and the Dark Side of the Judenfrage." *Studies in American Jewish Literature* 39, no. 1 (2020): 17–43.

Read, Jason. "Preemptive Strike (of a Philosophical Variety): Marx and Spinoza." *Crisis and Critique* 8, no. 1 (2021): 288–305.

Reason, Matthew. *Documentation, Disappearance and the Representation of Live Performance*. Basingstoke, UK: Palgrave Macmillan, 2006.

Reed, Anthony. *Soundworks: Race, Sound, and Poetry in Production*. Refiguring American Music. Durham, NC: Duke University Press, 2021.

Reinelt, Janelle G. "Is Performance Studies Imperialist? Part 2." *TDR: The Drama Review* 51, no. 3 (2007): 7–16.

Renton, David. *Labour's Antisemitism Crisis: What the Left Got Wrong and How to Learn from It*. Abingdon, UK: Routledge, 2022.

Reynolds, Simon. *Generation Ecstasy: Into the World of Techno and Rave Culture*. New York: Routledge, 1999.

Rheinberger, Hans-Jörg. *An Epistemology of the Concrete: Twentieth-Century Histories of Life*. Experimental Futures. Durham, NC: Duke University Press, 2010.

———. *Toward a History of Epistemic Things: Synthesizing Proteins in the Test Tube*. Writing Science. Stanford, CA: Stanford University Press, 1997.

Richards, Thomas. *Heart of Practice: Within the Workcenter of Jerzy Grotowski and Thomas Richards*. London: Routledge, 2008.

Richards, Thomas, and Jerzy Grotowski. *At Work with Grotowski on Physical Actions*. London: Routledge, 1995.

Rifkin, Mark. *Fictions of Land and Flesh: Blackness, Indigeneity, Speculation*. Durham, NC: Duke University Press, 2019.

———. "Indigeneity, Apartheid, Palestine: On the Transit of Political Metaphors." *Cultural Critique*, no. 95 (2017): 25–70.

———. "Indigenizing Agamben: Rethinking Sovereignty in Light of the 'Peculiar' Status of Native Peoples." *Cultural Critique* 73 (2009): 88–124.

———. "Queering Temporality and Moving beyond Settler Time (Episode 314)." *Green Dreamer* podcast, 2021. https://greendreamer.com/podcast/dr-mark-rifkin-beyond-settler-time.

———. *Speaking for the People: Native Writing and the Question of Political Form*. Durham, NC: Duke University Press, 2021.

Rigby, Kevin, Jr., and Hari Ziyad. "White People Have No Place in Black Liberation." *Racebaitr*, March 31, 2016. https://racebaitr.com/2016/03/31/white-people-no-place-black-liberation/.

Riles, Annelise, ed. *Documents: Artifacts of Modern Knowledge*. Ann Arbor: University of Michigan Press, 2006.

Riley, Shannon Rose, and Lynette Hunter. *Mapping Landscapes for Performance as Research: Scholarly Acts and Creative Cartographies.* Basingstoke, UK: Palgrave Macmillan, 2009.

Robinson, Dylan. *Hungry Listening: Resonant Theory for Indigenous Sound Studies.* Minneapolis: University of Minnesota Press, 2020.

Rogers, Amanda, and Ashley Thorpe. "A Controversial Company: Debating the Casting of the RSC's *The Orphan of Zhao.*" *Contemporary Theatre Review* 24, no. 4 (2014): 428–35.

Rosenberg, Jordana. "The Molecularization of Sexuality: On Some Primitivisms of the Present." *Theory and Event* 17, no. 2 (2014).

Rothberg, Michael. *Multidirectional Memory: Remembering the Holocaust in the Age of Decolonization.* Cultural Memory in the Present. Stanford, CA: Stanford University Press, 2009.

———. *The Implicated Subject: Beyond Victims and Perpetrators.* Cultural Memory in the Present. Stanford, CA: Stanford University Press, 2019.

Rouch, Jean. *Ciné-Ethnography.* Edited by Steven Feld. Minneapolis: University of Minnesota Press, 2003.

Saad, Layla F. *Me and White Supremacy: How to Recognise Your Privilege, Combat Racism and Change the World.* London: Quercus, 2022.

Sakolsky, Ronald B., and James Koehnline, eds. *Gone to Croatan: Origins of North American Dropout Culture.* Brooklyn, NY: Autonomedia, 1993.

Salata, Kris. *The Unwritten Grotowski: Theory and Practice of the Encounter.* Routledge Advances in Theatre and Performance Studies 26. New York: Routledge, 2012.

Saldanha, Arun. *Psychedelic White: Goa Trance and the Viscosity of Race.* Minneapolis: University of Minnesota Press, 2007.

———. "Reontologising Race: The Machinic Geography of Phenotype." *Environment and Planning D: Society and Space* 24 (2006): 9–24.

———. "So What *Is* Race?" Institute of Advanced Study. *Insights* 2, no. 12 (2009): 1–11.

Saldanha, Arun, and Jason Michael Adams, eds. *Deleuze and Race.* Edinburgh: Edinburgh University Press, 2013.

Sánchez, Raúl. "Writing." In *Decolonizing Rhetoric and Composition Studies: New Latinx Keywords for Theory and Pedagogy,* edited by Iris D. Ruiz and Raúl Sánchez, 77–89. Basingstoke, UK: Palgrave Macmillan, 2016.

Sant, Toni, ed. *Documenting Performance: The Context and Processes of Digital Curation and Archiving.* London: Bloomsbury Methuen Drama, 2017.

Schatzki, Theodore R., K. Knorr Cetina, and Eike von Savigny, eds. *The Practice Turn in Contemporary Theory.* New York: Routledge, 2001.

Schechner, Richard. "Double Edge Theatre in Its Ashfield Community: An Interview with Stacy Klein." *TDR: The Drama Review* 64, no. 4 (2020): 44–71.

———. "Oh, I Know I've Been Changed." *Theatre Research International* 46, no. 3 (2021): 346–70. https://doi.org/10.1017/S0307883321000304.

———. "Performers and Spectators Transported and Transformed." *Kenyon Review* 3, no. 4 (1981): 83–113.

Schechner, Richard, and Lisa Wolford, eds. *The Grotowski Sourcebook.* London: Routledge, 1997.

Schwab, Michael, ed. *Experimental Systems: Future Knowledge in Artistic Research*. Orpheus Institute Series. Leuven, Belgium: Leuven University Press, 2013.

Sexton, Jared. *Amalgamation Schemes: Antiblackness and the Critique of Multiracialism*. Minneapolis: University of Minnesota Press, 2008.

Sharpe, Christina. *In the Wake: On Blackness and Being*. Durham, NC: Duke University Press, 2016.

Shaviro, Steven. *The Cinematic Body*. Minneapolis: University of Minnesota Press, 1993.

Shotwell, Alexis. "Is It White Shame?" *Alexis Shotwell Blog*, August 13, 2017. https://alexisshotwell.com/2017/08/13/white-shame/.

———. *Knowing Otherwise: Race, Gender, and Implicit Understanding*. University Park: Penn State University Press, 2012.

Sicher, Efraim, ed. *Race, Color, Identity: Rethinking Discourses about "Jews" in the Twenty-First Century*. New York: Berghahn Books, 2013.

Simpson, Leanne Betasamosake. *As We Have Always Done: Indigenous Freedom through Radical Resistance*. Indigenous Americas. Minneapolis: University of Minnesota Press, 2017.

———. "Land as Pedagogy: Nishnaabeg Intelligence and Rebellious Transformation." *Decolonization: Indigeneity, Education & Society* 3, no. 3 (2014): 1–25.

Simpson, Leanne Betasamosake, Amanda Strong, and Spotted Fawn Productions. "Biidaaban (The Dawn Comes)." *Public: Art, Culture, Ideas*, no. 63 (2021): 101–11.

Slabodsky, Santiago. *Decolonial Judaism: Triumphal Failures of Barbaric Thinking*. New York: Palgrave Macmillan, 2014.

Sloterdijk, Peter. *You Must Change Your Life: On Anthropotechnics*. Translated by Wieland Hoban. Cambridge, UK: Polity, 2013.

Slowiak, James, and Jairo Cuesta. *Jerzy Grotowski*. 1st ed. Abingdon, UK: Routledge, 2018.

Smith, D Vance. "Africa Writes Back." *Aeon*, June 17, 2021. https://aeon.co/essays/africas-ancient-scripts-counter-european-ideas-of-literacy.

Snorton, C. Riley. *Black on Both Sides: A Racial History of Trans Identity*. Minneapolis: University of Minnesota Press, 2017.

Sobol, Richard, and Jeffrey A. Summit. *Abayudaya: The Jews of Uganda*. New York: Abbeville Press, 2002.

Social Science Research / University of Amsterdam. "Decolonising Europe #13: Decolonising Queerness." Podcast, March 18, 2021. https://www.youtube.com/watch?v=-ik0QM5QF5Q.

Spatz, Ben. "Artistic Research and the Queer Prophetic." *Text and Performance Quarterly* 41, no. 1–2 (2021): 81–105. https://doi.org/10.1080/10462937.2021.1908585.

———. *Blue Sky Body: Thresholds for Embodied Research*. New York: Routledge, 2020.

———. "Colors Like Knives: Embodied Research and Phenomenotechnique in Rite of the Butcher." *Contemporary Theatre Review* 27, no. 2 (2017): 195–215. https://doi.org/10.1080/10486801.2017.1300152.

———. "Earthing the Laboratory: Speculations for Doctoral Training." *Performance Research* 25, no. 8 (2020): 33–41. https://doi.org/10.1080/13528165 .2020.1909896.

———. "The Electronic Heart." BA thesis, Wesleyan University, 2001.

———. *Making a Laboratory: Dynamic Configurations with Transversal Video.* New York: Punctum Books, 2020.

———. "Molecular Identities: Digital Archives and Decolonial Judaism in a Laboratory of Song." *Performance Research* 24, no. 1 (2019): 66–79.

———. "Notes for Decolonizing Embodiment." *Journal of Dramatic Theory and Criticism* 33, no. 2 (2019): 9–22.

———. "To Open a Person: Song and Encounter at Gardzienice and the Workcenter." *Theatre Topics* 18, no. 2 (2008): 205–22. https://doi.org/10.1353/tt .0.0044.

———. *What a Body Can Do: Technique as Knowledge, Practice as Research.* London: Routledge, 2015.

Spatz, Ben, N. Eda Erçin, Caroline Gatt, and Agnieszka Mendel. "He Almost Forgets That There Is a Maker of the World." *Journal of Embodied Research* 4, no. 2 (2021): 32:06. https://doi.org/10.16995/jer.71.

Spatz, Ben, Nazlıhan Eda Erçin, Ilona Krawczyk, and Agnieszka Mendel. "whiteness." *Performance Philosophy* 7, no. 2 (2022): 169–72. https://doi.org/10 .21476/PP.2022.72349.

Spatz, Ben, Nazlıhan Eda Erçin, and Agnieszka Mendel. "ancestors: an illuminated video." *International Journal of Performance Arts and Digital Media* 17, no. 1 (2021): 46–55. https://doi.org/10.1080/14794713.2021.1880140.

Spatz, Ben, Nazlıhan Eda Erçin, Agnieszka Mendel, and Elaine Spatz-Rabinowitz. "Diaspora (An Illuminated Video Essay)." *Global Performance Studies* 2, no. 1 (2018): 30 min.

Stam, Robert, and Ella Shohat. *Race in Translation: Culture Wars around the Postcolonial Atlantic.* New York: New York University Press, 2012.

Stanger, Arabella. *Dancing on Violent Ground: Utopia as Dispossession in Euro-American Theater Dance.* Performance Works. Evanston, IL: Northwestern University Press, 2021.

Staniewski, Włodzimierz, and Alison Hodge. *Hidden Territories: The Theatre of Gardzienice.* London: Routledge, 2004.

Stein, Sharon, Vanessa Andreotti, Rene Suša, Sarah Amsler, Dallas Hunt, Cash Ahenakew, Elwood Jimmy, et al. "Gesturing Towards Decolonial Futures: Reflections on Our Learnings Thus Far." *Nordic Journal of Comparative and International Education (NJCIE)* 4, no. 1 (2020): 43–65. https://doi.org/10 .7577/njcie.3518.

Steinbock, Eliza. *Shimmering Images: Trans Cinema, Embodiment, and the Aesthetics of Change.* Durham, NC: Duke University Press, 2019.

Steinsaltz, Adin. *The Essential Talmud.* 30th anniversary ed. New York: Basic Books, 2006.

Stengers, Isabelle. *Cosmopolitics.* Posthumanities 9–10. Minneapolis: University of Minnesota Press, 2010.

Sterne, Jonathan. "The Theology of Sound: A Critique of Orality." *Canadian Journal of Communication* 36 (2011): 207–25.

Strings, Sabrina. *Fearing the Black Body: The Racial Origins of Fat Phobia*. New York: New York University Press, 2019.

Summit, Jeffrey A. "The Participating Observer: Fieldwork in Jewish Settings." *Musica Judaica* 20 (2014): 117–42.

TallBear, Kimberly. *Native American DNA: Tribal Belonging and the False Promise of Genetic Science*. Minneapolis: University of Minnesota Press, 2013.

Tamarkin, Noah. *Genetic Afterlives: Black Jewish Indigeneity in South Africa*. Theory in Forms. Durham, NC: Duke University Press, 2020.

Tan, Marcus Cheng Chye. "Double Take: Review of *Theatre and the World* by Rustom Bharucha." *Theatre Research International* 46, no. 1 (2021): 89–91. https://doi.org/10.1017/S0307883320000607.

Taylor, Diana. *The Archive and the Repertoire: Performing Cultural Memory in the Americas*. Durham, NC: Duke University Press, 2007.

Taylor, Keeanga-Yamahtta. *From #BlackLivesMatter to Black Liberation*. Chicago: Haymarket Books, 2016.

Taylor, Lucien. *Visualizing Theory: Selected Essays from V.A.R., 1990–1994*. New York: Routledge, 2014.

Tessman, Lisa, and Bat-Ami Bar On, eds. *Jewish Locations: Traversing Racialized Landscapes*. Lanham, MD: Rowman and Littlefield, 2001.

Teves, Stephanie Nohelani. "The Theorist and the Theorized: Indigenous Critiques of Performance Studies." *TDR: The Drama Review* 62, no. 4 (2018): 131–40.

Tharps, Lori L. "The Case for Black With a Capital B." *New York Times*, November 18, 2014. https://www.nytimes.com/2014/11/19/opinion/the-case-for-black-with-a-capital-b.html.

Thompson, Marie. "Whiteness and the Ontological Turn in Sound Studies." *Parallax* 23, no. 3 (2017): 266–82. https://doi.org/10.1080/13534645.2017.1339967.

Tinsley, Omise'eke Natasha. *Ezili's Mirrors: Imagining Black Queer Genders*. Durham, NC: Duke University Press, 2018.

Tomlinson, Gary. *The Singing of the New World: Indigenous Voice in the Era of European Contact*. New Perspectives in Music History and Criticism. Cambridge: Cambridge University Press, 2007.

Topolski, Anya. "The Dangerous Discourse of the 'Judaeo-Christian' Myth: Masking the Race–Religion Constellation in Europe." *Patterns of Prejudice* 54, no. 1–2 (2020): 71–90. https://doi.org/10.1080/0031322X.2019.1696049.

Towns, Armond R. "Toward a Black Media Philosophy." *Cultural Studies* 34, no. 6 (2020): 851–73. https://doi.org/10.1080/09502386.2020.1792524.

Traverso, Enzo. *The End of Jewish Modernity*. London: Pluto Press, 2016.

Truman, Sarah E. "The Intimacies of Doing Research-Creation: Sarah E. Truman in Conversation with Natalie Loveless, Erin Manning, Natasha Myers, and Stephanie Springgay." In *Knowings and Knots: Methodologies and Ecologies in Research-Creation*, edited by Nathalie Loveless. Edmonton: University of Alberta Press, 2019, 221–49.

Tuck, Eve, and Marcia McKenzie. *Place in Research: Theory, Methodology, and Methods*. London: Routledge, 2014.

Tuck, Eve, and K. Wayne Yang. "Decolonization Is Not a Metaphor." *Decolonization: Indigeneity, Education & Society* 1, no. 1 (2012): 1–40.

Ulehla, Julia. "Living Song: An Intergenerational Investigation of Moravian Folk Song." PhD diss., University of British Columbia, 2021. https://open.library .ubc.ca/soa/cIRcle/collections/ubctheses/24/items/1.0401497.

Urban Research Theater (2023), https://urbanresearchtheater.com/.

Vallejos, Lisa Xochitl. "The Dangerous Game of Calling Whiteness PTSD: A Response to Tada Hozumi." *Medium*, November 13, 2017. https://drlisavallejos .medium.com/the-dangerous-game-of-calling-whiteness-ptsd-a-response-to -tada-hozumi-d8bddccdc062.

Vaïs, Michel. "Lepage and Mnouchkine Collide with Cultural Appropriation." *PAJ: A Journal of Performance and Art*, no. 123 (2019): 71–74.

Vannini, Phillip, ed. *Non-Representational Methodologies: Re-Envisioning Research*. London: Routledge, 2015.

Veracini, Lorenzo. "Decolonizing Settler Colonialism: Kill the Settler in Him and Save the Man." *American Indian Culture and Research Journal* 41, no. 1 (2017): 1–18. https://doi.org/10.17953/aicrj.41.1.veracini.

Vertov, Dziga. *Kino-Eye: The Writings of Dziga Vertov*. Berkeley: University of California Press, 1984.

Watson, Ian. *Towards a Third Theatre: Eugenio Barba and the Odin Teatret*. London: Routledge, 1995.

Weheliye, Alexander G. *Habeas Viscus: Racializing Assemblages, Biopolitics, and Black Feminist Theories of the Human*. Durham, NC: Duke University Press, 2014.

———. *Phonographies: Grooves in Sonic Afro-Modernity*. Durham, NC: Duke University Press, 2005.

Weisenberg, Joey. *Building Singing Communities: A Practical Guide to Unlocking the Power of Music in Jewish Prayer*. New York: Mechon Hadar, 2011.

Wekker, Gloria. *White Innocence: Paradoxes of Colonialism and Race*. Durham, NC: Duke University Press, 2016.

Whittaker, Nicholas. "Case Sensitive: Why We Shouldn't Capitalize 'Black.'" *The Drift*, no. 5, September 17, 2021. https://www.thedriftmag.com/case-sensitive/.

Wiegman, Robyn. *Object Lessons*. Durham, NC: Duke University Press, 2012.

Wilderson, Frank B. *Red, White & Black: Cinema and the Structure of U.S. Antagonisms*. Durham, NC: Duke University Press, 2010.

Williams, Caroline Randall. "You Want a Confederate Monument? My Body Is a Confederate Monument." *New York Times*, June 26, 2020. https://www .nytimes.com/2020/06/26/opinion/confederate-monuments-racism.html.

Williams, Patrick, and Laura Chrisman, eds. *Colonial Discourse and Post-Colonial Theory: A Reader*. Harlow, UK: Pearson Education, 2011.

Wilson, Pamela, and Michelle Stewart. *Global Indigenous Media: Cultures, Poetics, and Politics*. Durham, NC: Duke University Press, 2008.

Wilson, Shawn. *Research Is Ceremony: Indigenous Research Methods*. Winnipeg: Fernwood Publishing, 2008.

Wolfe, Patrick. *Traces of History: Elementary Structures of Race*. London: Verso, 2016.

Wolford, Lisa. *Grotowski's Objective Drama Research*. Performance Studies. Jackson: University Press of Mississippi, 1996.

Womack, Veronica, Crystal Marie Fleming, and Jeffrey Proulx, eds. *Beyond White Mindfulness: Critical Perspectives on Racism, Well-Being and Liberation*. New York: Routledge Books, 2022.

Wood, Abigail. *And We're All Brothers: Singing in Yiddish in Contemporary North America*. SOAS Musicology Series. Farnham, UK: Ashgate, 2013.

Wright, Michelle M. *Physics of Blackness: Beyond the Middle Passage Epistemology*. Minneapolis: University of Minnesota Press, 2015.

Wynter, Sylvia. "The Ceremony Found: Towards the Autopoetic Turn/Overturn, Its Autonomy of Human Agency and Extraterritoriality of (Self-)Cognition." In *Black Knowledges/Black Struggles: Essays in Critical Epistemology*, edited by Jason R. Ambroise and Sabine Bröck-Sallah, 184–245. FORECAAST. Liverpool: Liverpool University Press, 2015.

———. "The Ceremony Must Be Found: After Humanism." *Boundary 2* 12, no. 3 (1984): 19. https://doi.org/10.2307/302808.

Yancy, George. *Look, a White! Philosophical Essays on Whiteness*. Philadelphia: Temple University Press, 2012.

———, ed. *White Self-Criticality beyond Anti-Racism: How Does It Feel to Be a White Problem?* Philosophy of Race. Lanham, MD: Lexington Books, 2015.

Zalta, Michael. "Hallucinatory Ethnicization." *Protocols*, no. 8 (2021). https://prtcls.com/article/hallucinatory-ethnicization/.

Ziyad, Hari. "My Gender Is Black." *Afropunk*, July 12, 2017. https://afropunk.com/2017/07/my-gender-is-black/.